Virginia Woolf and Capitalism

Virginia Woolf – Variations
Series editor: Derek Ryan

Recent books in the series
Virginia Woolf and the Anthropocene
Peter Adkins

Virginia Woolf and Capitalism
Clara Jones

Forthcoming
Virginia Woolf – Objects, Things, Matter
Laci Mattison

Virginia Woolf and Transnationalism
Shinjini Chattopadhyay

Virginia Woolf and Capitalism

Edited by Clara Jones

EDINBURGH
University Press

Edinburgh University Press is one of the leading university presses in the UK. We publish academic books and journals in our selected subject areas across the humanities and social sciences, combining cutting-edge scholarship with high editorial and production values to produce academic works of lasting importance. For more information visit our website: edinburghuniversitypress.com

© editorial matter and organisation, Clara Jones 2024, 2025
© the chapters their several authors 2024, 2025

Edinburgh University Press Ltd
13 Infirmary Street
Edinburgh EH1 1LT

First published in hardback by Edinburgh University Press 2024

Typeset in 11/13 Adobe Sabon by
IDSUK (DataConnection) Ltd

A CIP record for this book is available from the British Library

ISBN 978 1 3995 1408 8 (hardback)
ISBN 978 1 3995 1409 5 (paperback)
ISBN 978 1 3995 1410 1 (webready PDF)
ISBN 978 1 3995 1411 8 (epub)

The right of Clara Jones to be identified as the editor of this work has been asserted in accordance with the Copyright, Designs and Patents Act 1988, and the Copyright and Related Rights Regulations 2003 (SI No. 2498).

Contents

List of Figures	vii
Acknowledgements	viii
Series Preface	ix
Abbreviations	x
Notes on Contributors	xi

Woolf and Capitalism: Introduction   1
Clara Jones

PART I: CLASS, EMPIRE, CAPITAL

1. 'The eagle claws other peoples land, & goods': Virginia Woolf on the Desire to Dominate   29
   Michèle Barrett

2. Empire, Slavery and Capitalism   48
   Anna Snaith

3. 'my comfortable capitalistic head': Virginia Woolf on Consumption, Co-operation and Motherhood   70
   Charlotte Taylor Suppé

4. Biometric Feminism: *A Room of One's Own* and the Politics of Intelligence   92
   Natasha Periyan

5. 'Merchant of this city': Capitalism and the Liturgies of Peace and War in *Jacob's Room*   116
   Charles Andrews

PART II: LABOUR AND THE MARKETPLACE

6. Between the Houses: Woolf and the Property Market   137
   Rachel Bowlby

7. Publishing and Capitalism at the Hogarth Press 159
   Nicola Wilson

8. 'It's rather distinguished to be as ordinary as I am.' Woolf's Working Women Writers 182
   Bryony Randall

9. The Literary Public Sphere in Virginia Woolf's *Night and Day* 203
   Stanislava Dikova

10. Capitalism and Woolf's Beyond-Work 224
    Evelyn Tsz Yan Chan

11. Virginia Woolf: A Sound Investment 245
    Brenda R. Silver

CODA: CRITICAL/CREATIVE APPROACHES

12. Scrapbooking the Present Day: The *Three Guineas* Scrapbooks 269
    Helen Tyson

13. Work Cut Out 295
    Kabe Wilson

Index 305

Figures

12.1   Virginia Woolf, '3 volumes of press cuttings, manuscript and typed extracts relating to *Three Guineas*,' Monk's House Papers, University of Sussex Special Collections, the Keep, SxMs-18/2/B/16/F, vol. 1.   270

12.2   Virginia Woolf, '3 volumes of press cuttings, manuscript and typed extracts relating to *Three Guineas*,' Monk's House Papers, University of Sussex Special Collections, the Keep, SxMs-18/2/B/16/F, vol. 2.   271

12.3   Virginia Woolf, '3 volumes of press cuttings, manuscript and typed extracts relating to *Three Guineas*,' Monk's House Papers, University of Sussex Special Collections, the Keep, SxMs-18/2/B/16/F, vol. 3.   271

12.4   Virginia Woolf, '3 volumes of press cuttings, manuscript and typed extracts relating to *Three Guineas*,' Monk's House Papers, University of Sussex Special Collections, the Keep, SxMs-18/2/B/16/F, vol. 1, index.   276

12.5   Virginia Woolf, '3 volumes of press cuttings, manuscript and typed extracts relating to *Three Guineas*,' Monk's House Papers, University of Sussex Special Collections, the Keep, SxMs-18/2/B/16/F, vol. 1, 15.   277

12.6   Virginia Woolf, '3 volumes of press cuttings, manuscript and typed extracts relating to *Three Guineas*,' Monk's House Papers, University of Sussex Special Collections, the Keep, SxMs-18/2/B/16/F, vol. 2, 5.   279

All figures reproduced with thanks to the Society of Authors as the Literary Representative of the Estate of Virginia Woolf.

Acknowledgements

For their acute advice and warm support, thanks go to Natasha Periyan and Anna Snaith. Sincere thanks also to Susannah Butler, Fiona Conn, Elizabeth Fraser and Jackie Jones at Edinburgh University Press, who have been a pleasure to work with. Derek Ryan is a model series editor, and I am grateful to him for asking me to take on this project. Thanks to EUP's design team for the beautiful front cover, and to Ciaran Bermingham for suggesting the perfect image for it. I would like to acknowledge the Society of Authors as the Literary Representatives of the Estate of Virginia Woolf for their kind permission to reproduce images of Woolf's research scrapbooks for *Three Guineas* in Chapter 12. My deepest thanks go to the contributors to this volume; it has been a joy and an education to work with such a dynamic crew of Woolf scholars.

Series Editor's Preface

Virginia Woolf's 1937 BBC radio broadcast 'Craftsmanship' memorably describes how words live '[v]ariously and strangely, much as human beings live, by ranging hither and thither, by falling in love, and mating together' (*E6* 96). Her awareness of 'their need of change', their attempt to convey 'many-sided' truths (97), was strongly felt when she was composing her own works. In one diary entry, jotted down on Boxing Day 1929 as Woolf was 'blundering on at The Waves' (her seventh novel), she remarks: 'I write two pages of arrant nonsense, after straining; I write variations of every sentence; compromises; bad shots; possibilities' (*D3* 275). Itself one of those many-sided words, 'variations' famously characterise Woolf's Bloomsbury circle, this time – with an echo of her description in 'Craftsmanship' – 'on the theme of sex, and with such happy results' ('Old Bloomsbury', *MOB* 57).

This series, *Virginia Woolf – Variations*, explores the multiple ways in which Woolf's words, through their abundant variations upon theme and form, speak to urgent critical debates of the twenty-first century. Covering topics as diverse as the 'Anthropocene', 'Capitalism', 'Transnationalism', 'Objects, Things, Matter' and 'Health Humanities' (to name only a handful of the titles commissioned), its volumes present innovative, agenda-setting research by international scholars into the lasting historical, political, ethical and theoretical significance of Woolf's modernist aesthetics. Whether revisiting familiar questions from a fresh perspective or shifting our focus to new concerns, the books explore how Woolf's writing continues to incite provocative arguments about what it means to be human in the strangeness of a variously inhuman, posthuman or more-than-human world.

Derek Ryan

Abbreviations

AHH	*A Haunted House*
AROO	*A Room of One's Own*
BP	*Books and Portraits*
BTA	*Between the Acts*
CDB	*The Captain's Death Bed and Other Essays*
CE	*Collected Essays* (4 vols)
CR1	*The Common Reader*
CR2	*The Common Reader, Second Series*
CSF	*The Complete Shorter Fiction*
D	*The Diary of Virginia Woolf* (5 vols)
DM	*The Death of the Moth and Other Essays*
E	*The Essays of Virginia Woolf* (6 vols)
F	*Flush: A Biography*
FR	*Freshwater*
GR	*Granite & Rainbow: Essays*
JR	*Jacob's Room*
L	*The Letters of Virginia Woolf* (6 vols)
M	*The Moment and Other Essays*
MD	*Mrs Dalloway*
MEL	*Melymbrosia*
MOB	*Moments of Being*
MT	*Monday or Tuesday*
ND	*Night and Day*
OBI	*On Being Ill*
O	*Orlando: A Biography*
PA	*A Passionate Apprentice*
RF	*Roger Fry: A Biography*
TG	*Three Guineas*
TTL	*To the Lighthouse*
TW	*The Waves*
TY	*The Years*
VO	*The Voyage Out*

Notes on Contributors

Charles Andrews is Professor of English at Whitworth University. He is the author of *Writing against War: Literature, Activism, and the British Peace Movement* (Northwestern University Press 2017) as well as essays on peace studies approaches to writers including Virginia Woolf, Aldous Huxley, George Bernard Shaw, Vera Brittain and Sylvia Townsend Warner.

Michèle Barrett is an emeritus professor in the English department at Queen Mary University of London. She is the editor of Woolf's *A Room of One's Own and Three Guineas* (Penguin 1993), and of *Virginia Woolf on Women and Writing* (The Women's Press, 1979). She has recently undertaken a digital edition of Woolf's own reading and research notebooks, and related materials, which when complete will be hosted by King's College London. Her other research has included feminist and social theory. She has been active in examining the politics of commemoration in the First World War, and her research was, through the documentary film *Unremembered* (Channel 4, 2019), the catalyst for an official programme addressing the 'non commemoration' of African and other soldiers and porters.

Rachel Bowlby is Professor of Comparative Literature emeritus at UCL. Her most recent books are *Everyday Stories* (2016), *Talking Walking* (2018) and *Back to the Shops: The High Street in History and the Future* (2022), with a focus on the shops in *Mrs Dalloway*. *Feminist Destinations and Further Essays on Virginia Woolf* is published by Edinburgh University Press, as is *Unexpected Items* in the Feminist Library series.

Evelyn Tsz Yan Chan was previously Associate Professor in English at the Chinese University of Hong Kong. Her publications include *Virginia Woolf and the Professions* (2014), *The Humanities in Contemporary Chinese Contexts* (2016, as a contributor and co-editor) and *The Value of the Humanities in Higher Education: Perspectives from Hong Kong* (2020). Her primary research and teaching interests are in literary representations of work and of education, and in philosophical issues arising from such representations.

Stanislava Dikova is a postdoctoral researcher and a Visiting Fellow at the University of Essex. She has previously worked as a research associate at the University of East Anglia, a fixed-term lecturer at Essex, and a postdoctoral research associate at Keele University. Her work to date has been published in *the LSE Review of Books*, *The Modernist Review*, and *Feminist Modernist Studies*. She is also the co-editor of *Love and the Politics of Care* (Bloomsbury, 2022) and *Love and the Politics of Intimacy* (Bloomsbury 2023). Stanislava's research focuses on twentieth-century British fiction and political thought, with a special interest in women's writing relating to personal autonomy and state power.

Clara Jones is Senior Lecturer in Modern Literature at King's College London. She is the author of *Virginia Woolf: Ambivalent Activist* (Edinburgh University Press, 2016) and is currently at work on a new book on the politics of interwar women writers and activists including Rosamond Lehmann, Ellen Wilkinson, Elizbeth Bowen, Sylvia Townsend Warner and Amabel Williams-Ellis.

Natasha Periyan is a Lecturer in Modern English Literature at King's College London. Her first book is *The Politics of 1930s British Literature: Education, Gender, Class* (2018) and she has recently co-edited a special issue of *Women: A Cultural Review* with Clara Jones. She is currently writing a book on the concept of intelligence in interwar women's writing, a project which arises from her work as an AHRC Research Associate on 'Literary Culture, Meritocracy and the Assessment of Intelligence in Britain and America, 1880–1920' at the University of Kent.

Bryony Randall is Professor of Modernist Literature at the University of Glasgow. She has research interests in textual editing, women's writing, short fiction, and literature and the everyday, and has published across these fields. With Jane Goldman and Susan Sellers, she is co-General Editor of the Cambridge Edition of the Works of Virginia Woolf; is co-editing Woolf's short fiction for that edition; and is a volume editor for the Oxford University Press edition of the work of Dorothy Richardson. She is co-director of the Textual Editing Lab at the University of Glasgow, and edited a special issue of *Modernist Cultures* on the New Modernist Editing (2020), an output of the AHRC-funded Network of that name for which she was Principal Investigator. She is co-editor with Jane Goldman of *Virginia Woolf in Context* (2013), and author of *Modernism, Daily Time and Everyday Life* (2007).

Brenda R. Silver is Mary Brinsmead Wheelock Professor Emerita at Dartmouth College and a long-time Adjunct Professor of English at Trinity College Dublin. Her writings include *Virginia Woolf Icon*, *Virginia Woolf's Reading Notebooks*, and *Rape and Representation* (edited with Lynn A. Higgins), as well as her edition of *'Anon' and 'The Reader': Virginia Woolf's Last Essays*. She has published numerous articles on Woolf, as well as articles on Charlotte Brontë, E. M. Forster, John le Carré, the politics of anger, hypertext, Bloomsbury and psychoanalysis, the digital public sphere, and popular culture in the digital age.

Anna Snaith is Professor of Twentieth-Century Literature at King's College London. Her publications include *Modernist Voyages: Colonial Women Writers in London, 1890–1945* (2014), an edition of Virginia Woolf's *The Years* for the Cambridge University Press Edition of the Works of Virginia Woolf (2012), and of *A Room of One's Own and Three Guineas* for Oxford World's Classics (2015). She is the editor of *Sound and Literature* (2020) and is currently working on a Leverhulme-funded monograph entitled *Noisescapes: Writing Sound in Interwar Britain*.

Charlotte Taylor Suppé is an independent scholar whose work focuses on the way female authors write about motherhood. Her forthcoming book, entitled *Virginia Woolf and Motherhood* (Edinburgh University Press), examines Woolf's use of maternal discourses and characters within political, social and personal contexts. Charlotte is currently working on an extended study of women writers and maternity across literary history.

Helen Tyson is a Senior Lecturer in Twentieth- and Twenty-First-Century British Literature at the University of Sussex, where she is also a Co-Director of the Centre for Modernist Studies. Helen has published articles on modernism and psychoanalysis in *Critical Quarterly*, *Feminist Modernist Studies*, *Oxford Literary Review*, *Literature Compass* and *Textual Practice*. She is co-editor of the

Gradiva award-winning collection of essays *Wild Analysis: From the Couch to Cultural and Political Life* (Routledge, 2021) and of the book *English Studies: The State of the Discipline, Past, Present and Future* (Palgrave, 2015). Helen's first book, *Reading Modernism's Readers: Virginia Woolf, Psychoanalysis and the Bestseller* is forthcoming from Edinburgh University Press in 2024.

Kabe Wilson is a UK multimedia artist with a particular focus on adaptation across different forms. As part of an ongoing creative engagement with British modernism, especially the work of Virginia Woolf, he has produced *The Dreadlock Hoax*, a performance piece that adapted and inverted the infamous Dreadnought Hoax of 1910, *Olivia N'Gowfri – Of One Woman or So*, an extended experiment in literary recycling, 'On Being Still' (*The Modernist Review* #25), a series of paintings and writings that scrutinises his own engagement with the Bloomsbury Group, and *Looking for Virginia: An Artist's Journey through 100 Archives*, a multimedia archival project developed for his 2023 residency at the Centre for Modernist Studies at the University of Sussex.

Nicola Wilson is Associate Professor of Book and Publishing Studies at the University of Reading and Co-director of the Centre for Book Cultures and Publishing. She is author of *Home in British Working-Class Fiction* (2015), co-author of *Scholarly Adventures in Digital Humanities: Making the Modernist Archives Publishing Project* (2017) and General Editor of the Ethel Carnie Holdsworth series with Kennedy & Boyd.

Woolf and Capitalism: Introduction

Clara Jones

Virginia Woolf's first novel, *The Voyage Out* (1915), opens with a commentary on London's capitalist economics at the dawn of the twentieth century:

> The cab, by trotting steadily along the same road, soon withdrew them from the West End, and plunged them into London. It appeared that this was a great manufacturing place, where the people were engaged in making things, as though the West End, with its electric lamps, its vast plate-glass windows all shining yellow, its carefully-finished houses, and tiny live figures trotting on the pavement, or bowled along on wheels in the road, was the finished work. It appeared to her a very small bit of work for such an enormous factory to have made. For some reason it appeared to her as a small golden tassel on the edge of a vast black cloak.
> Observing that they passed no other hansom cab, but only vans and waggons, and that not one of the thousand men and women she saw was either a gentleman or a lady, Mrs. Ambrose understood that after all it is the ordinary thing to be poor, and that London is the city of innumerable poor people. Startled by this discovery and seeing herself pacing a circle all the days of her life round Piccadilly Circus she was greatly relieved to pass a building put up by the London County Council for Night Schools.[1]

The narrative perspective here is ambiguous. The episode is focalised by Helen Ambrose, whose upper-middle-class status puts her at an automatic remove from the place and people she encounters in London's East End. The frame of reference – the haberdasher's decorative 'golden tassel', the toy-like 'tiny live figures' – suggest Helen's naivety and complacency. The middle-class ignorance of poverty staged in this passage is understood by Woolf as a function of capitalist society. On the most basic level, the passage describes the scene and processes of industrial capitalism – London's East End is a 'great manufacturing place' in which labour is 'engaged in making' consumer and capital goods.[2] This is also a class-divided society: the men and women workers of the East End make possible the 'finished work' of the affluent West End, enjoyed by ladies and gentlemen. The reference to their 'carefully-finished houses' also foregrounds the significance of private property to this economic system.

What makes this more than a mere record of a capitalist society is precisely the narrative distance that at first glance seems merely to register Helen Ambrose's middle-class naivety. The repetition of 'appeared' draws attention to the spectacular dimensions of urban capitalism; the 'vast plate-glass windows all shining yellow' pointing to the ways in which commodities demand and command our gaze.[3] Helen's metaphor of the 'small golden tassel' also hints at the exploitation that undergirds this system: the wealth of the West End is enjoyed by very few at the direct expense of 'innumerable poor people' whose work 'makes' it. The prominence of 'appeared' introduces a note of caution too; things may appear to be one thing but be quite another. Woolf suggests that Helen's naivety is not her own individual failing but the result of a wider systematised process of mystification.[4] Her 'understanding that it is after all the ordinary thing to be poor' – 'after all' implying some indisputable logic – exposes the way in which a capitalist economic system naturalises, and in doing so obscures, the social conditions that facilitate capital accumulation.

As Anna Snaith has shown, this interrogation of London's capitalist economy sets the tone for the novel's scrutiny and exposure of the 'violent capitalist motivations behind colonialism'.[5] Snaith also shows how in this passage Woolf 'considers the gender implications of an inequitable economic system', with Helen imagining herself as a prostitute circling 'round Piccadilly Circus', another commodity in an all-encompassing market economy.[6] This identification and her revelations about the ubiquity of poverty under capitalism cause Helen momentary alarm. As Douglas Dowd notes, 'In a society where the poor masses were constantly reminded of the rich few for whom [...] they were producing great wealth' – 'vast plate-glass windows all shining yellow' and 'carefully-finished houses' – 'Who could be rich and not worry?'[7] It is telling that Helen's fears are quelled by a 'building put up by the London County Council for Night Schools'. The Night School is satirically aligned with bourgeois anxiety about the 'innumerable' poor and positioned as a middle-class 'authorised means of improving them'.⁸ This is an expression of Woolf's ambivalent attitude towards philanthropy, but it also registers her understanding that ostensibly ideologically neutral social and cultural institutions have a part to play in sustaining a capitalist status quo.

In Woolf's first novel we discover the dimensions that characterised her engagement with capitalism throughout her career, which this book charts: the economics of work, the stratifications of social class, gender as it mediates in a capitalist economy and the commoditisation of culture. Yet, drafted from 1907 and published in 1915, *The Voyage Out* was written during a different phase of capitalist production to her works of the interwar period. Part of what is fascinating and productive about considering Woolf through the critical lens of capitalism is the fact that her writing life spanned and directly interacted with different phases of capitalism in Britain. Born in 1882, amid a global economic depression, Woolf's childhood coincided with a turn away from classical political economy and the advent of a newly vitalised capitalist world system. As social and economic historians have noted, this was a moment of contradictions.⁹ The so-called 'high' industrial capitalism Woolf describes in *The Voyage Out* gave way to new patterns of consumption and the exploitation of mass markets. This moment was characterised by 'a shift in emphasis, in economic history and practice, from production to consumption, and from the satisfaction of stable needs to the creation of new desires'.¹⁰ The period 1875 to 1914 witnessed a new kind of economic imperialism which saw colonial expansion take hold, as capitalist powers sought raw materials and 'privileged access' to new markets.¹¹ This was also a period that heralded challenges to the capitalist status quo in Britain: the questioning of free trade orthodoxies, 'the strange death of Liberal England' and the rise of Labour as a social movement and its instatement as a parliamentary party; the emergence of class as a defining and galvanising political category and the appearance of a wholesale alternative to capitalism in the form of the 1917 Bolshevik Revolution. During Woolf's lifetime, capitalism was subjected to critiques from various positions on the Left.¹² As Mark Steven notes, it was a period before capitalism's complete ubiquity, when 'alternatives' were visible and imaginable.¹³ Capitalism had not yet succeeded in making '"capitalistic" [. . .] all elements of social existence'.¹⁴ World historical crises including two world wars and the stock market crash of 1929 were also crises in capitalism, and they were understood and critiqued as such by the writers, economists and thinkers that witnessed them, not least Woolf herself.

Virginia Woolf was deeply imbricated in the contradictions of the specific phase of capitalist development she lived and wrote through. A self-identified 'labour woman', Woolf's political and social involvement on the Left brought her close-up to contemporary critiques of capitalism, mounted by the co-operative and Fabian movements.[15] Writing in her editor's note to a book of Co-operative Guildswomen's memoirs, introduced by Woolf herself, Margaret Llewelyn Davies articulates the organisation's aim as the 'peaceful revolution from autocratic Capitalism to democratic Co-operation'.[16] At the 1933 Labour Party Conference Woolf recalls a conversation with Frederick Pethick-Lawrence about the European vested economic interests in re-armament: 'I said What an argument against Capitalism!'[17] The left-feminist critiques of capitalism we find in Woolf's fiction and polemics – from the critiques of exploitation in *The Voyage Out* to those of private property in *Three Guineas* – are written under the influence of these debates. But it is also the case – as with other of the era's sharpest anti-capitalist critics – that Woolf was a beneficiary of the system that she disparaged. She lived the life of a rentier, and as Rachel Bowlby's chapter on Woolf's summer of enthusiastic property speculations demonstrates, Woolf could be unself-conscious about the privileges this position afforded her.[18] Nicola Wilson's chapter shows that she was also an active participant in the market economy as the owner of a 'booming' (*D3* 260) publishing house, the Hogarth Press, even if it did do a good line in anti-capitalist writing. As Evelyn Tsz Yan Chan observes in her chapter, which revisits Woolf's literary treatment of earned and unearned wealth, there exists in Woolf's writing 'a real tug-of-war between representations of conserving the capitalist status quo, and of breaking free from it' (p. 237).

Rather than trying to resolve such contradictions or 'redeem' Woolf from them, this collection recognises them as crucial to the character of Woolf's relationship to capitalism. The chapters in this volume demonstrate the manifold and productive ways in which Woolf's literary output can be read through the lens of capitalism: the formal and thematic significance of capitalism to her work and her writing as a form of cultural capital. This collection owes much to decades of Woolf scholarship that has foregrounded Woolf's politics, in particular the pioneering feminists of the 1970s and 1980s who contended with the powerful popular and critical consensus that Woolf was an a-political aesthete.[19] The present collection is also of a piece with recent work in Woolf studies aiming to offer more precisely contextualised accounts of Woolf's ideas and ideals and her relationship to and activities in the 'real world'.[20]

It also responds to the wealth of existing scholarship that foregrounds Woolf's (sometimes vexed) engagements with social class.[21] Research on Woolf and her economic influences by Elena Gualtieri, Michael Tratner, Evelyn Tsz Yan Chan and Kathryn Simpson as well as work focusing specifically on Woolf and the economics of empire by Michèle Barrett, Anna Snaith and Patricia Novillo-Corvalán, has laid the groundwork for the present collection which takes as a given Woolf's interest in the political implications of economics.[22]

The book is arranged into three parts: 'Class, Empire, Capital'; 'Labour and the Marketplace' and 'Critical/Creative Responses'. Part I revisits key terms that have been central to the reappraisal of Woolf's politics over the last twenty years – class and empire – and considers their relationship to and function within the capitalist society in which Woolf lived. Part II turns our attention to Woolf on work, taking in the questions of labour, professionalism and amateurism that have co-animated recent work on this subject.[23] Chapters in this section explore Woolf's working life as an anti-capitalist publisher, her literary representations of labour, as well as her attitudes towards markets, literary and otherwise, and her own marketability as a present-day 'icon'. The closing Coda takes up questions of class, privilege and labour, in two pieces written from different pedagogical and creative perspectives. By concluding in this way, we aim to keep the question of 'Virginia Woolf and Capitalism' an open one. Helen Tyson's feminist scrapbooking with her undergraduate students and Kabe Wilson's found poem based on *Mrs Dalloway* model ways of re-reading Woolf's texts that underscore their disruptive political potential while also drawing attention to their occlusions. Tyson and her students find 'critical power' (p. 288) in Woolf's method of scrapbooking for *Three Guineas* even while their own productions reveal 'Woolf's struggle to think intersectionally about the role of class and race' (p. 287). By removing all words bar those that describe a character's social or working status from *Mrs Dalloway*, Wilson's 'work cut out' crystalises the novel's critique of class-divided capitalist society and its exploitative underbelly:

> Coal merchants. tradespeople.   Duke.   Princesses.
>   those poor girls in Piccadilly   stable boys
>   Lady   valet   little post at Court,
> looked after the King's cellars, polished the Imperial shoe-buckles,
> went about in knee-breeches and lace
> ruffes.   little job at Court!
>   secretary's   usher's job teaching little boys Latin, mandarin

As this passage shows, the poem also creates juxtapositions that raise questions about the visibility and invisibility of certain kinds of labour in the novel. In the typography of 'work cut out', the novel's three throw-away references to 'coolies' gain new critical prominence, drawing attention to the labour of indentured colonial people and asking critical questions of the urtext.

Virginia Woolf and Capitalism is arranged by theme rather than by chronology or genre, and resists implying a progressivist logic to Woolf's engagement with capitalism. There are chapters drawing attention to the social and political content of Virginia Stephen/Woolf's earliest literary ventures, like Stanislava Dikova's assessment of the literary public sphere in *Night and Day* and Bryony Randall's reading of Woolf's working women writer characters and their access to different kinds of interacting capital. There are others that explore the ethical blind spots and ambiguities of Woolf's 'mature' polemical writing, like Natasha Periyan's interrogation of the assumptions about class and race behind Woolf's 'statistical imagination' (p. 96) in *A Room of One's Own*, or Anna Snaith's assessment of Woolf's mobilisation of the economics of race and slavery in *A Room* and *Three Guineas*. The collection reconsiders the central tenets of Woolf's politics – her feminism, anti-imperialism, and pacifism – in the context of her engagements with capitalism. In her chapter on Woolf's chary relationship with the working-class feminists of the Women's Co-operative Guild, Charlotte Taylor Suppé shows how Woolf's self-identification as 'capitalist' operates both as a label of reproach and marker of difference and distinction. Charles Andrews's reading of *Jacob's Room* focuses on Woolf's critique of the 'integrated network of capitalism and civil religion' (p. 125) that produces young men like Jacob Flanders and then disposes of them in economically motivated wars. Throughout the collection, the reader is asked to consider Woolf in the context of our own late capitalist moment, whether in Evelyn Tsz Yan Chan's interrogation of contemporary postwork theories of basic income, or Brenda R. Silver's essay which, based on lectures given in the aftermath of the 2002 release of *The Hours*, focuses on Woolf's continuing star appeal and her treatment in contemporary literary 'fan' fiction.

The Virginia Woolf who emerges in this collection is a heterodox as well as prescient thinker about capitalism. The rest of this opening essay explores some textual examples that make this clear. Anticipating the cross-generic emphasis of the chapters that follow, my examples are drawn from short stories, essays, unpublished drafts and Woolf's personal writing. They offer introductions to some of

Woolf's interlocutors in her engagements with capitalism, as well as spotlight moments of specifically feminist resistance to its economic regime.

Virginia Woolf and Karl Marx

Even while critics have drawn attention to Woolf's negotiation of class, consumption and empire in her fiction and non-fiction works, 'capitalism' remains a comparatively under-used key term in Woolf studies. Part of the reason for this may lie in a reticence about reading Woolf through another critical paradigm – Marxism. This reticence may be read as the product of a larger-scale disenchantment with 'Marxist thinking, and the category of "capitalism" that over time it engendered', which, as Michèle Barrett observes in her chapter, 'went into a huge decline in the aftermath of the collapse of the Soviet Union in 1979 and the ending of the cold war' (p. 32). The question of Woolf's Marxist or Marxian credentials was at one time central to debates about her politics. Witness the critical disagreements of the 1970s and 1980s between feminist literary critic Jane Marcus and Woolf's nephew and biographer Quentin Bell. While Marcus characterised Woolf as a 'genteel Marxist', a writer who combined 'a Marxian economics with Freudian psychological insights and Wollstonecraft's revolutionary feminism',[24] Bell insisted that there was no evidence she had the faintest interest in Marx or Marxism. The disagreement between Marcus and Bell was about more than Marx or even Woolf's politics: it was an argument about the efficacy of a feminist-socialist literary critical practice. I have suggested elsewhere that this definitional argument meant that the details of Woolf's real-world political action went overlooked.[25] While I still think this is broadly true, Marcus's conjunction of Woolf and Marx in this debate is typically suggestive and one I want to pursue through some literary texts to see what they might tell us about Woolf's thinking about capitalism.

The arguments of Karl Marx took hold after his death in 1883. As Mark Steven notes, the 'cultural proliferation of Marxism' at the end of the nineteenth and through the first half of the twentieth century coincided with and was 'causally related' to the emergence of literary modernism.[26] The reach of Marx's ideas in this period was extensive; Dowd points out that anyone in the period interested in 'understanding capitalism' did so using 'analytical tools first forged by Marx'.[27] Woolf's reading of co-operative movement, Fabian and

Labour literature – including the work of Beatrice and Sidney Webb and R. H. Tawney – and perhaps most significantly her intellectual companionship with her husband, Leonard Woolf, who identified himself as a 'Marxian Socialist' in his writings on contemporary social and political history, will have provided Woolf with a live encounter with Marx's ideas.[28] Essays in this collection evidence this: Anna Snaith shows Woolf's 'intellectual synergies' with critics of empire who both followed and deviated from Marx, while Nicola Wilson considers the Hogarth Press's 'commitment to exploring contemporary crises in capitalism' (p. 169). Woolf's own early critics had little reticence about enlisting Marx as a political and cultural interlocutor. Writing about *A Room of One's Own* in 1933, one of Woolf's most acute readers, Winifred Holtby, remarks: 'Marx himself has hardly put the materialistic interpretation of psychology more clearly'.[29] By contrast, in a recent discussion of 'Marx and the Modernist Novel', Julian Murphet suggests readers will 'look in vain for overt signs of Marx's legacy in the canonical modernist novels of Woolf, Conrad, Faulkner, and James'.[30] Murphet's suggestion that residues of Marx's radical 'legacies' are only detectable on the level of aesthetics – what he describes as the 'underlying presuppositions of the new approach to form' – misses a trick when it comes to Woolf.

Marx makes a few brief appearances in Woolf's writing. He cuts an ambivalent figure each time and his placement reveals something about Woolf and capitalism. The instances I focus on here both come from late, contrasting texts. The first is the essay 'The Leaning Tower', originally a talk delivered in May 1940 to the Brighton Branch of the Workers' Educational Association, at that time presided over by the socialist historian R. H. Tawney.[31] This essay is not an unexpected place to find Marx; it is one of Woolf's most explicit statements on class, politics and economics and their influence on literary production. The other is the short story 'The Legacy', also written in 1940 on commission by *Harper's Bazaar*, which subsequently rejected it. 'The Legacy' tells the story of recently widowed MP, Gilbert Clandon, who discovers from reading his deceased wife's diaries that she had fallen in love with a socialist firebrand, 'B.M.', and killed herself upon hearing of her lover's own suicide. In some ways these texts could not be more different – one is a polemic on the concentration of capital in the hands of very few who are as a result able to produce art, whereas the other is a conventional, even melodramatic, story of a suicide pact, and something Woolf was incentivised to write by the offer of a substantial payment from a commercial magazine.

In 'The Leaning Tower' Marx features as the preferred reading matter of the new generation of political poets:

> In 1930 young men at college were forced to be aware of what was happening in Russia; in Germany; in Italy; in Spain. They could not go on discussing aesthetic emotions and personal relations. They could not confine their reading to the poets; they had to read the politicians. They read Marx.³²

The tone here is grudging. It is interesting that Marx is described as a politician, rather than as an economist or philosopher; he is clearly associated by Woolf with the leftist politics of the 'Leaning Tower Poets'. Marx is also identified with masculine forms of education and as a type of specialised knowledge – something these young men picked up at university and from which the mass of common readers, and here Woolf collapses any distinction between herself as a wealthy woman and her working-class audience, have been excluded. Woolf is unconvinced that custodians of Marx, Auden, Spender and MacNeice, with their 'self-pity' (*E6* 272) and posturing, are going to bring about the 'world without classes' (*E6* 275) she looks forward to at the end of the essay. And yet the redistributive model she imagines in the essay – with increased taxes undermining private property and asserting state-run, public institutions in their place – is inflected by a Marxian economics.

In 'The Legacy', Marx is again introduced as the author of improving reading for the bourgeoisie in need of ideological enlightenment. Angela Clandon's political conversion begins when she starts philanthropic work in Whitechapel and meets B.M. After initial 'heated argument[s] about socialism with B.M.' she comes around to his ways of thinking:

> B.M. told me the story of his childhood. His mother went out charring... When I think of it, I can hardly bear to go on living in such luxury... Three guineas for one hat!' If only she had discussed the matter with him, instead of puzzling her poor little head about questions that were much too difficult for her to understand! He had lent her books. Karl Marx. 'The Coming Revolution.'³³

The telegraphic syntax – 'Karl Marx. 'The Coming Revolution' – recalls the bathetic phrasing of 'The Leaning Tower': 'The read Marx'. Woolf is once again straining against the authoritative knowledge Marx appears to her to represent. It is telling that these late texts with their gestures to Marx were produced at a moment when Leonard was engaged with and 'up to a point' propounding a Marxian analysis of the contemporary crisis in 'western civilization' in his own writing.[34] Woolf's portrait of B.M. shares some of her husband's scepticism of the doctrinaire 'neo-Marxist', who would turn Marx from a great thinker of his time into a 'prophet', while perhaps also encoding some of her impatience with Leonard's own possession and reiteration of Marx's thought.[35] Both texts, however grudgingly, acknowledge the reach and significance of his influence.

The gender politics of this passage and of 'The Legacy' more broadly mean that its reference to Marx takes on a different guise. It is not reading Marx alone, or at all, that prompts Angela to rethink her politics but B.M.'s 'story of his childhood' and his mother's experiences of 'charring'. 'When I think of it, I can hardly bear to go on living in such luxury . . . Three guineas for one hat!' Angela's response is the product of her 'genius for sympathy', much touted by her patronising husband throughout the story.[36] The joke is on him: feminine sympathy is re-written as feminist solidarity, as Angela reveals just the socio-economic understanding with which her husband refuses to credit her. The emphasis is squarely on women's experiences of capitalism – as exploited workers and as conspicuous consumers of commodities. The price of Angela's hat – 'three guineas' – recalls the arguments about gender, private property and capital that Woolf made in her 1938 polemic of the same name. As Barrett points out in her chapter, Marx's theory of production 'tended to see the labourer as male' and ignore the specificities of women's position in a capitalist society. The proximity of B.M.'s charring mother, 'three guineas' and 'Karl Marx' needles this point. Angela has reached her own revolutionary conclusions about the wrongness of her life of luxury before we even reach Marx in the sentence. The feminist arguments of *Three Guineas* are enlisted in this passage to make an implied criticism of Marx, while the suggestive conjunction of Marx and 'three guineas' spotlights the critique of capitalism that Woolf stages in her 1938 polemic. 'The Legacy' shares *Three Guineas*'s interest in the role of women in a capitalist society, although it comes at this issue from a slightly different angle. As Anna Snaith notes, in *Three Guineas* Woolf writes from a 'consciously limited perspective', choosing to speak as an 'educated man's daughter', staying 'within the sphere of which she had first hand knowledge'.[37] 'The Legacy' considers the ways in which class mediates women's experiences under capitalism, as in this passage where Angela is forced to reflect on the economic relationship this system insists she shares with women of other classes.

Keynes, Woolf and The Cook

Quentin Bell once expressed his amazement that Woolf should be seen 'as a maker of political ideologies' comparable to John Maynard Keynes.[38] Adam Trexler has since argued that the two were in fact 'closely connected in their development of an economic representation of modernity' and he and other scholars have revealed the productive possibilities of reading Woolf in dialogue with her Bloomsbury peer.[39] Woolf's personal proximity to the twentieth century's most famous economist and the extent of her engagement with his ideas is a significant way into thinking about her attitudes towards capitalism, as Evelyn Tsz Yan Chan's chapter in this collection shows. Keynes assumed the role of a 'reluctant supporter' of capitalism, believing it was 'better than any conceivable alternative'.[40] This reformist attitude is evident in 'The End of *Laissez-Faire*':

> Many people, who are really objecting to capitalism as a way of life, argue as though they were objecting to it on the ground of its inefficiency in attaining its own objects. Contrariwise, devotees of capitalism are often unduly conservative, and reject reforms in its technique, which might really strengthen and preserve it, for fear that they may prove to be first steps away from capitalism itself [. . .] For my part, I think that capitalism, wisely managed, can probably be made more efficient for attaining economic ends than any alternative system yet in sight, but that in itself it is in many ways extremely objectionable. Our problem is to work out a social organisation which shall be as efficient as possible without offending our notions of a satisfactory way of life.[41]

Keynes was interested in adjusting the 'technique' of the capitalist system rather than upsetting the apple cart entirely. The damaging social consequences of capitalism are kept in view here – he acknowledges that while capitalism might be good at securing 'economic ends' it is 'extremely objectionable'. So, for Keynes what was necessary was a model of capitalism that created a reasonable balance between economic efficiency and the 'good life' for most people. Alex Zwerdling suggests that Keynes set out to challenge 'the Marxist dogma that capitalism is doomed', contrasting Keynes's 'unshakeable loyalty to his own class' with Woolf's own discomfort with her rentier privileges.[42]

Woolf's writing shows that she did not necessarily share Keynes's confidence in capitalism's ability to remake itself in a more sympathetic mould. Part of this, as Elena Gualtieri convincingly shows, is to do with Woolf's identification of a blind spot for gender in Keynesian economics. In *Three Guineas* she pursues precisely these questions, and it is perhaps not a surprise that Keynes was singularly unimpressed with Woolf's arguments in that essay.[43]

The fraught socio-economic and party-political moment of 1931 brings the critical dialogue between Woolf and Keynes into sharp focus. The onset of the Depression in Britain following the worldwide economic crash of 1929 coincided with the second minority Labour Government. It was not a 'radical government' but one which believed that a 'prospering capitalist industry would be the motor force of the transition to socialism'.[44] However, by 1931 with high levels of unemployment, the economic pressure of retaining a fixed exchange rate and a policy of free trade, it was clear that a 'budgetary crisis was looming'.[45] In July 1931 the May Committee, which had been investigating national expenditure, recommended massive cuts to public spending, including a twenty per cent reduction in unemployment benefit and the salaries of public servants. It was the failed attempts by Prime Minister Ramsay MacDonald and Chancellor Philip Snowden to persuade their cabinet to accept these and further cuts that led to the dissolution of the Labour Government and the formation of a majority conservative National Government, under the continued premiership of MacDonald.[46]

For Keynes, who sat on a number of government economic committees during this period, including the May committee, this was a moment of increased civic involvement and one during which he finessed the ideas about government intervention and spending that would be institutionalised as 'Keynesianism' decades later.[47] He was not in sympathy with the conventional wisdom that saving was the best policy in straightened economic times, and his journalism of the period makes this clear. He could be forceful, as in his reactions to the Budget and Economy Bills in September 1931, which he called 'replete with folly and injustice'.[48] But he could be playful too, as in a broadcast called 'Saving and Spending':

> Therefore, O patriotic housewives, sally out tomorrow early into the streets and go to the wonderful sales which are everywhere advertised, You will do yourselves good – for never were things so cheap, cheap beyond your dreams. Lay in a stock of household linen, of sheets and blankets to satisfy all your needs. And have the added

joy that you are increasing employment, adding to the wealth of the country because you are setting on foot useful activities, bringing a chance and a hope to Lancashire, Yorkshire, and Belfast.⁴⁹

Keynes sets out his belief in the power of consumption to redress the economic balance in affable style, speaking directly to British housewives via mock-heroic address. The tone is also patronisingly gendered, with its talk of 'the wonderful sales' where items are 'so cheap, cheap beyond your dreams'.

Virginia Woolf was also preoccupied with the political crisis of 1931.⁵⁰ An October letter to Margaret Llewelyn Davies, written ten days before the general election that was to prove devastating for Labour, shows her familiarity and impatience with contemporary economic debates:

> All the summer we had nothing but political arguments with Maynard and others; and I finally felt it so completely silly, futile, petty, personal and unreal – all this about money – that I retired to my room and read poetry in a rage.⁵¹

Woolf's 'Cook Sketch' – a three-page draft written entirely in the voice of a domestic cook – gives the lie to Woolf's rejection of the 'petty, personal and unreal' world of economic crises and party politics in this letter.⁵² Like Keynes, in this piece Woolf explores the economic implications of the contemporary tumult through the figure of the female consumer-shopper. Woolf's cook is a skilled domestic economist and politically savvy, rather different from the 'patriotic housewives' Keynes imagines going giddily about their shopping. The cook notes:

> Of course they've the old stock on hand now. They're not making a penny change different at the moment. But if the Budget rises, [they'll] rise too. Prices follow suit [. . .] though what the government is for if its [sic] not to protect us working classes I don't know I saw Mr Macdonald once myself – a disappointment he was too.⁵³

She is aware of the very recent Budget's impact on food prices and the presence of 'large quantities of unsold stocks' that were a fixture of the period.⁵⁴ The fraught contemporary debates in the Labour movement about what the parliamentary party 'is for' clearly inform the sketch. The cook's reflections on the government's debt to 'us working classes' is influenced by the painful spectacle of a

Labour Government proposing cuts to the dole and teachers' salaries in order to satisfy the economic orthodoxy of 'balancing the books'.[55] The 'Cook Sketch' emerges out of Woolf's impatience with her arguments with Keynes over the summer of 1931 about politics and money, meeting their abstraction and 'unreality' with a woman's lived experience of a crisis of capitalism.

'Emotional Capital' and Women's Labour

This final section considers the mobile way in which Woolf imagines and deploys the language and logic of capitalism outside its regular economic setting, focusing on examples from her diaries and letters. In these moments she appears to proleptically anticipate our present moment in which capitalism has made its way into every aspect of personal life, giving it the power to 'shape thought and feeling'.[56] Take the following example, in which Woolf records romantic advice she has offered to her young friend Alix Sargant-Florence in a letter to her sister:

> I never heard such a farce. Copulation every 10 days in order to free his suppressed instincts! I rather think she'll marry him in the end. She asked my advice – but nobody ever takes my advice. I told her on no account to copulate from a sense of duty, but to advise him to invest his capital either in a new theatre or picture gallery or string quartet and his instincts would be liberated spontaneously. (L2 319)

Here we find Woolf playing the unlikely dual roles of agony aunt and investment broker. Woolf is sceptical about the psychoanalytic cover used by H. T. J. Norton to pressure Sargant-Florence for sex. Woolf's comic reflections encode the concern she felt about her young women friends, which she expressed explicitly elsewhere, that while appearing to 'aboli[sh] private property' in their experimental love lives, their behaviour actually involved 'a reversion to the devoted submission of our grandmothers' (L2 214).[57] As with her pointed use of the phrase 'private property', Woolf's equation of sexual energy and capital in her letter to Vanessa is striking.[58] These passages show Woolf thinking about the intimate links between desire, 'instincts', property and capital and reveal an understanding of capitalism and its spheres of influence that goes beyond the narrowly economistic.

Woolf's most explicit reflections on capitalism in her diaries also comment on its psychic dimensions. Recording a conversation about Tolstoyan asceticism in 1918, Woolf writes:

> L. gave us a great many reasons why we should keep what we have, & do good work for nothing; I still feel, however, that my fire is too large for one person. I'm one of those who are hampered by the psychological hindrance of owning capital.[59]

It is an obvious point but one worth noting that this well-known passage focuses on the violence capitalism does to its supposed beneficiaries, people like Woolf herself with an excess of capital, rather than the exploited proletariat. This is a sentiment we find elsewhere – as in her talk of the middle classes being 'pinned down by their capital' in 'The Leaning Tower' (E6 269). Clearly such statements leave Woolf open to accusations of special pleading and ignorance of capitalism's primary victims. As I have suggested, they also acknowledge capitalism's pervasiveness, the way it conditions not only people's economic lives but their inner ones too.

The idea of an excess of capital appears again a few years later in a record of an event in Keynes's grand rooms in Cambridge: 'The party began after a few brilliancies on my part about religion; emotional [?] capital which I did not know how to invest, I said.'[60] The formulation 'emotional capital' is a suggestive one, even if it requires a cautious approach, as Anne Olivier Bell indicates that this is a questionable transcription. Reference to the original manuscript shows Woolf has deleted 'too much' and inserted 'emotional' in its place – creating an imaginative connection with her earlier claims about being 'hampered' by her wealth.[61] These reflections about religion as a form of capital register Woolf's understanding of the 'fusion' of capitalism and civil religion that Charles Andrews explores in his chapter in this collection. Her words were likely prompted by a visit that day to Fredegond Shove, who had been attending Catholic Mass and claimed to be 'happier & more full of vitality than before'. Woolf's trip to Cambridge threw up other prompts for reflection about the 'investment' of 'emotional capital'. Woolf said the following about her early evening with George and Dorothy Moore and their two children: 'Fine little cubs too, fat, hard, sturdy, likely to do us all credit when we are all dead. The elegiac note will creep in, & shall be justified if I have time.' The parenting of children is imagined as another way of investing emotional capital and deriving 'credit' – an investment that Woolf herself had not made, hence perhaps the 'elegiac note' she sounds here. This was also a period in which Woolf was making efforts on T. S. Eliot's behalf to secure him an annual income – significantly £500 a year – so that he could give up his post at Lloyd's and write full time.[62] It is little wonder, then, that at a moment when economic questions put pressure on her friendships and she and Leonard were reflecting on their status at middle-age and comparing themselves with their (near) contemporaries – G. E. Moore now the comfortable family man and Keynes, 'arrived & trim, yet our junior' (*D2* 232) – Woolf was thinking about the mobile nature of different forms of capital and their exchangeability.

But if the language of 'emotional capital' appears to accept the tenets of capitalist exchange into personal life, there is another more resistant strain of Woolf's work which both recognises and critiques what has since been defined as 'emotional labour'. Building on feminist critiques of Marx that drew attention to the unwaged work done by women in the home,[63] the concept of emotional labour focuses on capitalism as an 'emotional system', with women undertaking the bulk of work both in unpaid capacities in the home and increasingly in the marketplace, with the rise of the commercial sector in the twentieth and twenty-first centuries.[64] The self-sacrificing actions of the 'Angel in the House' in 'Professions for Women', Mrs Ramsay's exhausting displays of sympathy for her tyrannical husband and Angela Clandon's 'genius for sympathy' all read as a commentary on the particular kinds of 'emotion work' undertaken by middle-class women in domestic settings.[65] Woolf shows this work as indirectly reinforcing the capitalist status quo; in 'The Legacy' we are told that Angela had been the 'greatest of help' to her husband 'in his career' as, we assume, a Tory politician.[66] Among Woolf's last works, 'The Legacy' touches on the full range of women's paid and unpaid work under capitalism – Angela's sympathetic support of her husband, lower-middle-class secretary Minnie's precarious clerical work, and B.M.'s mother's grinding labour as a charwoman – and points to the interconnectedness of this work.

* * *

This introduction has shown the different and crucially interacting versions of capitalism circulating in Woolf's work throughout her career; it appears as economic order, political ideology and regulator of human relationships. The chapters that follow continue this work of exploring the dynamic and protean character of Woolf's engagement with and her critiques of capitalism. Galvanised by what existing Woolf scholarship has taught us about the place of economics, class, gender and empire in her writing, the work in this volume demonstrates how critically productive and provocative thinking about Woolf through the lens of capitalism can be.

Notes

1. Virginia Woolf, *The Voyage Out* (1915) (London: Penguin, 1992), 6.
2. This is subject matter Woolf would return to with a similarly sharp eye in her 'London Scene' essays, particularly 'The Docks of London'. For the treatment of capitalism and empire in this essay, see Anna Snaith and Michael Whitworth, 'Introduction', in *Locating Woolf: The Politics of Place and Space* (London: Palgrave Macmillan UK, 2007), 23–8.
3. Elizabeth Outka has discussed the prominence of the shop window display in *Night and Day* and that novel's 'commentary on modern consumerism'. *Consuming Traditions: Modernity, Modernism, and the Commodified Authentic* (Oxford: Oxford University Press, 2008), 130.
4. For more on the status and processes of mystification in Marx's theory of capitalism see Christopher Pierson, 'Introduction', in *The Marx Reader* (Cambridge: Polity, 1996), 16–17.
5. Anna Snaith, 'Leonard and Virginia Woolf: Writing Against Empire', *The Journal of Commonwealth Literature*, 50.1 (2015), 19–32 (19). David Bradshaw describes this passage as evidence of 'the socio-political outlook' that would characterise Woolf's fiction throughout her career. David Bradshaw, 'The Socio-Political Vision of the Novels', in *The Cambridge Companion to Virginia Woolf*, ed. by Susan Sellers, 2nd edn (Cambridge: Cambridge University Press, 2010), 124–41 (125).
6. Snaith, 'Leonard and Virginia Woolf', 23.
7. Douglas Dowd, *Capitalism and its Economics* (London: Pluto Press, 2004), 71.
8. Clara Jones, *Virginia Woolf: Ambivalent Activist* (Edinburgh: Edinburgh University Press, 2015), 44.
9. Eric Hobsbawm, *The Age of Empire* (London: Abacus, 1994), 37–8.
10. David Trotter, *The English Novel in History, 1895–1920* (London: Routledge, 1993), 11.
11. Hobsbawm, *The Age of Empire*, 60; Dowd, *Capitalism and its Economics*, 50.
12. For an account of economic critiques of capitalism in the modernist period see Adam Trexler, 'Economic Ideas and British Literature, 1900–1930: The Fabian Society, Bloomsbury, and *The New Age*', *Literature Compass*, 4 (2007), 862–87.

13. Mark Steven, 'Introduction', in *Understanding Marx, Understanding Modernism*, ed. by Mark Steven (London: Bloomsbury Academic, 2021), 6.
14. Dowd, *Capitalism and its Economics*, 90.
15. Virginia Woolf, *The Diary of Virginia Woolf, Volume Three: 1925–1930*, ed. by Anne Olivier Bell (Harmondsworth: Penguin, 1982), 198–9. Further page references will be given within the main text.
16. Margaret Llewelyn Davies, 'Editor's Note', in *Life As We Have Known It* (1931) (London: Virago, 2012), xii.
17. *The Diary of Virginia Woolf, Volume Four: 1931–1935*, ed. by Anne Olivier Bell (Harmondsworth: Penguin, 1983), 183. Further page references will be given within the main text.
18. For more on Woolf's finances, including her investments and inherited wealth, see: Elena Gualtieri, 'Woolf, Economics and Class Politics: Learning to Count', in *Virginia Woolf in Context*, ed. by Jane Goldman and Bryony Randall (Cambridge: Cambridge University Press, 2012), 183–92.
19. Writing in 1978 Michèle Barrett noted the sceptical attitude of left and Marxist literary critics and historians who considered Woolf's writing 'to lack any grip on the concrete, historical, fabric of society'. 'Towards a Sociology of Virginia Woolf Criticism', in Diana Laurenson (ed.), *The Sociology of Literature: Applied Studies* (Keele: University of Keele, 1978). See also Jane Marcus, *Virginia Woolf and the Languages of Patriarchy* (Indiana: Indiana University Press, 1987) and Rachel Bowlby, *Virginia Woolf: Feminist Destinations* (Edinburgh: Basil Blackwell, 1988).
20. Alex Zwerdling's *Virginia Woolf and the Real World* (Berkeley: University of California Press, 1986) is a crucial study in the development of historicist approaches to Woolf's writing. See Jessica Berman, *Modernist Fiction, Cosmopolitanism and the Politics of Community* (Cambridge: Cambridge University Press, 2001); Alice Wood, *Virginia Woolf's Late Cultural Criticism: The Genesis of The Years, Three Guineas and Between the Acts* (London: Bloomsbury, 2013); Natasha Periyan, '"Altering the Structure of Society": An Institutional Focus on Virginia Woolf and Working-Class Education', *Textual Practice*, 32 (2018), 1301–23.
21. See, for example, Mary M. Childers, 'Virginia Woolf on the Outside Looking Down: Reflections on the Class of Women', *Modern Fiction Studies*, 38 (1992), 61–79; Alison Light, *Mrs Woolf and the Servants* (London: Penguin, 2007); Mary Wilson, *The Labors of Modernism: Domesticity, Servants, and Authorship in Modernist Fiction* (London: Routledge, 2016); Ben Harker, 'On Different Levels Ourselves Went Forward: Pageantry, Class Politics and Narrative Form in Virginia Woolf's Late Writing', *ELH*, 78 (2011), 433–56; Anna Snaith, 'Wide Circles: The 'Three Guineas' Letters', *Woolf Studies Annual*, 6 (2000), 1–12.

22. Gualtieri, 'Learning to Count'; Michael Tratner, *Deficits and Desires: Economics and Sexuality in Twentieth-Century Literature* (Stanford: Stanford University Press, 2001); Evelyn Tsz Yan Chan, *Virginia Woolf and the Professions* (New York: Cambridge University Press, 2014); Kathryn Simpson, 'Economies and Desire: Gifts and the Market in *Moments of Being: 'Slater's Pins Have No Points'*", *Journal of Modern Literature*, 28.2 (2005), 18–37. Michèle Barrett, 'Virginia Woolf's Research for *Empire and Commerce in Africa* (Leonard Woolf, 1920)', *Woolf Studies Annual*, 19 (2013), 83–122; Snaith, 'Virginia and Leonard Woolf'; Patricia Novillo-Corvalán, 'Empire and Commerce in Latin America: Historicising Woolf's *The Voyage Out*', *Woolf Studies Annual*, 23 (2017), 33–60. Work exploring Woolf with a focus on consumption provides some gripping discussions of Woolf and capitalism, taking in her literary representations of commodity culture and shopping – see Rachel Bowlby, 'The Passer-by and the Shop Window', in *Carried Away: The Invention of Modern Shopping* (Columbia University Press, 2001), 49–78; and Reginald Abbott, 'What Miss Kilman's Petticoat Means: Virginia Woolf, Shopping, and Spectacle', *Modern Fiction Studies*, 38.1 (1992), 193–216; as well as her negotiation of the literary marketplace and market economies more broadly – see Jennifer Wicke, '*Mrs. Dalloway* Goes to Market: Woolf, Keynes, and Modern Markets', *NOVEL: A Forum on Fiction*, 28.1 (1994), 5–23; Alissa G. Carl, *Modernism and the Marketplace: Literary Culture and Consumer Capitalism in Rhys, Woolf, Stein, and Nella Larsen* (New York: Routledge, 2009); Elizabeth M. Sheehan, 'Consumer Culture', in *The Oxford Handbook of Virginia Woolf*, ed. by Jessica Berman (Oxford: Oxford University Press, 2021); Nicola Wilson, 'Virginia Woolf, Hugh Walpole, The Hogarth Press, and The Book Society', *ELH*, 79 (2012), 237–60.
23. See Chan, *Virginia Woolf and the Professions* and Victoria Baena, 'Labor, Thought, and the Work of Authorship: Virginia Woolf and Hannah Arendt', *Diacritics*, 48.1 (2020), 82–105.
24. Marcus, 'No More Horses: Virginia Woolf on Art and Propaganda', *Women's Studies*, 4 (1977), 265–89 (266, 274).
25. Jones, *Ambivalent Activist*, 13.
26. Steven, 'Introduction', 2, 1.
27. Dowd, *Capitalism and its Economics*, 101.
28. See Leonard Woolf, *Barbarians at the Gate* (London: Victor Gollancz, 1939), 123 and *The War for Peace* (London: Butler & Tanner Ltd, 1940), 152.
29. Winifred Holtby, *Virginia Woolf* (London: Wishart, 1932), 173.
30. Julian Murphet, 'Marx and the Modernist Novel', in *Understanding Marx, Understanding Modernism*, ed. by Mark Steven, 115–23 (121).
31. For more on the context of the talk see Periyan, 'Altering the Structure of Society', 1301–23.

32. Virginia Woolf, 'The Leaning Tower', in *The Essays of Virginia Woolf: Volume Six, 1933–1941*, ed. by Stuart N. Clarke (London: Hogarth Press, 2011), 259–83 (269). Further page references will be given within the main text.
33. Virginia Woolf, 'The Legacy', in *The Complete Shorter Fiction of Virginia Woolf*, ed. by Susan Dick (New York: Harcourt, Inc., 1989), 281–7 (286). Marx is not the author of a book with this title; Woolf appears to have borrowed it from a work by English socialist H. M. Hyndman, *The Coming Revolution in England* (1884).
34. Woolf, *Barbarians at the Gate*, 123, 99.
35. Woolf, *The War for Peace*, 152; Woolf, *Barbarians at the Gate*, 124.
36. In his appraisal of their 'remarkable record of political and organizational involvement', Raymond Williams describes the Bloomsbury group as engaging with and advocating for 'a lower class *as a matter of conscience*: not in solidarity, not in affiliation'. 'The Bloomsbury Fraction', in *Culture and Materialism* (London: Verso, 2005), 165–89 (173–4). By contrast, my reading of 'The Legacy' follows Jessica Berman, who insists on Woolf's interrogative interest in the problem of 'political solidarity' (*Modernist Fiction and Community*, 118) and her awareness of the distinctions between sympathy and solidarity.
37. Snaith, 'Wide Circles', 3–4.
38. Quentin Bell, 'Bloomsbury and "The Vulgar Passions"', *Critical Inquiry*, 6 (1979), 239–59 (243).
39. Trexler, 'Economic Ideas and British Literature', 877. Also see Mark Hussey, 'Mrs. Thatcher and Mrs. Woolf', *Modern Fiction Studies*, 50.1 (2004), 8–30; Wicke, '*Mrs. Dalloway* Goes to Market' and Tratner, *Deficits and Desires*.
40. Dowd, *Capitalism and its Economics*, 10, 131.
41. J. M. Keynes, 'The End of *Laissez-Faire*' (1926), in *Essays in Persuasion* (Edinburgh: Rupert Hart-Davies Ltd, 1951), 312–22 (320–1).
42. Zwerdling, *Virginia Woolf and the Real World*, 103.
43. Gualtieri, 'Learning to Count', 189–90.
44. Dudley Baines, 'The Onset of Depression', in *20th Century Britain: Economic, Social and Cultural Change*, ed. by Paul Johnson (London: Longman, 1994), 184; Andrew Thorpe, *A History of the British Labour Party* (London: Bloomsbury Publishing, 2015), 65.
45. Thorpe, *A History of the British Labour Party*, 77.
46. Ibid., 80.
47. For more on this period in Keynes's career see Robert Skidelsky, *John Maynard Keynes, Volume 2: The Economist as Saviour* (London: Viking, 1994), 343–400.
48. J. M. Keynes, 'The Economy Bill' (19 Sept 1931), in *Essays in Persuasion*, 162–7 (162).
49. J. M. Keynes, 'Saving and Spending' (Jan 1931), in *Essays in Persuasion*, 148–56 (152).

50. In their discussion of the contemporary writing project, 'The Docks of London', Snaith and Whitworth note that at a time of 'economic upheaval and uncertainty in Britain, questions of economics, trade and systems of government were uppermost in Woolf's mind'. 'Introduction', in *Locating Woolf*, 24.
51. *A Reflection of the Other Person: The Letters of Virginia Woolf, Volume Four, 1929–1931*, ed. by Nigel Nicolson and Joanne Trautmann (London: Hogarth Press, 1978), 392.
52. This draft appears in a notebook, mainly dedicated to a draft of Woolf's essay 'A Letter to a Young Poet', and dated '1931 Sept 24th', although Woolf's diary indicates she wrote the so-called 'Cook Sketch' a little later, on 14 October 1931. See Clara Jones, 'Virginia Woolf's 1931 "Cook Sketch"', *Woolf Studies Annual*, 20 (2014), 1–23.
53. Jones, 'Cook Sketch', 19–21.
54. Baines, 'The Onset of Depression', 181.
55. For this tumultuous moment in Labour history see Thorpe, *A History of the British Labour Party*, 77–80.
56. Dowd, *Capitalism and its Economics*, 2.
57. *A Question of Things Happening: The Letters of Virginia Woolf, Volume Two, 1912–1922*, ed. by Nigel Nicolson and Joanne Trautmann (London: Hogarth Press, 1976), 213–14. Further page references will be given within the main text.
58. It is possible to read Woolf's recommendation that Norton invest in a 'string quartet' as a satirical swipe at Keynes who was himself a famous patron of the arts.
59. *The Diary of Virginia Woolf, Volume One: 1915–1919*, ed. by Anne Olivier Bell (Harmondsworth: Penguin, 1979), 100–1.
60. *The Diary of Virginia Woolf, Volume Two: 1920–1924*, ed. by Anne Olivier Bell (Harmondsworth: Penguin, 1981), 231.
61. Falmer, The Keep, Monks House Papers, Virginia Woolf's diaries – copies, 1920–1928, Wednesday 7 February 1923, SxMs70/4/3/2.
62. For an account of Woolf's involvement with this fund for Eliot see Hermione Lee, *Virginia Woolf* (London: Vintage, 1997), 445–6.
63. In *Three Guineas*, Woolf herself can be read as anticipating many of the arguments of the 'Wages for Housework' movement. See Asako Nakai, 'Materialism, Autonomy, Intersectionality: Revisiting Virginia Woolf through the Wages for Housework Perspective', *Feminist Theory*, 24.4 (2023), 497–511.
64. See, for example, Arlie Hochschild, *The Managed Heart: Commercialization of Human Feeling* (Berkeley: University of California Press, 1979). In a more recent work, *Cold Intimacies: The Making of Emotional Capitalism* (London: Polity, 2007), Eva Illouz explores the interactions of emotional and economic relationships in contemporary Western society, charting the emergence of 'emotional intelligence' as a form of capital exploited for financial gain by middle classes.

65. See Arlie Hochschild, 'Emotion Work, Feeling Rules, and Social Structure', *American Journal of Sociology*, 85.3 (1979), 551–75.
66. Hochschild considers the relationship between emotional labour in the home and broader economic structures in 'Emotion Work, Feeling Rules', 551–75.

Works Cited

Abbott, Reginald. 'What Miss Kilman's Petticoat Means: Virginia Woolf, Shopping, and Spectacle'. *Modern Fiction Studies*, 38.1 (1992), 193–216.

Baena, Victoria. 'Labor, Thought, and the Work of Authorship: Virginia Woolf and Hannah Arendt'. *Diacritics*, 48.1 (2020), 82–105.

Barrett, Michèle. 'Towards a Sociology of Virginia Woolf Criticism'. In *The Sociology of Literature: Applied Studies*, ed. by Diana Laurenson, 145–60. Keele: University of Keele, 1978.

——, 'Virginia Woolf's Research for *Empire and Commerce in Africa* (Leonard Woolf, 1920)'. *Woolf Studies Annual*, 19 (2013), 83–122.

Bell, Quentin. 'Bloomsbury and "The Vulgar Passions"'. *Critical Inquiry*, 6 (1979), 239–59.

Berman, Jessica. *Modernist Fiction, Cosmopolitanism and the Politics of Community*. Cambridge: Cambridge University Press, 2001.

Bowlby, Rachel. 'The Passer-by and the Shop Window'. In Bowlby, *Carried Away: The Invention of Modern Shopping*, 49–78. New York: Columbia University Press, 2001.

——, *Virginia Woolf: Feminist Destinations*. Edinburgh: Basil Blackwell, 1988.

Bradshaw, David. 'The Socio-Political Vision of the Novels'. In *The Cambridge Companion to Virginia Woolf*, ed. by Susan Sellers, 2nd edn, 124–41. Cambridge: Cambridge University Press, 2010.

Carl, Alissa G. *Modernism and the Marketplace: Literary Culture and Consumer Capitalism in Rhys, Woolf, Stein, and Nella Larsen*. New York: Routledge, 2009.

Chan, Evelyn Tsz Yan. *Virginia Woolf and the Professions*. New York: Cambridge University Press, 2014.

Childers, Mary M. 'Virginia Woolf on the Outside Looking Down: Reflections on the Class of Women'. *Modern Fiction Studies*, 38 (1992), 61–79.

Dowd, Douglas. *Capitalism and its Economics*. London: Pluto Press, 2004.

Falmer. The Keep, Monks House Papers, Virginia Woolf's diaries – copies. 1920–1928. Wednesday 7 February 1923. SxMs70/4/3/2.

Gualtieri, Elena. 'Woolf, Economics and Class Politics: Learning to Count'. In *Virginia Woolf in Context*, ed. by Jane Goldman and Bryony Randall, 183–92. Cambridge: Cambridge University Press, 2012.

Harker, Ben. 'On Different Levels Ourselves Went Forward: Pageantry, Class Politics and Narrative Form in Virginia Woolf's Late Writing'. *ELH*, 78 (2011), 433–56.

Hobsbawm, Eric. *The Age of Empire*. London: Abacus, 1994.

Hochschild, Arlie. 'Emotion Work, Feeling Rules, and Social Structure'. *American Journal of Sociology*, 85.3 (1979), 551–75.

——, *The Managed Heart: Commercialization of Human Feeling*. Berkeley: University of California Press, 1979.

Holtby, Winifred. *Virginia Woolf*. London: Wishart, 1932.

Hussey, Mark. 'Mrs. Thatcher and Mrs. Woolf'. *Modern Fiction Studies*, 50.1 (2004), 8–30.

Illouz, Eva. *Cold Intimacies: The Making of Emotional Capitalism*. London: Polity, 2007.

Johnson, Paul (ed.). *20th Century Britain: Economic, Social and Cultural Change*. London: Longman, 1994.

Jones, Clara. 'Virginia Woolf's 1931 "Cook Sketch"'. *Woolf Studies Annual*, 20 (2014), 1–23.

——, *Virginia Woolf: Ambivalent Activist*. Edinburgh: Edinburgh University Press, 2015.

Keynes, J. M. *Essays in Persuasion*. Edinburgh: Rupert Hart-Davies Ltd, 1951.

Lee, Hermione. *Virginia Woolf*. London: Vintage, 1997.

Light, Alison. *Mrs Woolf and the Servants*. London: Penguin, 2007.

Llewelyn Davies, Margaret. 'Editor's Note'. In *Life As We Have Known It* (1931). London: Virago, 2012.

Marcus, Jane. 'No More Horses: Virginia Woolf on Art and Propaganda'. *Women's Studies*, 4 (1977), 265–89.

——, *Virginia Woolf and the Languages of Patriarchy*. Indiana: Indiana University Press, 1987.

Nakai, Asako. 'Materialism, Autonomy, Intersectionality: Revisiting Virginia Woolf through the Wages for Housework Perspective'. *Feminist Theory*, 24.4 (2023), 497–511.

Novillo-Corvalán, Patricia. 'Empire and Commerce in Latin America: Historicising Woolf's *The Voyage Out*'. *Woolf Studies Annual*, 23 (2017), 33–60.

Outka, Elizabeth. *Consuming Traditions: Modernity, Modernism, and the Commodified Authentic*. Oxford: Oxford University Press, 2008.

Periyan, Natasha. '"Altering the Structure of Society": An Institutional Focus on Virginia Woolf and Working-Class Education'. *Textual Practice*, 32 (2018), 1301–23.

Pierson, Christopher. 'Introduction'. In Pierson, *The Marx Reader*. Cambridge: Polity, 1996.

Sheehan, Elizabeth M. 'Consumer Culture'. In *The Oxford Handbook of Virginia Woolf*, ed. by Jessica Berman, 472–86. Oxford: Oxford University Press, 2021.

Simpson, Kathryn. 'Economies and Desire: Gifts and the Market in *Moments of Being: 'Slater's Pins Have No Points'*'. *Journal of Modern Literature*, 28.2 (2005), 18–37.

Skidelsky, Robert. *John Maynard Keynes, Vol. 2: The Economist as Saviour*. London: Viking, 1994.

Snaith, Anna. 'Leonard and Virginia Woolf: Writing Against Empire'. *The Journal of Commonwealth Literature*, 50.1 (2015), 19–32.

Snaith, Anna. 'Wide Circles: The "Three Guineas" Letters'. *Woolf Studies Annual*, 6 (2000), 1–12.

Snaith, Anna and Michael Whitworth, eds. 'Introduction'. In *Locating Woolf: The Politics of Place and Space*. London: Palgrave Macmillan, 2007.

Steven, Mark (ed.). *Understanding Marx, Understanding Modernism*. London: Bloomsbury Academic, 2021.

Thorpe, Andrew. *A History of the British Labour Party*. London: Bloomsbury Publishing, 2015.

Tratner, Michael. *Deficits and Desires: Economics and Sexuality in Twentieth-Century Literature*. Stanford: Stanford University Press, 2001.

Trexler, Adam. 'Economic Ideas and British Literature, 1900–1930: The Fabian Society, Bloomsbury, and *The New Age*'. *Literature Compass*, 4 (2007), 862–87.

Trotter, David. *The English Novel in History, 1895–1920*. London: Routledge, 1993.

Wicke, Jennifer. '*Mrs. Dalloway* Goes to Market: Woolf, Keynes, and Modern Markets'. *NOVEL: A Forum on Fiction*, 28.1 (1994), 5–23.

Williams, Raymond. *Culture and Materialism*. London: Verso, 2005.

Wilson, Mary. *The Labors of Modernism: Domesticity, Servants, and Authorship in Modernist Fiction*. London: Routledge, 2016.

Wilson, Nicola. 'Virginia Woolf, Hugh Walpole, the Hogarth Press, and The Book Society'. *ELH*, 79 (2012), 237–60.

Wood, Alice. *Virginia Woolf's Late Cultural Criticism: The Genesis of The Years, Three Guineas and Between the Acts*. London: Bloomsbury, 2013.

Woolf, Leonard. *Barbarians at the Gate*. London: Victor Gollancz, 1939.

Woolf, Leonard. *The War for Peace*. London: Butler & Tanner Ltd., 1940.

Woolf, Virginia. *The Complete Shorter Fiction of Virginia Woolf*, ed. by Susan Dick. New York: Harcourt, Inc., 1989.

——, *The Diary of Virginia Woolf, Volume One: 1915–1919*, ed. by Anne Olivier Bell. Harmondsworth: Penguin, 1979.

——, *The Diary of Virginia Woolf, Volume Two: 1920–1924*, ed. by Anne Olivier Bell. Harmondsworth: Penguin, 1981.

——, *The Diary of Virginia Woolf, Volume Three: 1925–1930*, ed. by Anne Olivier Bell. Harmondsworth: Penguin, 1982.

——, *The Diary of Virginia Woolf, Volume Four: 1931–1935*, ed. by Anne Olivier Bell. Harmondsworth: Penguin, 1983.

——, *The Essays of Virginia Woolf: Volume Six, 1933–1941*, ed. by Stuart N. Clarke. London: Hogarth Press, 2011.

———, *The Question of Things Happening: The Letters of Virginia Woolf, Volume Two, 1912–1922*, ed. by Nigel Nicolson and Joanne Trautmann. London: Hogarth Press, 1976.
———, *A Reflection of the Other Person: The Letters of Virginia Woolf, Volume Four, 1929–1931*, ed. by Nigel Nicolson and Joanne Trautmann. London: Hogarth Press, 1978.
———, *A Room of One's Own and Three Guineas*, ed. by Michèle Barrett. London: Penguin, 1993.
———, *The Voyage Out* (1915). London: Penguin, 1992.
Zwerdling, Alex. *Virginia Woolf and the Real World*. Berkeley: University of California Press, 1986.

Part I

Class, Empire, Capital

Chapter 1

'The eagle claws other peoples land, & goods': Virginia Woolf on the Desire to Dominate

Michèle Barrett

'The moulds are filled nightly': *Jacob's Room* (1922)

One of the most eloquent examples of a socially critical impetus in Woolf's writing is her description, in *Jacob's Room*, of a night at the opera. Even before we get into London's famous opera house, we learn the economic geography of how people go home – of all the carriages, 'not one turns eastward'.[1] The audience is made up exclusively of people from west of Covent Garden, rather than from the much poorer neighbourhoods of London's East End.

Inside the opera house, a more complex stratification is in play. Woolf's narrator announces blandly that 'nature and society between them have arranged a system of classification which is simplicity itself; stalls, boxes, amphitheatre, gallery. The moulds are filled nightly' (*JR* 57). London's main opera house has not changed much since 1922. Woolf refers to 'two thousand hearts in the semi-darkness', which is comparable to the current (2022) capacity of the Royal Opera House, which seats 2,256 people. If you wanted to see the current production of *Norma* you could pay £225 for a seat in the orchestra stalls, or again £225 for one seat in a box in the Grand Tier (though you have to buy 4 of them). The amphitheatre prices range from £96 down to £11, depending on how good the view of the stage is and whether you actually get a seat to sit on or have to stand. Woolf's 'gallery' is presumably what is now called the balcony, where seats (or standing room) can be as little as £11, similarly reflecting a poor view and lack of comfort, as well as great height above the stage. Edward Whittaker, just the kind of poor music-lover who is encouraged to use the cheapest tickets, is 'suspended' in the gallery, and 'surreptitiously held a torch to his miniature score' (*JR* 57). Another young man in a cheap seat, 'set a little apart from his fellows by the influence of the music', is making his way 'down the stone stairs' (*JR* 58) at the end of the opera. The carpeted stairs are for the expensive areas, and the balcony seats (the gallery in Woolf) are reached via a hard stone staircase.

At the other end of the social scale, in Woolf's account, 'a Royal hand attached to an invisible body' signifies the presence of royalty in the opera house. Royalty engenders sentimental patriotism – 'the Queen of England' (like Miss Isobel Pole in *Mrs Dalloway*) 'seemed a name worth dying for' (*JR* 56). The image of the royal hand at the opera brings to mind Virginia Stephen's earlier experience:

> Every other night, I look into the middle box on the pit tier, and see Beatrice [Thynne], black and red, resting an imperious fist on the ledge. She looks as though she were ruling modern society; like a Roman Empress, with a drop of hot Tartar blood.[2]

As Emma Sutton writes 'Woolf grew up immersed in music. As a young woman, she attended operas and concerts at the Royal Opera House three or four times a week – sometimes every night.'[3] Woolf's description of the patrons of the opera, with their 'pink faces and glittering breasts', and the 'bald distinguished men with gold-headed canes' strolling down the thickly carpeted 'crimson avenues' between the stalls, conjures a world of affluence and conspicuous consumption.

But what does this opera scene in *Jacob's Room*, so clearly 'about' social class, tell us about Woolf and capitalism, the subject of this book? The rich and the poor obviously exist in many social systems, not only in capitalism. Woolf is here merely observing these differences of social class, not probing their interconnections. The opera scene is prefaced by the enigmatic remark 'as some believe, the city loves her prostitutes' (*JR* 56), located towards the East End and not admitted to the opera house. The pink faces and glittering breasts of the men at the opera bring to mind Hugh Whitbread in *Mrs Dalloway*, accused of being 'responsible for the plight of those poor girls in Piccadilly', but no such argument is made here.[4] Woolf's model, in this instance, of the social system is drawn from observation rather than analysis; it describes social difference. It revolves around resources, but it does not particularly convey a relationship of exploitation between the rich and the poor.

'wherever I seat myself, I die in exile'

Readers familiar with the scene will realise that I have not yet revealed Woolf's trump card – the narrator's extraordinary outburst at the end: 'The moulds are filled nightly. There is no need to distinguish details. But the difficulty remains – one has to choose' (*JR* 57). The narrator tells us that they [she?] would like to sit beside the Queen, hear the Prime Minister's gossip, penetrate the 'massive fronts of the respectable' to see what codes they conceal, assume for a moment the lives and imaginations of others. 'But no – we must choose. Never was there a harsher necessity! or one which entails greater pain, more certain disaster; for wherever I seat myself, I die in exile. Whittaker in his lodging-house; Lady Charles at the Manor' (*JR* 57). This narrator is outspoken – in Christine Froula's words, is 'anything but an exemplary subject', ignoring 'culture's hailings into the proper, conventional, normative feminine positions'.[5]

This vocabulary brings back the Althusserian model of the subject, and the way the (individual) subject is 'hailed' or 'interpellated', by ideology, into their place in the social order: 'Hey, you there!', as Froula quotes from Althusser.[6] Woolf's form of words, 'the moulds are filled nightly', is, like Althusser's, a rather sociological formulation. Woolf's father, Leslie Stephen, passed that approach on to his daughter, as Brenda R. Silver explains.[7] Stephen's view was that historical context and an awareness of social conditions were key to reading literature. However, Woolf's idea of 'the moulds' is much more determinist – social roles exist, and people fill them. They are procrustean beds, to which individuals conform. There are resonances here of the once-influential 'social reproduction' thesis in Marxist thinking about capitalism. This model, also derived from Althusser, saw social institutions such 'the family' or the school system as 'ideological state apparatuses' (ideological as opposed to repressive) that were important for the reproduction of capitalism.[8]

'[W]herever I seat myself, I die in exile.' An emotional and phenomenological response from the narrator, and one which is positively melodramatic. It is easy to attribute this to Woolf's own passionate interest in the lives of others, and to the desires she evinced as a writer to engage with the experiences of others. But the statement is so forceful that it leaves open the door to an argument that these 'moulds', the social segregation based on money, are an example of a social system that should be criticised as it is shown working 'at its most intense'. Woolf is here presenting not merely a set of observations about the social stratification of London's opera house, but a violent response to it as engendering a fatal exile, presumably from shared humanity.

Capitalism and Marxist thought

The usual dictionary definition of capitalism is that it is a system based on private property and profit, rather than the state: 'an economic and political system in which a country's trade and industry are controlled by private owners for profit'.[9] Capitalism is

> an economic system characterized by private or corporate ownership of capital goods, by investments that are determined by private decision, and by prices, production, and the distribution of goods that are determined mainly by competition in a free market.[10]

In turn, the dictionary says 'capital' is 'wealth – that is, money and goods – that's used to produce more wealth'. These definitions are reasonable in themselves, but do pave the way for thinking about capitalism as a descriptor or codeword for money. The term 'capitalism' can be stripped of its emphasis on exploitation, and operate as a signifier for anything to do with money, hence if we speak of stocks and shares, exchange rates, international trade arrangements and so on, we are necessarily talking about capitalism.

A Dictionary of Marxist Thought has a long entry on capitalism, from which we can excerpt 'Whatever the form, it is the private ownership of capital in the hands of a class – the class of capitalists to the exclusion of the mass of the population – which is a central feature of capitalism as a mode of production'.[11] The *Dictionary* points out that the word 'capitalism' is rarely used by non-Marxist schools of economics, and this is true more broadly. Sociology, for the many years I taught it in UK universities, was divided into those who, influenced by Marxist thinking, talked about 'capitalism' and those who, holding to other paradigms, such as those drawn from the work of Max Weber, talked about 'modern industrial society'. Marxist thinking, and the category of 'capitalism' that over time it engendered, went into decline in the aftermath of the collapse of the Soviet Union in 1979 and the ending of the cold war.

I've mentioned that Woolf is presenting in her fiction some aspects of a social system that are not what are usually thought of when the language of social class is deployed. It's time to look at what Marx himself said, as this is the primary locus of the argument about capitalism. Marx developed his understanding of class through an analysis of *labour*, which he considered as a defining characteristic of humanity. Humans have the ability to transform nature through their labour, they can plan their projects, and are not limited by instinct. As critics have pointed out, this is a form of humanist 'triumphalism', sadly at odds with what we now know of the damage these humans have inflicted on nature. Raymond Williams also pointed out that it corresponds to and repeats the basic concepts of capitalism and imperialism – 'limitless and conquering expansion; reduction of the labour process to the appropriation and transformation of raw materials'.[12]

In theory the capacity to labour is seen as a quality of all humans; in practice, Marx tended to see the labourer as male, as feminists pointed out.[13] Work done by women in the home was not counted as productive, and that idea led to the perception of women workers as damaging the earning capacity of men – a perception that lingered long in the trades unions in Britain. The division of labour between men and women might have been created by the economic requirements of capitalism, but the form it took reflected ideas about what was appropriate for men, women and children.

Marx saw the wage system in terms of a dynamic of exploitation. This is not a description, it is an analysis, or theory: the 'labour theory of value'. Capitalism is grounded in the accumulation of capital, which happens when surplus value is extracted from wage labourers. Workers do not sell products, they sell their ability to work for a certain amount of time, in return for a wage. But in the time they work, they produce goods worth more than their wages. That is because wages are set according to the cost of those workers' food, housing, etc., not according to the value of what they produce. The difference between what the capitalist has to pay for their wages, and the value of what is produced, is called 'surplus value'. When sold, it is realised as profit. Marx went on to explain the different forms of extracting surplus value. This can be done 'absolutely', simply by making the workers work for longer hours, or 'relatively', by making production more efficient.[14]

Marx's analyses of how capitalism works were published in German in 1867 and translated into English in 1887. Marx died in 1883, and the take-up of his ideas in the English-speaking world occurred after his death. Huge changes in production and technology make the simple two-class model, so powerful as an analytic tool to examine the factory system of nineteenth-century Britain, simply not up to the task of accounting for current inequalities. And nothing could have less power now than the binary and reductive model that 'the labour theory of value' was to become in the hands and manifestos of many political forces. This means that a Marxist analysis of capitalism in Britain around the time of Woolf s birth in 1882 doesn't really make much sense by 1941 when she died, let alone now. Woolf, in her fiction, wishes to draw attention to issues other than the class relation that Marx says is not only central but exclusively important. We can see this in the following discussion of *Mrs Dalloway* and psychiatry: it appears to be partly about class, but is also partly about suffering, and war, taken out of that context.

It is, of course, possible to find fascinating material on the subject of capitalism in Woolf's biographical papers, perhaps the most dramatic being her diary thoughts in 1918 that it might be necessary, 'psychologically', to renounce inherited wealth, 'if one is to abolish capitalism'. Notwithstanding her husband's view that inherited wealth should be kept, so that they could do 'good work for nothing', Virginia Woolf records that she still feels that 'my fire is too large for one person. I'm one of those who are hampered by the psychological hindrance of owning capital.'[15] Woolf's feelings about inherited wealth contribute to the contradictory and sometimes ambivalent stances she takes up, in her non-fiction writings particularly, on questions of money, material conditions and politics.[16]

'[T]o criticise the social system': *Mrs Dalloway* (1925)

I'd like to examine again Woolf's much-quoted statement in her diary that she wanted in her fiction 'to criticize the social system, and to show it at work, at its most intense'. Alex Zwerdling, author of *Virginia Woolf and the Real World*, suggests that Woolf 'observes, describes, connects, provides the materials for a judgment about society and social issues'.[17] Many Woolf critics, including myself, have seen Woolf's reference to criticising the social system, in her diary plans for *Mrs Dalloway*, as implicitly radical, particularly with regard to social class. But, is the social system that she is criticising capitalism? The quotation is sandwiched between two statements that deflect attention away from the social system. It reads: 'I have almost too many ideas. I want to give life & death, sanity & insanity; I want to criticize the social system, & to show it at its most intense – But here I may be posing'.[18] Life and death, sanity and insanity, are different from 'the social system', albeit part of it and regulated by it. It might be possible to read the 'posing' question as a touch of imposter syndrome on Woolf's part, but there is a more constructive way to look at it. In an important passage in *The Pargiters* she talks about the rival merits of history and fiction, concluding that 'I prefer, where truth is important, to write fiction'.[19] Perhaps the sociological stance is being seen as a pose, while fiction is needed to approach truth.

Is *Mrs Dalloway* principally about social class? Is the social system shown here capitalist? Is it an anti-capitalist novel? I'm going to begin to answer those questions by looking at two aspects of the novel: the extended criticism of psychiatry, and Clarissa Dalloway's ignorance about the plight of Armenians. Neither of these is reducible to social class as we normally understand it.

Woolf sets up, in the criticisms of Sir William Bradshaw and Dr Holmes for their treatment of Septimus Warren Smith, a narrative that describes these doctors in terms of class and status: 'Holmes and Bradshaw, men who never weighed less than eleven stone six, who sent their wives to Court, men who made ten thousand a year' (*MD* 162). The psychiatrist Bradshaw has a car that is 'low, powerful, grey, with plain initials interlocked on the panel'; furs and rugs were 'heaped in it' to keep his wife warm. Lady Bradshaw waits in the car while Sir William visits 'the rich, the afflicted, who could afford the very large fee which Sir William very properly charged for his advice' (*MD* 103). 'The upkeep of that motor car alone must cost him quite a lot, said Septimus, when they got out into the street' (*MD* 108). Septimus, whose overcoat is 'shabby' (*MD* 15), and his wife Rezia live in a Bloomsbury lodging-house, then a relatively down-at-heel area of London (*MD* 163).

Septimus is a shell-shocked veteran of the First World War, who figures as a double for Clarissa Dalloway herself. Woolf's notes in October 1922 record the development of her plans. On October 14 she said: 'I adumbrate here a study of insanity & suicide: the world seen by the sane & the insane side by side – something like that'. Two days later the plan incorporated a crucial clarification – the notion of the possibility of an 'insane truth':

> Suppose it to be connected in this way: Sanity and insanity. Mrs. D. seeing the truth, SS seeing the insane truth. The pace to be given by the gradual increase of S's insanity on the one side; by the approach of the party on the other.[20]

Sir Willam's mantra is 'proportion':

> Worshipping proportion, Sir William not only prospered himself but made England prosper, secluded her lunatics, forbade childbirth,

penalized despair, made it impossible for the unfit to propagate their views until they, too, shared his sense of proportion. (*MD* 109)

It hardly needs adding that Woolf herself had been subjected to some of this treatment. It's hard not to feel the anger behind the narrator's conclusion to this passage of the novel:

Naked, defenceless, the exhausted, the friendless received the impress of Sir William's will. He swooped; he devoured. He shut people up. It was this combination of decision and humanity that endeared Sir William so greatly to the relations of his victims. (*MD* 112)

The outspoken critique of psychiatry in this section of the novel is eloquent. In choosing insanity, and the valence of 'insane truth', as a major focus of the text, Woolf may have dressed Sir William and Septimus in the ordinary clothes of social class, but she is pointing to something important that is beyond class. *Mrs Dalloway* is an exercise in the criticism of power more generally. It is nearer to Foucault than to Marx. As Foucault said:

To put it very simply, psychiatric internment, the mental normalization of individuals, and penal institutions have no doubt a fairly limited importance if one is only looking for their economic significance. On the other hand, they are undoubtedly essential to the general functioning of the wheels of power.[21]

Woolf's attack on psychiatry also pulls in a significant undertow of hostility towards colonial attitudes and assumptions. Bradshaw's ostensibly benign 'proportion' has a sister. She is 'less smiling, more formidable' and 'even now engaged – in the heat and sands of India, the mud and swamp of Africa, the purlieus of London' in 'dashing down shrines, smashing idols, and setting up in their place her own stern countenance' (*MD* 109). 'Conversion is her name and she feasts on the wills of the weakly' (*MD* 109). In a few sentences Woolf here conjures up the sinister arrogance of the British colonialists and missionaries who sought to impose their religion onto the peoples whose land and resources they had taken. Conversion 'offers help, but desires power', and she too was in Sir William's heart, albeit concealed 'as she mostly is' by 'some plausible disguise; some venerable name; love, duty, self-sacrifice' (*MD* 110). Here Woolf articulates something much more powerful than observation or description – she is producing an analysis of the relations of exploitation at work.

Woolf invokes 'conversion' as a 'fastidious Goddess' who 'loves blood better than brick, and feasts most subtly on the human will' (*MD* 110). Her critique of psychiatry aired straightforward descriptions of social class and used them to point to the way in which power operates to subjugate and destroy the vulnerable Septimus. In making an analogy between the values of proportion and the more aggressive 'conversion' that forms part of colonialism, Woolf refuses to restrict herself to social class, as traditionally understood, and, emphasising mental domination, draws a parallel between the destruction of the vulnerable in London, and in India and Africa. Anna Snaith sees this as a connection that was evident in Woolf's writing from the beginning: 'From her very first novel [*The Voyage Out*, 1915], she was figuring the capitalist underside of imperialism and was linking imperial control to the workings of patriarchy and religion.'[22]

Back with the Dalloways: Mr Richard Dalloway has returned to his political committee work after lunch with his wife. He has given her some roses and told her to have a rest, as ordered by the doctor. '"Some committee?" she asked him. "Armenians", he said; or perhaps it was "Albanians"' (*MD* 131). Clarissa Dalloway is soon interrogating herself about who it was:

> He was already half-way to the House of Commons, to his Armenians, his Albanians, having settled her on the sofa, looking at his roses. And people would say, 'Clarissa Dalloway is spoilt.' She cared much more for her roses than for the Armenians. Hunted out of existence, maimed, frozen, the victims of cruelty and injustice (she had heard Richard say so over and over again) – no she could feel nothing for the Albanians, or was it the Armenians? but she loved her roses (didn't that help the Armenians?) – the only flowers she could bear to see cut. (*MD* 132)

Richard Dalloway's sympathy for the Armenians echoes that of Leonard Woolf, who described in his autobiography how at the age of fourteen, 'I could almost see the helpless Armenians being bayoneted by the Turkish soldiers and the women and children fleeing and floundering through the snowdrifts'.[23]

Trudi Tate has argued that Woolf is here both satirising and condemning Clarissa Dalloway's 'preposterous' childishness and refusal of responsibility. Tate points out that June 1923, when *Mrs Dalloway* is set, was precisely a key moment in Britain's history of betrayal of the Armenians.[24] We know from Virginia Woolf's own research notes (now digitised for the website WoolfNotes.com), that she was herself extremely well informed about the massacres in Armenia in the late nineteenth century, as she had read and taken notes from all the British Consular Reports from Turkey of that period.[25] As I've suggested before, Tate's argument must be correct; not only was Woolf herself extremely well informed about the Armenian genocide (as we would now call it), she also had personal reasons to be familiar with Albania.[26]

It's easy enough to point to aspects of *Mrs Dalloway* that are an indictment of a social system working against vulnerable people. The most powerful one is the impassioned critique of psychiatry, particularly in the person of the bloated Sir William. And if we accept Tate's argument about Clarissa Dalloway, then we can see her as an example of the female patriotic ignorance that helped to take Britain to war in 1914. It brings to mind the scene in *The Voyage Out*, where an earlier fictional iteration of Clarissa Dalloway responded to the sight of the British Mediterranean Fleet at sea by 'convulsively' squeezing Rachel Vinrace's hand and saying '"Aren't you glad to be English?"'[27]

But is the issue itself about class and capitalism? Surely not. The critique of psychiatry could have been set in another socio-economic location. Mrs Dalloway's ignorance of Armenian politics is more about foreign policy than 'capitalism' as such.

WoolfNotes.com

Woolf's newly available reading and research notes throw light on her views about capitalism.[28] Notebook 21 includes Woolf's notes made in 1939–40 on Freud's *Group Psychology and the Analysis of the Ego*.[29] Woolf notes that 'every individual is ruled by these attitudes of the group mind wh[ich] exhibit themselves in such forms as racial characteristics, class prejudice, public opinion'. Woolf artlessly asks 'Suppose we add sex prejudice?', getting to the nub of her thoughts about Freud.

This notebook also contains some of Woolf's early thoughts on women, men, and war for what was to become her essay 'Thoughts on Peace in an Air Raid', published in October 1940. The ideas appear to take off from the Freud essay, but venture into some unusual thoughts about capitalism. The notes contain the following lines:

> In the present war we are fighting for liberty. But we can only get it if we destroy the male attributes. Thus the woman[s] part is to achieve

the emancipation of man. In that lies her only hope of permanent peace. Said to be a capitalist war. Capitalism only the result of certain human desires. She has had to suppress them.[30]

In December 1939, *Forum*, an American magazine, asked Woolf to write about peace, but she did not complete that essay. Thinking about peace, she consulted Sheena, Lady Simon about what she might write, as she feared that 'living in the country' she might become 'angular and eccentric'.[31] In May 1940 she made a strange entry in her diary: 'This idea struck me: the army is the body: I am the brain. Thinking is my fighting.'[32] Although 'thinking is my fighting' is a common, sometimes vaunted, way to characterise intellectual work, the preceding idea is very odd. Woolf was generally opposed to what we might call mind/body dualism, and so this fleeting contrast between (the army as) body and (herself as) brain is particularly recondite.

The essay entitled 'Thoughts on Peace in an Air Raid' was published in *New Republic* in October 1940. Woolf's letter to Sheena Simon, in January 1940, explains in some detail how she was thinking about the plan to 'destroy' male attributes. She was thinking about how to break down the sexual division of labour.

'[D]o cast your mind further that way', she wrote:

> about sharing life after the war: about pooling men's and women's work: about the possibility, if disarmament comes, of removing men's disabilities. Can one change sex characteristics? How far is the women's movement a remarkable experiment in that transformation? Mustn't our next task be the emancipation of man? How can we alter the crest and the spur of the fighting cock? Thats the one hope in this war: his soberer hues, and the unreality, (so I feel, and I think he feels) of glory. No talk of white feathers anyhow; and the dullness comes through the gilt much more than last time. So it looks as if sexes can adapt themselves: and here (thats our work) we can, or the young women can, bring immense influence to bear. So many of the young men, could they get prestige and admiration, would give up glory and develop whats now so stunted – I mean the life of natural happiness. (L6 380)

The 'unreality' of glory in war is presented here in a way that calls to mind Paul Fussell's interpretation of the First World War in terms of modern irony. The theme of glory had preoccupied Woolf for some while, as *Orlando* (1928) uses humour to joke about it: Nick Greene keeps adverting to 'gloire', which he mispronounces as '"Glawr" (Orlando could have wished him a better accent.)'.[33]

The argument of 'Thoughts of Peace in an Air Raid' (now published as a booklet in the Penguin Books Great Ideas series) throws light on Woolf's enigmatic note: 'Said to be a capitalist war. Capitalism only the result of certain human desires.' These desires, according to Woolf, are 'the desire for aggression; the desire to dominate and enslave'. She speaks of a young airman up in the sky, who is 'driven by voices in himself – ancient instincts, instincts fostered and cherished by tradition and education'.[34] The word 'instinct' is being used to underline the ancient and intractable nature of the aggression. In the manuscript draft of *A Room of One's Own*, which was published in1992 as *Women and Fiction*, Woolf had used the term 'possessive instinct' – 'The eagle claws other peoples land, & goods', she had originally written, 'killing one's sisters & cousins in order to get it from them'.[35] Another connection between the thinking underlying 'Thoughts on Peace in an Air Raid', in 1940, and Woolf's approach to *A Room of One's Own* in 1928/9, can be seen in this emphasis on instinct. Men, she says, 'are driven by instincts which are not within their control' – 'the instinct for possession, the rage for acquisition which drives them to desire other people's fields and goods perpetually; to make frontiers and flags; battleships and poison gas; to offer up their own lives and their children's lives' (*AROO* 35).

The Desire to Dominate and Enslave

The desire for aggression, the desire to dominate and enslave. For Woolf, they are human desires or instincts that underlie capitalism, as well as pre-date it. Perhaps this is why she turns so frequently to the naked expression of these in the violent colonialism of her time. Certainly, the research contribution that she made to Leonard Woolf's *Empire and Commerce in Africa* centred on the so-called 'scramble for Africa', where the European powers stole 'other peoples land, & goods' in colonising the continent.[36] Now that Woolf studies has caught up with her in understanding the importance of colonial violence, we can better see these themes in her fiction.[37]

But where does that leave us with Woolf and capitalism? It seems that the substantive conflict between the two classes of nineteenth century capitalism, based on the exploitation of the labour of one class by the other, is not so powerfully figured in her fiction as the exploitation of indigenous peoples by their colonisers. There is one area, however, where current thinking about capitalism, and Woolf's vision, coincide: this is what we might call 'ecological Marxism'.

This is a generational issue. A survey in 2021 found that 75 per cent of young people in Britain 'blame capitalism for the climate crisis' and 73 per cent believe that capitalism fuels 'selfishness, greed and materialism'. What's more, 71 per cent also believe that 'capitalism fuels racism'.[38] Climate campaigner Greta Thunberg made a powerful anti-capitalist speech at the Glasgow Climate Change Conference, in 2021, and has now publicly thrown in her lot with anti-capitalism. She argued that the climate and ecological crisis dates back to 'colonialism and beyond', to the idea that some people are worth more than others.[39]

I might have to eat my words here, casting our minds back to the transatlantic disputes of the 1980s about how radical Woolf was. I tended to argue then that her politics were characterised by ambivalence and contradiction. In 1993, editing *A Room of One's Own and Three Guineas*, I suggested that the traditional view of Woolf as an elitist aesthete had been decisively displaced by feminist interpretations that stressed her anti-patriarchal stance and commitment to a range of radical ideas and politics. 'Yet', I insisted, 'it would be a big mistake to construct Virginia Woolf as an ideologically simple anarchist, lesbian, ecological, socialist, anti-racist feminist.'[40] At present the ecofeminist interpretation of Woolf is in the ascendent. Thinking back over the complicated arguments of *Three Guineas*, this is perhaps a better way to think about Woolf's politics. She was certainly not a 'Marxist' of any recognisable stripe. In some respects Woolf's thinking could have been of interest to Marxists of her time, but they did not perceive the relevance of her ideas. Her argument about women having no investment in their country is somewhat out of date, but her conclusion remains a classic ringing endorsement of a global approach: 'as a woman, I have no country. As a woman I want no country. As a woman my country is the whole world' (*TG* 234).

Three Guineas also provides us with an instance in which Woolf's social and political understanding is imaginative and nuanced. She is addressing a middle-aged barrister, a man, linking sexism and patriarchalism to the rise of fascism in the 1930s.

> You are feeling in your own persons what your mothers felt when they were shut out, when they were shut up, because they were women. Now you are being shut out, you are being shut up, because you are Jews, because you are democrats, because of race, because of religion. It is not a photograph that you look upon any longer: there you go, trapesing along in the procession yourselves. And that makes a difference.

Woolf concludes that 'the whole iniquity of dictatorship, whether in Oxford or Cambridge, in Whitehall or Downing Street, against Jews or against women, in England, or in Germany, in Italy or in Spain is now apparent to you' (*TG* 228).

Woolf, in 1938, is thinking in the terms that are now thought of as intersectionality. Perhaps what is most powerful about the image of the procession is that it refuses to settle on one axis of exclusion, it includes race, religion and antisemitism as well as feminism. Interestingly, it does not include social class, other than in the allusion to the middle-class barrister now being drawn into the politics of tyranny emanating from Hitler and Mussolini. In this most impassioned of her political writings, *Three Guineas*, the politics of social class are overshadowed by what she saw as a broader iniquity. The 'desire to dominate and enslave', as she put it in 'Thoughts on Peace in an Air Raid', which in her mind was a human desire pre-dating the historical social and economic form of capitalism.

Notes

My warm thanks to Clara Jones, who suggested I might write this piece, and has given much useful advice. I would also like to thank Gilly Furse, the technical director of the WoolfNotes project, for her labours, including research, above and beyond the call of duty.

1. Virginia Woolf, *Jacob's Room* (1922) (London: Penguin, 1992), 56. Further references will be included within the main text.
2. Virginia Woolf, *The Flight of the Mind: The Letters of Virginia Woolf, Volume One: 1888–1912*, ed. by Nigel Nicolson and Joanne Trautmann (London: The Hogarth Press, 1975), 394. Further references will be included within the main text.
3. Emma Sutton, 'How Virginia Woolf's work was Shaped by Music', *The Conversation*, 26 March 2021 <https://theconversation.com/how-virginia-woolfs-work-was-shaped-by-music-157998> [accessed 31 October 2023].
4. Virginia Woolf, *Mrs Dalloway* (1925) (London: Penguin, 2000), 80. Further references will be included within the main text.
5. Christine Froula, *Virginia Woolf and the Bloomsbury Avant-Garde* (New York: Columbia University Press, 2005), 79.
6. Louis Althusser, 'Ideology and Ideological State Apparatuses', in *Lenin and Philosophy and Other Essays* (London: New Left Books, 1971); Froula, *Virginia Woolf*, 79.
7. Brenda R. Silver, *Virginia Woolf's Reading Notebooks* (Princeton: Princeton University Press, 1983), 27–8.

8. For a discussion of those issues, see my essay 'Althusser's Marx, Althusser's Lacan', in *The Politics of Truth: From Marx to Foucault* (Cambridge: Polity Press, 1991), 96–110.
9. Entry for 'capitalism, n.2', OED Online, September 2022, Oxford University Press <https://www.oed.com/view/Entry/27454?rskey=zPHa1U&result=2&isAdvanced=false> [accessed 31 October 2023].
10. Entry for 'capitalism', Merriam-Webster.com Dictionary, s.v. <https://www.merriam-webster.com/dictionary/capitalism> [accessed 31 October 2023].
11. *A Dictionary of Marxist Thought*, 2nd edn, ed. by T. B. Bottomore (Oxford, Blackwell, 1991), 71–4.
12. Raymond Williams, 'Problems of Materialism', *New Left Review*, 109 (1978), 8–9.
13. See Michèle Barrett and Mary McIntosh, 'The "Family Wage": Some Problems for Socialists and Feminists', in *Capital and Class*, 11, 1980; Michèle Barrett, *Women's Oppression Today: Problems in Marxist Feminist Analysis* (London: Verso, 1980); Michèle Barrett, 'Marxist-Feminism and the Work of Karl Marx', in *Feminism and Equality*, ed. by A. Phillips (Oxford: Blackwell, 1987).
14. For a more detailed account of the labour theory of value, mainly drawn from Volume 1 of Marx's *Capital*, see Michèle Barrett, *Women's Oppression Today* (London: Verso, 1980), 163–7.
15. Virginia Woolf, *The Diary of Virginia Woolf: Volume One, 1915–1919*, ed. by Anne Olivier Bell (London: Hogarth Press, 1977), 100–10.
16. These issues are discussed further in *Virginia Woolf: Women and Writing*, introduced by Michèle Barrett (London: The Women's Press, 1979), 15–16; Virginia Woolf, *A Room of One's Own and Three Guineas*, ed. and introduced by Michèle Barrett (London, Penguin, 1993); Clara Jones, *Virginia Woolf: Ambivalent Activist* (Edinburgh: Edinburgh University Press, 2016); Clara Jones, 'Virginia Woolf's *A Room of One's Own* and the Problem of Inherited Wealth', in *Influence and Inheritance in Feminist English Studies*, ed. by Clara Jones and Emily J. Hogg (Basingstoke: Palgrave Macmillan, 2015), 20–33.
17. Alex Zwerdling, '*Mrs Dalloway* and the Social System', *PMLA*, 92.1 (January 1977), 69–82.
18. Virginia Woolf, *The Diary of Virginia Woolf: Volume Two, 1920–1924*, ed. by Anne Olivier Bell (New York: Harcourt Brace Jovanovich, 1980), 248.
19. Virginia Woolf, *The Pargiters: The Novel-Essay Portion of The Years*, ed. by Mitchell A. Leaska (London: The Hogarth Press, 1978), 9.
20. Quoted in Elaine Showalter, 'Introduction', in *Mrs Dalloway*, xxvii.
21. Michel Foucault, 'Truth and Power', in *Power/Knowledge*, ed. by Colin Gordon (Brighton: Harvester, 1980), 116. For a discussion of Woolf in relation to Foucault's ideas, see Michèle Barrett, 'Virginia Woolf Meets

Michel Foucault', in Barrett, *Imagination in Theory: Essays on Writing and Culture* (Cambridge: Polity 1999), 186–204.
22. Anna Snaith, 'Leonard and Virginia Woolf: Writing Against Empire', *Journal of Commonwealth Literature*, 50.1 (2015), 19–32 (30).
23. Leonard Woolf, *The Journey Not the Arrival Matters: An Autobiography of the Years 1939–1969* (London: The Hogarth Press, 1969), 388.
24. Trudi Tate, 'Mrs Dalloway and the Armenian Question', in *Modernism, History and the First World War*, ed. by Trudi Tate (Manchester: Manchester University Press, 1998).
25. Michèle Barrett, 'Virginia Woolf's Research for *Empire and Commerce in Africa* (Leonard Woolf, 1920)', *Woolf Studies Annual*, 9 (2013), 83–122.
26. This is discussed in more detail in Michèle Barrett, 'WoolfNotes: Virginia Woolf's Reading and Research Notes Online', in *Historicizing Modernists: Approaches to 'Archivalism'*, ed. by Matthew Feldman, Anna Svendsen and Erik Tonning (London: Bloomsbury Academic, 2021), 24–51.
27. Virginia Woolf, *The Voyage Out* (1915) (London: Penguin, 1992), 60.
28. <https://www.WoolfNotes.com> is a collaboration between Brenda R. Silver, author of *Virginia Woolf's Reading Notebooks* (1983); Michèle Barrett, Project Lead, WoolfNotes; Gilly Furse, Technical Director, WoolfNotes.com; and Clara Jones, WoolfNotes team. It was launched in summer 2023, and includes high-specification scans of Woolf's reading notebooks, including two found subsequent to the 67 described in Silver's 1983 book, and substantial additional reading and research materials.
29. Sigmund Freud, *Group Psychology and the Analysis of the Ego*, trans. by James Strachey (International Psycho-Analytic Press, 1922), 2nd edn (London: The Hogarth Press, 1940).
30. See <https://WoolfNotes.com>, Silver index, Notebook 21, p. 13 of 26 [accessed 2 June 2023].
31. Virginia Woolf, *Leave the Letters Till We're Dead: The Letters of Virginia Woolf, Volume Six, 1936–1941*, ed. by Nigel Nicholson and Joanne Trautmann (London: The Hogarth Press, 1980), 375. Further references will be included within the main text.
32. Virginia Woolf, *The Diary of Virginia Woolf, Volume Five, 1936–1941*, ed. by Anne Olivier Bell (London: Penguin, 1985), 285.
33. Virginia Woolf, *Orlando* (1928) (London: Penguin, 1992), 63.
34. Virginia Woolf, *Thoughts on Peace in an Air Raid* (London: Penguin, 2009), 3–4.
35. Virginia Woolf, *Women and Fiction: The Manuscript Versions of* A Room of One's Own, ed. by S. P. Rosenbaum (Oxford: Blackwell, 1993), 59–60.
36. See Barrett, 'Virginia Woolf's Research'.
37. See, for example, Snaith, 'Writing Against Empire'; Jane Marcus, 'Britannia Rules *The Waves*', in *Hearts of Darkness: White Women Write Race* (New Brunswick: Rutgers University Press, 2004).

38. Kristian Niemietz, 'Left turn ahead: Surveying attitudes of young people towards capitalism and socialism', Institute of Economic Affairs, 6 July 2021 <https://iea.org.uk/publications/left-turn-aheadsurveying-attitudes-of-young-people-towards-capitalism-and-socialism> [accessed 31 October 2023].
39. Mark L. Friedman, 'Powerful Anti-Capitalist Speech by Greta Thunberg at Glasgow Climate Change Conference' <https://sevenseasmedia.org/powerful-anti-capitalist-speech-by-greta-thunberg-at-glasgow-climate-change-conference> [accessed 8 December 2022].
40. Michèle Barrett, 'Introduction', in *A Room of One's Own and Three Guineas* (London: Penguin, 1993), xlv. Further references will be included within the main text.

Works Cited

Entry for 'capitalism, n.2'. OED Online. September 2022. Oxford University Press <https://www.oed.com/view/Entry/27454?rskey=zPHa1U&result=2&isAdvanced=false> [accessed 31 October 2023].

Entry for 'capitalism'. Merriam-Webster.com Dictionary, s.v. <https://www.merriam-webster.com/dictionary/capitalism> [accessed 31 October 2023].

Barrett, Michèle. *The Politics of Truth: From Marx to Foucault*. Cambridge: Polity Press, 1991.

——, 'Virginia Woolf Meets Michel Foucault'. In *Imagination in Theory: Essays on Writing and Culture*, 186–204. Cambridge: Polity, 1999.

——, 'Virginia Woolf's Research for *Empire and Commerce in Africa* (Leonard Woolf, 1920)'. *Woolf Studies Annual*, 19 (2013), 83–122.

——, *Women's Oppression Today: Problems in Marxist Feminist Analysis*. London: Verso, 1980.

——, 'WoolfNotes: Virginia Woolf's Reading and Research Notes Online'. In *Historicizing Modernists: Approaches to 'Archivalism'*, ed. by Matthew Feldman, Anna Svendsen and Erik Tonning, 24–51. London: Bloomsbury Academic, 2021.

Bottomore, T. B. et al. (eds.). *A Dictionary of Marxist Thought*. 2nd edn. Oxford: Blackwell, 1991.

Foucault, Michel. 'Truth and Power'. In Foucault, *Power/Knowledge*, ed. by Colin Gordon. Brighton: Harvester, 1980.

Freud, Sigmund. *Group Psychology and the Analysis of the Ego*. London: The Hogarth Press, 1940.

Friedman, Mark L. 'Powerful Anti-Capitalist Speech by Greta Thunberg at Glasgow Climate Change Conference' <https://sevenseasmedia.org/powerful-anti-capitalist-speech-by-greta-thunberg-at-glasgow-climate-change-conference> [accessed 8 December 2022].

Froula, Christine. *Virginia Woolf and the Bloomsbury Avant-Garde*. New York: Columbia University Press, 2005.

Jones, Clara. 'Virginia Woolf's *A Room of One's* Own and the Problem of Inherited Wealth'. In *Influence and Inheritance in Feminist English Studies*, ed. by Clara Jones and Emily J. Hogg, 20–33. Basingstoke: Palgrave Macmillan, 2015.

——, *Virginia Woolf: Ambivalent Activist*. Edinburgh: Edinburgh University Press, 2016.

Lee, Hermione. *Virginia Woolf*. London: Chatto & Windus, 1996.

Marcus, Jane. *Hearts of Darkness: White Women Write Race*. New York: New Brunswick: Rutgers University Press, 2004.

Marx, Karl. *Capital: A Critical Analysis of Capitalist Production, Volume One*. London: Allen and Unwin, 1971.

——, 'Estranged Labour'. In *Economic and Philosophic Manuscripts of 1844*, trans. by Martin Milligan. Guildford, CT: Prometheus Books, 1988.

Niemietz, Kristian. 'Left turn ahead: Surveying attitudes of young people towards capitalism and socialism'. Institute of Economic Affairs, 6 July 2021 <https://iea.org.uk/publications/left-turn-aheadsurveying-attitudes-of-young-people-towards-capitalism-and-socialism> [accessed 31 October 2023].

Silver, Brenda. *Virginia Woolf's Reading Notebooks*. Princeton: Princeton University Press, 1983.

Snaith, Anna. 'Leonard and Virginia Woolf: Writing against Empire'. *Journal of Commonwealth Literature*, 50.1 (2015), 19–32.

Sutton, Emma. 'How Virginia Woolf's work was Shaped by Music'. *The Conversation*, 26 March 2021 <https://theconversation.com/how-virginia-woolfs-work-was-shaped-by-music-157998> [accessed 31 October 2023].

Tate, Trudi. '*Mrs Dalloway* and the Armenian Question'. In *Modernism, History and the First World War*, ed. by Trudi Tate, 160–82. Manchester: Manchester University Press, 1998.

Williams, Raymond. 'Problems of Materialism'. *New Left Review*, 109 (1978), 3–7.

Woolf, Leonard. *The Journey Not the Arrival Matters: An Autobiography of the Years 1939–1969*. London: The Hogarth Press, 1969.

Woolf, Virginia. *The Diary of Virginia Woolf: Volume One, 1915–1919*, ed. by Anne Olivier Bell. London: The Hogarth Press, 1977.

——, *The Diary of Virginia Woolf: Volume Two, 1920–1924*, ed. by Anne Olivier Bell. New York: Harcourt Brace Jovanovich, 1980.

——, *The Diary of Virginia Woolf: Volume Five, 1936–1941*, ed. by Anne Olivier Bell. London: Penguin, 1985.

——, *The Flight of the Mind: The Letters of Virginia Woolf, Volume One, 1888–1912*, ed. by Nigel Nicolson and Joanne Trautmann. London: The Hogarth Press, 1975.

——, *Jacob's Room*. London: Penguin, 1992.

——, *Leave the Letters Till We're Dead: The Letters of Virginia Woolf, Volume Six, 1936–1941*, ed. by Nigel Nicolson and Joanne Trautmann. London: The Hogarth Press, 1980.

——, *Mrs Dalloway*, ed. and introduced by Elaine Showalter. London: Penguin, 2000.
——, *Orlando*. London: Penguin, 1972.
——, *The Pargiters: The Novel-Essay Portion of The Years*, ed. by Mitchell A. Leaska. London: The Hogarth Press, 1978.
——, *A Room of One's Own and Three Guineas*, ed. and introduced by Michèle Barrett. London: Penguin, 1993.
——, *Thoughts on Peace in an Air Raid*. London: Penguin, 2009.
——, *Virginia Woolf: Women and Writing*, ed. and introduced by Michèle Barrett. London: The Women's Press, 1979.
——, *The Voyage Out*. London: Penguin, 1992.
——, *Women and Fiction: The Manuscript Versions of A Room of One's Own*, ed. by S. P. Rosenbaum. Oxford: Blackwell, 1993.
Zwerdling, Alex. '*Mrs Dalloway* and the Social System'. *PMLA*, 92.1 (January 1977).

Chapter 2

Empire, Slavery and Capitalism

Anna Snaith

Virginia Woolf has become iconic for the inventiveness of her radical, materialist feminism. But that feminism universalises whiteness, and some of its central tropes and figures are predicated on the capitalist gains of empire. I wish, in this chapter, and with a full acknowledgement of my own privilege and positionality, to explore the representation of empire and slavery in Woolf's major essays, *A Room of One's Own* (1929) and *Three Guineas* (1938): topics which demand renewed attention in the wake of the 2020 Black Lives Matter protests.[1] The history of racial violence occupies a haunting presence in these texts, surfacing in fleeting yet pivotal metaphors. While Woolf stopped short of representing Black lives or colonised subjectivity, her focus was consistently on the exploitative economics of imperial extraction alongside more culturally-based forms of conquest and control. I argue that investigating her critique of capitalist imperialism is perhaps where we find her greatest contribution to issues of global inequality, or, put another way, her most sustained and consistent engagement with capitalist modernity centres on the arena of empire. Placing these two essays in the context of work by prominent anti-imperialists such as J. A. Hobson and Leonard Woolf illuminates the complexity of her representation of the ideology and economics of empire, but also shows how her focus on *gender* and capital fills a gap in their thinking. Then, in considering how we might approach the racially problematic aspects of these texts, I turn to Black writers such as Alice Walker, Sylvia Wynter and Saidiya Hartman for whom Woolf's feminist methodologies and strategies of representation and resistance in *A Room of One's Own* have been a point of resonance as well as departure.

Part of the materialism of Woolf's feminist politics can be found in her recurring reference to capital, the impacts of its uneven distribution, and the gendered conditions of unwaged labour. Hermione Lee calls *A Room of One's Own* Woolf's 'economic autobiography', and *Three Guineas* is even more reliant on a language of economics to buttress its arguments.[2] This concentration on money is invariably tied to an awareness of global systems of capitalist imperialist exploitation and their impacts on women. In Woolf's first novel, *The Voyage Out* (1915), the exploitative conditions of the Anglo-South American trade in rubber underpins narratives of individual and national development just as it parallels the oppression of women and their trade on the marriage market.[3] At the other end of her career, in her *London Scene* essays, she turned to 'The Docks of London' (1931) to emphasise the connections between raw materials imported from colonial locations and market economics: the tastes and fashions of consumers in the heart of London. This emphasis on and exposure of the profit motive, or surplus value, as the primary driver of imperialism demonstrates her intellectual synergies with Leonard Woolf and those close to him in the Labour Party, especially E. D Morel, H. N. Brailsford and J. A. Hobson. Economic imperialism was, in the early twentieth century, a novel way of considering the function and future of the British Empire that united liberal and Marxist anti-imperialists.

As Robert Young outlines, 'anti-colonialism goes back to the beginnings of colonialism itself' particularly in the mobilisation of humanitarian, moral or religious arguments.[4] But with Marx, we see a shift towards an economic perspective with 'European expansion as both a cause and effect of the development of capitalism'.[5] Marx emphasised the global dimension of capitalism on which later thinkers would expand. While he was not alive to witness the Berlin conference and the 'scramble for Africa', Marx located the beginnings of industrial capitalism in the search for raw materials and new markets in the colonial space:

> the discovery of gold and silver in America, the extirpation, enslavement and entombment in mines of the indigenous population of that continent, the beginnings of the conquest and plunder of India, and the conversion of Africa into a preserve for the commercial hunting of blackskins, are all things which characterize the dawn of the era of capitalist production.[6]

He saw colonialism as 'both a ruthless system of economic exploitation and a significant positive move towards a utopian future'.[7]

The Woolfs were connected to those British intellectuals engaged in producing the first systematic analyses of the capitalist underpinnings of the 'new' imperialism, or the competitive expansion of European empires in the latter part of the nineteenth century. J. A. Hobson, an economist who had been in South Africa covering the Boer War for the *Manchester Guardian*, followed Marx in emphasising the economic drivers of imperialism. In *Imperialism: A Study* (1902), he set out to expose the way its 'economic taproot' was veiled by moral or religious discourse. Young calls Hobson's 'the first theoretical analysis of imperialism as an economic, political and institutional practice which [. . .] was fundamentally irrational'.[8] His theory, briefly put, was that during the nineteenth-century development of monopoly capitalism, the exhaustion of opportunities for domestic investment caused financiers and industrialists to seek new markets and investment potential for their surplus capital. He had witnessed this under-consumption first-hand in the context of the South African mining industry and the careers of profiteers such as Cecil Rhodes. As seen in the European 'scramble' for African land and resources, this 'aggressive Imperialism' discouraged international co-operation and encouraged forms of hyper-nationalism, thereby leading to war and conflict, as Charles Andrews explores in his chapter on *JR* in this volume.[9] As Hobson put it, the 'conditions of modern capitalist production [. . .] compel an ever keener "fight for markets"'.[10] This meant that the machinery of government worked in the interests of a small group of businessmen and professionals at great public expense and loss. Hobson questioned Marx's insistence on the inevitability of this stage of capitalism by including data to demonstrate that external trade was 'by no means essential to the industrial progress of a nation'.[11] His proposed solutions ranged from socialist ideas about wealth redistribution and progressive taxation to various forms of imperial federation. Scholars have drawn attention to the drawbacks and inconsistencies of Hobson's thinking, including his reference to the '"lower races"', his continued advocacy of racial hierarchies and the antisemitism of his characterisation of Jewish financiers. Hobson came from a liberal rather than revolutionary tradition, but his ideas were taken up by Marxist intellectuals, most notably Vladimir Lenin whose *Imperialism: The Highest Stage of Capitalism* (1917) drew directly on Hobson's empirical data and ideas.

Leonard Woolf knew Hobson through the Union of Democratic Control and later the Independent Labour Party. Hobson's influence on Leonard can be seen most clearly in the latter's substantial work, *Empire and Commerce in Africa* (1920), which demonstrates the late nineteenth-century shift to the rule of 'commerce, industry, and finance' in European imperial foreign policy and critiques the notion that the purpose of the state is 'the promotion of the commercial interests of the nation'.[12] What distinguishes Woolf's study from Hobson's is the sheer amount of empirical evidence and his detailed analysis of the partition of North and East Africa by European powers. Like Hobson, Woolf's data, drawn from consular reports, demonstrates the economic and national disbenefits to colonialism. Unlike Hobson, he includes a closing section on the impact of economic imperialism on African peoples, stressing the 'disastrous' effects of land grabs and exploitative labour conditions and slavery: 'by fraud or force the native chiefs and rulers were swindled or robbed of their dominions'.[13]

Leonard Woolf was one of the foremost British anti-imperialists of the interwar period: a position formed by his experience as a colonial administrator in Sri Lanka (then Ceylon). He was Secretary to the Labour Party's Advisory Committee on Imperial Questions set up in 1924 and

> he was ahead of most of the party leaders, as well as the trade-union movement, in advocating independence for India, Ceylon, Egypt, and Ireland after the First World War. Virtually every party document on the empire issued from the 1920s to the 1940s bore his imprint.[14]

While, like Hobson, his writing is marred by its paternalism and reference to 'non-adult' races, Woolf advocated internationalism to support African countries towards increased independence. He was unusual in his intellectual circles for stating that 'the capitalist system in Europe produces the exploitation of Africa' and for seeing the colonised person 'as a human being with a right to his own land and his own life, with a right even to be educated and to determine his own destiny'.[15]

Virginia Woolf, we now know, might well have been named as a co-author on *Empire and Commerce in Africa* given her extensive work as researcher for the book. Michèle Barrett's discovery of 783 notecards in Virginia Woolf's hand demonstrates the depth of her knowledge of international trade with the African continent, European foreign economic policy and anti-imperialism.[16] She was reading and taking copious notes on source texts on East and North Africa and creating tabular records of imports and exports from British Consular Reports. As Barrett notes, this work demonstrates her alignment with Leonard's anti-imperial views and 'if anything, her notes are more anti-imperialist, more tending towards the damning quotation, than the final book he published'.[17]

This research also evidences her familiarity with the economics of empire, which, I suggest, is a crucial context for approaching the materialist feminism of *A Room of One's Own* as well as its haunting by more or less overt references to race and slavery. In particular, Woolf augments work by Hobson and Leonard Woolf through her concentration on women's alienation and suppression by the machinations of capitalist imperialist patriarchy.

In *A Room of One's Own*, Woolf launches a complex argument about women's exclusion from the capitalist imperialist system with its self-perpetuating power structures. As she also argues in *Three Guineas*, this is both a cause of women's subordination as well as central to their ability to think beyond and against the structures themselves. Whereas Hobson and Leonard Woolf focused on the accumulation of capital by the middle and upper classes, Woolf investigates the implication for *women* of this concentration of capital and the surplus value which their free domestic and reproductive labour provides. The obstacles to women's creative production, in Woolf's formulation, are absolutely tied to the violence of empire. No sooner has the text begun than Woolf reminds the reader that accumulated capital underpins Oxbridge: the university is literally founded on 'an unending stream of gold and silver' (*AROO* 7). Buildings, lectureships, endowments were made possible by 'the coffers of kings and queens and great nobles' and, in the age of industry, from the 'great financial magnates of our own time [who] came and laid cheques and bonds' (*AROO* 8, 15). Woolf recognises the bedrock of intellectual and creative endeavour in the profits of slavery and colonial trade, a subject whose details are only just being investigated in, for example, the University of Cambridge's 'Legacies of Enslavement' Report.[18] By contrast, as evidenced in the meagre fare at Fernham, women have existed in 'poverty and insecurity' without the opportunity to earn money or, if they could work, 'the law denied them the right to possess what money they earned'.[19] The narrator tracks the stultifying and exclusionary effects of wealth and chooses the sum of £500 (the cornerstone of her argument about the basic requirements for the woman writer) carefully: enough to live on but not about profit and wealth.

For Woolf, the drive to colonise is bound up with hyper-masculinity and the figure of 'Man'. The narrator finds these crystallised in Kipling's poetry:

Mr Kipling's officers who turn their backs; and his Sowers who sow the Seed; and his Men who are alone with their Work; and the Flag – one blushes at all these capital letters as if one had been caught eavesdropping at some purely masculine orgy (*AROO* 77).

Women, like colonial subjects, are abused, silenced and alienated in their own nation. The rage to preserve wealth and superiority creates the vociferous insistence on the inferiority of women which the narrator documents so comprehensively: 'rich people [...] are often angry because they suspect that the poor want to seize their wealth' (*AROO* 27). *A Room of One's Own* connects the forces which have denigrated and marginalised women to global structures of capitalist finance and their foundation in the construction of particular forms of masculinity.

She traces the perpetuation of imperial ideology in culture, education, the family and the professions which resonates with Hobson's identification of the central role of not just financiers and industrialists in the capitalist imperialist system but 'all the professions, military and civil, the army, diplomacy, the church, the bar, teaching and engineering'.[20] The empire provides employment and opportunity for professional men, he argues, creating 'an interested bias towards Imperialism throughout the educated circles'.[21] Imperialism masquerades as patriotism and compromises 'intellectual liberty' given that 'the church, the press, the schools and colleges, the political machine, the four chief instruments of popular education, are accommodated to its service'.[22] Hobson specifically singles out the university with its reliance on endowments and patrons who in turn limit intellectual freedom by dictating who teaches and what is taught. Woolf will explore the limits on 'intellectual liberty' in greater depth in *Three Guineas*, but in *A Room of One's Own* she echoes Hobson and Leonard Woolf by connecting patriarchal power to imperialism: 'the instinct for possession, the rage for acquisition which drives them to desire other people's fields and goods perpetually; to make frontiers and flags; battleships and poison gas' (*AROO* 30). Hobson, too, had characterised imperialism as the 'lusts of struggle, domination, and acquisitiveness'.[23]

But with this context in mind, we return to the text's central trope: the £500 annual legacy left the narrator by her aunt, Mary Beton, who 'died by a fall from her horse when she was riding out to take the air in Bombay' (*AROO* 29). The narrator has previously made her living 'by cadging odd jobs from newspapers, by reporting a donkey show here or a wedding there' but is now able to write freely: in fact, to write the text we are reading (*AROO* 29). That said, the foundational image concerns unearned funds gained through the violence of colonialism: the very system that the narrator denounces elsewhere in the text. The trope draws on Julia Stephen's Anglo-Indian background and anticipates Percival's fall from a horse in India in *The Waves* (1931): as Jane Marcus notes, the fall is 'the original imperialist historical sin'.[24] Woolf's Quaker aunt, Caroline Emelia Stephen, who left her a lump-sum legacy of £2,500 in 1909 (the interest on which would have been much less than £500), had no connections to India but other members of her family did, including Woolf's cousin, Dorothea Stephen who was a missionary in India and her uncle, James Fitzjames Stephen, a lawyer whose work in India included drafting and codifying numerous Indian laws. On one level, Woolf celebrates the aunt's autonomy over her money which contrasts with Mary Seton and the impoverished women's college, but on another, female emancipation is propelled by inherited wealth which is complicit in colonial domination. Money is always tainted, she seems to suggest, and women stand implicated.

Bombay/Mumbai sits at the heart of Woolf's essay, then, but an unrealised, empty colonial location inhabited only by a privileged white woman. And her feminist arguments are underpinned by racial violence in other ways: namely, the co-option of the language of slavery. On her father's side, Woolf had family members involved in the slave trade as well as its abolition. Her paternal great grandfather, James (Jem) Stephen (1758–1832), was a lawyer whose presence at a slave auction in St Kitts turned him into an abolitionist. He then worked with his brother-in-law, William Wilberforce, on the 1807 Slave Trade Act which prohibited the slave trade in the British Empire and his writings on abolition included *England Enslaved by her Own Slave Colonies* (1826).[25] His son, Leslie Stephen's father, also James Stephen (1789–1859), was Undersecretary for the Colonies, helped to draft the 1833 Abolition Bill and was known as 'Mr. Mother-Country Stephen' for his insistence on the 'family' of empire.[26] While Woolf was born into a family whose members had been engaged in different ways in the work of empire, *A Room of One's Own* bypasses the legacies of the slave trade or attention to women of colour in favour of a metaphorical focus on the enslavement of white women within marriage. She was 'the property of her husband', 'the slave of any boy whose parents forced a ring upon her finger' (*AROO* 34). In fact, Woolf argues, women have always been poor and had 'less intellectual freedom than the sons of Athenian slaves' (*AROO* 81). Here, Woolf is drawing on a long tradition of feminist discourse from Mary

Wollstonecraft's *Vindication of the Rights of Women* (1792) to John Stuart Mill's *The Subjection of Women* (1869). Wollstonecraft articulated women's slavery in political and civil terms and Mill argued that post-abolition, 'the only slaves that remained were the ones married to men under British law'.[27] Woolf, too, defines women's slavery through their status as their husband's property and their own historic exclusion from property ownership.

As Vron Ware has discussed, in the early nineteenth century white women abolitionists drew on a language of united sisterhood, as well as discourses of sin and morality, to argue for the end of slavery, but post-abolition, 'women were able to exploit the power of the slavery analogy in interpreting their own servitude but without needing any longer to refer to the slaves whose bondage had once outraged and inspired them'.[28] In *A Room of One's Own*, too, the lack of reference to the Atlantic slave trade is particularly curious given that women's public and political subjecthood was co-constituted with abolitionist advocacy. Also, many of the white women involved in abolitionism in the early nineteenth century came from the Quaker tradition of Woolf's own family. *A Room of One's Own* is, in many ways, founded upon awareness of global systems of violence and subjection but without acknowledgement of the lived experience of that injustice. Her rhetoric of enslavement both evokes but also obscures a history of racial oppression as slavery is called up and harnessed to the oppression of white British women. *A Room of One's Own* emerges out of a reformist context but one which also limits Woolf's 'capacity to see black women as women, or women from the colonies as Englishwomen'.[29]

And this is exactly what occurs in the much-discussed passage of trans-racial encounter, worth quoting in full:

> They are not even now as concerned about the health of their fame as men are, and, speaking generally, will pass a tombstone or a signpost without feeling an irresistible desire to cut their names on it, as Alf, Bert or Chas. must do in obedience to their instinct, which murmurs if it sees a fine woman go by, or even a dog, Ce chien est à moi. And, of course, it may not be a dog, I thought, remembering Parliament Square, the Sieges Allee and other avenues; it may be a piece of land or a man with curly black hair. It is one of the great advantages of being a woman that one can pass even a very fine negress without wishing to make an Englishwoman of her (*AROO* 38–9).

The Black woman is silenced and stands outside the category of Englishwoman. She is denied citizenship, erasing the long history of

Black people in Britain. Jane Marcus, in *Hearts of Darkness: White Women Write Race*, offers a full discussion of this passage in part as a corrective to her earlier work on Woolf's anti-imperialism: 'I have been complicit as a critic in producing a radical and sympathetic "Virginia Woolf" for readers who want to hear that voice.'[30] As Marcus notes, 'feminism's installation in the academy and the vexed field of feminist criticism and theory are haunted by the still, proud figure of the black woman caught in the white woman's gaze'.[31] She focuses not only on the black woman's otherness, but also the adjective 'fine' which evokes the slave auction or bill of sale and a 'possessive, measuring, and judging gaze'.[32] In addition, the phrase 'even a very fine' suggests a hierarchy of Black people in terms of those 'worthy' of colonisation or inclusion within the nation space. As Ellen Bayuk Rosenman suggests, 'while Woolf's woman writer might not want to colonise the black woman, neither does she identify with her. The flexible selfhood of women writers does not, apparently, extend to other races.'[33] The passage offers no attempt at trans-racial solidarity or interest in the Black woman's history. To quote Urmila Seshagiri: 'Woolf's anti-imperialism rarely manifests itself through claims about racial or cultural equality.'[34]

The passage builds on Woolf's argument about masculinity, patriarchal power and colonisation. The male desire to inscribe and own, developed in the home, the classroom and the professions, is on a continuum with men's objectification of women and their glorification of imperialism through statues such as in Berlin's Sieges Allee or London's Parliament Square. In this complex passage, Woolf's narrator excavates the psychology of colonialism and its perpetuation through the spectacle of nationalism. But the occlusion is all the more striking given this insistence on women's refusal of such desires. Women are applauded for their non-territorial response to the sight of a Black woman, but the moment of encounter stops there. The narrator's shift from the Black male victim of colonialism to the Black woman suggests a level of gender affinity but not one that extends beyond ignoring her. This is curious, too, when Woolf's novels are full of women imperialists such as Lady Bruton in *Mrs Dalloway* with her emigration schemes: 'if ever a woman could have worn the helmet and shot the arrow, could have led troops to attack, ruled with indomitable justice barbarian hordes [. . .] that woman was Millicent Bruton'.[35] In a similar vein, Marcus asks why the narrator rushes to 'extricate herself from sharing the guilt of imperialism with white men. Her own relatives' stories made that complicity [. . .] clear'.[36] Woolf's point, it seems, is not that women are absolved of colonial guilt but that they have historically stood outside the institutions and structures which have perpetuated imperial ideology.

Another way to approach this passage is to consider, as others have, the phrase – 'Ce chien est à moi' – from Blaise Pascal's *Pensées*. Given that this is one of the epigraphs to Leonard Woolf's *Empire and Commerce in Africa*, it connects the representation of empire and slavery in *A Room of One's Own* to a wider body of writing on economic imperialism. This, in turn, suggests that the refusal to mark, own and conquer at the heart of this passage, then, is not just about gendered behaviours but a more pervasive political act of resistance. We might turn back to Leonard Woolf's excoriating critique of colonialism as a reminder of the freight of Woolf's moment of trans-racial encounter: 'Slavery, drink and rifles, and the bloodshed and degradation which capitalism, in its hunger for profits and dividends [. . .] has carried into every bay and river and forest of Africa, can never be atoned for.'[37] For Jane Goldman, this passage continues the braiding together of canine and female identities around a set of tropes concerning slavery and empire that occurs throughout the text. The early reference to a 'collar' suggests not only a canine identity but slavery: 'that collar I have spoken of, women and fiction, the need to coming to some conclusion on a subject that raises all sorts of prejudices and passions, bowed my head to the ground' (*AROO* 4). Goldman focuses on the shifting identity positions and the mobility between subject and object which characterises the passage and complicates any fixed hierarchies. The dog is both defacing, or urinating on, the tombstone or signpost, but also being owned and possessed: 'a marked and marking being'.[38] The same goes, she argues, for the narrator: 'how far is she speaking as a woman at all (she is pointedly not a self-designated "*English-woman*")'.[39] In a text all about the slipperiness of identity and voice, the pronoun 'one' also distances the narrator from easy affiliation or alignment. Goldman draws our attention to the continuous pluralising mobility of binary categories of race, gender or species. She writes:

> I am not interested in indicting Woolf or *A Room of One's Own* as racist, or indeed in rescuing either from such indictments; but I am interested in the ways Woolf's writing [. . .] encourages her readers to engage actively in the quite canine business of chasing, unearthing, and *turning* its dense metaphors and tropes.[40]

The layers of allusive signification in Woolf's prose do not erase the problematics of this passage but call attention to the contingency of the categories and contexts out of which its encounter arises.

In *Three Guineas*, written nearly a decade later, and in a very different political and economic climate, Woolf returns to the construction of man as dictator and tyrant and makes the connections between patriarchy and imperialism even more overt. The narrator investigates how universities and the professions are training grounds for nationalism, patriotism and the arts of war and how this is buttressed by the ceremonial and spectacular performance of power and hierarchy. She imagines an experimental college which will not teach 'the arts of dominating other people' nor 'the arts of ruling, of killing, of acquiring land and capital'.[41] In Hobson's *Imperialism*, he too traces the roots of jingoism in an education system which cultivates 'the savage survivals of combativeness' and 'poisons' childrens' 'early understanding of history by false ideals and pseudo-heroes'.[42] This is, he argues, 'as foul an abuse of education as it is possible to conceive'.[43]

Woolf also elaborates on women's relationship to imperialism. Without means of her own, and given that marriage was the only profession open to women, she was forced to 'accept their views and fall in with their decrees': 'all her conscious effort must be in favour of what Lady Lovelace called "our splendid Empire"' (*TG* 123). With increased financial and intellectual autonomy, Woolf explores how women are to use their 'outsiderness', or their alternative training, to prevent war and injustice. As Helen Tyson observes in her chapter in this collection, Woolf envisions entry to the professions leading to a shift from being 'victims of the patriarchal system' to 'champions of the capitalist system': the words '"For God and Empire" will very likely be written, like the address on a dog-collar, round your neck' (*TG* 150, 152). To prevent this, the narrator gives a guinea to help women enter the professions only if she commits to in no way hinder the access of 'any other human being, whether man or woman, white or black' (*TG* 149). Entry must come with conditions: poverty, chastity (refusal to 'sell your brain'), derision (refusal of fame and praise), freedom from the unreal loyalties of 'pride and nationality' (including 'religious pride, college pride, school pride, family pride, sex pride') (*TG* 161). Anti-imperialism is central to that outsiderness: refuse 'all such ceremonies as encourage the desire to impose "our" civilisation or "our" dominion upon other people' (*TG* 186).

Three Guineas also contains a range of references to slavery, both metaphoric and literal. Women's exploitative and unwaged domestic labour is akin to slavery, but Woolf also underscores the discrepancy in gendered capital by comparing funds available to the Women's Social and Political Union and the Society for the Abolition of Slavery for the 'abolition of *that* slavery' (*TG* 128 my emphasis). The causes are connected but the scope of their work is vastly different due to women's lack of access to financial resource. And the repeated reference to money, including currency, salaries, donations, is central to the feminist socialism of *TG*. The pages are littered with pound signs and money provides a language for talking about inequity: an irrefutable marker of disparity. In *Wages Against Housework*, Silvia Federici writes: 'to want wages for housework means to refuse that work as an expression of our nature, and therefore to refuse precisely the female role that capital has invented for us'.[44] Nearly four decades earlier, Woolf made similar points about the place of women's unpaid domestic and reproductive labour in the capitalist system: 'wives and mothers and daughters who work all day and every day, without whose work the State would collapse and fall to pieces, without whose work your sons, sir, would cease to exist, are paid nothing whatever' (*TG* 136). She references particular campaigns such as 'pensions for spinsters' (150) and 'equal pay for equal work', drawing on Eleanor Rathbone's campaigning, via the National Union of Women's Suffrage Societies, for a 'national endowment of motherhood' (*TG* 150).[45] In arguing for a fair wage for women she raises the question of a living wage ('how much money is needed to live upon in England today') and what is the 'mean' between 'excessive wealth' and 'excessive poverty' (*TG* 151). Woolf explores the gendered implications of capitalism, but also fundamentally challenges the supposed 'taint' of paid work and the taboo which prohibited women from even speaking about money and wages.

While numbers populate *Three Guineas*, the guinea is the unit of currency at its heart. As with *A Room of One's Own*, this titular trope acknowledges the history of slavery and the middle passage. Her choice of currency was deliberate and freighted. In the 1930s the guinea was no longer in circulation as a coin but was a unit of currency (worth £1.05 or 21 shillings) used for professional services such as medical or legal fees, horse racing or subscriptions and paid for by cheque (as on the book's original cover). By using this term instead of pounds or shillings, Woolf employs the language of her stated audience: the upper-middle-class barrister and the 'daughters of educated men'. But the guinea is also a currency which came into being because of the slave trade, named unofficially after the Guinea Coast of West Africa, and another way in which the foundation of Woolf's text is haunted by racial injustice. The guinea was first minted in 1663 for the Royal African Company, the English company which held a monopoly on trade with West Africa until the early eighteenth century. Gold exported by the RAC from West Africa was made into guineas by the Royal Mint and 'between 1673 and 1713 over five hundred thousand guineas were struck' bearing an elephant, icon of the RAC.[46] The coin was out of circulation after 1814 but was still used as a unit of value. The guinea, like the £500, is contaminated, particularly given that the term 'guinea' or 'guineamen' was also used to refer to the vessels, sites of violence and terror, that transported slaves across the Atlantic. As Naomi Black has argued, the guinea represents 'the English ruling class, whose female members are excluded from power, but it represents as well the exploitation, the corruption that underlies that power'.[47] The talismanic connection of the coin passed from person to person here becomes a more abstracted sign of exchange: both of privilege and donation. Money is the material form of the social relations of production, and here the symbol of feminist agency is haunted by the capitalist gains of empire and slavery.

Woolf's major essays are marked by occlusions and silences around race, slavery and empire. They are also deeply radical and creative explorations of capitalist imperialism and its impacts on women's lives. One way of assessing the longevity and contemporary currency of these texts is by turning to their influence on Black artists and writers. In this final section, I consider such responses to *A Room of One's Own* by Alice Walker, Sylvia Wynter and Saidiya Hartman. In Alice Walker's 'Saving the Life That is Your Own: The Importance of Models in the Artist's Life' she emphasises the importance of recovering Black women writers – 'abandoned, discredited, maligned, nearly lost' – as foundational for her own writing life. Alongside Zora Neale Hurston and Toni Morrison, Walker cites 'Virginia Woolf – who has saved so many of us' as a model of radicalism.[48] Walker's extends Woolf's call to think back through our mothers by recovering those women silenced by Woolf's own recovery project. Walker takes her dialogue with *A Room of One's Own* further in 'In Search of Our Mothers' Gardens' by literally inserting her own text into Woolf's: '"any woman born with a great gift in the sixteenth century [insert "eighteenth century," insert "black woman," insert "born or made a slave"] would have certainly gone crazed'.[49] As Tuzyline Jita Allan has argued, Walker re-animates the text for a Black female voice to demonstrate that 'not all women are created equal': 'the reloaded text, then, is discharged bearing the double image of Woolf's "thwarted and hindered" but unenslaved female artist in sixteenth-century England *and* Walker's talented, brutally silenced black bondwoman in eighteenth-century America'.[50] She asks how Woolf's central idea about money and private space would apply to a Black woman writer like Phillis Wheatley, 'a slave, who owned not even herself'.[51] Walker relates Woolf's celebration of the 'suppressed poet', the 'mute and inglorious' woman writer, to generations of Black women engaged in artistry such as quilting and gardening, again extending Woolf's redefinition of artistry. Walker both unravels and writes over the central terms of *A Room of One's Own* while simultaneously acknowledging the tools and strategies of feminist recovery.

The Jamaican writer, Sylvia Wynter, who studied at King's College London several decades after Woolf, is another Black intellectual who has engaged with *A Room of One's Own*. Among Wynter's frequent references to radical Black thinkers such as Aimé Césaire, Frantz Fanon and C. L. R. James, Woolf stands out. But the tools Woolf used to de-naturalise patriarchal power resonate with Wynter's own project of excavating the genres through which hierarchies of the 'human' have been constructed. Wynter's wide-ranging and allusive writing returns often to the question of why white, Western man has become the norm against which all other forms of being are measured: our current 'ethnoclass (ie Western bourgeois) conception of the human, Man [. . .] overrepresents itself as if it were the human itself'.[52] In her essay 'Unsettling the Coloniality of Being/Power/Truth/Freedom: Towards the Human, After Man, Its Overrepresentation: An Argument', Wynter moves through the various stages of constructions of the human and their foundation in colonial violence. The medieval, theocentric conception of the human revolved around a Spirit/Flesh dichotomy whereby humans are unified in a common enslavement through sin. The 'de-supernaturalizing of our modes of being human' emerged in Renaissance humanism, the rise of the natural and physical sciences and 'the new rational/irrational organising principle and master code'.[53] During this period Man is invented as a political subject (Man1). Then, in the nineteenth century, a biocentric or bioevolutionary conception of the human (Man2) was inaugurated with race as its central defining and ordering category: a 'new principle of non-homogeneity, that of DuBois' Color Line in its white/nonwhite, Men/Natives form [. . .] will now be drawn as a "Space of Otherness"'.[54] As Wynter sets out, the ascendance of white Western Man is reliant on the colonial project and the mercantile systems of global trade which would lead to the horrors of plantation slavery.

Wynter turns to Woolf when considering the role of representation in understandings of the human. She argues, as did Woolf, that the illusion of the superiority of Western man relies on constant repetition and reinforcement: 'it must ensure the functioning of strategic mechanisms that can repress all knowledge of the fact that its biocentric descriptive statement is a descriptive statement'.[55] She turns to *A Room of One's Own* not only for its denaturalising of patriarchy but also its exploration of the symbolic means by which patriarchy asserts its power: 'The stigmatizing portrayal of women as intellectually inferior, made by "angry male professors" that Virginia Woolf had brilliantly zeroed in on (in her essay *A Room of One's Own*).'[56] The narrator of *A Room of One's Own* gradually exposes the pervasive workings of patriarchy – 'his was the power and the money and the influence' (*AROO* 26) – but reveals the systematic denigration of women (to which Wynter alludes) to be a product of the precarity of power: when the angry professor 'insisted a little too emphatically on the inferiority of women, he was concerned not with their inferiority, but with his own superiority' (*AROO* 27). In 'Unsettling', as well as in 'The Ceremony Must Be Found: After Humanism' (1984), Wynter locates Woolf in a line of thinkers who expose the artificiality of this 'ontological order of value' that others and excludes.[57] She compares Woolf's detailed charting of the 'effects of discouragement' on women (*AROO* 40) to Carter G. Woodson's *The Miseducation of the Negro* (1933) in which he argues that Black people are being indoctrinated rather than educated and taught to view themselves as inferior. Whether it's 'thinking back through our mothers' or learning about Black history and culture, countering these 'demotivating processes' is essential to defamiliarising and resisting these discourses of negation.[58] As Wynter writes, we can see 'Woolf and Woodson's insights as insights into the workings of the symbolic representation processes instituting of our present genre of the human, Man' as well as 'the overall system of knowledge that is enacting of these processes'.[59]

In 'The Re-enchantment of Humanism: An Interview with Sylvia Wynter' (2000), Wynter, in conversation with David Scott, refers again to Woolf and *A Room of One's Own* in the context of a process she terms, via anthropologist Maurice Goldelier, 'occultation'. Here she expands on the work of 1960s feminists, acknowledging their intervention in naming and exposing patriarchy but also calling out their Euro-American blindnesses: 'because they could experience the issue of gender from their already privileged perspective as an urgent and unique issue, they introduced an entirely new opening'.[60] They named patriarchy as a continually self-perpetuating social order which privileges men over women, but also showed how 'mechanisms of occultation' keep its authorship opaque.[61] But 'even before the sixties' feminism', Wynter argues, 'if you go back and read that powerful 1929 essay, *A Room of One's Own*, by Virginia Woolf, you can see that it is this Godelier-type issue, as it applies to gender roles, that she is already opening'.[62]

Wynter here pinpoints Woolf's feminist project of defamiliarising the ways in which women's 'inferiority' is made to seem natural or essentialised. One thinks here of *Three Guineas*, not mentioned by Wynter, but the text in which Woolf more fully explores the constructedness of the patriarch as dictator or tyrant and the literal and epistemic violence required to maintain the gendered hierarchy: 'he is Man himself, the quintessence of virility, the perfect type of which all the others are imperfect adumbrations' (*TG* 214). Woolf's detailed excavation of the material and ideological reinforcing of male supremacy through the university, state, army, judiciary and the home acts as a precursor, in the field of gender, to Wynter's more abstracted and globalised account. While Woolf does not think through decoloniality in the way Wynter does, she makes the connection to imperialism and its exploitative and violent operations. Both remain committed to a revised, or planetary, humanism and place 'genre' or representation at the centre of their thinking about dispossession.

Wynter turns to Woolf for a methodology of resistance as does Saidiya Hartman in her recent work *Wayward Lives: Beautiful Experiments* (2019). Hartman's project is to reanimate the lives of early twentieth-century, young, Black women whose archival traces are found in sociological surveys, parole or social workers' records. She presents these dispossessed woman as 'sexual modernists, free lovers, radicals, and anarchists' and in their intimate histories finds rebellion, riotous conduct and 'the beautiful plot against the plantation she waged each and every day'.[63] In her 'A Note on Method' to *Wayward Lives*, Hartman describes how she 'pressed at the limits of the case file and the document, speculated about what might have been, imagined the things whispered in dark bedrooms, and amplified moments of withholding, escape and possibility'.[64] The violence and limits of the archive can be met with 'critical fabulation', which acts as a counter-narrative to one of surveillance, degradation and pathology.[65] Writing about her methodological influences, Hartman cites a tradition of Black radical thought as well as 'the model of the possible offered in the work of Marguerite Duras, Virginia Woolf'.[66] Woolf spent her writing life uncovering and speculating about the lives of obscure women: whether the shop girl whose biography she'd prefer to Napoleon's, the queer scientists Chloe and Olivia or the 'creative force' which permeates the walls surrounding those women imprisoned in the domestic sphere (*AROO* 68, 63, 66). Throughout her writing life as an essayist, Woolf engaged in critical fabulation to draw her readers to women's histories. And of course, in Shakespeare's sister she imagined a life where the archive lay silent. Hartman writes of her 'mode of close narration, a style which places the voice of narrator and character in inseparable relation' which also echoes *A Room of One's Own*.[67] Woolf's polyvocal narrator references the Scottish ballad, 'Mary Hamilton' or the 'Fower Marys' about four ladies-in-waiting to Mary, Queen of Scots, one of whom has killed her child after becoming pregnant by the king. The 'Mary Seaton', 'Mary Beaton' and 'Mary Carmichael' in the ballad becomes characters in the text (Fernham's principle, the narrator's aunt and a novelist respectively), thus blurring subject and object. Woolf deliberately utilises a communal voice, stretching back through history, just as Hartman celebrates the radical potential of the choral:

> the chorus is the vehicle for another kind of story, not of the great man or the tragic hero, but one in which [. . .] mutual aid provides the resource for collective action, not leader and mass, where the untranslatable songs and seeming nonsense make good the promise of revolution.[68]

Woolf's commitment to communality made her fear the iconicity which has 'fixed' a text like *A Room of One's Own*, turning it into soundbites or slogans. That fixity undermines the rhetorical strategies of interruption and openness which are so central to the text's inclusion of other voices and anticipation of critique. *A Room of One's Own* embraces its audience: inviting them to engage in various recovery projects and to 'write all kinds of books' (*AROO* 82). Woolf's essay continues to prompt reworkings and rethinkings in relation to race and contemporary society, in the spirit Woolf imagined, some of which take creative fuel from those very moments of arrest and exclusion. Jo Hamya's *Three Rooms* (2021), for example, is explicit about its debt to Woolf but also explores issues of precarity and the impossibility of attaining a 'room of one's own' through the eyes of its young, Black, educated protagonist. Kabe Wilson's performance piece *The Dreadlock Hoax* (19 May 2014) emerged out of his artwork, *Olivia N'Gowfri – Of One Woman or So*, composed over five years by rearranging the words of *A Room of One's Own*. This recycled work traces the experience of a Black woman at Cambridge radicalised by reading Black intellectuals and whose plan of arson is interrupted by her interaction with *A Room of One's Own* and her realisation that 'destruction cannot undo the difficulties of the past; only by reworking, restructuring and recycling material can the present account for the past and create possibilities of a different future'.[69] Wilson has described how the impetus for the project came from Woolf's reference to the Black woman and how the 'uneasy furtiveness' of the original usage became an 'explosive critical moment'.[70] Moments of textual difficulty, even revulsion, can be generative as Woolf's texts continue to be remixed, re-read and challenged. And that, after all, was the model of creativity, as communal and accretive, that she put forward so compellingly in *A Room of One's Own*.

Notes

1. I pursue this focus also because much of the excellent work on Woolf and empire tends to concentrate on her fiction: see, for example, Kathy J. Phillips, *Virginia Woolf Against Empire* (Knoxville: University of Tennessee Press, 1994).
2. Hermione Lee, *Virginia Woolf* (London: Vintage, 1997), 556.
3. See Anna Snaith, 'Another Tale of Rubber: À Propos of The Voyage Out', *Critical Quarterly*, 61.4 (2019), 80–9 and 'Leonard and Virginia Woolf: Writing Against Empire', *Journal of Commonwealth Literature*, 50.1 (2015), 19–32.
4. Robert J. C. Young, *Postcolonialism: An Historical Introduction* (Oxford: Blackwell, 2001), 74.
5. Young, *Postcolonialism*, 102.
6. Karl Marx, *Capital*, Volume 1, trans. by Ben Fowkes (Harmondsworth: Penguin, 1976), 915.
7. Young, *Postcolonialism*, 109. See 101–12 for a full discussion of Marx on colonialism and imperialism.
8. Young, *Postcolonialism*, 98.
9. J. A. Hobson, *Imperialism: A Study* (Nottingham: Spokesman, 2011), 50.
10. Hobson, *Imperialism*, 51.
11. Ibid., 66.
12. Leonard Woolf, *Empire and Commerce in Africa: A Study in Economic Imperialism* (London: Routledge, 1998), 24, 7.
13. Woolf, *Empire*, 343, 353.
14. Fred Leventhal and Peter Stansky, *Leonard Woolf: Bloomsbury Socialist* (Oxford: Oxford University Press, 2019), 112.
15. Woolf, *Empire*, 362, 359.
16. See Michèle Barrett, 'Virginia Woolf's Research for *Empire and Commerce in Africa* (Leonard Woolf, 1920)', *Woolf Studies Annual*, 19 (2013).
17. Barrett, 'Woolf's Research', 113.
18. See <https://www.cam.ac.uk/about-the-university/history/legacies-of-enslavement> [accessed 31 October 2023].

19. Virginia Woolf, *A Room of One's Own and Three Guineas*, ed. by Anna Snaith (Oxford: Oxford University Press, 2015), 19. Further references will be included within the main text.
20. Hobson, *Imperialism*, 82.
21. Ibid., 82.
22. Ibid., 206, 203.
23. Ibid., 207.
24. Jane Marcus, *Hearts of Darkness: White Women Write Race* (New Brunswick: Rutgers University Press, 2004), 42.
25. See Jane de Gay, 'James Stephen's Anti-Slavery Politics: A Woolfian Inheritance', in *Virginia Woolf and the (Common)wealth Reader*, ed. by Helen Wussow and Mary Ann Gillies (Clemson: Clemson University Press, 2014), 27–38.
26. Marcus, *Hearts*, 71.
27. Vron Ware, *Beyond the Pale: White Women, Racism and History* (London: Verso, 2015), 106.
28. Ware, *Beyond*, 109.
29. Marcus, *Hearts*, 21.
30. Ibid., 13.
31. Ibid., 31.
32. Ibid., 47.
33. Ellen Bayuk Rosenman, *A Room of One's Own: Women Writers and the Politics of Creativity* (New York: Twayne, 1995), 114.
34. Urmila Seshagiri, *Race and the Modernist Imagination* (Ithaca: Cornell University Press, 2010), 143.
35. Virginia Woolf, *Mrs Dalloway*, ed. by Anne E. Fernald (Cambridge: Cambridge University Press, 2015), 161.
36. Marcus, *Hearts*, 32.
37. Woolf, *Empire*, 259.
38. Jane Goldman, '"Ce chien est à moi": Virginia Woolf and the Signifying Dog', *Woolf Studies Annual*, 13 (2007), 70.
39. Goldman, 'Signifying', 72.
40. Ibid., 51. Goldman also, like Marcus, draws attention to the implied reference to race and slavery in Woolf's inclusion of Aphra Behn, author of *Oronooko: or, the Royal Slave* (1688).
41. Virginia Woolf, *A Room of One's Own and Three Guineas*, ed. by Anna Snaith (Oxford: Oxford University Press, 2015), 118. Further references will be included within the main text.
42. Hobson, *Imperialism*, 204.
43. Ibid., 205.
44. Silvia Federici, *Wages Against Housework* (Bristol: Falling Wall Press, 1975), 4. See also Asako Nakai's 'Materialism, Autonomy, Intersectionality: Revisiting Virginia Woolf through the Wages for Housework Perspective', *Feminist Theory*, 24.4 (2023), 497–511.
45. See Eleanor Rathbone, *The Disinherited Family* (London: E. Arnold & Co., 1924).

46. Colleen E. Kriger, *Making Money: Life, Death, and Early Modern Trade on Africa's Guinea Coast* (Athens: Ohio University Press, 2017), 59.
47. Naomi Black, *Virginia Woolf as Feminist* (Ithaca: Cornell University Press, 2004), 176.
48. Alice Walker, 'Saving the Life That Is Your Own: The Importance of Models in the Artist's Life', *In Search of Our Mothers' Gardens: Womanist Prose* (London: Phoenix, 2005), 9, 14.
49. Walker, *Search*, 235.
50. Tuzyline Jita Allan, 'A Voice of One's Own: Implications of Impersonality in the Essays of Virginia Woolf and Alice Walker', *The Politics of the Essay: Feminist Perspectives*, ed. by Ruth-Ellen Boetcher Joeres and Elizabeth Mittman (Bloomington: Indiana University Press, 1993), 131–2.
51. Walker, *Search*, 235.
52. Sylvia Wynter, 'Unsettling the Coloniality of Being/Power/Truth/Freedom: Towards the Human, After Man, Its Overrepresentation: An Argument', *CR: The New Centennial Review*, 3.3 (2003), 260.
53. Wynter, 'Unsettling', 263–4, 300.
54. Ibid., 322.
55. Ibid., 326.
56. Ibid., 326.
57. Sylvia Wynter, 'The Ceremony Must Be Found: After Humanism', *Boundary*, 2 Vol. 12–13 (1984), 42.
58. Wynter, 'Unsettling', 326.
59. Ibid., 327.
60. David Scott, 'The Re-enchantment of Humanism: An Interview with Sylvia Wynter', *Small Axe*, 8 (2000), 184.
61. Scott, 'Re-enchantment', 184.
62. Ibid., 185.
63. Saidiya Hartman, *Wayward Lives, Beautiful Experiments: Intimate Histories of Social Upheaval* (London: Serpent's Tale, 2019), xv, 34.
64. Hartman, *Wayward*, xiv–xv.
65. Saidiya Hartman, 'Venus in Two Acts', *Small Axe*, 26, 12.2 (2008), 11.
66. Saidiya Hartman, 'Intimate History, Radical Narrative', *Black Perspectives*, 22 May 2020 <https://www.aaihs.org/intimate-history-radical-narrative> [accessed 31 October 2023].
67. Hartman, *Wayward*, xiii.
68. Ibid., 348.
69. Kabe Wilson and Susan Stanford Friedman, 'Of Words, Worlds and Woolf: Recycling A Room of One's Own into Of One Woman or So', *Recycling Virginia Woolf in Contemporary Art and Culture*, ed. by Monica Latham, Caroline Marie and Anne-Laure Rigeade (London: Routledge, 2021), 184–5.
70. Wilson and Friedman, 'Recycling', 194–5.

Works Cited

Allan, Tuzyline Jita, 'A Voice of One's Own: Implications of Impersonality in the Essays of Virginia Woolf and Alice Walker'. In *The Politics of the Essay: Feminist Perspectives*, ed. by Ruth-Ellen Boetcher Joeres and Elizabeth Mittman, 131–50. Bloomington: Indiana University Press, 1993.

Barrett, Michèle. 'Virginia Woolf's Research for *Empire and Commerce in Africa* (Leonard Woolf, 1920)'. *Woolf Studies Annual*, 19 (2013), 83–122.

Black, Naomi. *Virginia Woolf as Feminist*. Ithaca: Cornell University Press, 2004.

Federici, Silvia. *Wages Against Housework*. Bristol: Falling Wall Press, 1975.

Goldman, Jane. '"Ce chien est à moi": Virginia Woolf and the Signifying Dog'. *Woolf Studies Annual*, 13 (2007), 49–86.

Hartman, Saidiya. 'Intimate History, Radical Narrative'. *Black Perspectives*, 22 May 2020 <https://www.aaihs.org/intimate-history-radical-narrative> [accessed 31 October 2023].

——, 'Venus in Two Acts'. *Small Axe*, 26, 12.2 (2008), 1–14.

——, *Wayward Lives, Beautiful Experiments: Intimate Histories of Social Upheaval*. London: Serpent's Tale, 2019.

Hobson, J. A. *Imperialism: A Study*. Nottingham: Spokesman, 2011.

Kriger, Colleen E. *Making Money: Life, Death, and Early Modern Trade on Africa's Guinea Coast*. Athens: Ohio University Press, 2017.

Lee, Hermione. *Virginia Woolf*. London: Vintage, 1997.

Lenin, V. I. *Imperialism: The Highest Stage of Capitalism*. London: Union Books, 2015.

Leventhal, Fred and Peter Stansky. *Leonard Woolf: Bloomsbury Socialist*. Oxford: Oxford University Press, 2019.

Marcus, Jane. *Hearts of Darkness: White Women Write Race*. New Brunswick: Rutgers University Press, 2004.

Marx, Karl. *Capital*, Volume 1. Trans. by Ben Fowkes. Harmondsworth: Penguin, 1976.

Phillips, Kathy J. *Virginia Woolf Against Empire*. Knoxville: University of Tennessee Press, 1994.

Rosenman, Ellen Bayuk. *A Room of One's Own: Women Writers and the Politics of Creativity*. New York: Twayne, 1995.

Scott, David. 'The Re-enchantment of Humanism: An Interview with Sylvia Wynter'. *Small Axe*, 8 (2000), 119–207.

Seshagiri, Urmila. *Race and the Modernist Imagination*. Ithaca: Cornell University Press, 2010.

Walker, Alice. 'Saving the Life That Is Your Own: The Importance of Models in the Artist's Life'. *In Search of Our Mothers' Gardens: Womanist Prose*, 3–14. London: Phoenix, 2005.

——, 'In Search of Our Mothers' Gardens'. *In Search of Our Mothers' Gardens: Womanist Prose*, 231–43. London: Phoenix, 2005.
Ware, Vron. *Beyond the Pale: White Women, Racism and History*. London: Verso, 2015.
Wilson, Kabe and Susan Stanford Friedman. 'Of Words, Worlds and Woolf: Recycling A Room of One's Own into Of One Woman or So'. In *Recycling Virginia Woolf in Contemporary Art and Culture*, ed. by Monica Latham, Caroline Marie, Anne-Laure Rigeade, 183–268. London: Routledge, 2021.
Woolf, Leonard. *Empire and Commerce in Africa: A Study in Economic Imperialism*. London: Routledge, 1998.
Woolf, Virginia. *Mrs Dalloway*, ed. by Anne E. Fernald. Cambridge: Cambridge University Press, 2015.
——, *A Room of One's Own and Three Guineas*, ed. by Anna Snaith. Oxford: Oxford University Press, 2015.
——, *The Voyage Out*. London: Penguin, 1970.
Wynter, Sylvia. 'The Ceremony Must Be Found: After Humanism'. *Boundary 2*, Vol. 12–13 (1984), 19–70.
——, 'Unsettling the Coloniality of Being/Power/Truth/Freedom: Towards the Human, After Man, Its Overrepresentation: An Argument'. *CR: The New Centennial Review*, 3.3 (2003), 257–337.
Young, Robert J. C. *Postcolonialism: An Historical Introduction*. Oxford: Blackwell, 2001.

Chapter 3

'my comfortable capitalistic head': Virginia Woolf on Consumption, Co-operation and Motherhood

Charlotte Taylor Suppé

From the age of thirty, Virginia Woolf spent eleven years learning about and working within the Women's Co-operative Guild (WCG). Her commitment to this movement has found a well-deserved place in recent Woolf criticism, yet the culture of the WCG was largely at odds with the rest of her social and intellectual life. Where the WCG was a society of mothers that exercised working-class women's economic influence and directly campaigned for political change, Woolf was a child-free woman who fostered a feminism based on upper-middle-class women's professional autonomy and embraced ambivalence in her textual politics.[1] Thus, there is still much to be understood about Woolf's involvement with a group whose politics and economics she understood so well, but about whose members she could be scathing.

Given how involved she was with the organisation it is unsurprising to find that Woolf mentions Guild meetings frequently in her diaries and letters. One particular diary passage exemplifies her disparagement of both her WCG work and the Guildswomen themselves:

> we dined early & had the Guild. Mr Adams spoke. The level is certainly not a high one [. . .] as usual it was only when talk drifted near food that one of the women broke silence. She wanted a bread shop [. . .] for a time they all spoke at once – stories of their own ill treatment & of their neighbours. Oddly phlegmatic these women for the most part; with a passive sort of pleasure in sitting there & watching like so many pale grey sea anemones stuck to their rocks. Still, the children, the housework – excuses enough if one troubled to look. (*D1* 112)

A notable element of this passage is Woolf's description of the women as 'passive' and her denigration of their desire for a Co-operative 'bread shop'. Food shopping was a central tenet of the WCG's ethos and such an appeal fell well within its policy of using consumption and co-operation to actively affect change. Not only was Woolf fully acquainted with WCG economic strategies but, as Michael Tratner has shown, she adapted co-operative principles to make a point in her own writing.[2] However, she could not reconcile her feelings about the Guildswomen with her progressive, co-operative economic leanings. At its core, Woolf's sharpness was driven not by the Guild's political or economic policies but by her prejudices towards its working-class members. There were what she perceived to be irreconcilable differences between herself and the Guildswomen; where they had motherhood and housework, she had a command of language and an active artist's mind. These biases appear across Woolf's work, as do negative connections between working-class women, motherhood and consumption, and such associations are a valuable lens through which to view Woolf's position on class.

'my Mothers': The Homemakers of the WCG

Woolf's primary connection with the WCG was through its general secretary Margaret Llewelyn Davies. The pair were introduced in 1909 by their mutual friend Janet Case although Woolf only became involved in Guild politics after her marriage to Leonard. The WCG was an integral part of Leonard's work and, alongside him, Woolf cultivated a thorough understanding of the movement. In 1913 she attended the Guild annual congress and visited factories, in 1914 she read Co-operative movement manuals and, between 1916 and 1923, she hosted, organised speakers and acted as secretary for the Richmond branch meetings. Clara Jones and Alice Wood have shown how committed Woolf was to the Guild yet it was difficult for her to entirely empathise with a society of 'mothers' established on the importance of working-class women's economic influence.[3] Motherhood is a prevalent theme in Woolf's writing, with mother and non-mother characters, maternalist discourse and maternal imagery found throughout her oeuvre from her earliest short stories (as Bryony Randall's chapter in this collection shows) to her final novel, *Between the Acts*. Her writing employs maternal and domestic activities to explore women's autonomy and creativity, with maternity repeatedly impeding artistic creation. Motherhood is also associated with systemic political and social strictures that prevent women from fulfilling their potential. While different types of mother characters populate Woolf's work – from 'unmaternal' Clarissa Dalloway to *The Waves*' 'unscrupulous' and 'jealous' maternal archetype Susan – those that value or pursue motherhood are overwhelmingly champions of patriarchal, nationalistic or Victorian values.[4] Motherhood was also a fraught topic on a personal level and Woolf's letters and diaries reveal her personal resistance to 'the maternal passion'.[5] The competition she felt with her sister Vanessa, the premature death of their mother and the Woolfs' decision not to have children can also be traced in the links Woolf drew between maternity, femininity, self-worth and the creative process.

Woolf unequivocally saw the Guildswomen as mothers. She referred to the Richmond branch as 'the Mothers' or 'my Mothers' and wrote to a prospective speaker: 'The audience consists of about 12 mothers of families.'[6] After a disastrous talk on venereal disease, Woolf told Llewelyn Davies how one member had berated the lecturer, admonishing 'it was a most cruel speech, and only a childless woman could have made it "for we mothers try to forget what our sons have to go through"' (*L2* 139). Moreover, the Guildswomen overwhelmingly *were* mothers, as Gillian Scott records in her history of the WCG: 'Guild branches recruited from the women who shopped at the Co-op stores [. . .] The typical Guildswoman was married [. . .] and in her middle age.' The Guild's 1893 Annual Report indicates that most of the 6,412 members were wives and mothers and, Scott notes, 'this pattern became more pronounced as the Guild grew in size'.[7] Woolf also had some professional experience that caused her to associate the WCG with maternity. In 1915 Llewelyn Davies approached her with a collection of Guildswomen's letters concerning the strain of bearing too many children in reduced circumstances. Woolf proposed turning these letters into a book, unsuccessfully trying to involve Gerald Duckworth in their publication. In the end the Guild self-published the collection, calling it *Maternity: Letters from Working-Women*.

In addition to finding it difficult to identify with working-class mothers, Woolf struggled to empathise with a culture that was built on the economic impact of food shopping. While shopping is a theme in Woolf's work that has garnered interest in recent decades,[8] there is a noticeable difference between her writing of middle-class women stepping out into the world to buy non-essential, desirable consumer goods – Clarissa Dalloway, for example, shopping for flowers, or the protagonist in 'Street Haunting' buying a lead pencil – and working-class women buying the basic goods required to feed a family. These two divergent types of consumption have been defined by Rachel Bowlby as 'going shopping' and 'doing the shopping'. Bowlby notes that, from their advent in the mid-nineteenth-century, '(f)ood shopping was associated with necessity and routine, whereas department stores had promoted a sense of goods that engendered new desires and possibilities'.[9] Accordingly, when Woolf's middle-class characters 'go shopping' they explore the impact of modernity on women's social interactions. 'Doing the shopping' on the other hand – whether in a material working-class sense or from the administrative perspective of a middle-class mistress – is, like cooking, an exploration of old-fashioned domesticity.[10]

On a personal level Woolf found food shopping 'disagreeable', especially 'when done in a mass' (*D1* 102). After a 1915 shopping trip she recorded, 'some counters are besieged by three rows of women. I always choose the empty shops, where I suppose, one pays 1/2[d] a lb. more'. That Woolf didn't know the price of goods and guessed that the quieter shops were more expensive shows not only her distance from working-class shoppers but also how infrequently she went 'marketing' (*D1* 5). Another revealing diary entry early in 1915 notes:

> L. went off to Hampstead to give the first of his lectures to the Women's Guild. He did not seem nervous: he is speaking at this moment. We rather think that old Mr Davies is dying [...] & his life prevents Margaret from much work. I bought my fish & meat in the High Street – a degrading but rather amusing business. I dislike the sight of women shopping. They take it so seriously. (*D1* 7–8)

Given the stream of Woolf's thoughts from Guild activism to shopping it seems fair to suggest that the degradation and amusement she associated with buying her own dinner was linked, albeit subconsciously, with the WCG. In other words, the 'they' who take shopping so seriously are, for Woolf, the working-class Guildswomen.

Co-operative Shopping and the Economics of Co-operation

Woolf was right, the Guildswomen did take shopping seriously. Co-operative stores were the grassroots of the Co-operative movement and since, as Gillian Scott notes, 'the stores were dependent upon the trading loyalty of the working-class housewife for their survival and growth', the WCG had a powerful voice within this movement.[11] Shopping was also important to individual Guildswomen who often had to feed large families. In a 1913 article, Leonard Woolf described the average Guild member in the following way:

> no one receives a more terrible or perpetual schooling, than the woman whose husband hands over to her on Saturday a sum which may be as small as 12s or 13s, and leaves it entirely to her to feed him and clothe him, to pay his rent, and to bring up his children.[12]

In the same year, the Fabian Society (of which Leonard was an active member) published a short book investigating the food budgets of just such a working-class family. This pamphlet, entitled *Round About a Pound a Week*, notes: 'Without doubt, the chief article of diet in a 20s. budget is bread. A long way after bread come potatoes, meat and fish.'[13]

Given the central place of bread in the working-class diet it is no wonder that the Guildswomen wanted to open a bread shop. Indeed, this proposal embodied the very heart of the co-operative ethos of establishing stores which shared their profits among the community via regular dividends. In the first issue of *The Co-operator* magazine, in 1828, founder William King wrote: 'We *must* go to a shop every day to buy food and necessaries – why then should we not go to our own shop?'[14] More than a century later co-operation had achieved resounding success, with Llewelyn Davies explaining: 'Men and women, as members of their local Co-operative Societies, own the shops where they buy [. . .] and manage their business through elected committees and members' meetings.' The Co-operative movement was a powerful economic force. While co-operation began on a local level – with working-class women's basket-power at the movement's beating heart – collectively these small enterprises formed large conglomerations. Llewelyn Davies recorded how 'the England and Scottish Co-operative Wholesale Societies [. . .] form one of the largest trading and manufacturing concerns in Great Britain' and the Guild used this influence for both domestic and international lobbying. As Llewelyn Davies noted: 'Guildswomen, starting from buying bread and butter on revolutionary principles, have reached an international outlook.'[15]

Unlike capitalism – which favours those that stockpile wealth – and socialism – which prioritises the worker and communalises wealth – co-operation foregrounds the consumer, placing them in the primary position of economic power. In his book *Co-operation and the Future of Industry*, Leonard Woolf explored why he found co-operation preferable to both capitalism and socialism, writing:

> A system of industry which throws the control into the hands of the owners of capital can never be truly and fully democratic, and the same is true of a system which would throw it into the hands of the workers. The owners of capital will always be only a small minority of the whole community, and industrial workers can never be more than a large majority. But every one, man, woman and child, is in the nature of things a consumer. In a sense therefore the co-operator consumers represent the whole community in a way in which the capitalists or the workers could never represent it.[16]

Michael Tratner provides an excellent account of how, for the Woolfs, co-operation was far more than simply an economic theory but rather represented the key to a more peaceful future.[17] In the period before, during and after the First World War progressive thinkers were looking for solutions to the aggression flourishing in capitalist Europe. Co-operation sparked the interest of some social activists and economists;[18] not only was it egalitarian but it had a moderating effect on the economy. This meant that by simply doing their shopping the community was protected from the ills of unbound wealth accumulation but still had a revenue stream that could liberate the working class from crippling poverty and fund public services. Historian Ian MacPherson has noted that from very early on in the history of co-operative thought its economic model was considered an 'antidote to social discord and the descent into war' because it offered 'a germ of empowerment and social cohesion that could multiply and grow, dulling competitive instincts and helping to create more equitable communities'.[19]

As a pacifist who criticised the bolstering of competitive instincts, Woolf valued co-operation and Tratner has demonstrated how she adapted its economics to fit her textual politics. In *Three Guineas*, Woolf discredits the capitalist enterprise of wealth gain (asking: 'what Harley Street specialist has time to understand the body, let alone the mind or both in combination, when he is a slave to thirteen thousand a year?').[20] *Three Guineas* also probes the poverty that counterpoises capitalist hoarding (making an example of Scottish novelist Margaret Oliphant who, Woolf states, 'sold her brain, her very admirable brain, prostituted her culture and enslaved her intellectual liberty in order that she might earn her living' (*TG* 217)). Rejecting these extremes, Woolf offers co-operation as an alternative. By showing her spending (rather than saving) her available money – a limited but influential amount in the form of its titular coins – *Three Guineas* both combats capitalism, fascism and war through consumption and cultivates those areas of culture valued by non-competitive, upper-middle-class women or, as Woolf calls them, 'the daughters of educated men'. As Tratner notes; 'if women controlled the surpluses generated by a thriving economy, they could use it for "education, pleasure and philanthropy" and hence avoid the dangers of hoarding'.

While Tratner successfully establishes that Woolf adopted cooperative economic theory and integrated it into her unique feminist stance, his research also uncovers an uncomfortable paradox, for she did not associate the Guildswomen with such transformative purchasing power. Where the upper-middle-class woman is Woolf's ideal shopper due to her limited personal wealth and educated choices, the Guildswomen do not enjoy the same financial and educational opportunities and therefore cannot be progressive or exert effective co-operative influence. Tratner highlights the importance of education within the strategic consumerism of *Three Guineas*, noting that 'one needs to develop the mind and body in order to have the best pleasures'.[21] (If this seems at all incongruous in a work that rails against the paucity of upper-middle-class women's schooling it is important to remember that Woolf is not discounting education but critiquing the imbalanced social and educational systems of her class while questioning how women can forge new systems.) The role that educated refinement plays in Woolf's co-operative theory causes her to appropriate WCG economic principles while using the Guildswomen's poverty to repeatedly deny them the revolutionary possibilities of their own ethos. Hesitations about working-class women's consumption can be seen particularly well in 'Memories of a Working Women's Guild', where the 'mothers' of the WCG are repeatedly shown as conservative and conventional while the upper-middle-class narrator displays her purchasing power and progressive taste.

'Memories of a Working Women's Guild'

'Memories of a Working Women's Guild' began life in 1929 when Margaret Llewelyn Davies asked Woolf to write the introduction to a WCG's collection of working-class women's memoirs (later titled *Life as We Have Known It*). Woolf was already a well-known author, and the preface may have been Llewelyn Davies's practical way to draw attention to a book that she feared would struggle to attract a readership. The pair had a complex relationship, Llewelyn Davies was not only a colleague but a good friend of Leonard's, and had been a valued support during Woolf's 1913–1915 breakdowns. Indeed, in 1915, when Woolf was recovering, Llewelyn Davies was one of the few people she consistently wrote to, dictating letters to Leonard when she could not manage to write herself. These correspondences are among some of the most sensitive in the volumes of Woolf's collected letters. She was incredibly grateful to Llewelyn Davies for her attentions, writing on one occasion:

> You saved Leonard I think, for which I shall always bless you, by giving him things to do. It seems odd, for I know you so little, but I felt you had a grasp on me, and I could not utterly sink. I write this because I do not want to say it, and yet I think you will like to know it [...] Dear Margaret, I so often think of you, and thank you for what you have done for us both, and one cd. do nothing to show what it meant. (*L2* 60)

On another occasion Woolf declares: 'No one is really [...] quite so inspiring to see, as you are', noting of Llewelyn Davies's visits; 'they were the saving of life to me' (*L2* 70). From 1916 onwards Woolf's letters to Llewelyn Davies became more formal and diplomatic, with the pair not always seeing eye to eye. After the 1919 publication of *Night and Day*, which Llewelyn Davies did not particularly enjoy, Woolf was compelled to reply: 'You'll never like my books, but then shall I ever understand your Guild? Probably not' (*L2* 399). By early 1930, around the time Woolf wrote 'Memories', her attitude changed again, with one particularly bleak diary entry finding Llewelyn Davies's ageing a 'tragedy' and her 'shapelessness, & shabbiness & dreariness & drabness unspeakable'.[22] Despite this, Woolf still felt a compunction to visit and, until the end of her life, repeatedly recorded feeling sorry that Llewelyn Davies had lost the drive and vigour she radiated in her prime. It is important to understand this relationship because it had a bearing on Woolf's work for the WCG and on her promise to write the introduction, both tasks she may have accepted, at least in part, out of a sense of duty to Llewelyn Davies, Leonard and the community in which she lived. This is not to undermine the impact working for the Guild had on Woolf but rather to understand that her motivations in undertaking this work may not have been solely political.

Woolf initially wrote to Llewelyn Davies that she felt 'rather doubtful about doing a preface'.[23] She claimed that the Guildswomen's memoirs did not need an introduction and that she did not know enough about the subject matter; a claim in keeping with her general reticence about fictionalising the lived realities of working-class women.²⁴ Woolf's doubts about the introduction were never laid to rest, continuing even as the book went to print. They were joined by her discomfort at the editing process. She explained to Llewelyn Davies that the changes she was being asked to make at the insistence of the Guildswomen made her writing feel disingenuous, and wrote in her diary: 'Never – this is the moral – do a kindness in writing. Never agree to use one's art as an act of friendship' (*D3* 307). There were further underlying worries about time (it was written 'with great plodding' (*D3* 304)), the artistic merit of the endeavour, and the reception it might have. In private, she could be vicious about the project, telling Vanessa: 'I have to write about working women all morning – which is as if you had to sew canopies round chamber pots' (*L4* 175). However, the introduction explores a domain her texts generally avoided and, having accepted the task, she may also have recognised the difference between private snobbery and the opportunity to write something honest that had a 'chance to get rid of conventionalities' (*L4* 229). As Mary Childers notes, 'Woolf confirms her support for the purposes of the Guild by agreeing to have Hogarth Press publish the collection and by including in her preface several paragraphs that acknowledge the moving content of the volume'.²⁵ Arguably, the process of writing, editing and publishing something as 'full of difficulties' (*L4* 191) as the introduction encouraged Woolf in her experiments voicing the inner lives of working-class characters. Though she was already practising such characters in the drafts of *The Waves*, it was only after the publication of *Life as We Have Known It* that she felt secure enough to explore these interior monologues in published works, including them in *The Years* and *Between the Acts*.²⁶

In order not to make the preface a traditional introduction or lay opinion piece, Woolf framed it as a letter to Llewelyn Davies. When finished she sent one copy to the *Yale Review* because she had promised them an article, and one copy to the WCG. Llewelyn Davies's reply was generally complimentary but asked for several revisions, while the *Yale Review* answered that they wanted to publish it immediately. Woolf then asked if Llewelyn Davies minded her publishing an unedited version in America, if 'I suppressed all real names, did not mention you or Lillian, and made it my personal view of congresses in general?' (*L4* 191). Consequently, the letter was published in two different versions; the essay 'Memories of a Working Women's Guild', initially printed in the *Yale Review*, and the 'Introductory Letter to Margaret Llewelyn Davies' in *Life as We Have Known It*.

Both the 'Introductory Letter' and 'Memories' are essays of two parts. In the first Woolf recalls a WCG conference (ostensibly the 1913 conference she attended with Leonard) using her social and emotional distance from the Guildswomen to present an abstract view of their political and economic desires. The second half employs fragments of the women's memoirs to explore working-class women's lives and the WCG's place in them. After editing, the essays remained remarkably similar, with both forms using inflammatory language and exhibiting anxiety regarding interaction with, and writing about, working-class lives. Both have provoked a range of reactions depending on how much sincerity any given reader affords their narrative tone.[27]

An aspect where the essays differed considerably was in their editing process. While Woolf opposed the changes suggested by Llewelyn Davies (on behalf of the Guildswomen), this resistance is absent in her letters to Helen McAfee, the editor of the *Yale Review*. Against Llewelyn Davies's revisions Woolf argues: 'One has to be "sympathetic" and polite and therefore one is uneasy and insincere' (*L4* 229), yet she writes to McAfee: 'I think your suggestion of a title is very good and have adopted it' (*L4* 193) and 'I quite agree to your alterations, and I see the point about [the] letter quoted on page 22' (*L4* 201). Woolf was not paid for the 'Introductory Letter', writing it for free and donating her modest royalties to the WCG, noting, with a somewhat bland compliment: 'They must want money for something or other, and I should only feel I was paying my due for the immense interest their letters gave me.' However she was 'handsomely paid' (*L4* 286) by the *Yale Review*, with 'Memories' being one in a series of articles they bought and published.

An indication that Woolf may have felt some discomfort at the disparity between the production, purpose and reach of the two different publications can be seen in a change she made when editing the 'Introductory Letter'. Speaking of the concerns the Guildswomen raise at their conference, 'Memories' states: 'If every reform they demand was granted this very instant it would not matter to me a single jot',[28] while the 'Introductory Letter' offers: 'If every reform they demand was granted this very instant it would not touch one hair of my comfortable capitalistic head.'[29] While Woolf's feelings about her place as a wealthy woman in a capitalist society (which she was by 1929) have been explored from many different angles in this volume, describing herself as such is unexpected and may have been a self-conscious reaction to her working-class 'editors' and readers.[30] 'Memories' was written against the backdrop of an economic crisis which did not particularly affect Woolf. As the owner of the Hogarth Press and one of its most successful authors she felt pride at the fact that her writing kept '7 people fed and housed [. . .] they live on my words' (*D3* 221). Concurrently, 'Memories' conveyed the anger she felt when the WCG conference-goers used their speeches to 'deride ladies and to imitate [. . .] their mincing speech and little knowledge of what it pleases them to call "reality"' (*E5* 231). By using the word capitalist to describe herself – whether in an ironic way or not – Woolf perhaps indicates not only a disquiet inherent in relationships between people of different classes, particularly where money is involved, but also her discomfort at the relationship she had with the WCG and their perceived inability or refusal to acknowledge her and her contemporaries' use to society.

'dressed in their best clothes': Mrs Giles of Durham and the Working-Class Consumer

In *A Room of One's Own* Woolf advises the young author Mary Carmichael to investigate her

> relation to the ever-changing and turning world of gloves and shoes and stuffs swaying up and down among the faint scents that come through chemists' bottles down arcades of dress material over a floor of pseudo-marble [. . .] for it is a sight that would lend itself to the pen as fittingly as any snowy peak or rocky gorge in the Andes.[31]

The suggestion that a shopping trip might constitute the ideal medium for a writer is characteristic of Woolf's upper-middle-class, feminist textual politics. By putting this advice into practice in texts such as *Mrs Dalloway*, Woolf moved beyond the individual's experience of cultural participation to the broader topics of global trade, international economics, colonialism, pacifism and war. In 'Memories', however, Woolf focuses on the Guildswomen's meagre purchasing power and repeatedly signals that they are not the adventurous shoppers of her novels. The WCG conference-goers are 'women who scrubbed and cooked and bargained and knew to a penny what they had to spend' (*E5* 178) and Woolf emphasises how infrequently they can afford (or need) to shop for clothing. Not only do the Guildswomen prepare for many months, storing 'hat, shoes, and dress' to appear at the congress, but there is 'an air of discreet novelty' about their outfits (*E5* 177). Woolf twice describes the conference-goers as being in their 'best clothes' (*E5* 180 & 184) and records how they returned home, 'hung their clothes in the wardrobe and plunged their hands in the wash tub again' (*E5* 180). This meagre material consumption is compared directly with the far more profligate expenditure of 'Ladies in evening dress' (*E5* 182) and 'the middle classes wearing tail coats and silk stockings' (*E5* 183). Measured against the impermanence of silk stockings and the cost of inhabiting the 'ever-changing and turning world' of fashionable evening dress, the paucity of the Guildswomen's apparel is made especially conspicuous.

'Memories' focuses on various types of shopping, with clothing, food and cultural consumption all prominent. Woolf does not include these upper-middle-class 'ladies' and their clothes merely to show the trappings of capitalist commodity culture, but goes on to depict these contemporaries as idealised shoppers who 'desire Mozart and Cézanne and Shakespeare; and not merely money and hot water laid on' (*E5* 182). When the educated customer spends money on the arts – here represented by three of Woolf's favourite musicians, painters and writers – they are using co-operation to invest in a culture that spreads empathy and tolerance (indeed, during WW1, Woolf wrote of Mozart's *Magic Flute* that she 'thought rather better of humanity for having that in them' (*D1* 153–4)). The second part of this phrase – 'not merely money and hot water laid on' – is also significant for it exemplifies Woolf's thoughts about the Guildswomen's economic inclinations. She observes how, when they 'get together communally they always talk about baths and money: they always show the least desirable of their characteristics – their lust for conquest and their desire for possessions' (*E5* 182). For Woolf, the Guildswomen are not informed co-operators but frustrated capitalists. Their desire for baths and money – a representation of their capitalist aspirations – becomes a theme throughout the essay, mentioned no less than six times in a variety of forms. Woolf may have adapted this idea about the Guildswomen's pecuniary inclinations from Leonard's work. In *Co-operation and the Future of Industry* he describes early, and heavily socialist, co-operative experiments where: 'Success was, in fact, almost as quickly fatal to them as failure, for, owing to the poverty of the members, the temptation to revert to individualism and withdraw any capital which accumulated was strong.'[32] Whether her own or an adopted idea, it is striking that Woolf associates the negative aspects of capitalism (such as greed) not with her own 'capitalistic head', but with her working-class comrades.

Ironically, Woolf distances herself from the Guildswoman because of their individualistic, capitalist desires. Given their poverty, Woolf explains how difficult it is for her and her contemporaries to understand the WCG conference-goers:

> To expect us, whose minds, such as they are, fly free at the end of a short length of capital, to tie ourselves down again upon that narrow plot of acquisitiveness and desire is impossible. We have baths and money. Society has supplied us with all we need in that direction. (*E5* 182)

A small annuity, spent constructively/co-operatively on items of pleasure rather than necessity, rids Woolf's ideal consumer of her capitalist desire to possess. This allowance had, of course, already been valued at £500 in *A Room of One's Own* where Woolf explores 'the poison of fear and bitterness' (*AROO* 34) that poverty breeds in the creative individual. This 'poison' and having to work for one's living leads to a lack of vision and ultimately the inability to make art.[33]

It is an unintended paradox of 'Memories' that although economic liberty leads to creative freedoms – the ability to think and write for example – Woolf's narrator and the 'ladies' she associates with cannot envisage life in a working-class woman's shoes. Woolf makes a point of trying, and failing, to empathise with the Guildswomen. At the conference she engages in 'a childish game' of 'Let's pretend', putting herself in the place of one of the speakers before concluding that: 'One could not be Mrs Giles of Durham because one's body had not stood at the wash-tub; one's hands had never wrung and scrubbed and chopped up whatever the meat may be that makes a miner's dinner' (*E5* 179). While Woolf may not have cooked often, and would have been able to afford better cuts of meat than the working-class woman she describes, she certainly had cooked meat. In 1929 she wrote to Vita Sackville-West 'I cooked veal cutlets and cake today' (*L4* 93) and within the year she would write the unpublished 'Cook Sketch', putting herself in the place of a working-class protagonist and, as Clara Jones notes, revealing a 'scrupulous knowledge of various cuts of meat and understanding of wider issues in domestic economy'.[34] Given this, Woolf's unmitigated denial of the sensory understanding of this working-class wife's experience is remarkable. Alison Light has called the above passage 'excessively distancing', especially given that in *The Waves* (which was written concurrently) Woolf was 'imagining the lives of three different men – one homosexual – relying, presumably, on aesthetic sympathy'.[35]

'no right to bring a child into the world': The Evolution of a Co-operator

Throughout 'Memories' Woolf creates distance between herself and the WCG members. She is 'untouched [. . .] irretrievably cut off from the actors [. . .] an outcast from the flock' (*E5* 178). Woolf's detachment from the Guildswomen focuses on their maternal and domestic responsibilities and their conservative values. Unlike Woolf and her contemporaries, these women with 'hot babies in their arms' are 'not in the least detached and cosmopolitan' (*E5* 180). They cannot act as informed co-operative consumers and cannot create art – 'this book is not a book' (*E5* 176), notes Woolf of *Life* – but instead have willingly produced children to uphold a flawed capitalist system. Woolf expressed similar opinions in her letters, noting of the Guildswomen: 'The melancholy thing is that they seem perfectly respectable and content, rather like old gentlemen in Clubs [. . .] I cant help thinking that fiery reformers fly completely over their heads' (*L2* 19). Similarly, when writing to Llewelyn Davies about the edits the WCG requested, Woolf argues:

> If they [. . .] cant be told that they weigh on an average 12 stone – which is largely because they scrub so hard and have so many children – and are shocked by the word 'impure' how can you say that they face 'reality'? [. . .] What depresses me is that the workers seem to have taken on all the middle class respectabilities which we – at any rate if we are any good at writing or painting – have faced and thrown out [. . .] For you see, it is that to my thinking that now makes the chief barrier between us [. . .] And why, with such a chance to get rid of conventionalities, do they cling to them? (*L4* 228–9)

In private, Woolf did not see the potential for activism in the everyday Guildswomen because she saw them as conventional housewives and mothers. However, while Woolf couldn't see the WCG women as consumers or creators, in the idealistic tradition of *A Room of One's Own* – which proclaims of Mary Carmichael 'Give her another hundred years [. . .] She will be a poet' (*AROO* 85) – she did see an evolutionary path towards a moment where they might develop such abilities. In order to explore this, she used one of the accounts contained within the collection: the memoir of hat-worker Nellie Scott.

In Woolf's writing motherhood is often an act performed by women with Victorian morals in support of a nationalistic society.[36] 'Memories' reiterates this view through the retelling of Scott's journey from a childhood spent working in a hat factory to becoming a magistrate and Co-operative conference delegate. Woolf reworks the memoir, adopting its themes to explore the potential evolution of working-class women from conservative (with both lowercase and capital Cs) to liberal free thinkers and co-operators. In the beginning Woolf describes the Guildswomen's antecedents:

> women in Christie's hat factory [. . .] who worked for 'honour'. They gave their lives to the cause of putting straight stitches into the bindings of men's hat brims [. . .] And as they drove in their straight stitches they reverenced Queen Victoria and thanked God [. . .] that they were all married to good Conservative working men. (E5 186)

These traditionalist workers are described with Woolf's typical irony, they demonstrate an 'incorrigible idealism of the human mind' and she drives home their nationalistic, warmongering sympathies, noting how 'the highest ideals of duty flourish in an obscure hat factory as surely as on a battlefield' (E5 186). Change comes when the workers start to read voraciously; indeed, 'they read with the indiscriminate greed of a hungry appetite that crams itself with toffee and beef and tarts and vinegar and champagne all in one gulp' (E5 186). While the authors of *Life as We Have Known It* were all avid readers with lists of their favourite books included in the collection, Woolf's description of their haphazard and uncontrollable literary urges reveal further flaws in their capacity as consumers. Woolf rebukes them for not following an unwritten syllabus implicitly understood by the more culture-savvy 'ladies'. This criticism is rather incongruous for a woman who, in the 1925 essay 'How Should One Read a Book?', wrote 'the only advice [. . .] that one person can give another about reading is to take no advice, to follow your own instincts, to use your own reason' (E5 573), but it once again highlights her antipathy to working-class consumption.[37]

Despite its chaotic nature the Guildswomen's reading sparks a change in their ideals. Suddenly, the:

> younger generation had the audacity to say that Queen Victoria was no better than an honest charwoman who had brought up her children respectably. They had the temerity to doubt whether to sew straight stitches into men's hat brims should be the sole aim and end of a woman's life [. . .] Ideas, indeed, were seething in their brains. A girl, for instance, would reason, as she walked along the streets of a factory town, that she had no right to bring a child into the world if that child must earn its living in a mill. (E5 186–7)

Deciding not to become a mother forms the apex of Woolf's working-class woman's evolution. This is reflected in Scott's memoir when not only does she choose to remain child-free, but she records an open discussion of it with her conservative workmates:

> the Irish girl came one Monday and said: 'Nellie, the priest said last night all married people who had no children would go to hell,' and I retorted: 'I should think I deserved to go to hell if I had brought some of the children into the world I have seen.'[38]

In addition to this exchange Scott alludes to the contraceptive movement by recalling her own mother's interest in the controversial birth control advocates Charles Bradlaugh and Annie Besant. As noted, Woolf felt that motherhood curtailed women's freedom and as such she was interested in reproductive control. Indeed, it may well be that what attracted her to Scott's memoir in the first place was her insistence that she would not have children.

Woolf does not stop her evolutionary retelling of the memoir at contraceptive freedom and its attendant intellectual emancipation. After deciding not to bear children, the working-class woman is finally on her way to becoming a true co-operator. She begins to 'dream of future cities where there were to be baths and kitchens and wash houses and art galleries and museums and parks' (*E5* 187). With access to not only baths and other domestic necessities but also leisurely recreations, she moves to become one of Woolf's urbane consumers, albeit one who consumes culture that is predominantly free (although this should not be read into too deeply as Woolf took this list directly from Scott's memoir). At this point in her evolutionary narrative Woolf introduces the moment when the Guild 'crept [. . .] into existence', offering working-class women 'the rarest of all possessions – a room where they could sit down and think remote from boiling saucepans and crying children' (*E5* 187). Ultimately, in this room of their own, even the working-class women who have children manage to find enough distance from their maternal identities to write their life stories.

Woolf's retelling of Scott's memoir is fascinating both in its own right and in combination with other evolutionary narratives she creates (such as that of Mary Carmichael). However, this chronicle of growth and realisation is not a history and it does not accurately describe the life of her Guild contemporaries. Instead it is a fantastical weaving of past, present and future that portrays her feelings about some imaginable potential that might be realised in an ideal world.

For Woolf, there was a difference between the capable women at the head of the WCG dictating its policy and 'controlling the masses' (*L2* 19), and the general WCG members who she described as conservative mothers with little money to spend and little understanding of how to spend it.

Woolf understood that the aim of *Life as We Have Known It* – much like the Guild conference – was to stimulate not art but political change. Combining her own biases and political postulations with a need to reflect upon the material realities of *Life*'s memoirs made writing 'Memories' a difficult task she did not enjoy. Nonetheless, its place as a piece of work undertaken as a commission for the WCG caused her beliefs and theories to be confronted with alternate value systems and realities. This undertaking did not leave Woolf unchanged. As noted, after completing 'Memories' she went on to create work (both published and unpublished) that included significantly more working-class voices. *The Years*, for example, not only includes brief insights into the thoughts of domestic servants Baxter and Crosby, but an entire meal with the Robson family. Indeed, not only did Woolf base Mr Robson on the linguist Joseph Wright but she included the detail that Mr Wright's mother was a Guildswoman. During another curious and relatively prosaic moment in *The Years*, Eleanor thinks: 'The streets were crowded; women were swarming in and out of shops with their shopping baskets [. . .] She, too, was going to her work.'[39] Given an understanding of Woolf's previous writing on working-class consumption and co-operative economics this acknowledgement of 'doing the shopping' as 'work' is powerful and hints at a change in Woolf's thinking (although, as with so much of Woolf's work, this moment is double-edged as it also may reflect on the domestic nature of Eleanor's philanthropic pursuits). In *Between the Acts* Woolf includes some rather wonderfully self-aware references to the feelings of the domestic staff at Pointz Hall. During a scene in which Lucy Swithin makes sandwiches with Mrs Sands the cook, the former, vocalising her free-flowing inner monologue, feels: 'It was soothing, it was consolidating, this handwork together' while the latter, remaining silent, 'registered, as her lips showed, a grudge she mustn't speak against people making work in the kitchen'.[40] Perhaps the most telling change is when the mind of La Trobe (the book's creative voice and a woman who herself transcends class) is made 'fertile' (*BTA* 125) by the talk of the working-class drinkers in the village public house. By linking motherhood, consumption and co-operative economics, 'Memories' and 'Introductory Letter' touch on topics that were important parts of Woolf's everyday lived experience but also changed her social awareness. Exploring the lives of working-class women, these essays are an invaluable part of Woolf's oeuvre, illuminating not only her economic understanding and position on the WCG, but also the class-based tensions that are a significant part of her work even when such women are absent.

Notes

1. It could be argued that Woolf embraced ambivalence in every area of her writing. Anna Snaith explains of Woolf's multivocal formal stratagems: 'Rather than imposing form or unity on this multiplicity, Woolf accepts plurality as such and seeks structures in her writing which will allow ambiguity' (Anna, Snaith, *Public and Private Negotiations* (Basingstoke: Palgrave Macmillan, 2000), 86). For two differing yet complimentary discussions of Woolf's feminism, ambivalence and politics see Judith Allen, 'Feminist Politics' and Lisa Coleman, 'Woolf and Feminist Theory', both in *Virginia Woolf in Context*, ed. by Bryony Randall and Jane Goldman (Cambridge: Cambridge University Press, 2012).
2. Michael Tratner, *Deficits and Desires: Economics and Sexuality in Twentieth-Century Literature* (Stanford: Stanford University Press, 2002).
3. Clara Jones, *Virginia Woolf: Ambivalent Activist* (Edinburgh: Edinburgh University Press, 2016); Alice Wood, 'Facing *Life as We Have Known It*: Virginia Woolf and the Women's Co-operative Guild', *Literature & History*, 23.2 (2014), 18–34.
4. Virginia Woolf, *Mrs Dalloway* (1925) (London: Penguin, 2000), 209; *The Waves* (1931) (London: Penguin, 2000), 174. Further page references will be given within the main text.
   Jacob's Room's Betty Flanders, for example, is a parody of a war-mother who encourages her sons in a patriarchal, competitive education, tells them stories of wartime violence and encourages them to keep knives to defend themselves against the chickens. Betty ensures her sons have a capitalist role model with the mis-labelled tombstone of her dead husband, and finds a violent, imperialist father figure in the form of Captain Barfoot.
5. Virginia Woolf, *The Letters of Virginia Woolf, Volume Three, 1923–1928*, ed. by Nigel Nicholson and Joanne Trautmann (New York: Harcourt Brace Jovanovich, 1978), 365. Further page references will be given within the main text.
6. Virginia Woolf, *The Letters of Virginia Woolf, Volume Two, 1912–1922*, ed. by Nigel Nicholson and Joanne Trautmann (New York: Harcourt

Brace Jovanovich, 1978), 231, 238, 155. Further page references will be given within the main text.

7. Gillian Scott, *Feminism and the Politics of Working Women* (London: UCL Press, 1998), 16.
8. See, for example, Reginald Abbott 'What Miss Kilman's Petticoat Means', *Modern Fiction Studies*, 38.1 (1992), 193–216 and Elizabeth Outka, '"The Shop Windows Were Full of Sparkling Chains": Consumer Desire and Woolf's *Night and Day*', in *Virginia Woolf Out of Bounds*, ed. by Jessica Schiff Berman and Jane Goldman (New York: Pace University Press, 2001).
9. Rachel Bowlby, *Carried Away: The Invention of Modern Shopping* (New York: Columbia University Press, 2001), 8.
10. This domesticity dulls the creative mind. An example of this can be seen in *Between the Acts* where Isa Oliver orders fish while making abortive attempts at writing poetry.
11. Scott, *Feminism*, 11.
12. Leonard Woolf, 'A Democracy of Working Women', *New Statesman*, 21 June 1913 (328–9), 329.
13. Maud Pember Reeves, *Round About a Pound a Week* (London: G. Bell, 1914), 94.
14. King, *The Co-operator*, 1 May 1828, 1–4 (3).
15. Margaret Llewelyn Davies, *Life as We Have Known It: The Voices of Working-Class Women* (London: Hogarth, 1931; repr. London: Virago, 2012) x, xii–xiii.
16. Leonard Woolf, *Co-operation and the Future of Industry* (London: George Allan & Unwin, 1918), 36.
17. Tratner, *Deficits and Desires*, 91–5.
18. Such as the academic G. D. H. Cole and the Fabians Sydney and Beatrice Webb.
19. Ian MacPherson, 'The International Co-operative Movement & Peace: Questions Drawn from its Early History', in *Co-operatives and the Pursuit of Peace*, ed. by Joy Emmanuel and Ian MacPherson (Victoria: New Rochdale Press, 2007), 40.
20. Virginia Woolf, *A Room of One's Own and Three Guineas* (London: Penguin, 2000), 196. Further page references will be given within the main text.
21. Tratner, *Deficits and Desires*, 98.
22. Virginia Woolf, *The Diary of Virginia Woolf, Volume Three, 1925–1930*, ed. by Anne Olivier Bell (London: The Hogarth Press, 1981), 297. Further page references will be given within the main text.
23. Virginia Woolf, *The Letters of Virginia Woolf, Volume Four, 1929–1931*, ed. by Nigel Nicholson and Joanne Trautmann (New York: Harcourt Brace Jovanovich, 1979), 65.
24. For more on Woolf's elimination of working-class characters see Finn Fordham, *I Do, I Undo, I Redo: The Textual Genesis of Modernist*

Selves in Hopkins, Yeats, Conrad, Forster, Joyce, and Woolf (Oxford: Oxford University Press, 2010).
25. Mary M. Childers, 'Virginia Woolf on the Outside Looking Down: Reflections on the Class of Women', *Modern Fiction Studies*, 38.1 (1992), 61–79 (71).
26. Examples from both *The Years* and *Between the Acts* will be given at the end of the chapter.
27. Hermione Lee, for example, calls 'both versions [. . .] honest' and 'uneasy', while Regenia Gagnier notes: 'Woolf's confrontation with the Co-operative Working Women is one of the most penetrating class confrontations in modern British discourse.' Lee, *Virginia Woolf* (London: Vintage, 1997), 361; Gagnier, 'Between Women: A Cross-Class Analysis of Status and Anarchic Humor', *Women's Studies*, 15 (1988), 135–48 (139).
28. Virginia Woolf, 'Memories of a Working Women's Guild', in *The Essays of Virginia Woolf, Volume Five, 1929–1932*, ed. by Stuart N. Clarke (London: Chatto & Windus, 2009), 176–94 (178). Further page references will be given within the main text.
29. Virginia Woolf, 'Introductory Letter to Margaret Llewelyn Davies', in *The Essays of Virginia Woolf, Volume Five*, 225–40 (227). Further page references will be given within the main text.
30. For more on Woolf's finances see Diane Gillespie, 'Adventures in Common: Investing with Woolfs and "Securitas"', in *Virginia Woolf and the Common(Wealth) Reader*, ed. by Helen Wussow and Mary Ann Gillies (Liverpool: Liverpool University Press, 2014).
31. Virginia Woolf, *A Room of One's Own and Three Guineas* (London: Penguin, 2000), 81. Further page references will be given within the main text.
32. Leonard Woolf, *Co-operation and the Future of Industry*, 21. Given her opposition towards aggressive individualism it may have been difficult for Woolf to reconcile what she saw as the Guildswomen's individualist, capitalist tendencies with their staunch pacifism – however she does not mention any such reservations.
33. Though they have 'dauntless energy which no amount of childbirth and washing up can quench entirely' (*E5* 186), the Guildswomen's creative abilities have been doused by these undertakings. Rather than reading their work as literary creations, Woolf notes that the voices of the working-class memoirists are 'beginning only now to emerge from silence into half articulate speech' (*E5* 189).
34. Jones, *Ambivalent Activist*, 139.
35. Alison Light, *Mrs Woolf and the Servants* (London: Penguin, 2007), 204.
36. In addition to Betty Flanders, other examples of such mothers include *The Voyage Out*'s early rendering of Clarissa Dalloway who admires Royal Navy warships, talks at length about the superiority of men and yearns to have a son.

37. Another example of this is a scene from *The Waves* set in a working-class eating house.
38. Scott, *Life as We Have Known It*, 89.
39. Virginia Woolf, *The Years* (1937) (London: Penguin, 1998), 91.
40. Virginia Woolf, *Between the Acts* (1941) (London: Penguin, 1992), 23. Further page references will be given within the main text.

Works Cited

Abbott, Reginald. 'What Miss Kilman's Petticoat Means: Virginia Woolf, Shopping, and Spectacle'. *Modern Fiction Studies*, 38.1 (1992), 193–216.

Allen, Judith. 'Feminist Politics: "Repetition" and "Burning" in *Three Guineas* (Making it New)'. In *Virginia Woolf in Context*, ed. by Bryony Randall and Jane Goldman. Cambridge: Cambridge University Press, 2012.

Bowlby, Rachel. *Carried Away: The Invention of Modern Shopping*. New York: Columbia University Press, 2001.

Childers, Mary M. 'Virginia Woolf on the Outside Looking Down: Reflections on the Class of Women'. *Modern Fiction Studies*, 38.1 (1992), 61–79.

Coleman, Lisa. 'Woolf and Feminist Theory: Woolf's Feminism Comes in Waves'. In *Virginia Woolf in Context*, ed. by Bryony Randall and Jane Goldman. Cambridge: Cambridge University Press, 2012.

Fordham, Finn. *I Do, I Undo, I Redo: The Textual Genesis of Modernist Selves in Hopkins, Yeats, Conrad, Forster, Joyce, and Woolf*. Oxford: Oxford University Press, 2010.

Gagnier, Regenia. 'Between Women: A Cross-Class Analysis of Status and Anarchic Humor'. *Women's Studies*, 15 (1988), 135–48.

Gillespie, Diane. 'Adventures in Common: Investing with Woolfs and "Securitas"'. In *Virginia Woolf and the Common(Wealth) Reader*, ed. by Helen Wussow and Mary Ann Gillies. Liverpool: Liverpool University Press, 2014.

Jones, Clara. *Virginia Woolf: Ambivalent Activist*. Edinburgh: Edinburgh University Press, 2016.

King, William. *The Co-operator*, 1 May 1828, 1–4.

Lee, Hermione. *Virginia Woolf*. London: Vintage, 1997.

Light, Alison. *Mrs Woolf and the Servants*. London: Penguin Books, 2008.

Llewelyn Davies, Margaret (ed.). *Life as We Have Known It: The Voices of Working-Class Women*. London: Hogarth, 1931; repr. London: Virago, 2012.

MacPherson, Ian. 'The International Co-operative Movement & Peace: Questions Drawn from its Early History'. In *Co-operatives and the Pursuit of Peace*, ed. by Joy Emmanuel and Ian MacPherson. Victoria: New Rochdale Press, 2007.

Outka, Elizabeth. '"The Shop Windows Were Full of Sparkling Chains": Consumer Desire and Woolf's *Night and Day*'. In *Virginia Woolf Out of Bounds*, ed. by Jessica Schiff Berman and Jane Goldman. New York: Pace University Press, 2001.

Pember Reeves, Maud. *Round About a Pound a Week*. London: G. Bell, 1914.

Scott, Gillian. *Feminism and the Politics of Working Women*. London: UCL Press, 1998.

Snaith, Anna. *Virginia Woolf: Public and Private Negotiations*. Basingstoke: Palgrave Macmillan, 2000.

Tratner, Michael. *Deficits and Desires: Economics and Sexuality in Twentieth-Century Literature*. Stanford: Stanford University Press, 2002.

Wood, Alice. 'Facing *Life as We Have Known It*: Virginia Woolf and the Women's Co-operative Guild'. *Literature & History*, 23.2 (2014), 18–34.

Woolf, Leonard. *Co-operation and the Future of Industry*. London: George Allan & Unwin, 1918.

——, 'A Democracy of Working Women'. *New Statesman*, 21 June, 1913, 328–9.

Woolf, Virginia. *Between the Acts*, ed. by Stella McNichol with an introduction and notes by Gillian Beer. London: Penguin, 1992.

——, *The Diary of Virginia Woolf, Volume One, 1915–1919*, ed. by Anne Olivier Bell. London: The Hogarth Press, 1977.

——, *The Diary of Virginia Woolf, Volume Three, 1925–1930*, ed. by Anne Olivier Bell. London: The Hogarth Press, 1981.

——, *The Essays of Virginia Woolf, Volume Five, 1929–1932*, ed. by Stuart N. Clarke. London: Chatto & Windus, 2009.

——, *The Letters of Virginia Woolf, Volume Two, 1912–1922*, ed. by Nigel Nicholson and Joanne Trautmann. New York: Harcourt Brace Jovanovich, 1978.

——, *The Letters of Virginia Woolf, Volume Four, 1929–1931*, ed. by Nigel Nicholson and Joanne Trautmann. New York: Harcourt Brace Jovanovich, 1979.

——, *Mrs Dalloway*, ed. by Stella McNichol with an introduction and notes by Elaine Showalter. London: Penguin, 2000.

——, *A Room of One's Own and Three Guineas*, ed. by Stella McNichol with an introduction and notes by Michèle Barrett. London: Penguin, 2000.

——, *The Waves*, ed. by and with an introduction and notes by Kate Flint. London: Penguin, 2000.

——, *The Years*, ed. by Stella McNichol with an introduction and notes by Jeri Johnson. London: Penguin, 1998.

Chapter 4

Biometric Feminism: *A Room of One's Own* and the Politics of Intelligence

Natasha Periyan

Introduction: Intelligence, Capitalism and Meritocracy

A complicated reality underpins the mnemonic dictate of *A Room of One's Own* which finds that a woman needs 'a room of her own and five hundred a year' to facilitate creative production. As Michèle Barrett argues:

> although Woolf may have argued that the majority of writers were cushioned by their parents' money, one can produce many instances of writers being inspired by adversity and overcoming extremely inauspicious circumstances. So the basic thesis of *A Room of One's Own* is not an uncontentious one.[1]

Barrett's observation gets to the heart of the romantic origins of creativity that held genius to be detached from material means, innate and inviolable, as opposed to a more materialist take on the circumstances that would best facilitate writers' work. The debate finds new force in the early twentieth century. In *A Room of One's Own*, Woolf was weighing in on a particular (and contentious) contemporaneous debate: the role of environment in determining intelligence. In both her resistance to – and engagement with – discourses surrounding intelligence, there is a biometric dimension to Woolf's feminist politics that has been hitherto unconsidered. For historians of science and psychology, intelligence is a 'brashly modern notion' with the term 'intelligent' a 'scientific buzz word' in the early years of the twentieth century.[2] The concept of 'intelligence' was absorbed into psychology from nineteenth-century evolutionary biology, which perceived 'cognition as essentially layered or graded', and conceptualised man's intelligence on a scale with animal.³ Darwin's *The Descent of Man* identified women's intelligence as inferior to men's and was indebted to the statistical research of Francis Galton whose *Hereditary Genius* (1869) examined 'eminent men of modern days' to argue that intellectual ability was inherited.⁴ Francis Galton was a figure that haunted Woolf. Her father's family were included as a case study in *Hereditary Genius*, a work that she references in *Night and Day*, and, as a teenager, she included Galton's work in her reading lists. Galton's commitment to nature in shaping intellectual ability held implications for the feminist debate on intelligence.⁵ Woolf's materialist argument for literary production therefore occurs in a context that denies women's intellectual ability based on a conception of mental ability as based in nature, not nurture. Such an argument would thus perceive the discrepancy in male/female literary achievement as resulting from a lack of women's ability, rather than unpropitious circumstances.

Capital is central to *A Room of One's Own*'s examination of the environmental factors that shape female creativity. The feminist-materialist critique of literary production in *A Room* has a thorny relationship to capitalism. As Clara Jones notes, 'inherited wealth [. . .] [is] a problem that repeatedly rears its head to unsettle and queer the pitch of an essay so well-known for its ease and charm'.⁶ The narrator of *A Room of One's Own* received her inheritance from an aunt who died falling from her horse in Bombay: 'she had left me five hundred pounds a year for ever'.⁷ While the narrator secures her freedom of mind from inherited wealth, the text's 'vexed engagement with inherited wealth' is further figured on the level of how precisely the text's audience should acquire their five hundred pounds.⁸ While the text's refrain remains consistent in its demands surrounding five hundred a year and a room of one's own, there is an inconsistency to how this might be achieved. Woolf's repeated deployment of the capacious verb 'to have' allows for a lack of specificity to the means through which the text's advocacy of material means might be achieved: 'have five hundred a year of your own' (*AROO* 33), 'have five hundred a year each of us and rooms of our own' (*AROO* 102). The looseness of the verb 'to have' allows Woolf to avoid straightforwardly advocating inherited wealth (and thus a quasi-aristocratic writer class). Yet there is, at the end of Chapter 5, the possible allusion to inherited capital in the injunction to 'give her a room of her own and five hundred a year' (*AROO* 85). Inherited capital as the source of financial freedom is eschewed, however, elsewhere in the text. *A Room of One's*

Own also includes the edict to 'Earn five hundred a year by your wits' (*AROO* 60), which is repeated towards the end of the text's conclusion:

> there must be at this moment some two thousand women capable of earning over five hundred a year in one way or another, you will agree that the excuse of lack of opportunity, training, encouragement, leisure and money no longer holds good. (*AROO* 101)

After an examination of the barriers to women's intellectual achievement, the text is satirical in its identification of so small a number of women who are suggested to be unhampered by material means.

The reference to women earning money through their 'wits' and being 'capable' reflects a meritocratic form of wealth acquisition. The mechanism for meritocracy – intelligence – gained scientific logic in the early twentieth century when, in 1909, the intelligence test, developed by Binet-Simon, claimed to offer a way of quantifying innate intelligence and making it measurable. The engine for a burgeoning early twentieth-century meritocracy, the intelligence test was instrumentalised by educational systems in the scholarship ladder and became the basis for grammar school selection. Meritocracy offered a biological solution to the capriciousness of inherited capital. As Perkin suggests, it provided a rationale for selection beyond the 'blind selection of the market'.[9] It also 'challenged the aristocratic ideal of the primacy of passive property' as 'selection by merit[,] [was] measured no longer by aristocratic opinion, the competition of the market or popular vote but by the judgment of the qualified expert'.[10] In the interwar period, intelligence also became associated with a response to capitalism. The introduction to this volume quotes Keynes's framing of the 'problem' of finding a solution to *laissez-faire* social capitalism: 'to work out a social organisation which shall be as efficient as possible without offending our notions of a satisfactory way of life'.[11] Advocates of positive eugenics, including Keynes himself, who was Director of the British Eugenics Society (1937–1944), understood the crisis of capitalist reproduction as biological and economic. Motivated by the perception that more intelligent, middle-class citizens (and class and intelligence were inextricably linked by eugenicists in this period) were restricting their family size and thus threatening the survival of the economic system, positive eugenics became a byword for ensuring national efficiency. Such ideas could, in Keynes's words, threaten to 'offend[ing] our notions of a satisfactory way of life'.

Meritocrats always held an uneasy relationship with the Left. Meritocracy originally seemed a progressive solution to the problem of inherited wealth: while anti-egalitarian in basis, it provided opportunities to redistribute wealth based on the advantages gained by intellectual ability rather than those gained by capitalist inheritance. Wooldridge suggests that 'Meritocratic mobility [. . .] offered a means of reconciling elitism with democracy', although in effect, meritocracy replaced an economic elite with an intellectual elite.[12] Against a debate surrounding the relative weight of nature vs. nurture in determining intelligence, interwar communist biologists, including J. B. S. Haldane, Naomi Mitchison's brother, were keen to approach meritocracy with a scientific concern for accuracy by controlling environmental variables. The 1939 Geneticists' Manifesto advocated a levelling of environmental factors to get a true read on intelligence. It was felt that merit could only be adequately gauged when environment was equal.[13] For these scientists, true meritocracy was deferred until the achievement of a socialist state. Woolf's essay 'The Niece of an Earl' anticipates elements of this argument. First published in the October 1928 edition of *Life and Letters*, contemporaneous with Woolf's speeches at Girton and Newnham, the essay established the possibility of a socialist future: 'class distinctions were not always so hard and fast as they have now become [. . .] In another century or so, none of these distinctions may hold good.'[14] In this future, a meritocratic vision is presented where 'Only natural differences such as those of brain and character will serve to distinguish us' (*E4* 563). Woolf's vision of the future implies that differences of nurture and environment would have been equalised. In this context, the emphasis on five hundred a year and a room of one's own for literary production is striking. There is an equality to the demand as Woolf's refrain calls for a particular kind of levelling of environmental factors to ensure that everyone has the same material resources as a prerequisite to creative work.

Virginia Woolf's argument in *A Room* is lauded and has been a cherished pillar of her materialist politics. Woolf's feminist-socialist politics are more complex when read in the context of her lifelong interest in and ambivalence about mental ability and measurement. The text gets its specifically feminist appeal in its negotiation of, and indeed marginalisation of, the place of relative male versus female intelligence in literary production. Woolf focuses the debate on female intelligence to consider environmental factors, not innate ability, and in so doing resists succumbing to the 'decrees of the measurers' (*AROO* 96). A biometric understanding of Woolf's feminism also supports a reading that is sensitive to social class and race. While Woolf resists the impulse to classify and rank intellectually, she is susceptible to the pervasive influence of the intelligence testers in her statistical imagination which demonstrates a concern with the 'typical', a focus which also elucidates the text's conscious, and unconscious, blind spots on class and race. Woolf remains far more cognisant of her work's dialogue with the metrical impulse of mental ability than her reviewers, however, who evidenced the gender-based stereotyping surrounding intelligence that Woolf's work resisted.

Gender, Environment and Intelligence in *A Room of One's Own*

A Room of One's Own explores the impairment of the female intellect that a discrepancy in educational opportunities creates.[15] In *A Room of One's Own* the sibling divide is figured through the fantastical conceit of Shakespeare's sister, Judith, who, Woolf's narrator suggests, shares her brother's genius. This 'wonderfully' (*AROO* 42) and 'extraordinarily gifted sister' (*AROO* 43) has a dire fate: 'any woman born with a great gift in the sixteenth century would certainly have gone crazed, shot herself' (*AROO* 45). She did not go to the 'grammar school' (*AROO* 43) and learn Ovid, Virgil and Horace, like her brother, despite being 'as adventurous, as imaginative, as agog to see the world as he was' (*AROO* 43). Woolf's construction of Shakespeare as indebted to classical training at his grammar school critiques prevailing formulations of the nature of his genius. Logan Pearsall Smith notes that, through the efforts of figures such as Edward Young, Shakespeare 'came more and more to be regarded as the great example of the "natural" genius, who by the power of his inborn gifts alone, quite unassisted by art or learning, reached the most sublime levels of artistic achievement'.[16] The establishment of parity of intellectual appetite between Judith and her brother is significant: '*as* adventurous, *as* imaginative, *as* agog to see the world as he was' (emphases added, *AROO* 43). Manuscript insertions Woolf made to the text between April and May 1929 clarify the areas of the argument that *A Room* does not focus on: the relative intelligence of men and women.[17] Woolf inserted a passage that demonstrates a keen rebuttal to the dictates of the mental measurers. The addition reinforces the text's efforts to shift the terms of the debate to focus on environmental inhibitors of female intelligence:

No opinion has been expressed, you may say, upon the comparative merits of the sexes even as writers. That was done purposely, because, even if the time had come for such a valuation – and it is far more important at the moment to know how much money women had and how many rooms than to theorise about their capacities – even if the time had come I do not believe that gifts, whether of mind or character, can be weighed like sugar and butter, not even in Cambridge, where they are so adept at putting people into classes and fixing caps on their heads and letters after their names [. . .] All this pitting of sex against sex, of quality against quality; all this claiming of superiority and imputing of inferiority, belong to the private-school stage of human existence where there are 'sides', and it is necessary for one side to beat another side, and of the utmost importance to walk up to a platform and receive from the hands of the Headmaster himself a highly ornamental pot. As people mature they cease to believe in sides or in Headmasters or in highly ornamental pots [. . .] No, *delightful as the pastime of measuring may be, it is the most futile of all occupations, and to submit to the decrees of the measurers the most servile of attitudes.* So long as you write what you wish to write, that is all that matters; and whether it matters for ages or only for hours, nobody can say. But to sacrifice a hair of the head of your vision, a shade of its colour, in deference to some Headmaster with a silver pot in his hand or to some professor with a measuring-rod up his sleeve, is the most abject treachery, and the sacrifice of wealth and chastity which used to be said to be the greatest of human disasters, a mere flea-bite in comparison. (*AROO* 95–6, emphases added)

The domestic simile, 'weighed like sugar and butter' (95), deflates the impulse to rank and classify 'gifts' (95) of 'mind and character' (95). Woolf alludes to the school prize-giving ceremony and its tradition of ranking and rewarding the exceptional in the reference to the 'Headmaster with a silver pot' and Headmaster with a 'highly ornamental pot'. The narrator finds that, even if desirable, a gender-based comparison of the talents of men and women is impossible because women 'remain even at this moment almost unclassified' (*AROO* 77). There are no metrics by which women's capacity to fill their roles are graded: 'no yard measures [. . .] can lay against the qualities of a good mother or the devotion of a daughter, or the fidelity of a sister, or the capacity of a housekeeper' (*AROO* 77), while '[f]ew women even now have been graded at the universities; the great trials of the professions, army and navy, trade, politics and diplomacy have hardly tested them' (*AROO* 77). Woolf alludes to women's historic exclusion from the university and the civil service; the traditional arenas in which men's ability were measured through the mechanism of the competitive examination. The meritocratic, competitive examination gained momentum in the 1850s. The 1853 India Act made examination a condition of entry to the civil service, and, in the same decade, Oxford and Cambridge established entrance exams.[18] This modern examination system constituted a shift from a medieval examination system which, Ansgar Allen notes, 'cultivated the self – involving comparisons between the self being worked upon and surrounding tradition as exemplified by craft masters' to a system which, as devised by Jeremy Bentham, would involve a 'different form' of 'comparisons [. . .] between individual learners', and which could 'engender tensions between individuals'.[19] Woolf's narrator's resistance to these models of assessment, her sense that 'the pastime of measuring [. . .] is the most futile of all occupations [. . .] to submit to the decrees of the measurers the most servile of attitudes' (*AROO* 95–6) is accompanied by the contention that women are excluded from such statistical modes of understanding the self that renders them marginalised in relation to the meritocratic order.

However, rather than calling for women's ability to be measured in the intelligence test, Woolf's narrator instead suggests that the environmental factors that hamper intelligence should be quantified: 'the psychologists of Newnham and Girton might come to our help [. . .] For surely it is time that the effect of discouragement upon the mind of the artist should be measured' (*AROO* 48). Amendments made between the draft version of *A Room of One's Own* and the published text reinforce Woolf's interest in the effects of educational opportunity on female intelligence. Margaret of Newcastle is described in the Fitzwilliam manuscript as having a 'wild, generous, [——] hard intelligence'[20] and this is amended in the final version to 'wild, generous, untutored intelligence' (*AROO* 56). The shift in emphasis in the omission of 'hard' and replacement with 'untutored' reinforces the unpropitious educational conditions that inhibit the female intellect.

A Room of One's Own and Class

While *A Room of One's Own* reconfigures the terms of the debate on female intelligence to focus not on questions of relative male and female intellect but the material barriers to the female intellect, the reception of the text indicated a resistance to these arguments and the persistence of stereotyped notions surrounding female intelligence. Most notable was a review by Lyn Irvine, a Girton graduate and eventual Hogarth author (the Press published her first book *Ten Letter Writers* in 1931), in the books' pages of the *Nation and Athenaeum*, edited by Leonard Woolf. The review focuses on mental ability and is worth examining in detail because it signals a persistent ambivalence about the quality and potential of women's intellect, despite Woolf's manifesto for the environmental factors that have inhibited its development.

Irvine comments that 'upon the face of it' the argument that finds 'the female of the species is inferior to the male, is ludicrous', before suggesting that, if certain evidence is selected, it is 'less easy to dispatch' Professor von X with his 'monumental work upon "The Mental, Moral, and Physical Inferiority of the Female Sex"'.[21] Engaging with the nature vs. nurture debate on intelligence, Irvine notes that 'every child inherits mental capacities from both its male and female ancestors, if it inherits any at all'.[22] Irvine's circumspect phrasing reflects the shifting position of biologists such as J. B. S. Haldane in the interwar period as the provenance of intelligence was examined.[23] Irvine's provisional language continues: 'if everything depends upon environment, then there is no need for the modern woman to start at a disadvantage', citing the 'comparative ease with which women adapted themselves to university training in one generation' as proof, a comment which, of course, does not acknowledge the statistical difference in the number of men and women at university at the time.[24] Irvine suggests that a lack of mental resources rendered women subject to the unappetising cuisine Woolf's narrator famously observes in *A Room*: 'is lack of means alone responsible, and not perhaps lack of something else? The poorest imaginable community of men [...] would use their imaginations and invent a pudding as cheap as prunes and custard, but edible, even delectable', in a rather literal rendering of Woolf's conceit.[25]

Woolf's response to the review in the letters pages of *The Nation and Athenaeum* on 16 November 1929 highlights Irvine's imputation that it is inferior intellectual aptitude that inhibits women's ability to summon up a more delicious diet. Woolf counters Irvine's misogynistic insistence that men would have used their imagination to avoid a diet of prunes and custard and thus have 'some desirable power that women lack' by noting that 'the majority of Englishmen are sitting down at this moment to such a diet. The working-class man does not possess either £500 a year or a room of his own.'[26] Woolf's comments underpin her conception that the problem is one of means (not ability) and implicitly align women with the state of the working-class man. They also reflect a sensitivity to social class which critical accounts have argued is marginalised in *A Room of One's Own*.[27] This marginalisation is conscious, in much the same way as *Three Guineas* focuses on the daughters of educated men, while consigning consideration of working-class women to the text's notes in order to reinforce the strength of its polemic.[28] In *A Room of One's Own*, Woolf points up the limits of her argument by making evident to her reader the slippages in her logic which co-opt the impoverished conditions of the working class to stand in for the lives of women:

> Sir Arthur Quiller-Couch writes:
> '[. . .] [T]he poor poet has not in these days, nor has had for two hundred years, a dog's chance. *Believe me – and I have spent a great part of ten years watching some three hundred and twenty elementary schools – we may prate of democracy, but actually, a poor child* in England has little more hope than had the son of an Athenian slave to be emancipated into that intellectual freedom of which great writings are born.'
> Nobody could put the point more plainly. 'The poor poet has not in these days, nor has had for two hundred years, *a dog's chance. . . a poor child* in England has little more hope than had the son of an Athenian slave to be emancipated into that intellectual freedom of which great writings are born.' That is it. Intellectual freedom depends upon material things. Poetry depends on intellectual freedom. And women have always been poor [. . .] Women, then, have not had a dog's chance of writing poetry. (*AROO* 97, emphases added)

Woolf's ellipses highlight the jump between her source text, which focuses on the circumstances that have limited the creative output of the working-class child, and her own conclusions that explore how women's material (and intellectual) impoverishment excludes them from literary work. The rhetorical slippage is allowed to stand.

Woolf addressed issues surrounding class, writing and education more directly in two contexts around the time of the production of *A Room of One's Own*. The first was in 'The Niece of an Earl', which associates education with a form of class displacement that troubles the position of the working-class writer: 'For it is impossible, it would seem, for working men to write in their own language about their own lives. Such education as the act of writing implies at once makes them self-conscious, or removes them from their own class' (*E4* 562–3).[29] The second was in the school scenes of *The Waves Holograph I*, which were written between July and November 1929, shortly after the April–May 1929 manuscript insertion to *A Room of One's Own* that satirises the 'private-school stage of human existence' (*AROO* 95)

Biometric Feminism 101

and the school prize-giving ceremony. The school scenes of the novel's drafts return to the imagery of the prize-giving ceremony to consider, less markers of the 'comparative merits' (*AROO* 95) of the genders, but rather class-based markers of civic initiation through ceremonies of academic attainment:

> Innumerable children, or as they now began to be called 'future citizens', we Toms Charles Harris Ellen, Alices Dorothys, & so on [...] & to each the Dr. gave a book, & Miss Lambert gave a book, with an inscription in their rapid scholastic hands. – ~~save of course, Florrie Staples, the kitchenmaid.~~[30]

The elision of male and female names in the school prize-giving ceremony puts the emphasis on class, rather than gender, division. The name of the 'kitchenmaid', Florrie, is visibly erased from the educational ceremony that initiates new 'citizens' into the intellectual and social order through the bestowal of a book, as literacy is aligned with citizenship.

Where *A Room of One's Own* does consider the intelligence of working-class women, it does so to regret the textual neglect of working-class women's lives. The text takes a demographic perspective tainted by a eugenicist conviction of the differential fertility rate between the working and middle class, as it notes the 'innumerably populated' (*AROO* 80) 'long streets somewhere south of the river' (*AROO* 80). As Jones identifies, there is a 'humane' element to the description of working-class women's lives, but Woolf's description of working-class life also contains elements of the eccentricity of the carnivalesque:[31]

> feeling in imagination the pressure of dumbness, the accumulation of unrecorded life, whether from the women at the street corners with their arms akimbo, and the rings embedded in their fat swollen fingers, talking with a gesticulation like the swing of Shakespeare's words; or from the violet-sellers and match-sellers and old crones stationed under doorways; or from drifting girls whose faces, like waves in sun and cloud, signal the coming of men and women and the flickering lights of shop windows. All that you will have to explore, I said to Mary Carmichael, holding your torch firm in your hand. (*AROO* 81)

The depiction of the working-class women's lives is engaged with as a problem of narrative representation. The women are associated with a form of ignorant stupidity ('dumbness') that is felt as a form of artistic responsibility to record lives hitherto 'unrecorded'. The passage anticipates elements of the 'Introductory Letter'. The striking phrase 'feeling in imagination' pre-dates the fraught examination of sympathetic entanglement that the later text's middle-class narrator explores as she recalls the working-class women at a Women's Co-operative Guild conference: 'It was aesthetic sympathy, the sympathy of the eye and of the imagination, not of the heart and of the nerves; and such sympathy is always physically uncomfortable.'[32] In the above passage, the heightened language in the description of the 'drifting girls' suggests a merely 'aesthetic sympathy': there is a lyrical beauty in the simile that likens their faces to 'waves in sun and cloud'. However, as the 'Introductory Letter' suggests, there is also something 'uncomfortable' about this description. The ambiguous identity of these girls, potentially shop girls, but also, the language suggests, in the sexualised punning of 'coming', potentially prostitutes, seems to aestheticise economic and sexual exploitation. The physically expressive women with 'arms akimbo' seem graceless, like the 'thick-set and muscular' women of the 'Introductory Letter' (*E5* 229). The description of these women, who embody a physical and verbal language evocative of Shakespeare, as they 'talk[ing] with a gesticulation like the swing of Shakespeare's words', also anticipates the women of the 'Introductory Letter': 'the quality that they have, judging from a phrase caught here and there, from a laugh, or a gesture seen in passing, is precisely the quality that Shakespeare would have enjoyed' (*E5* 232). In the usage of the term 'crone', the text performs an act of 'aesthetic sympathy' as it mirrors the vivid form of expression evocative of an older lexicon that is associated with the text's subjects. The term 'crone' is archaic; its long etymology dates back to Middle English Chaucerian usage.[33] As so often in Woolf's work, there is an association of working-class life with an atavistic form of existence. The description is evocative of the 'ancient song' of the 'battered old woman with one hand exposed for coppers' in *Mrs Dalloway* (1925), who is associated with the 'primeval', the 'passing generations', and the 'age of tusk and mammoth'.[34]

Confronted with these problems of identification and expression that are so familiar when Woolf depicts working-class lives and voices, the text performs an act of narrative abdication. Elsewhere Woolf's narrative abdication takes the form of a proleptic deferment of democratic aesthetic and social forms, and here it becomes a gesture of artistic opportunity: 'all that you will have to explore, I said to Mary Carmichael, holding your torch firm in your hand' (*AROO* 81).[35] Woolf's awareness of the limitations of her own position has been analysed in relation to the polemical reach of *Three Guineas*.³⁶ In *A Room of One's Own* this limitation can be construed as artistic possibility: 'All these infinitely obscure lives remain to be recorded' (*AROO* 81).

Morley College and Social Class

Where *A Room of One's Own* encounters the 'pressure of dumbness' as a form of narrative responsibility, Woolf's 1905 'Morley Sketch' is alive to the intelligence of working-class women. Previously titled 'A Report on Teaching at Morley College', Jones rechristened the sketch in order to draw attention to the elements of performativity in the writing as Woolf 'tries out the various roles of dedicated teacher, social investigator and anti-authoritarian maverick', and in trialling these different narrative positions the text directly addresses the intelligence of working-class women.³⁷

Stephen's diaries demonstrate a clear respect for the mental ability of her students at Morley, even if they threw her planned lessons off course: 'meditating how on earth to discuss Sir T[homas]. Browne [. . .] & two women – nice & intelligent – came finally, but were readier to talk than listen'.³⁸ In the 'Morley Sketch', the women are characterised as incredulous and receptive: 'The faithful pair of friends sat receptive & open mouthed as usual.'³⁹ The comments suggest a vacant gormlessness in the women that, only on occasion, is outweighed by evidence of their mental ability as they attempt to synthesise the information presented to them: 'Pictures I showed them, & I lent them books; sometimes they seemed to gape not in {sheer} <mere impotent> wonder {to be} but to be trying to piece together what they heard; to seek reasons; to connect ideas.'⁴⁰ As if sensitive to the inflammatory connotations of the verb 'gape', a later passage cancels this term as it assessed the suitability of a series of planned lectures by George Trevelyan for the women's education:

> Meanwhile, my four women, {are to be} <can> hear eight lectures on the French Revolution if they wish to continue their historical learning: {& then? Which from a knowledge of the state of their minds I conceive will be wholly useless to them. It will be another temptation to them to.} And what, I ask, will be the use of that? Eight lectures dropped into their minds, {without any <which are wholly unable to>} like meteors from another sphere infringing on

> this planet, {& which [has has] merely time to gape for a moment & ask what are you to whence? before they} <dissolving into dust again>. {So fragmentary and disconnected will these eight} Such disconnected fragments will these eight lectures be: to people who {se mind} <have> absolutely no power of receiving them as part of a whole, & {applying the} applying them {in} to their proper ends.[41]

As Jones suggests, the insistence that the women would find it difficult to engage with Trevelyan's lectures 'might seem like proof of her belief in their intellectual inferiority'.[42] Revisions to the manuscript suggest an attempt to mitigate negative expressions of the women's mental ability and to focus instead on the limitations of Trevelyan's curriculum. The cancelled phrases '{& then? which from a knowledge of the state of their minds I conceive will be wholly useless to them. It will be another temptation to them to.}', '[minds]{without any <which are wholly unable to>}'; '{& which [has has] merely time to gape for a moment & ask what are you to whence? before they}', all focus on the perceived deficiencies of the women, while the emendations and retained phrases focus on the qualities of the lectures themselves.[43]

The language implies that the difficulties the women might have in synthesising the lectures, in 'receiving them as part of a whole', can be attributed to failures of curriculum. In the 'Morley Sketch' the imagery suggests both the estranging nature of the lectures ('like meteors from another sphere infringing on this planet') and their incoherence ('disconnected fragments').[44] Notably one of Woolf's own lectures on aspects of Italian culture had a more idiosyncratic focus, 'upon our journey in Italy' (*PA* 225) and contextualised Venice against a hook that would grab her students' attention: 'the kind of thing they really enjoy [. . .] whether there were fleas in the beds at Venice. I shall have to invent some' (*PA* 225). In the passage above, there is also evidence of a shift from the mental to a broader sociological critique. The deletion of the specific reference to the students' 'mind[s]' in the allusion to them being part of a 'people who{se mind} <have> absolutely no power of receiving' the lectures suggests a shift of focus away from solely mental ability to a political and social disempowerment in the broader focus on 'power' in general. This reading receives fresh impetus from the earlier observation in the 'Sketch' that the women were primed full of potential: 'it would not be hard to educate them sufficiently to give them a new interest in life'.[45]

While there is evidence of an attempt to mitigate comments that negatively assess the students' intelligence, the 'Morley Sketch' also demonstrates Stephen's interest in grading the minds of her students. Stephen's concern with the women's intelligence comes during a period of research into the nature and quality of intelligence. Her comments occur the year after Charles Spearman published on the concept of 'general factor' intelligence (or 'g'), which Spearman associated with the 'mental energy' required for the performance of mental tests, and they come more than a decade after Edward Cattell first introduced the idea of 'mental tests and measurements' in 1890 as a means of establishing individual differences.[46] Woolf ranks the students' minds as she suggests of Miss Williams, a reporter and reviewer for a clerical paper: 'she was certainly of a higher {level} level of intelligence than the other women'.[47] Stephen resists standardised models of understanding mental ability as she assesses the women's intelligence:

> {In spite of warning, I found them of a higher standard on the whole} On the whole they were possessed of more intelligence than I expected; though that intelligence was almost wholly uncultivated. But of this I am convinced; that it would not be hard to educate them sufficiently to give them a new interest in life; {whether it were history, language music, – or} They have {[as it]} tentacles languidly stretching forth from their minds, feeling vaguely for substance, & easily applied by a guiding hand to something that {would} <could> really <grasp> {nourish them}.[48]

The deletion ('{In spite of warning, I found them of a higher standard on the whole}') suggests that Stephen's own estimation of the women's intelligence was formed in the context of a rather cynical institutional assessment of their abilities.[49] The language of cultivation reflects an interest in environmental factors that nurture genius. The zoological and botanical term 'tentacles' can be seen to dehumanise the women, but it also is part of a familiar semantic field that associates vegetable matter with mental potential, as I shall consider in greater depth in relation to *A Room of One's Own*. Stephen frames her role as teacher as more than a mechanism for quantifying intelligence, but rather a facilitator 'guiding' her students.[50] However, at the same time, the revisions she makes to the manuscript, the deletion of the term 'nourish them' and the focus on the women's own mental 'grasp' moderates her own nurturing role as educator to amplify the women's own empowerment and mental reach.[51] Anticipating the concerns of *A Room of One's Own*, the text is engaged with an awareness of the social and economic conditions that inhibit the fulfilment of the women's intellectual potential: Stephen observed of one of the students that 'she could write grammatical sentences, which followed each other {logical} logically enough; and she had evidently some facility of expression; in other circumstances I suppose, she would have been a writer!'[52]

The 'Typical' Woman: Class and Race in *A Room of One's Own*

Woolf's response to Irvine's review of *A Room of One's Own* in *The Nation and Athenaeum* suggests her concern to address her arguments to a perceived 'typical' middle-class woman. Irvine's review ends with a rhetorical move that calls on her reader to 'imagine the Brontë sisters born nearly a century later, leaving Haworth to win scholarships at Fernham, afterwards with good degrees becoming mistresses at Roedean and Cheltenham'.[53] For Irvine, those that benefit most from the higher education of women are not the Brontë sisters, 'but the Smith sisters and the Jones sisters and all the other sisters whose Victorian prototypes never thought about rebelling against the lot of woman', while Charlotte Brontë 'teaching at Cheltenham, is still troubled with dreams'.[54] Woolf's reply to Irvine argues that *A Room* explores the conditions necessary for the 'typical' to become the 'remarkable':

> in no circumstances could the Brontë sisters have been either typical schoolmistresses or typical globe-trotters. They remain rare and remarkable women. And my argument was that if we wish to increase the supply of rare and remarkable women like the Brontës we should give the Joneses and the Smiths rooms of their own and five hundred a year. One cannot grow fine flowers in a thin soil. And hitherto the soil – I mean no disrespect to Miss Smith and Miss Jones – has been very starved and very stony.[55]

Woolf deploys a well-established tradition that examines discourses of genius through the lens of vegetable matter and natural growth. The lexical register from which this metaphor is drawn echoes that of Addison, and was later expanded upon by Young in his *Conjectures on Original Composition* (1759).[56] Addison distinguishes between two classes of genius; the wild, untutored genius and the genius refined by learning:

> the first is like a rich Soil in a happy Climate, that produces a whole Wilderness of noble Plants rising in a thousand beautiful Landskips

[sic] without any certain Order or Regularity. In the other it is the same rich Soil under the same happy Climate, that has been laid out in Walks and Parterres, and cut into Shape and Beauty by the Skill of the Gardener.[57]

Unlike Addison, Woolf is not concerned with different categories of genius, but rather the general environmental conditions (the soil) that hamper the intellect.[58]

Manuscript additions Woolf made to the description of Mary Carmichael (modelled on Marie Stopes), who is praised for the unself-conscious nature of her writing (she 'wrote as a woman, but as a woman who has forgotten that she is a woman' (*AROO* 84)), demonstrate her concern with dealing with the 'typical'. Woolf is at pains to establish Mary Carmichael's unremarkable intellect in two additions to the Monk's House Manuscript that are found in the final version of the text and which clarify Mary Carmichael's intellectual status: 'She was no "genius" – that was evident' (*AROO* 83); 'Considering that Mary Carmichael was no genius [. . .] without enough of those desirable things, time, money and idleness, she did not do so badly' (*AROO* 85). Woolf repeats Mary Carmichael's lack of 'genius' in order to reinforce her contention that if she is 'give[n] [. . .] a room of her own and five hundred a year [. . .] she will write a better book one of these days' (*AROO* 85). In establishing Mary Carmichael as 'no more than a clever girl whose books will no doubt be pulped by the publishers in ten years' time' (*AROO* 83), Woolf puts the emphasis on the material conditions that support creative writing rather than Romantic notions of creative genius.

This concern for dealing with the 'typical' extends also to an attempt to determine an 'average' as Woolf establishes a quantitative basis for *A Room*'s arguments. Woolf defines the 'average' in socio-economic terms which naturalise her initial Cambridge audience, and a middle-class readership. The norm is defined in the manuscripts of *A Room of One's Own* as 'the average woman, the middle class woman' (*AROO* 72) and 'middle class women, ordinary women' (*AROO* 99). Amendments Woolf made in the writing process reinforce a conception of the average as being a class-based measure. The Fitzwilliam manuscript suggests that 'by no possible means could ~~a woman~~ <women,> ~~have taken part in~~ average women, women who had nothing but their brains or their character to commend them, have taken part in any one of the great movements',[59] while in the final version the notion of the 'average' is marked by a measure of social class: 'by no possible means could middle-class women with nothing but brains and character at their command have taken part in any of the great movements [...] of the past' (*AROO* 41). Both versions make reference to the 'average woman in the time of Shakespeare' and the 'average Elizabethan woman' (*AROO* 41).[60] Woolf's concern with the 'average' and the 'typical' suggests a statistical imagination that reflects the pioneering work of Karl Pearson, Galton's disciple. Pearson founded courses on statistics at UCL in his Biometric Laboratory and established the principle of the normal distribution curve, which visualised the mean measurement in graphic form.[61]

The text's notion of an 'average' is one that is also shaped by race. As Snaith argues, '[t]he intersection of race and gender is one of the text's blind spots'.[62] The comment that 'It is one of the great advantages of being a woman that one can pass even a very fine negress without wishing to make an Englishwoman of her' (*AROO* 46) effaces the idea of a Black British population, as Barrett notes, and as Jones observes, the comment 'reproduces the objectifying gaze of the coloniser'.[63] The specific terms of this objectification represent an uneasy intersection of Woolf's queer gaze with her feminist and anti-colonial politics. This comment was introduced into the text from the manuscript drafts which do not include this comment.[64] This textual addition suggests the unevenness of the terms within which Woolf was aware of the limitations of her position. While she provides some visions of the working class that can be considered humane (see Jones), her sense of Black women is exoticising (see Barrett).[65] Such moves further normalise the text's 'average' addressee as the white, middle-class woman.

Coda

Winifred Holtby situated an analysis of Woolf's politics within a metric understanding of male and female relationships that reflected a contemporaneous concern with intellectual ability:

> The difficulty of sex-differentiation is overcome by taking as criterion some measure of value greater than the measure of sexual difference. That criterion is the relationship of the individual to reality – a relationship which men and women share alike. By concentrating on intellectual likeness instead of physiological difference, she achieves her knowledge of unity [...] [t]he barriers dividing man from man, man from God, sex from sex, race from race and class from class

have become transparent and dissolved in the light of reality [. . .] fears, hatreds and misunderstandings of division disappear.[66]

Holtby's claim that Woolf sees 'intellectual likeness' between the sexes is supported by *A Room of One's Own*'s marginalisation of clichéd notions of the inferiority of women's intellect and an advocacy of an androgynous mind: 'one must be woman-manly or man-womanly' (*AROO* 94).[67] Other markers of social difference that Holtby suggests are 'transparent and dissolved' in the text, are points of tension that, I have argued in this chapter, naturalise a white, middle-class, female audience.[68] While Holtby suggests that Woolf overcomes the barriers of sex, race and class alike, the charm and inventiveness that enables Woolf to envisage a solution to sex difference falters in relation to race and class, where, with varying degrees of cognisance, Woolf's vision of 'unity' breaks down.[69] A biometric reading of Woolf's feminism demonstrates the fraught place of intelligence in interwar Britain. At the intersection of gender, class and race, the new scientific understanding of intelligence marked a departure from capitalism to underpin a new meritocratic elite, with, as I have suggested here, its own 'misunderstandings of division'.[70]

Notes

1. Michèle Barrett, 'Introduction', in Virginia Woolf, *A Room of One's Own and Three Guineas* (London: Penguin, 1993), ix–liii (xx).
2. Lorraine Daston, 'The Naturalized Female Intellect', *Science in Context*, 5.2 (1992), 209–35 (211); Kurt Danziger, *Naming the Mind: How Psychology Found Its Language* (London: Sage, 1997), 66.
3. Danziger, *Naming the Mind*, 69.
4. Francis Galton, *Hereditary Genius* (London: Macmillan, 1869), 3.
5. Flavia Alaya, 'Victorian Science and the "Genius" of Woman', *Journal of the History of Ideas*, 38.2 (1977), 261–80 (267).
6. Clara Jones, 'Virginia Woolf's *A Room of One's Own* and the Problem of Inherited Wealth', in *Influence and Inheritance in Feminist English Studies*, ed. by Emily J. Hogg and Clara Jones (Basingstoke: Palgrave Macmillan, 2015), 20–33 (23).
7. Virginia Woolf, *A Room of One's Own and Three Guineas* (London: Penguin, 1993), 34. Further page references will be given within the main text.
8. Jones, 'The Problem of Inherited Wealth', 31.
9. Harold Perkin, *The Rise of Professional Society: England Since 1880* (London: Routledge, 2002 [1990]), 380.

10. Perkin, *The Rise of Professional Society*, 380.
11. J. M. Keynes, 'The End of *Laissez-Faire*', in *Essays in Persuasion* (London: Macmillan and Co., 1931), 186–212 (210).
12. Adrian Wooldridge, *Measuring the Mind: Education and Psychology in England, c. 1860–c. 1990* (Cambridge: Cambridge University Press, 1994), 175.
13. H. Gruenberg, 'Men and Mice at Edinburgh: Reports from the Genetics Conference' [*The Geneticists' Manifesto*], *The Journal of Heredity*, 30.9 (1939), 371–74.
14. Virginia Woolf, 'The Niece of an Earl', in *The Essays of Virginia Woolf, Volume Four, 1925–1928*, ed. by Andrew McNeillie (London: Hogarth Press, 1994), 559–63 (563). Further page references will be given within the main text.
15. As Snaith notes, this was figured in the form of a sibling divide in texts such as *The Years*. This specific framing of educational experience was one that had autobiographical urgency for Woolf who, aside from attending short courses at King's College Ladies' Department between 1897 and 1901, was largely educated at home while her brothers, Adrian and Thoby, attended school. Anna Snaith, *Virginia Woolf: Public and Private Negotiations* (Basingstoke: Palgrave, 2016 [2000]), 97; Anna Snaith and Christine Kenyon-Jones, 'Tilting at Universities: Virginia Woolf at King's College London', *Woolf Studies Annual*, 16 (2010), 1–44.
16. Logan Pearsall Smith, *Four Words: Romantic, Originality, Creative, Genius* (Oxford: Clarendon Press, 1924), 25.
17. See S. P. Rosenbaum, 'Introduction', in *Virginia Woolf, Women & Fiction: The Manuscript Versions of A Room of One's Own*, transcribed and edited by S. P. Rosenbaum (London: Blackwell Publishers, 1992), xiii–xlii (xl).
18. Ansgar Allen, *Benign Violence: Education In and Beyond the Age of Reason* (Basingstoke: Palgrave Macmillan, 2014), 17.
19. Allen, *Benign Violence*, 16.
20. Rosenbaum, *Virginia Woolf, Women & Fiction*, 95.
21. Lyn Ll. Irvine, 'Virginia Woolf Upon Women', *The Nation and Athenaeum*, 9 November 1929, 201–3, (202).
22. Irvine, 'Virginia Woolf Upon Women', 202.
23. For an outline of J. B. S. Haldane's position on the role of environment in shaping intelligence see Natasha Periyan, 'Naomi Mitchison, Eugenics and the Community: The Class and Gender Politics of Intelligence', in *The 1930s: A Decade of Modern British Fiction*, ed. by Nick Hubble, Luke Seaber and Elinor Taylor (London: Bloomsbury, 2021), 91–122 (93–5).
24. Irvine, 'Virginia Woolf Upon Women', 202. As Dyhouse notes, figures from the University Grants Committee demonstrate that women represented 16 per cent of the student population of Great Britain in 1900,

24 per cent in 1920, and 27 per cent in 1930. Carol Dyhouse, *No Distinction of Sex? Women in British Universities, 1870 – 1939* (London: UCL Press, 1995), 17.
25. Irvine, 'Virginia Woolf Upon Women', 202.
26. Virginia Woolf, 'Women and Leisure', 'Letters to the Editor', *The Nation and Athenaeum*, 16 November 1929, 248.
27. Snaith asks '[w]hat kind of "women" does the essay speak for and to?'; Sean Latham notes that 'This feminist manifesto severely restricts itself from the outset, for it imagines that this money and this room will only be granted to women of Woolf's own social class' while Michèle Barrett reads Woolf's class-based focus as a strategic decision to reinforce her polemic as she argues that Woolf takes the 'decision of the feminist' in *A Room of One's Own* 'to prioritize specific needs of (middle-class) women over the more general (socialist) desirability of abolishing capitalism'. Anna Snaith, 'Introduction', in Virginia Woolf, *A Room of One's Own and Three Guineas* (Oxford: Oxford University Press, 2015), xi–xxxvi (xxii); Sean Latham, *Am I a Snob?: Modernism and the Novel* (Ithaca: Cornell University Press, 2018), 110–11; Michèle Barrett, 'Introduction', xxi.
28. Natasha Periyan, *The Politics of 1930s British Literature: Education, Class, Gender* (London: Bloomsbury, 2018), 169–74.
29. Natasha Periyan, 'Democratic Art or Working-Class Literature? Virginia Woolf, the Women's Cooperative Guild and Literary Value in the "Introductory Letter"', in *Working-Class Writing: Theory and Practice*, ed. by Nick Hubble and Ben Clarke (London: Palgrave Macmillan, 2018), 99–119 (105–107).
30. Virginia Woolf, *The Waves The Two Holograph Drafts*, ed. by J. W. Graham (London: The Hogarth Press, 1976), 137.
31. Clara Jones, 'Preface', in Virginia Woolf, *A Room of One's Own* (London: Persephone, 2019), v–xvii (xv).
32. Virginia Woolf, 'Introductory Letter to Margaret Llewelyn Davies', *The Essays of Virginia Woolf, Volume Five: 1929–1932*, ed. by Stuart N. Clarke (London: Hogarth Press, 2009), 225–41 (231). Further page references will be given within the main text.
33. See <https://0-www-oed-com.catalogue.libraries.london.ac.uk/view/Entry/44723?rskey=OMsYuh&result=1&isAdvanced=false#eid> [accessed 31 October 2023].
34. Virginia Woolf, *Mrs Dalloway* (London: Penguin, 1996), 91, 92, 90.
35. See Periyan, 'Democratic Art or Working-Class Literature?'.
36. Commenting on *Three Guineas*, Snaith argues that Woolf's refusal to advocate for the working class was a 'deliberate political stance' that revealed her 'consciousness of the limitations of her own class position', leading her to speak only to and about 'that class of women of which she has had experience'. Anna Snaith, *Virginia Woolf*, 114.

37. Clara Jones, *Virginia Woolf: Ambivalent Activist* (Edinburgh: Edinburgh University Press, 2016), 24.
38. Virginia Woolf, *A Passionate Apprentice: The Early Journals 1897–1909* (London: Pimlico, 2004), 224. Further page references will be given within the main text.
39. 'Appendix 1: The Morley Sketch', in *Virginia Woolf: Ambivalent Activist*, 210–15 (212).
40. 'Morley Sketch', 213.
41. Ibid., 213.
42. Jones, *Ambivalent Activist*, 34.
43. 'Morley Sketch', 213.
44. Ibid., 213.
45. Ibid., 213.
46. Gregory Richard Langton (ed.), *Oxford Companion to the Mind* (Oxford: Oxford University Press, 2004), 473; See Nikolas Rose, 'The Psychological Complex: Mental Measurement and Social Administration', *Ideology and Consciousness*, 5 (1979), 5–68 (49) for more on Cattell and mental measurement.
47. 'Morley Sketch', 212.
48. 'Ibid., 213.
49. Ibid., 213.
50. Ibid., 213.
51. Ibid., 213.
52. Ibid., 212.
53. Irvine, 'Virginia Woolf Upon Women', 202, 202.
54. Ibid., 202–3, 203.
55. Woolf, 'Women and Leisure', 248.
56. See M. H. Abrams, *The Mirror and the Lamp: Romantic Theory and the Critical Tradition* (Oxford: Oxford University Press, 1971 [1953]), 198–212 for Young and ideas linking genius and vegetable matter, with discussion of German theories of genius.
57. *The Spectator*, CLXI, 3 September 1711, unnumbered page.
58. This imagery was, notably, also used to assess Woolf's creative calibre. Storm Jameson, reviewing *Orlando*, associated her skills more with the carefully tended garden than the wildflower meadow: 'she lacks humanity. She is in some way, or by some word laid on her, outside humanity [...] She has no roots in our common earth. Her genius, carefully tended, pruned, enriched, has no roots in our common earth.' Storm Jameson, 'The Georgian Novel and Mr Robinson', *Bookman* (New York), July 1929, 449–63, in *Virginia Woolf: Critical Heritage* (London: Routledge & Kegan Paul, 1975), 244–5 (245).
59. Rosenbaum, *Virginia Woolf, Women & Fiction*, 69.
60. Ibid., 71.
61. See Daniel Kevles, *In the Name of Eugenics: Genetics and the Uses of Human Heredity* (Berkeley: University of California Press, 1986

[1985]), 20–40 for Pearson's role as a pioneer of biometrics and the institutor of statistical modes of enquiry in the university.
62. Snaith, 'Introduction', xxii. See Snaith's discussion of Alice Walker's insertion of Black women into the narrative of *A Room of One's Own* in *In My Mother's Garden*, xxii.
63. Barrett, 'Editor's Notes', in Virginia Woolf, *A Room of One's Own and Three Guineas* (London: Penguin, 1993), 108; Jones, 'Preface', xiv.
64. Rosenbaum, *Virginia Woolf, Women & Fiction*, 84.
65. Jones, 'Preface', xv; Barrett, 'Editor's Notes', 108.
66. Winifred Holtby, *Virginia Woolf: A Critical Memoir* (London: Continuum, 2007 [1932]), 185.
67. Holtby, *Virginia Woolf*, 185.
68. Ibid., 185.
69. Ibid., 185.
70. Ibid., 185.

Works Cited

Abrams, M. H. *The Mirror and the Lamp: Romantic Theory and the Critical Tradition*. Oxford: Oxford University Press, 1971 [1953].
Addison, Joseph. *The Spectator*, CLXI, 3 September 1711, unnumbered page.
Alaya, Flavia. 'Victorian Science and the "Genius" of Woman'. *Journal of the History of Ideas*, 38.2 (1977), 261–80.
Allen, Ansgar. *Benign Violence: Education In and Beyond the Age of Reason*. Basingstoke: Palgrave Macmillan, 2014.
Barrett, Michèle. 'Introduction'. In Virginia Woolf, *A Room of One's Own and Three Guineas*, ix–liii. London: Penguin, 1993.
Danziger, Kurt. *Naming the Mind: How Psychology Found Its Language*. London: Sage, 1997.
Daston, Lorraine. 'The Naturalized Female Intellect'. *Science in Context*, 5.2 (1992), 209–35.
Dyhouse, Carol. *No Distinction of Sex? Women in British Universities, 1870–1939*. London: UCL Press, 1995.
Holtby, Winifred. *Virginia Woolf: A Critical Memoir*. London: Continuum, 2007 [1932].
Galton, Francis. *Hereditary Genius*. London: Macmillan, 1869.
Gruenberg, H. 'Men and Mice at Edinburgh: Reports from the Genetics Conference' [*The Geneticists' Manifesto*]. *The Journal of Heredity*, 30.9 (1939), 371–4.
Irvine, Lyn Ll. 'Virginia Woolf Upon Women'. *The Nation and Athenaeum*, 9 November 1929, 201–3.
Jameson, Storm, 'The Georgian Novel and Mr Robinson'. *Bookman* (New York), July 1929, 449–63. In *Virginia Woolf: Critical Heritage*, 244–5. London: Routledge & Kegan Paul, 1975.

Jones, Clara. 'Preface'. In Virginia Woolf, *A Room of One's Own*, v–xvii. London: Persephone, 2019.

———, *Virginia Woolf: Ambivalent Activist*. Edinburgh: Edinburgh University Press, 2016.

———, 'Virginia Woolf's *A Room of One's Own* and the Problem of Inherited Wealth'. In *Influence and Inheritance in Feminist English Studies*, ed. by Emily J. Hogg and Clara Jones, 20–33. Basingstoke: Palgrave Macmillan, 2015.

Kevles, Daniel. *In the Name of Eugenics: Genetics and the Uses of Human Heredity*. Berkeley: University of California Press, 1986 [1985].

Keynes, J. M., 'The End of *Laissez-Faire*'. In *Essays in Persuasion*, 186–212. London: Macmillan and Co., 1931.

Langton, Gregory Richard (ed.). *Oxford Companion to the Mind*. Oxford: Oxford University Press, 2004.

Latham, Sean. *Am I a Snob?: Modernism and the Novel*. Ithaca: Cornell University Press, 2018.

Oxford English Dictionary Online <www.oed.com> [accessed 31/10/23]

Periyan, Natasha. 'Democratic Art or Working-Class Literature? Virginia Woolf, the Women's Cooperative Guild and Literary Value in the "Introductory Letter"'. In *Working-Class Writing: Theory and Practice*, ed. by Nick Hubble and Ben Clarke, 99–119. London: Palgrave Macmillan, 2018.

———, 'Naomi Mitchison, Eugenics and the Community: The Class and Gender Politics of Intelligence'. In *The 1930s: A Decade of Modern British Fiction*, ed. by Nick Hubble, Luke Seaber and Elinor Taylor, 91–122. London: Bloomsbury, 2021.

———, *The Politics of 1930s British Literature: Education, Class, Gender*. London: Bloomsbury, 2018.

Perkin, Harold. *The Rise of Professional Society: England Since 1880*. London: Routledge, 2002 [1990].

Rose, Nikolas. 'The Psychological Complex: Mental Measurement and Social Administration'. *Ideology and Consciousness*, 5 (1979), 5–68.

Rosenbaum, S. P. 'Introduction'. In *Virginia Woolf, Women & Fiction: The Manuscript Versions of A Room of One's Own*, transcribed and edited by S. P. Rosenbaum, xiii–xlii. London: Blackwell Publishers, 1992.

Snaith, Anna. 'Introduction'. In Virginia Woolf, *A Room of One's Own and Three Guineas*, xi–xxxvi. Oxford: Oxford University Press, 2015.

———, and Christine Kenyon-Jones. 'Tilting at Universities: Virginia Woolf at King's College London'. *Woolf Studies Annual*, 16 (2010), 1–44.

———, *Virginia Woolf: Public and Private Negotiations*. Basingstoke: Palgrave, 2016 [2000].

Smith, Logan Pearsall. *Four Words: Romantic, Originality, Creative, Genius*. Oxford: Clarendon Press, 1924.

Wooldridge, Adrian. *Measuring the Mind: Education and Psychology in England, c. 1860–c. 1990*. Cambridge: Cambridge University Press, 1994.

Woolf, Virginia. 'Appendix 1: The Morley Sketch'. In Clara Jones, *Virginia Woolf: Ambivalent Activist*, 210–15. Edinburgh: Edinburgh University Press, 2016.

——, 'Introductory Letter to Margaret Llewelyn Davies'. *The Essays of Virginia Woolf, Volume Five: 1929–1932*, ed. by Stuart N. Clarke, 225–41. London: Hogarth Press, 2009.

——, *Mrs Dalloway*. London: Penguin, 1996.

——, 'The Niece of an Earl'. *The Essays of Virginia Woolf, Volume Four, 1925–1928*, ed. by Andrew McNeillie, 559–63. London: Hogarth Press, 1994.

——, *A Passionate Apprentice: The Early Journals 1897–1909*. London: Pimlico, 2004.

——, *A Room of One's Own and Three Guineas*. London: Penguin, 1993.

——, *The Waves The Two Holograph Drafts*, ed. by J. W. Graham. London: The Hogarth Press, 1976.

——, 'Women and Leisure'. 'Letters to the Editor'. *The Nation and Athenaeum*, 16 November 1929, 248.

Chapter 5

'Merchant of this city': Capitalism and the Liturgies of Peace and War in *Jacob's Room*

Charles Andrews

In an essay for the *Times* in August of 1916, Virginia Woolf described walking the South Downs and hearing 'the beating of gigantic carpets by gigantic women, at a distance'.[1] Gunfire in France accompanies her experience of the Downs, a 'sinister sound of far-off beating' that she associates with the 'desire to be somehow impossibly, and therefore all the more mysteriously, concerned in secret affairs of national importance' that 'is very strong at the present moment' (*E2* 40). She notes that people of this region maintain a mystical belief that war and nature are interdependent: 'no one limits the action of the guns to the addling of a few hen's eggs; the very sun in the sky, they assert, has been somehow deranged in his mechanism by our thunder on earth' (*E2* 41). Entire weather systems have been disrupted by the war, and the allusion to addled hen's eggs acknowledges the impact on the local farming economy. Even more miraculous, however, is 'the behaviour of the church bell' which historically has predicted the end of war: 'the bell belongs to a church which stands solitary upon a hill in the midst of wild marshes, and is gifted with the power of foretelling the return of peace by dropping from the belfry exactly three months before peace is declared' (*E2* 41). The bell dropped in May of 1916, 'to the delight of all beholders', but Woolf remarks that as she writes in mid-August, 'you may still hear the guns from the top of the Downs' (*E2* 41). Though portents of peace may be failing, she admits that we might still believe 'with a deeper conviction than before that we live in a world full of mysteries' (*E2* 42).

This mysterious world of unseen but nevertheless potent connections among nature, war, economy and church establishes some of the preoccupations that would grow throughout her postwar writings, emerging with particular force and imaginative power in

Jacob's Room (1922) as I will argue in this chapter. Her essay about the South Downs is a minor effort at travel writing and local anthropology, cataloguing some of the quaint beliefs from rural England during wartime, but its fusion of several key ideological systems gestures towards Woolf's later, richer, and more thoroughgoing efforts to capture this social and political construct in fiction. Though she is presumably less enthralled by wartime superstitions than the locals, Woolf still writes about them with interest, and her attention to these beliefs and practices shows deep awareness of the power of public ritual for comprehending the war, signifying 'national importance', and building collective identity. Christianity informs these rituals – the town, after all, orients around its church bell – but the specific beliefs and their effect on 'the beholders' is abstracted from orthodox Christian practices and made into something more generalised and nationalistic. The term for this phenomenon is 'civil religion', the collective assent to a set of ritualised convictions that produces communal, national identity in local forms. Civil religion manifests in 'cultural liturgies', as James K. A. Smith describes them, becoming '*rituals of ultimate concern*: rituals that are formative for identity, that inculcate particular visions of the good life, and do so in a way that means to trump other ritual formations'.[2] While the cultural formations Woolf describes in the South Downs are intriguing and fanciful, her continued exploration of cultural liturgies through fiction would show ambivalence, challenge, and protest – especially against the liturgies that support and sustain militarism and war.

Reading *Jacob's Room* as Woolf's response to some of the most significant cultural liturgies that guide our lives can offer a new way to understand the novel as well as offer insights into how we might best live within the pressures of ideological systems that interpellate us. Capitalism, militarism, imperialism and civil religion fuse together, and the novel shows how Jacob and his family are ensnared by national liturgies. Eugene McCarraher has argued that capitalism became 'the religion of modernity', and his analysis of this modern religion demonstrates the association between capitalist enterprise and the violence of the nation-state:

> far from being an agent of 'disenchantment,' capitalism [. . .] has been a regime of enchantment [. . .] Even if many (if not most) of us believe in a disenchanted, de-sacralized cosmos – a universe devoid of spirits and other immaterial but animate beings – capitalism has assumed, in its way, the status of an enchanted world. Like the blood-sacrificial rites of nationalism that sanctify the modern state,

capitalism represents what the theologian William Cavanaugh has called a 'migration of the holy', a forced march of sanctity and devotion toward new, putatively secular objects of reverence.[3]

In McCarraher's account, the supposed progression of secularity in modernity is a misconception; the loss of traditional religious belief does not signal a turn towards rationalism but rather indicates the transferal of sacredness and enchanted belief to the marketplace. *Jacob's Room* is filled with signs of this transference as well as the associations between an enchanted market and a sanctified nation-state that collude to enable global warfare.

This collusion of forces produces what Stanley Hauerwas and Romand Coles describe as 'the politics of death' through interconnected ideologies and institutions that create 'a dense, dynamic, and finely woven mesh of destruction and fear'.[4] Against this 'woven mesh', they advocate for 'an alternative politics that cares for the commonalities, differences, and emergent irregularities of life [which] must also be dense, molecular, supple, mobile, and trickster-like in its modes'.[5] Woolf's experimental prose style in *Jacob's Room*, I would argue, achieves this 'supple, mobile, and trickster-like' modality through using what Stuart N. Clarke and Susan Sellers call its 'narrative arabesques', an associative style that emphasises the radical ordinary.[6] Instead of straightforward narrative progression or detailed, 'objective' character description, Woolf employs small, telling details, fragments, impressions and images that require her reader to make connections among sometimes seemingly disparate ideas. Her web-like narrative exposes how powerful ideologies and cultural liturgies interact and affect us. While Jacob is at Cambridge, for example, he sits in the King's College Chapel aloof and detached from the ritual surrounding him, unmoved by the sight of men processing – 'young men rise in white gowns; while the subservient eagle bears up for inspection the great white book'.[7] Yet Jacob's detachment cannot free him entirely from this religious rite that functions to discipline young men like him and mould them into leaders of industry, government, empire, military and church. From the ritual of the chapel Woolf pivots to the forest outside where her narrator imagines a lantern that attracts 'every insect in the forest' and the impression that 'something senseless inspires them' (*JR* 49) – a blinding attraction that echoes the candle-lit sodality of the chapel and the rote conscription of the young men within but will also return near the end of the novel in her image of London's financial district where bankers and businessmen also swarm like bugs: 'each insect carries a globe of the world in his head, and the webs of the forest are schemes evolved for the smooth conduct of business; and honey is treasure of one sort and another' (*JR* 266–7). A tree falls with the sound of 'a terrifying volley of pistol-shots', linking chapel, nature, finance and violence, and finally we return to Jacob's mind where he is distracted by thoughts of women rendered through material commodities: 'if the mind wanders it is because several hat shops and cupboards of coloured dresses are displayed upon rush-bottomed chairs' (*JR* 50). Even in a short passage such as Jacob's university chapel experience, the intricate network of associated images reveals the 'woven-mesh' that creates the politics of death, and no part of Jacob – his mind, body, and libido – is free from this cultural web. *Jacob's Room* requires its readers to attend to the many elements that shape us as we and the novel's characters strive to understand Jacob and his actions. The world of the book is fixated on a politics of death, and no simple alternative emerges to overthrow the enchantments of the capitalist state.

That refusal to supply easy political alternatives or even a satisfying narrative closure has led to a common understanding of the novel as an 'elegy'. While crafting *To the Lighthouse*, Woolf would famously ponder 'a new name for my books to supplant "novel" [. . .] But what? Elegy?'[8] From this cue, many readers have viewed *Jacob's Room* in the tradition of the elegy.[9] Judith Martin, for example, observes that it 'is at once a sincere expression of bereavement and grief in the wake of the loss of life in World War I, as well as a critique of England's educational, political, and social institutions' and that 'Woolf takes up the concept of irrevocable loss not merely as a subject but also as a guiding formal principle'.[10] 'Elegy' is also an apt term because it suggests a liturgical alternative to nationalist modes of ritual commemoration that abounded in postwar culture. Rather than a neutral litany of mourning, lamentation for the dead – and exposing the forces that caused this death – becomes protest by opposing celebratory national commemorations that refashion military death as honourable sacrifice. The nation demands fealty and devotion, and military sacrifice is, perhaps, the highest form of worship – martyrdom for the state in witness to its power. Woolf's fictional elegy, therefore, is not neutral but is a pointed critique of postwar ideologies and practices. The public work of an elegy is often to transform the chaos of grief into orderly expression, an artistic effort towards redemption. But *Jacob's Room* resists any salvific telos; its world is too broken, too prone towards destruction to be salvaged even through a rich work of mourning.[11] Its profound sadness and loss becomes protest against the matrix of militarism, capitalism, imperialism and civil religion, and it offers glimpses of counter-liturgies for peace.

Describing Woolf's fiction as political liturgy and protest risks flouting her own statements about the value and essence of literature, especially in the 1920s when she was refining her new experimental style. Though her relationship with political art would change and develop through the 1930s, her comments about the autonomy of literary expression in the 1920s have been crucial to understanding modernism and her own complex handling of politics and history in fiction. Her famous accusation, for instance, that Edwardians such as H. G. Wells, Arnold Bennett and John Galsworthy wrote books of 'incompleteness and dissatisfaction' rather than novels has long shaped our understanding of modernist fiction.[12] Incomplete books that require political actions from their readers are troubling to Woolf because they seem to diminish the uniqueness of aesthetic objects. Treatises, manifestos, essays and pamphlets might serve just as well and perhaps even better to convey political 'messages'; art has its own mode and sphere of existence that can be flattened and diminished by didacticism.

And yet, her experimental form remains politically engaged through attempting to capture a full panoply of interconnected experiences and ideologies. As Judith C. Brown contends, war and capitalism merge, and Woolf's formal innovations – her attempts at totality – grapple with this new economic and political reality: 'The Great War, as Keynes understands it, would auger the slow collapse of the imperial order, and the shift toward an internationalised economy, or global capitalism; Woolf steps into this breach and gestures toward a new order.'[13] Her fiction, Brown argues 'attempts to express a comprehensive economy' and 'Woolf makes everything her subject, thus making totalizing desire the overwhelming question at the center of her fictional world'.[14] Nearly every paragraph shows a complex interweaving of the novel's themes as well as the political and ideological forces that determine the characters. *Jacob's Room* persistently foreshadows war, but that foreshadowing is not only in the gestures towards death and violence that occur in its myriad images of ruin. Woolf's style creates associations among Christianity, militarism, nationalism, imperialism and capitalism – forces that conspire to plunge the world into the war that claims Jacob's life. By analysing *Jacob's Room* within this complex network of associated ideologies, we might see the thoroughness of her depiction of a politics of death as well as her protest against its ravages.

In a small but important moment early in the novel, Betty Flanders decides without much deliberation to inscribe her late husband's tombstone with the phrase 'Merchant of this city' (*JR* 21). Scholarly investigation has shown her inaccuracy – 'Scarborough is not a city', note

Stuart N. Clarke and Jane Goldman – but little has been written about the ideological weight of Betty's inscription.[15] She is far from being a shill for the managerial class, yet when Betty grasps for something meaningful to encapsulate her spouse's life, an elevated claim about his commercial status seems to her most fitting. Her reasoning is vague, and the notion of Seabrook as a 'merchant' does not square with the town's perception of him as a dabbler in ranching, hunting, farming and other outdoor pursuits that 'run a little wild' (*JR* 21). Seabrook 'had only sat behind an office window for three months' late in his career, but Betty feels that this image of her husband is 'an example for the boys' (*JR* 22). Betty is not particularly committed to a capitalist vision of her spouse and family, but a mercantile sensibility shapes her actions as she grasps for a ritual way to manage her grief. She likewise does not seem especially religious, yet that mercantilism fuses with Christian ritual in the absence of other modes of public commemoration. During their marriage Betty feels Seabrook to be 'part of herself', but in death 'he had merged with the grass' and become 'one of a company' amid 'the decayed wreaths, the crosses of green tin, the narrow yellow paths, and the lilacs that drooped in April, with a scent like that of an invalid's bedroom, over the churchyard wall' (*JR* 22). There are competing forces in this image of Seabrook's burial place. Christian symbols in a graveyard by a church show human efforts to make sense of death through religious ritual, but the natural world overtakes these gestures towards immortality as everything surrounding the grave slides into decay. In Betty's mind, the fusion of natural order, religious rite and commercial identity sustains her memory of her husband, and the public activity of the church reinforces his posthumous presence: 'when, with her skirt hitched up, feeding the chickens, she heard the bell for service or funeral, that was Seabrook's voice – the voice of the dead' (*JR* 22). The association of Seabrook's gravestone and its public liturgy with violent death is amplified by Archer Flanders's interjection into Betty's thoughts: '"Wouldn't you like my knife, mother?" said Archer' (*JR* 22). Like so many moments throughout the novel, this brief and mundane mention of death, violence and weaponry projects beyond itself in a foreshadowing of war, and Betty seems vaguely aware of the connections between civil religious practices and violence: 'sounding at the same moment as the bell, her son's voice mixed life and death inextricably, exhilaratingly' (*JR* 22). Archer will remain alive at the novel's end, but like his brother he will be deployed to combat and lost to Betty, and the mixture of his voice – a semi-serious offer to use his knife against their rooster who attacks Betty during her chicken feedings – links combat with the commemoration for their dead father. Buried in a churchyard, commemorated by crosses and wreaths, and honoured as a 'merchant', Seabrook Flanders becomes in his afterlife an emblem of national commerce – a significant factor in Britain's imperial enterprises and the war that will eventually claim his sons. Seabrook Flanders's grave is one of many instances where civil religious liturgy fuses with capitalism and foreshadows war. The description of his memorial and Betty's relationship with his memory is a clear moment of elegy, foreshadowing the death and memorialisation to come in the novel, but it mounts little of the protest that Jacob's death elicits. Instead, Woolf establishes early in the novel how peacetime is casually and banally replete with the forces that produce English identity and the inescapable presence of Christian institutions and practices. Though gravemarkers and church bells do not seem as threatening as fiery celebrations or political rallies, Woolf shows how the tapestry of English life is preparing itself for the violent, militaristic, hot forms of nationalism that will later erupt.[16]

The novel opens with a glimpse of the Flanders family, rendered in Woolf's impressionistic style where small details create a tableaux with profound political significance. We are introduced to Betty as she writes a letter to Captain Barfoot using a pen with a 'gold nib' (*JR* 7). Ostentatious luxury is not one of Betty's prominent characteristics, but she is immediately presented with an indulgence in commodity culture, using a tool that signals wealth far beyond its particular use value. Betty's tear-blurred eyes while writing connect with her participation in capitalist structures of commodification and in turn link with her feelings for Captain Barfoot, a figure of naval commerce who also forges one of the novel's earliest relationships with the symbols of warfare. At the children's bedtime, Archer asks his mother, 'won't that steamer sink?' and Betty assures him that 'it won't' because 'the Captain's in bed long ago' (*JR* 16). The child's question, as Vara Neverow points out, foreshadows the coming war, not only through the general sense of destruction but with the specific connection to Archer himself who will ultimately serve in the King's Navy.[17] Images of and allusions to naval warfare recur throughout the novel, beginning with the setting in Scarborough which was the site of the first naval attack by Germany in the First World War.[18] Not many specific details are given about the Captain, his history or his current work, but the associations attached to him nonetheless suggest the inter-related web of commercial seafaring and naval warfare. Betty's tears at the beginning of the novel have their counterpart in her grief-stricken paralysis in the final chapter, confused and disoriented by the war's consuming of her sons.

War and commerce conjoin in Woolf's depiction of Betty's world, and the cultural force of Christianity shapes English nationalism and contributes to its politics of death. Betty's emotions distort her vision as she writes to Captain Barfoot, looking about with watery eyes. 'Tears made all the dahlias in her garden undulate in red waves and flashed the glass house in her eyes, and spangled the kitchen with bright knives', the narrator reports in an imagistic and distorted description that is psychedelic and reflected through consumer goods such as kitchen knives that metaphorically evoke tears (*JR* 8). This sentence shifts midway, however, from Betty's perspective to that of 'Mrs. Jarvis, the rector's wife' who knows of Betty's grief – or at least fancies that she does – and 'think[s] at church, while the hymn-tune played and Mrs. Flanders bent low over her little boys' heads, that marriage is a fortress and widows stray solitary in the open fields, picking up stones, gleaning a few golden straws, lonely, unprotected, poor creatures' (*JR* 8). Betty's particular experience of grief is thus consumed by a narrative informed by a religious authority whose position as 'rector's wife' seemingly gives her purview over the gendered space of motherhood. Religious ritual gives shape to the lives of Betty and her family, but little in this moment suggests a religious sensibility that is compassionate, sustaining or communal. The community here is only a function of 'proper' social order, where the rector's wife seems more judgemental than concerned. Through Woolf's free indirect style, we gather that Mrs Jarvis understands marriage not as a relationship or even as a moral institution but, in a distinctly martial metaphor, as a fortress to protect the otherwise vulnerable and possibly wayward single woman. Her image of vulnerability and poverty for the widow has biblical overtones, portraying her as a gleaner in echo of the figures of Ruth and Naomi from the Hebrew scriptures. The biblical story of Ruth rests on a base where economics are essential to the story's premise and narrative outcome. Widows without familial caretakers have almost no chance for survival apart from gleaning, and a marriage plot emerges from this basis. Though Betty does not seem as destitute as Ruth, she is still framed as economically vulnerable and in need of marriage – at least in the eyes of the rector's wife – and the loss of her sons to war robs her of one of her few familial support systems. Thus, Betty's emotional state fuses with commercial enterprises, the latent militarism building towards war, and the sense of social order crafted by the church. Consciously or not, she participates in liturgy that shapes her social world. It is a Christian liturgy of church worship and hymn singing, but the dimension of this liturgy that rises to the surface in Woolf's portrayal is its disciplining of social relations in language drawn from the military.

Christian liturgy is explicitly part of the narrative, but these religious references join with other cultural liturgies as part of Jacob's formation. In a description of other bathers at the seaside, the narrator tells of 'an enormous man and woman', whose size is presumably enlarged by the child's point of view (*JR* 11). Their presence is explained in a parenthetical aside that is likely not from Jacob's consciousness: '(it was early-closing day)' (*JR* 11). While the child plays on the beach as an unencumbered youth, the adults around him can only absorb such miniature holidays because the corporate cycles allow some freedom from work. We know little about this man and woman other than their grotesque appearance in Jacob's eyes, but the narrator's intrusion on the free indirect discourse reasserts the pervasiveness of capitalism. The seaside shifts from natural environment for childhood exploration to designated space for holiday, a reminder that adult leisure is entirely governed by the economic system that determines times of rest and times of mandatory labour. There is nothing particularly violent or belligerent in the specific appearance of the people enacting this capitalist liturgy, but Jacob is immediately terrified by the growing power of the ocean and rushes for his nanny whose stalwart presence comforts him despite his surging emotions, which, like his mother's, distort the world through their prism. It is in this moment that Jacob spots the skull that becomes one of the chapter's most indelible images: 'Sobbing, but absent-mindedly, he ran farther and farther away until he held the skull in his arms' (*JR* 12). From the subtle reminder that capitalism forms us, even in spaces dominated by natural power, the narrator presents one of the most potent images where death is implied, foreshadowed and embraced. Jacob's combination of fearful tears and absent-mindedness capture well the character traits that will persist with him into adulthood, his emotionalism matched by his distraction. Such traits make him beguiling to friends and lovers but also are a puzzlement. These are also the traits that solidify his path towards war, as he distractedly joins the military effort only to be cut down before we learn much about his feelings or any of his battle experiences. By holding the skull, the boy is united with death, and though his child's mind does not register the full meaning of this *memento mori* or take conscious account of the shaping force of capitalism on his experience at the sea, both elements fuse through Woolf's narrative style. In a striking coda, as Jacob sleeps in his bed with his feet by 'the sheep's jaw with the big yellow teeth', there is pouring rain outside that falls into a 'child's bucket [that] was half-full of rain water' and an 'opal-shelled crab slowly circled round the bottom, trying with its weakly legs to climb the steep side; trying again and falling back, and trying again and again' (*JR* 19). While Jacob sleeps he is surrounded by reminders of death and of living things caught in systems they cannot escape, doomed to repeat patterns that slowly kill them, and enthralled by enslaving liturgies.

Jacob is a notable example of this enthralment since he is so resolutely dissatisfied, aloof and non-committal. He is not a passionate agent of capitalist desire or of patriotic devotion. His 'faith', it would seem, is tenuous and minimal, and he ought to be the paradigmatic secular modern subject. But he is captured nevertheless by the enchantments of capitalism, the possessiveness of imperialism, and ultimately the blood sacrifice of nationalism. *Jacob's Room* exhibits an integrated network of capitalism and civil religion that primes him for leadership in the empire and sends him to the western front and his death. Though *Jacob's Room* offers glimpses of some alternatives to the 'politics of death' such as Woolf's rendering of the natural world and the underlying, unseen connections among people in community across time and space, the dominant feature of the novel is its portrayal of how Jacob is constituted in ways that lead to death. As is so often the case throughout *Jacob's Room*, the ideologies that claim us are shown to be inescapable and not something we can simply choose our way out of. Jacob's aloofness and disengagement appear as insufficient strategies for countering the politics of death.

That politics of death which emerges through the woven mesh of capitalism, militarism and civil religion acquires global resonance through Jacob's imperialist attitudes. A significant feature of Jacob's belief system is his casual embrace of empire that manifests through his approach to global citizenship. On the morning after Jacob's 'coronation' during the Guy Fawkes Day celebrations, he seeks respite from jingoistic displays through conversation with his friend Timmy Durrant with whom he can indulge a self-congratulatory and sophomoric appreciation of classical Greek literature. With abandon they shout quotations from Sophocles and Aeschylus on Haverstock Hill in the early hours of the morning. As if attempting to elevate himself above the masses and their political liturgies, Jacob meets his friend with a show of erudition: 'it seemed to both that they had read every book in the world; known every sin, passion, and joy. Civilizations stood round them like flowers ready for picking' (*JR* 122). Besides the self-aggrandisement of their boasts, their passion also drips with imperial possessiveness, a will to claim and own the regions they study and master; Jacob declares that he and his friend 'are the only people in the world who know what the Greeks meant' (*JR* 122). Education and knowledge have not expanded Jacob and Timmy's sensitivity or openness to the world; their learning is a mode of conquest. Rejecting the foolishness of the Guy Fawkes celebrations, Jacob reverts to another mode of jingoism, and his enthusiasm is ironically misunderstood by a stall-keeper who sells the young men their morning coffee: 'Taking Jacob for a military gentleman, the stall-keeper told him about his boy at Gibraltar' (*JR* 123). The stall-keeper misunderstands the intent of Jacob and Timmy's declarations about Greece – they are thinking literarily and philosophically – but he has in fact intuited their subtext. Pride of global ownership manifests in their fancies, and the stall-keeper recognises in their speech the tone of military conquest. In response to the stall-keeper, 'Jacob cursed the British army and praised the Duke of Wellington' (*JR* 123) – a form of impotent protest pitched to offend the old man that does little to separate Jacob from the imperial and militaristic ideologies that impose themselves on him. It is a subtle and unremarkable moment of daily conscription in the long foreshadowing arc where ceremony and liturgy, even when they are unwanted and casually resisted, still shape a person and portend his ceremonial death in war.[19] The central thrust of Woolf's novel are the myriad ways in which Jacob Flanders – heir to social success, elite education, economic comfort, imperial ambition, patriarchal satisfaction and military valour – is senselessly killed by these very forces of 'success'.

Jacob's privilege, economic power and imperialist attitudes are especially pronounced in the final sections of the novel where he goes on tour through Greece and Italy. Tourism, as Jacob performs it, is laced with imperialist values and through Woolf's formal style includes meaningful associations with global war and the market economy. Because of Jacob's early death in war, his youthful tourist experiences are among his final acts and defining features. We will never know if his attitudes towards the world beyond England could have changed as he aged, so we are left with a sense that his mode of global encounter – grasping at and consuming experiences and famous sites – is the sum total of his convictions. Through these associations, Woolf suggests that Jacob's attitude towards international relations is consistent with the descent into global violence that soon overtakes him. During his tour, Jacob thinks that 'after doing Greece he was going to knock off Rome', a possessive, dismissive and aggressive way of imagining global experience, and his view of Rome is largely shaped by his conquest of a region known for its once mighty empire (*JR* 220). He imagines writing about his experiences, but in a mode that would reinforce the sense of conquest along with barbs about the current state of British politics: 'it might turn to an essay upon civilization. A comparison between the ancients and moderns, with some pretty sharp hits at Mr. Asquith – something in the style of Gibbon' (*JR* 221). Italy was bad – 'all fierceness, bareness, exposure, and black priests shuffling along the roads' – but English 'civilization' is even worse (*JR* 220). These aspersions with imperialist overtones and gestures towards the religious life of the nation – those priests on the roadways – flash through Jacob's mind when he sees 'a lean Italian sportsman with a gun' on his way to the Parthenon, a moment of proleptic military violence associated with tourism (*JR* 222). Among the sights, Jacob also registers 'advertisements of corsets and of Maggi's consommé', images of commerce that seem to make as much of an impression on him as the historical ruins and global opportunities (*JR* 223). The sense that Jacob's tourism is spurred by imperialist sentiments is reinforced by the narrator's side commentary on his motives:

> at the age of twelve or so, having given up dolls and broken our steam engines, France, but much more probably Italy, and India almost for a certainty, draws the superfluous imagination [. . .] Jacob, no doubt, thought something in this fashion, the *Daily Mail* crumpled in his hand. (*JR* 223)

Reading a conservative English newspaper (that will later stoke anti-German sentiments), bored and distracted, Jacob feels the imaginative pull of empire where his fantasies grow ever more 'exotic' in the 'certainty' that India should be among his conquests, and his tourism is freighted with participation in the capitalist economy. His travel conquests are both imperialist and erotic – Sandra Wentworth Williams thinks about the 'English boy on tour' with desire (*JR* 233). As Judith Brown provocatively argues, '[t]he economies Woolf represents entwine the financial realities of the world with the libidinal economies of her characters that extend, like empire, around the world'.[20] Jacob's grasp on the world, cultural knowledge, and the people around him operates from a place of consumerist avarice, signs of his enmeshment in imperialism, militarism and global capitalism.

Near the novel's conclusion, Woolf draws together the public sounds of religious worship, the heights of finance capital and the ground bass of war. There is global sweep to her description of morning in Athens through the sounds that 'rouse most cities with their interpretation of the day's meaning' (*JR* 265). Christianity, through the morning church bells that we have also heard in London and Scarborough, 'interprets' first, but 'less melodiously, dissenters of different sects issue a cantankerous emendation' (*JR* 265). Those other 'sects' are not coded as traditional religions but rather appear to be the sounds made by industry and war: 'steamers, resounding like giant tuning forks [. . .] the thin voice of duty, piping in a white thread from the top of a funnel' and 'a long-drawn sigh between hammer-strokes' that one can hear 'from an open window even in the heart of London' (*JR* 265). Athens and London join with other cities of the world in this shared sense that Christianity, while remaining present in the background of urban life, is but one voice among many signs of labour that mix into a chorus with those 'hammer-strokes' – ambiguous noises that are either workers or gunfire.[21] In her report on the sounds of war from the South Downs, Woolf stated that a well-known writer called the blasts 'the hammer stroke of Fate', and here in *Jacob's Room* those hammer-strokes link industry with warfare in a dissenting chorus with the church (*E2* 40). While those sounds of work, religion and war define the urban space at its working-class strata, Woolf immediately moves from these sounds to Mrs Grandage's kettle, an aural link between the streets below and the powerbrokers such as Tom Grandage, who 'reads the golfing article in the *Times*, sips his coffee, wipes his moustaches, and is off to the office, where he is the greatest authority upon the foreign exchanges and marked for promotion' (*JR* 266). The public ritual of church bells joined with industrial labour and war thus forms a counterpoint to the people who nonchalantly oversee the international finance that affects so many other labourers. So often Woolf's fiction uses these kinds of unseen connections to suggest our underlying unity and the surprising relationships that persist even within a fragmentary and isolating modernity, but here the unseen connections are more sinister. Rising over the London skyline is 'the Bank of England', purview of Tom Grandage and his colleagues, whose inattention to the people he affects will contribute to global catastrophe (*JR* 267). Mundane elements of modernity such as 'shaving-glasses; and gleaming brass cans [and] all the jolly trappings of the day' have seemingly taken us beyond 'the melancholy medieval mists' and 'vanquished chaos' of the violent past, but the narrator's optimism about this modernity is ironically undercut by the knowledge that modern war has already erupted (*JR* 267). 'The conduct of daily life', she contends, 'is better than the old pageant of armies drawn out in battle array upon the plain', but we know that such pageantry is already underway and will engulf Jacob and his generation (*JR* 267).[22]

One of the novel's most explicit images of war integrates naval commerce and global industry in a description of the manoeuvres of 'battleships [that] ray out over the North Sea' (*JR* 254). There is some ambiguity in the description of these ships; it is unclear whether this is gunnery practice or a temporal flash forward to an actual battle, and the nationality of the military is also uncertain.[23] Regardless, the military action is dispassionate and destructive. The gunship's 'target [. . .] flames into splinters' at the command of the 'master gunner [who] counts the seconds, watch in hand – at the sixth he looks up' (*JR* 254). Six seconds of cold calculation lead to an explosion while the crew of 'a dozen young men in the prime of life descend with composed faces into the depths of the sea; and there impassively (though with perfect mastery of machinery) suffocate uncomplainingly together' (*JR* 254). The dozen men are of Jacob's generation, and their fate, whether dying or becoming impassive and machine-like weapons, will soon be his. On a hillside visible through field glasses, 'like blocks of tin soldiers', an army is destroyed, presumably by the ship's firepower, and some of these flattened men 'still agitate up and down like fragments of broken matchsticks' (*JR* 254). Little else in all of Woolf's oeuvre is as explicit about the battlefield, but even here the catastrophic violence is displaced onto metaphors where the dying men appear in the distance like toys and matches. The coldness of the scene and its abundance of metaphor creates irony that amplifies the sense of protest. Viewed dispassionately through binoculars, war looks like child's play – an echo and mirror image of the novel's opening where Jacob and Archer's play on the beach carries premonitions of violent death. But this scene of battleships is not an isolated image of war. Immediately, Woolf explains that 'these actions' – the devastations of warfare – bond 'together with the incessant commerce of banks, laboratories, chancellories, and houses of business' to become 'the strokes which oar the world forward, they say' (*JR* 254–5). The unidentified 'they' at the end of this sentence recurs through the paragraph, signalling the narrator's separation from the ideology she describes, calling into question whether the world is advanced by this fusion of military power and national finance. Business, science, banking and the government's exchequer are unequivocally fused with the violence at sea, and the narrator concludes the section with more opinions from conventional wisdom about the failure of artists to effectively contend with these political and economic realities. 'It is thus that we live, they say, driven by an unseizable force', the narrator reports: 'They say that the novelists never catch it; that it goes hurtling through their nets and leaves them torn to ribbons. This, they say, is what we live by – this unseizable force' (*JR* 255). This section of the novel begins with metafictional commentary about the challenges of capturing Jacob's character and ends with an unidentified 'they' – presumably the voices of public opinion and powerbrokers – refuting the capacity of fiction to grasp such powerful ideologies. Woolf begins with a statement about the aesthetic challenge she has set for herself, revealing an elusive character through indirection as a form of elegiac protest, and concludes with a counter-argument and rebuttal from a voice that insists on the inadequacies of fiction to be realistically political.

Jacob's Room stands as evidence for Woolf's confrontation with these twin challenges, and her exposure of the ways in which military and capitalist liturgies destroy people like Jacob becomes her mode of peace witness. By concluding in a space where Jacob and the narrative itself are 'unredeemed', Woolf offers a provocative vision that refuses to call for any singular 'solution' that might be redemptive.[24] Our grief at the despair Jacob leaves behind is the possible source for a new politics with liturgies that do not insist on prior regimes' versions of salvation. Woolf's first novel-length work of experimental fiction achieves a great deal of its power from a swirling array of images that create associations and impressions rather than the 'objective' and external descriptions familiar from realism, and this experimental form enables her to portray the dense and dynamic forces that captivate us and perpetuate cultures of death. Her response to this powerful matrix is a narrative that is 'supple, mobile, and trickster-like' as well, calling readers not into specific political action but into a heightened awareness of the powers that destroy and into a mode of lamentation as protest.[25] While the villagers Woolf encountered in the South Downs staked their hopes for a ceasefire on the magical enchantments of their church bell, *Jacob's Room* imagines a more complex, agonised, contentious and durable vision of peace.

Notes

1. Virginia Woolf, 'Heard on the Downs: The Genesis of Myth', *The Essays of Virginia Woolf, Volume Two, 1912–1918*, ed. by Andrew McNeillie (San Diego: Harcourt Brace Jovanovich, 1987), 40–2 (40). Further references will be included within the main text.

2. James K. A. Smith, *Desiring the Kingdom: Worship, Worldview, and Cultural Formation; Volume 1 of Cultural Liturgies* (Grand Rapids: Baker Academic, 2009), 86.
3. Eugene McCarraher, *The Enchantments of Mammon: How Capitalism Became the Religion of Modernity* (Cambridge, MA: Belknap, 2019), 4. See also William T. Cavanaugh, *Migrations of the Holy: God, State, and the Political Meaning of the Church* (Grand Rapids: Eerdmans, 2011).
4. Stanley Hauerwas and Romand Coles, *Christianity, Democracy, and the Radical Ordinary: Conversations Between a Radical Democrat and a Christian* (Eugene: Cascade Books, 2008), 8.
5. Hauerwas and Coles, *Christianity*, 8.
6. Stuart N. Clarke and Susan Sellers, 'Introduction', to *Jacob's Room: The Cambridge Edition of the Works of Virginia Woolf* (Cambridge: Cambridge University Press, 2020), xxxviii.
7. Virginia Woolf, *Jacob's Room: The Cambridge Edition of the Works of Virginia Woolf*, ed. by Stuart N. Clarke and David Bradshaw (Cambridge: Cambridge University Press, 2020), 48. Further references will be included within the main text.
8. Virginia Woolf, *The Diary of Virginia Woolf, Volume Three: 1925–1930*, ed. by Anne Olivier Bell (Harmondsworth: Penguin, 1982), 34.
9. Debates remain about the irony and sincerity of this elegy. See, for example Alex Zwerdling, '*Jacob's Room*: Woolf's Satiric Elegy', *ELH*, 48. 4 (Winter 1981), 894–913; Kathleen Wall, 'Significant Form in *Jacob's Room*: Ekphrasis and the Elegy', *Texas Studies in Literature and Language*, 44.3 (2002), 302–23; Kelly S. Walsh, 'The Unbearable Openness of Death: Elegies of Rilke and Woolf', *Journal of Modern Literature*, 32.4 (2009), 1–21; Erin Penner, *Character and Mourning: Woolf, Faulkner, and the Novel Elegy of the First World War* (Charlottesville: University of Virginia Press, 2019).
10. Judith Martin, 'Elegy and the Unknowable Mind in *Jacob's Room*', *Studies in the Novel*, 47.2 (Summer 2015), 176–92 (179, 176).
11. Sanja Bahun argues that much of modernist literature can be understood as enacting a tension about representing 'the melancholic utterance', manifesting in what Bahun calls 'countermourning' (13). For Woolf's late fiction specifically, Bahun focuses on her 'ambivalence of feelings' that integrates with her complex politics (157). My reading of *Jacob's Room* resonates with this sense that simplistic modes of mourning might have less political force and in effect be too consistent with the nationalistic versions of commemoration. See Bahun, *Modernism and Melancholia: Writing as Countermourning* (Oxford: Oxford University Press, 2014).
12. Virginia Woolf, 'Character in Fiction', *The Essays of Virginia Woolf, Volume Three, 1919–1924*, ed. by Andrew McNeillie (San Diego: Harcourt Brace Jovanovich, 1988), 420–38 (427).

13. Judith C. Brown, '"This Globe, Full of Figures": Woolf's Comprehensive Economy', *Yearbook of Comparative Literature*, 60 (2014), 105–23 (107).
14. Brown, 'Woolf's Comprehensive Economy', 107.
15. Clarke and Goldman, 'Explanatory Notes', to *Jacob's Room: The Cambridge Edition of the Works of Virginia Woolf* (Cambridge: Cambridge University Press, 2020), 329.
16. For detailed analysis of 'hot' versus 'banal' nationalism, see Michael Billig, *Banal Nationalism* (London: Sage, 1995).
17. Vara Neverow, 'Notes to *Jacob's Room*', in Virginia Woolf, *Jacob's Room*, ed. by Vara Neverow (Orlando: Harcourt, 2008), 192.
18. See Masami Usui, 'The German Raid on Scarborough in *Jacob's Room*', *Virginia Woolf Miscellany*, 35 (Fall 1990), 7.
19. For more on the power of 'daily conscription' see Judith Butler, *Frames of War: When Is Life Grievable?* (London: Verso, 2009).
20. Brown, 'This Globe, Full of Figures', 114.
21. Neverow suggests that this is either gunnery practice or actual combat audible through the open windows in August 1914 ('Notes', 299).
22. Vincent Sherry argues that in this moment 'Woolf is putting the practices of liberal rationalist language on the line', calling into question the decrease in international violence that modernity ought to supposedly bring (74). Sherry, '*Jacob's Room*: Occasions of War, Representations of History', in *A Companion to Virginia Woolf*, ed. by Jessica Berman (Oxford: Wiley-Blackwell, 2016), 67–78.
23. Clarke and Goldman, 'Explanatory Notes', 664–5.
24. On the political power of embracing 'unredemption', see Karen Bray, *Grave Attending: A Political Theology for the Unredeemed* (New York: Fordham University Press, 2019).
25. Hauerwas and Coles, *Christianity, Democracy, and the Radical Ordinary*, 8.

Works Cited

Bahun, Sanja. *Modernism and Melancholia: Writing as Countermourning*. Oxford: Oxford University Press, 2014.

Billig, Michael. *Banal Nationalism*. London: Sage, 1995.

Bray, Karen. *Grave Attending: A Political Theology for the Unredeemed*. New York: Fordham University Press, 2019.

Brown, Judith C. '"This Globe, Full of Figures": Woolf's Comprehensive Economy'. *Yearbook of Comparative Literature*, 60 (2014), 105–23.

Butler, Judith. *Frames of War: When Is Life Grievable?* London: Verso, 2009.

Cavanaugh, William T. *Migrations of the Holy: God, State, and the Political Meaning of the Church*. Grand Rapids: Eerdmans, 2011.

Clarke, Stuart N. and Jane Goldman. Explanatory notes to *Jacob's Room*, by Virginia Woolf, 291–723. Cambridge: Cambridge University Press, 2020.

Clarke, Stuart N. and Susan Sellers. 'Introduction' to *Jacob's Room*, by Virginia Woolf, xxxvii–xcvi. Cambridge: Cambridge University Press, 2020.

Hauerwas, Stanley and Romand Coles. *Christianity, Democracy, and the Radical Ordinary: Conversations Between a Radical Democrat and a Christian*. Eugene: Cascade Books, 2008.

McCarraher, Eugene. *The Enchantments of Mammon: How Capitalism Became the Religion of Modernity*. Cambridge, MA: Belknap, 2019.

Martin, Judith. 'Elegy and the Unknowable Mind in *Jacob's Room*'. *Studies in the Novel*, 47.2 (Summer 2015), 176–92.

Neverow, Vara. 'Introduction' to *Jacob's Room*, by Virginia Woolf, xxxvii–xciv. Orlando: Harcourt, 2008.

Penner, Erin. *Character and Mourning: Woolf, Faulkner, and the Novel Elegy of the First World War*. Charlottesville: University of Virginia Press, 2019.

Sherry, Vincent. '*Jacob's Room*: Occasions of War, Representations of History'. In *A Companion to Virginia Woolf*, ed. by Jessica Berman, 67–78. Oxford: Wiley-Blackwell, 2016.

Smith, James K. A. *Desiring the Kingdom: Worship, Worldview, and Cultural Formation; Volume 1 of Cultural Liturgies*. Grand Rapids: Baker Academic, 2009.

Usui, Masami. 'The German Raid on Scarborough in *Jacob's Room*'. *Virginia Woolf Miscellany*, 35 (Fall 1990), 7.

Wall, Kathleen. 'Significant Form in *Jacob's Room*: Ekphrasis and the Elegy'. *Texas Studies in Literature and Language*, 44.3 (2002), 302–23.

Walsh, Kelly S. 'The Unbearable Openness of Death: Elegies of Rilke and Woolf'. *Journal of Modern Literature*, 32.4 (2009), 1–21.

Woolf, Virginia. *The Diary of Virginia Woolf: Volume Three, 1925–1930*, ed. by Anne Olivier Bell. Harmondsworth: Penguin, 1982.

——, *The Essays of Virginia Woolf, Volume Two, 1912–1918*, ed. by Andrew McNeillie. San Diego: Harcourt Brace Jovanovich, 1987.

——, *The Essays of Virginia Woolf, Volume Three, 1919–1924*, ed. by Andrew McNeillie. San Diego: Harcourt Brace Jovanovich, 1988.

——, *Jacob's Room: The Cambridge Edition of the Works of Virginia Woolf*, 1922, ed. by Stuart N. Clarke with the participation of David Bradshaw. Cambridge: Cambridge University Press, 2020.

Zwerdling, Alex. '*Jacob's Room*: Woolf's Satiric Elegy'. *ELH*, 48.4 (Winter 1981), 894–913.

Part II

Labour and the Marketplace

Chapter 6

Between the Houses: Woolf and the Property Market

Rachel Bowlby

'Driving past, people said to each other: "I wonder if that'll ever come into the market?"'[1] Taken from *Between the Acts*, this remark relates to a pretty old house in the countryside – Pointz Hall, where the opening scene of the novel has just been recounted and where all the subsequent scenes will be set. Rather than being spoken by any particular character, or at any specified time, it is offered generically, as simply the sort of thing that gets said.

The ready comment encapsulates a quintessentially twentieth-century perspective on an age-old sight. More and more, what is seen in a house is not merely a building but a monetary value and a potential object of exchange. However unique and exclusive, houses seen from this point of view are not fixed in their one location but move intermittently into a space known as 'the market'. This paradoxical mobility of *l'immobilier* – goods that, by definition, do not move – says everything about the slow but sure transition, now taken for granted, from a world in which houses are most naturally identified with their place and their occupants, to present-day times, market-driven, when anything, houses included, may be put into circulation, given a price, and moved from one owner to the next. Motoring past, what 'people' see is not a home and a history, so much as a future prospect of purchase, with all that that entails. They see a dream house: a fantasy also taking the form of an investment. The past and the beauty add to the value of that – a value which, even more paradoxically, may factor in the nostalgia for a former time in which pretty old houses were not yet primarily seen as potential objects of purchase.

These complex but now conventional ways of seeing are further pointed up by the first part of the paragraph in which the viewing vignette so fleetingly appears:

> Pointz Hall was seen in the light of an early summer morning to be a middle-sized house. It did not rank among the houses that are mentioned in guide books. It was too homely. But this whitish house with the grey roof [...] was a desirable house to live in. Driving past, people said to each other: 'I wonder if that'll ever come into the market?' And to the chauffeur: 'Who lives there?' (*BTA* 7)

The strikingly formal passive construction – 'was seen' – is like a pastiche of the style of the 'guide books'. But then, as if taking in the more 'homely' associations attributed to the house that fails to qualify as guidebook material, the scene shifts into the momentarily adjacent interior of a passing motor car, to eavesdrop on the kind of thing 'people' in such spaces supposedly always say, directly quoted. That 'desirable' verdict references the typical formulation of an estate agent's promotional description, now embedded into people's own judgement – or rating – of what they see; in that context, the casual speculation about coming into the market follows as if automatically.

The house's desirability is about what it would be like 'to live in', rather than purely because of its market value. But the very word seems to keep the house itself at the distance from which (as here) it is seen; or (in the case of an estate agent's description) from which it is described. A desired object is what someone does desire, but a desirable object is the kind of thing people are thought to desire, in a likely or typical situation. Thus the attractiveness of the 'des. res.', in the advertising abbreviation of the period, is part of its market value, as presented to any potential buyer. A desired object will no longer be desired in the same way once it has been obtained; whereas a 'desirable' object (and they may be one and the same) remains a desirable object after you have bought it and moved in. Which in itself, by a further twist of promotional logic, may be part of the reason why you desired it in the first place, or why it can be enjoyed, in all senses, once it has been acquired and the buyer now lives there for real.

The final words of the paragraph point out a further division, both inside the car and in terms of the house's perception. 'And to the chauffeur' introduces a character presumed to have local knowledge of a kind that the car's other occupants do not. He has not been included in the exchange about the house coming into the market; that is what such people say 'to each other'. He may (though it turns out he can't) be able to answer the question 'Who lives there?' The chauffeur's treatment reinforces the social distance between him and the 'people' he is driving, and the question put to him leads to the spelling out of a conventional kind of distinction between the residents of a rural area:

> The chauffeur didn't know. The Olivers, who had bought the place something over a century ago, had no connection with the Warings, the Elveys, the Mannerings or the Burnets; the old families who had all inter-married, and lay in their deaths inter-twisted, like the ivy roots, beneath the churchyard wall. (*BTA* 7)

In one way the ivy image abolishes worldly differences: all these people are now mixed up, without individual or even human identity (they resemble the roots of a plant). But in another way, the social differences remain as they were in the living, above-ground world. Only certain named families 'inter-married' and dwell and decay together in the same part of the churchyard. Their inferiority – below ground, almost as though below stairs – confirms their difference from 'The Olivers', distinctively on their own, who came from elsewhere (and have probably found their spouses, since they came, from beyond this particular parish).

On the surface of the passage, however, is the contrast between long-established villagers, whose roots are here, and those still perceived as having arrived from elsewhere: '*Only* something over a hundred and twenty years the Olivers had been there' (*BTA* 7). This must be in part a joke about the difference between urban and rural understandings of local histories, as well as the clichés of comment upon that supposed difference: as if a century were no time at all in this place untouched by change. But it is vital that when these Olivers turned up they 'bought the place'. It had 'come into the market' back then, already.

Later in the novel, the difference is stated again, or rather enacted, as the two sorts of well-to-do family sit apart at the village pageant:

> The audience were assembling [. . .] Among them [. . .] were representatives of our most respected families – the Dyces of Denton; the Wickhams of Owlswick; and so on. Some had been there for centuries, never selling an acre. On the other hand there were new comers, the Manresas, bringing the old houses up to date, adding bathrooms. (*BTA* 46–7)

So the distinction between the families and the newcomers is directly mapped onto a supplementary distinction between, on the one hand, those who have simply continued to live and die exactly where their ancestors did the same, without reference to real estate ('never selling an acre'); and on the other, those who turned up from elsewhere and took over a bit of it, making it modern. They came, they saw, they bought (and they added bathrooms).

Houses are perfect manifestations of the symbolic force of capitalism as invisible organiser and transformer of cultural perceptions. On the face of it, they are physical buildings to be lived in and occupied; as such, they stay where they are, in one place. At the same time, they move into another zone once they 'come into the market'. This market occurs in a different sphere from those weekly events for the buying and selling of produce and livestock (and which contribute still to the retro attractions of rural living). Rather – by this mid-twentieth-century time – 'the market' refers to the governing economic system that shapes almost every human transaction and situation; those that it doesn't stand out by their very exception or exemption.[2] Taking its cue from the passing attention in *Between the Acts* to a house that might one day be for sale, this essay begins to reflect on Woolf's occasional representations of the property market: the bought and the sold, the lived in and left, the rented and rented out.

The property market itself is both thoroughly *sui generis* – other things are portable, but in this case the buyer must move to what they have bought – and at the same time representative of larger and abstract changes in the practices and norms of an increasingly capitalistic economy.[3] Such changes do not just affect how things are done and described, but also get into the corners of everyday experience and anyone's sense of who they are. In that seemingly casual comment about a nice house that might someday be purchasable are the roots – in a newly entangled sense – of a whole mode of mythical modern aspiration whereby something called a property 'ladder' is meant to take you up in the world, level by level, one rung at a time. Enter that classic modern character known as the 'prospective' buyer.

The property market is an exemplary and also highly peculiar segment of the fast-moving market economy of Britain between the wars and after. It is peculiar in that every property for sale, unlike almost every other type of modern commodity, is a one-off. For any given residential unit there is no exact equivalent. Even with the most standard of 'little boxes', whether houses or flats, each residence has its own unique position on the grid, or within the building, with different aspects of light or sound and other environmental features. Yet property is also exemplary rather than exceptional, in that it demonstrates the power of the market to make everything, anything, everywhere (especially) into a commodity. A town, any town, can be shown as worth visiting, or worth moving to (worth paying money to look at it or live in it). A house, any house, can be seen as having a market value, to be regarded as a desirable object or site of purchase or investment.

Woolf herself, as we shall see, was an experienced participant in the country property market. From the start of their marriage she and Leonard maintained a second home in the East Sussex countryside, while living mainly in London. This was a couple who, in the now consecrated phrase for a form of privileged migration, routinely 'divided their time' between the primary home in the city and the country retreat. In part it was a pattern sustained from Woolf's own childhood years, with long summer holidays in Cornwall. That pattern in turn has something in common with the centuries-old seasonal movement of the upper classes between a country seat and a town house. From the modern side, it also belongs with the now standard alternation of work and vacation, pressure and peacefulness.

Yet despite this common social ground, in *Between the Acts* Woolf's narrator is at a remove from the generic would-be buyers of the 'desirable' old residence. On other writing occasions, in essays and letters especially, there is a further separation when she shows an unargued contempt for another type of home, not the unique old pile but the masses of newly built residences now visible both across the countryside and in the recently developed suburbs of south London. Often but not always, the disparagement is directed against the lower-middle-class occupants of little houses in the outer suburbs of the city – some hapless clerk going home to his dreary dwelling in Croydon or Surbiton. In countryside settings, this attitude sometimes transfers straightforwardly to the proliferation of new-build small houses that Woolf observes on car journeys in Sussex.[4] There is praise in *Between the Acts* for the 'light of evening that reveals depths in water and makes even the red brick bungalow radiant' (*BTA* 116); with that 'even' the bungalows are both redeemed and damned again, since the word makes them into a worst-case sight that would otherwise – in a clearer light – constitute a disturbance to the picture of tranquillity. And as Clara Jones has described, there is an equally negative attitude in relation to the larger 'villas' constructed in country areas for wealthier customers.[5]

The social territory of *Between the Acts* is ambiguous in a further way. Pointz Hall is no new-build excrescence, but a house that has been there for centuries. Yet its twentieth-century occupants have urban as much as pastoral connections. Thus the 'stockbroker' Giles, personification of capitalist speculation, commutes to the city from the country house where he looks the part of the farmer he wishes he was, as in an older type of economy. For city dwellers in the countryside – those who go back and forth, whether daily or at longer intervals – the country is valued because it is regarded as free from or still unaffected by the stresses of modern living, conceived in terms of a constant demand for hurry. Thus the countryside is appreciated as much for the difference of time as the difference of place. The view is more beautiful; but also, the pace is slower. The modern life from which the metropolitan people may seek to disencumber themselves is characterised by its relentless movement, as if in a forward direction; the country world, on the other hand, keeps calmly on, as the days and the seasons go round. Its inhabitants stay where they are, in their one place; but it is from the vantage point of modernity – in the car that speeds past, for instance – that their continuity shows up. That stability is visible only because of the mobile perspective epitomised by the travelling visitor or 'new comer' – a term that already includes both the movement and the change that drive the modern economy.

For in *Between the Acts* the pastoral idyll, imagined as timeless, is already interrupted by the counter-demands – or attractions – of contemporary efficiency and inventions. If the congregation at the church is dwindling, then that is why, and the vicar knows it and states it with slogan-like certainty: 'The motor bike, the motor bus, and the movies – when Mr Streatfield called his roll call, he laid the blame on them' (*BTA* 47). An actual motor bike turns up early on in the novel, when Giles's wife Isa orders fish for lunch by telephone – a new technology, and an instant connection at a distance. The fish is delivered, not much later, by 'Mitchell's boy', who 'jumped off his motor bike', prompting a historical comparison with times gone by: 'There was no feeding the pony with lumps of sugar at the kitchen door, nor time for gossip, since his round had been increased' (*BTA* 21). The extended round is a matter of countable productivity, a modern demand for speed which the motor bike both fulfils and sets in motion. The lingering gossip and lumps of sugar then frame that modern efficiency, appearing now as a wistful image of slower times gone by.

At a later point in the novel this opposition between the olden days and modern performance is brought out once again, but with the opposite emphasis. Prompted by the village pageant's survey of English history, some elderly members of the audience are talking about what has changed in their living memory:

> Well, look at my daughter. To the right, just behind you. Forty, but slim as a wand. Each flat has its refrigerator . . . It took my mother half the morning to order dinner . . . We were eleven. Counting servants, eighteen in the family . . . Now they simply ring up the Stores . . . (*BTA* 95)

Again, the present time is viewed by reference to a comparison with the past, but here that past is represented as over-demanding, rather than leisurely. For 'my mother', every task took for ever, whereas younger women of today can simply phone up the shop and have food delivered, as Isa does. Also, the daughter's flat might be anywhere; the conveniences of modern life are independent of where in particular she happens to live. For Mitchell's boy, on the other hand, time has become a scarce resource; he can no longer stop and chat when he has to keep to a schedule.

Woolf's novels often incorporate detailed descriptions of the dwellings in which their characters live – from the decaying Scottish holiday house in *To the Lighthouse* (1927) to the London town house of *Mrs Dalloway*; other obvious instances include Jacob's titular 'room', and Orlando's (365-room) mansion. *The Years* has an instance of aristocratic migration between the country place and the London house, with Kitty making the northwards journey on an overnight sleeper train from King's Cross: it is the grander version, unrelated to working life, of what happens weekly with modern businessmen like Giles who travel between the place of work in the city and the home in the country. But despite the frequent suggestion of movements between or back to homes of various kinds, there are few Woolfian references to the finding of somewhere to live in the first place, or to the other (trade) side of that process.

One partial exception to the first of these absences is a sympathetic representation of a single, older woman who is thinking about a place to buy to live. With that concentration of focus, the 'driving past' scenario shifts into seeing a house as a possible future identity, as well as an object of purchase. So it is that with the family home about to be sold, and with an easy modern mobility, the Eleanor of 1911 in *The Years* is passing through Dorsetshire villages and thinking of where, with her newfound freedom and financial means, she might choose to put herself:

> What shall I do now? Live there? she asked herself, as she passed a very respectable Georgian villa in the middle of a street. No, not a village she said to herself; and they jogged through the village. What

about that house then, she said to herself, looking at a house with a verandah among some trees. But then, she thought, I should turn into a grey-haired lady cutting flowers with a pair of scissors and tapping at cottage doors.[6]

'What about that house then?' A new house, for the one who makes the move, now becomes a decision about what kind of person to be (or to dream of being): a lifestyle choice. So many options, anywhere and everywhere. As many possible selves to choose to be, or not to be.

For the second theme, it is true that *Mrs Dalloway*'s Septimus Smith worked before the war at the firm of 'Sibleys and Arrowsmiths, auctioneers, valuers, land and estate agents' (the string of stated functions is standard at the time). He did it well and was promoted, but otherwise no details are given of the job or its setting.[7] There is also one protracted scene of *The Years* which takes place in an estate agent's office. This is the culminating London party that occupies most of the long Present Day section at the end. But perhaps what is most remarkable about this episode is that it is possible not to notice its setting at all. The party has nothing to do with the businesses in whose premises it partly takes place, in the spillover downstairs part of the house. 'They've let these rooms, I suppose' (*TY* 263) is how one guest puts it when she arrives – referring to her hosts, who live in and own the house as a whole.

That offices are what the venue normally is only comes to light at a point when a detail of that setting leads to a misunderstanding. There is a poster on the wall that an elderly Irish guest misidentifies as a 'manifesto' making some kind of political statement – 'I don't join societies, I don't sign any of these' (*TY* 306). In reality it is an advertisement for a house for sale in a Sussex coastal town – as North Pargiter discovers when he takes a look at it later: 'He turned his back and pretended to read the particulars of a desirable property at Bexhill, which Patrick had called for some reason "a manifesto"' (*TY* 307).[8] Comically, this muddle of 'money and politics' (*TY* 304), as North has just characterised the topics of the party conversations, might then suggest an unspoken clash between radical activism and the property market. Bang in the middle of the 1930s (the novel was published in 1937), the mix-up hints at conflations endemic to the promotional culture that posters epitomised at the time. In what is already a juxtaposition of commerce and hospitality, workplace and leisure venue, public and private spaces, this incident then makes its own kind of background statement, within the novel, about the emerging predominance of a culture of buying and selling – of everything and anything, all the time.

The distinctiveness of this odd office party shows up in other ways if we contrast its basic setting, the ultra-functional function room, with that of the event that takes place at the end of *Mrs Dalloway*, a decade earlier. The finale of both novels is a gathering of people, and people's pasts, for a special occasion at a specific time. But the grand location for the Dalloways' largesse is reduced in *The Years* to a one-night-only commercial timeshare, involving office premises that are rented out within the house of the hosts. This later party happens in adjoining spaces that are used by purveyors of standard mid-twentieth-century commercial and legal services (there is a solicitor's office as well as the estate agent's rooms).

A further contrast can be made with the 'des. res.' of *Between the Acts*. In that novel the prospective buyers (as they briefly become) are *in situ*, glimpsing the actual place that, if only for now, appears to them as the object of their dreams. In *The Years*, on the other hand, the Bexhill placard is many motor-car miles from the place it is advertising, and it elicits no sign of desire or even interest from any of the people who happen to pass it over the course of the pages and hours that take place in the room where it is on display. It is not described; it must be a common enough kind of design. But it is also an indication of the type of direction that the dreams of 'ordinary people' (an expression that the novel uses more than once) are encouraged to take.[9]

The combination of the quasi-touristic scene (in *Between the Acts*) and the long-distance advertising of a house for sale (in *The Years*) is indicative now of the growing importance of buying and selling houses. Yet it remains the case that Woolf's novels do not feature the property market of her time in any extensive way, any more than they feature the share-trading world of the stockbroker, say. From inside the cars driving past Pointz Hall, the interest evoked by the sight of an attractive old house is partly, already, financial, and stated as such ('the market'); but it is fleeting and conventional. What is said is the sort of thing that 'people' of a certain class do say at such moments, and it does make the house and its view inextricable from their possible marketability. But the buying and selling of country houses is not represented as being at the centre of their thoughts, whether in general or on this particular day out. In this context the hints in Woolf's last two novels of a preoccupation with property seem suitably prophetic, but also decidedly minor. By way of contrast to this relative absence, shops and shopping, the places and behaviours that form the background of everyday monetary exchanges, are present in all

Woolf's novels, and sometimes emphatically. 'Mrs Dalloway said she would buy the flowers herself', in the famous opening; the novel goes on to display a full range of retailing formats and buying experiences, from the upmarket florist's to the impoverished flower-seller on the street. Beyond these small-scale enterprises, the novel also explores the largest and latest modes of commercial expansion. It features a department store, that institution that takes over the functions of specialist shops, to sell 'all the commodities in the world'; there is also an aeroplane taking over the sky itself to promote a brand of confectionery via the latest mode of advertising (*MD* 113, 18–19).[10] The stress on the shops seems natural in the light of their significance in the daily life of the time – women's especially. Equally, by this logic of social reflection, the relative absence of real-estate interests would seem to conform to the habits of interwar middle-class society. This is not yet, far from it, the British culture of sixty years later, with its fervent promotion of universal home ownership.

So far, so muted, then. Yet pause again, and suddenly, where you least expect it, out of the pages of other Woolfian writings there steps a quite different buying character and a quite different level of attention to the property market as a spur to its own special dramas of freak desire joined to resolute calculation. The protagonist of this story is none other than Mrs Woolf herself, as she describes what she did and how she felt in the early summer of 1919 – a period during which, in rapid succession, she bought not one house but two, one after the other – with the second abruptly taking the place of the first as an object of new desire, and the first sold on without her and Leonard ever having lived in it. Put like this it is a story that might better suit a person in the business of twenty-first-century property development, seeking primarily to make a swift profit. Which she did, as it happens, and took some pleasure in that supplementary outcome. But this is only one element of an extraordinary swirl of events and feelings that make up this house-buying adventure of the middle of 1919, as recounted if not re-staged by the principal character herself in her diary and letters at the time. Decades before either *The Years* or *Between the Acts*, Woolf was living through and writing down a house-purchase story that leaves far behind those novels' gentle suggestions of the peculiarities of the property market.

The story has multiple points of entry, but one beginning is this. In the late spring of 1919, Leonard and Virginia Woolf knew they would have to leave Asheham House, the country house in Sussex which they had been renting for several years. They had been making preliminary enquiries with a view to finding another place. Then one day Virginia happened upon a house which she bought on impulse. In a letter to her sister: 'I saw a house in Lewes on Monday and we've offered to buy it freehold for £300 – very old, small, but rather charming – however some one else is after it and has probably got it.'[11] In her diary, Woolf recounts a longer version of how it was that she had come across this unusual place, the Round House. It reads as an exemplary story of the build-up of buying desire, exposing the step-by-step process of a pre-purchase seduction. There is nothing like it in any of her novels.

To begin with, there was a visit to an estate agency in Lewes, unplanned and casual and introduced as such:

> To pass the time, more than anything, I asked Mrs Wycherley about houses; & she, after tepidly recommending some that were impossible & sketching the difficulties of the situation, bethought her of one newly on the market, small, old, actually in Lewes, & perhaps a little humble for one used to lodge at Asheham. I pricked my ears, since this is always the way one is told of what one wants.[12]

The commentary goes in two seemingly contradictory directions as Woolf first interprets Mrs Wycherley's remark as a shrewd marketing tactic and then, straight after, casts the narrative into the mode of something like an ironic fairy tale (bewyched!). So the intrepid hero makes the journey as directed,

> Off I went, up Pipes Passage, under the clock, & saw rising at the top of the sloping path a singular shaped roof, rising into a point, & spreading out in a circular petticoat all round it. (*D1* 279)

Upon arrival she encounters another ambiguous helper figure, which moves the story on: 'Then things began to go a little quicker. An elderly and humble cottage woman the owner, showed me over.' Now at the later time of telling the tale, Woolf wonders about the promptings of her feelings then:

> How far my satisfaction with the small rooms, & the view, & the ancient walls, & the wide sitting room, & the general oddity & character of the whole place were the result of finding something that would do, that one could conceive living in, that was cheap (freehold £300) I don't know; but as I inspected the rooms I became conscious of a rising desire to settle here; to have done with looking about; to take this place, & make it one's permanent lodging. (*D1* 279)

The tick-box list of appealing features in the first half of this long sentence balances and makes way for the contrasting excitement and different logic of the 'rising desire' of the second, now with a drive towards completion, 'to have done' with the quest and to find an eternal or 'permanent' place to stay. The next sentence carries on to even greater heights, in effect making no fewer than three separate versions and times of Virginia, as the diarist now ruefully sets herself at a future distance from the character whose emotions at that time are being described. Like a limbering up for the nebulous genre, as yet unnamed, of property porn, this may be the most comically erotic passage in any of Woolf's writing: 'Perhaps later', she says, 'it will amuse me to read how I went from one grade to another of desire; till I felt physically hot & ardent, ready to surmount all obstacles.'

Ready. 'In short I took it there & then, being egged on by Wycherley's hesitation, & hints of a purchaser who had already asked for the refusal.' This rival, real or not, performs a clinching role. The mere suggestion of their existence persuades the present prospective purchaser, decisively overcoming the 'hesitation' that she chooses to see as 'Wycherley's' rather than her own. And in fact it is she not Mr Wycherley who deals with potential drawbacks as well as positive aspects, in the phase just before the final capitulation. At that point, with a slight change of mood, she reflects more calmly on the objective qualities of the place. The sense of omnipotence, 'ready to surmount all obstacles', gives way to a simpler statement of the property's location up and away from the town:

> I liked the way the town dropped from the garden leaving us on a triangular island, vegetables one side, grass the other; the path encircling the round house amused me; nor are we overlooked. (*D1* 279)

Those last four words shift the tone as though from the storybook tale of an enchanted hilltop castle to a homeowner's practical statement of privacy; it is the difference between a limitless 'view', looking out, that special feature already noted, and the reverse issue of containment and constraint through being on view yourself, to neighbours or passers-by.

The episode stands as a superb textbook case of the four-stage sequence of selling recommended by marketing practitioners in every manual of salesmanship at this time, for application to any type of goods. The process consists of inducing and noting a standard series of changes in the customer's state of mind with regard to the purchase in view. If all goes according to plan, she will move smoothly along a line that goes from an initial Attraction, then on to Interest, then Desire, and finally Action, which is the moment of deciding to buy.[13] Stress is laid on what the salesman is meant to do to procure a progression on to the next level up of this individual campaign. In particular, he must make suggestions – how nice this would look in your home! – and he must overcome objections – it's all right, you really can pay for it, thanks to our simple instalment plan.

But with the Round House little active intervention occurs; the prospect (Mrs Woolf) appears to have taken herself through each stage pretty much on her own, as she goes once again through the mental process in her later report to herself of that day. All it takes from the salesman – but it is decisive – is the tiny, lingering tweak of the possible pre-existing buyer. A passage from *How to Be a Successful Estate Agent*, a handbook published in 1904, summarises, from the agent's perspective, the attitude to adopt at the closing stage:

> you should endeavour to convey suggestions to your prospective client in such a way as to make him feel sure that the property you are showing him is just what he wants – that he cannot get along without it, and that the present time is almost his last chance to secure it. Work your own mind up to believe these things and, if possible, convey this feeling to your customer by acts as well as words.[14]

'Just what he wants', and the 'last chance to secure it': the two urgencies capture exactly the coexisting states of a pre-buying mind that Woolf identifies in herself. There is the 'hot and ardent' sensation of rising desire; at the same time there is the tired longing to 'have done with looking about'.

Why was Woolf so 'ready' – susceptible and fearless, and on the brink? Aside from the quirks of the place itself, the magical geometries of the encircling path, the curving rooms and the 'triangular island' up there, there is also – to use the textbook language – a pre-existing disposition on the part of this potential buyer. The primary reason for this is the need that summer to move out of Asheham House: the landlord had given notice. There was therefore time pressure along with the need and desire to find another country home.

Earlier that afternoon Woolf had entered the office of a different Lewes estate agent, Powell's. She was dishevelled after a muddy walk into the town and more amused than embarrassed to think of the misleading impression she may have created in the mind of the person she spoke to:

> such mud that when I went into Powell, the land agent, the sleek little clerk looked from my head to my boots in expostulation – as if such a figure couldn't possibly require a house with 7 bedrooms & a bathroom. Unhappily there seems little chance of finding one. (*D1* 250)

Lost to the property-rating sensibilities of a century later is the fact that at this time the grandness that goes against this customer's mucky presentation is not in the number of bedrooms so much as the specification of 'a bathroom', that sought-after new feature. (Two decades on, that is the one improvement – 'adding bathrooms' – that is mentioned, in the passage quoted earlier, for the property-purchasing arrivals to the village of *Between the Acts*.) And in effect, Woolf also turns round the negative up-down appraisal of herself as a client by her counter-disparagement of the man behind the desk as not just 'little' but 'sleek' – which mocks him for making the effort she hasn't. Apart from the class condescension, it is as if her own dirt and disarray can be cancelled out by his overdoing of the proper appearances.

As well as the existing wish to find a new residence quickly, there is a further precipitating factor, on the day itself, for the sudden outcome when Woolf ventures fatefully to her viewing of the Round House. For she had just come away from a nasty argument with her sister Vanessa at Charleston, her home nearby; this had put Virginia in a tense frame of mind for seeing, initially and as already planned, a different house. This prior viewing is narrated as the immediate sequel to the sister incident; it is the episode that precedes the Round House adventure:

> Anyhow I left in rather a crumpled condition, & paused in Lewes, on L.'s advice, to see a house on the hill. A degree of that refinement & smug efficiency which one finds in Surrey houses set me against the White House, & I trudged down into Lewes again in no cheerful mood, with three hours, moreover, to spend there. (*D1* 279)

With its irritable dismissal of a species called 'Surrey houses', this dipping moment confirms the prelude to a turnaround in the story of the momentous day. By the end Woolf will have come full circle: it is at this point of descent, with multiple causes for feeling low, that the culminating Round House story begins – 'To pass the time, more than anything, I asked Mrs. Wycherley about houses. . .'. The unhappy background means that its positive outcome becomes – on a magnified scale – like an over-the-top case of purchasing therapy.

Fight with big sister; 'rather a crumpled condition'. Viewing of horrible house; even more down. Viewing of better house; buy it!

The low points of the quarrel with Vanessa and the depressing Surrey-style house serve to set in relief the high point of the surprise second house. But behind and before the chances of this one June day, it is the notice to quit Asheham House and the first approaches to finding another place that form the longer-term prelude to the sudden dénouement. 'The end of the story,' says Woolf, 'is that we have bought the Round House.' Even more than that, she goes on, slowing down to an almost liturgical solemnity, she and Leonard 'are now secure of a lodging on earth so long as we need sleep or sit anywhere' (*D1* 279). Nothing – no landlord – can ever again make them move.

So there they lived happily ever after? Well, not quite. A further episode awaits, in which this seemingly finished story then comes to function as no more than the precursor to a follow-up. It supersedes it not only with a further house but also by putting on show yet more features of the latest twentieth-century consumer psychology. Moving on just a few weeks in the diary entries, there is this: 'We own Monks House (this is almost the first time I've written a name which I hope to write many thousands of times before I'm done with it) for ever.' Fickle woman! Although this time, as it turned out, the place really did become the forever home, the eternal dwelling, its name to be written many thousands of times not just by herself but, beyond her death, by generations of Woolf fans and Bloomsbury tourists to come. Since 1980 Monk's House has been under the care of the National Trust, whose mission excludes any of its properties being put up for sale.

Back in the middle of things, Woolf continues and begins the new story – 'It happened thus' – on the day at the end of June that Leonard is down in Lewes to see – for the very first time! – the house they have bought together as a result of Virginia's moment of house-buying passion. Here is how she tells it:

> As we walked up the steep road from the station last Thursday on the way to inspect the Round House, we both read out a placard stuck on the auctioneers wall. Lot 1. Monks House, Rodmell. An old-fashioned house standing in three quarters of an acre of land to be sold with possession. The sale we noted was on Tuesday; to take place at the White Hart. That would have suited us exactly, L. said as we passed, & I, loyal to the Round House, murmured something about the drawbacks of Rodmell, but suggested anyhow a visit to the place; & so we went on. (*D1* 286)

Once again, no textbook of marketing practice could have set this up more simply – or for that matter more implausibly. Stick up a poster to sell a house which your prospects will pass on their way to the one they will now, being aware of the better option, turn against:

> the Round House no longer seemed so radiant and unattainable when we examined it as owners. I thought L. a little disappointed, though just & polite even to its merits. The day lacked sun. The bedrooms were very small. The garden not a country garden. Anyhow it seemed well to plan a visit to Rodmell on the following day. (*D1* 286)

All too clearly the first house is 'no longer' the 'unattainable' object of desire (it has been attained), and the significant rival in the situation is no longer a competing fellow purchaser but a solid and far more desirable other house. 'Anyhow it seemed well' – almost as if the 'no longer' wanted but completed purchase could just be popped into a pre-paid envelope marked Return.

Woolf's first reactions to Monk's House are consciously cooler than when she was shown the Round House: 'This time I flatter myself that I kept my optimism in check.' There follows a list of what the place lacks – no bathroom facilities, for instance. Again, the same turn of phrase: 'These prudent objections kept excitement at bay.' Optimism in check, excitement at bay: the wording acknowledges that an emotion of pleasure is making its presence felt in a not unwelcome way. In this carefully controlled mental environment, the plan to bid at the auction can then take the form of a rational calculation, despite the extraordinary situation of having only just chosen and even bought a different property: 'In short, we decided walking home to buy if we could, & sell Round House, as we conjecture we can. Eight hundred we made our limit' (*D1* 287).

The 'prudent objections' and the emotionless recounting, this time, of the viewing come across in stark contrast to the Round House moment of magically lifting spirits. But then after all, it is as if this sensible discussion of the pros and cons of the advertised house is no more than a matter of sober restraint, for when it comes to the scene of the auction, the diary shifts into dramatic mode. With their budget set at that ceiling of £800, the Woolfs have decided to delegate their bidding to the experienced Mr Wycherley. But they go along to the White Hart all the same to witness the scene. Once again, there is the effect of being 'egged on'. Once again, there is the thrill of a rising tension, this time attached to the shouting of sums of money, rather than to the visual appeal of a building.

> The auctioneer egged us on. I daresay there were six voices speaking, though after £600, 4 of them dropped out, & left only a Mr Tattersall competing with Mr Wycherley. We were allowed to bid in twenties; then tens; then fives . . . Seven hundred reached, there was a pause; the auctioneer raised his hammer, very slowly. (*D1* 287)

And that's it, the house is theirs for £700, as Woolf repeats in letters to friends – although the local newspaper reported the price achieved as £750, a considerable discrepancy.[15] At all events, 'I don't suppose many spaces of five minutes in the course of my life have been so close packed with sensation' (*D1* 287).

But even that outcome – owning two houses at once – was not the whole story, and not a one-off aberration either. A short while before the early June day in Lewes, Woolf was writing to a friend of 'our three cottages in Cornwall' – referring to the result of a recent long-distance transaction in regard to some houses that had been recently rented out to one D. H. Lawrence. During his time there this tenant had written a novel called *Women in Love*. Lawrence for his part had put out feelers for doing a house swap with the Woolfs' place in Richmond. The inclusion of these Cornwall cottages means that at the high point of July and August 1919 the Woolfs had no fewer than six places to their name, the others being the Round House, Monk's House and Hogarth House (in Richmond), their principal residence. Nor is *this* all. To these six might be added three more. There was Woolf's part ownership of the large London house in which she grew up, 22 Hyde Park Gate (it was sold a few years later). There was Little Talland House, in Firle, on which she had taken out a lease in 1911; it had been sublet shortly after that. And finally there was Asheham House, which was still theirs during the midsummer months of acquiring the five new places (*L2* 382).[16] By my count that makes a total of nine – not bad going for an accidental property portfolio.

Nor is the situation of possessing multiple homes one that Woolf finds, in principle, awkward. On the contrary, there are practical thoughts of how to make the most of such a position, even to make it a project in its own right. In April, writing to Duncan Grant, she refers to an available house that he said he had heard about, and thence to a plan for her and Leonard to be absentee landlords of that and a Cornwall cottage: 'We think we might take 2: and always have one let; one in Cornwall, the other in Sussex, and make the rent of both' (*L2* 350). 'We think we might take 2'! – well, why not?

On another occasion, now with the Cornwall cottages in the mix, the thoughts are more lifestyle than income as Woolf speculates about having places in all three locations, long-term: London for living in, Sussex for weekends, Cornwall for longer breaks:

> of course Cornwall is almost irresistible; so I've written to find out, and we rather think, if we take them, of moving all our furniture and books down there from Asheham, and taking a tiny cottage in Firle or thereabouts as a week end place. (*L2* 340)

Occasionally, a touch of self-mockery does appear in recounting the summer's extraordinary sequence of real-estate events. To her old classics teacher, Janet Case, towards the end of July, Woolf writes:

> Did Leonard tell you how we bought a house in Lewes, and then saw one we liked better at Rodmell, and so bought that, and have now sold the first house, and have only 3 cottages in Cornwall, and Asheham, and the house at Rodmell and Hogarth House to live in? (*L2* 379)

By this time the Woolfs had succeeded in selling on the Round House, without having ever lived there. They walked away not just with no financial loss, but with a considerable profit.

The £320 resale price obtained for a house bought just a few weeks before represents a rate of increase rarely attained in even the wildest of property booms, before or since. That wasn't why they did it. But still, it gives this story something of the flavour of a mad morality or immorality tale of speculative risk and rescue, way out of the expected Woolfian character on either side. In all of Leonard's lifelong care with the managing of their money, there is nothing to rival this midsummer gamble. And in all of Virginia's novels, is there any episode that can match the house-purchase diary entries for sheer dramatic tension and narrative push? This is what buying and selling houses did for (or to) the woman – transformative in its crazy capitalist way. From a letter to Lady Ottoline Morrell:

> We are down here [in Sussex] involved in so many dealings with houses that we may well find ourselves bankrupt; and then the first person I shall come to for refuge will be you, of course. But why, when we've just bought a house, should another appear much more desirable, – . . . ? (*L2* 372, ellipsis mine)

Why indeed?

In describing Woolf's own reporting of the moods and swings of that momentous summer I have refrained from offering any critique – in part because the matter is one of personal confession in writings that were not intended for general readership, and in part because many of the property-seeking mentalities that she evokes have slipped into the fabric of events in the world of a century later. Who are we to judge, or to claim to stand apart? In the 1980s the government of Margaret Thatcher fervently advocated a 'right to buy' aspiration to home ownership, to include all social classes and, crucially, social housing which had never before been open to market transactions. Unlike some other controversial precepts of that period, notably 'Clause 28', which banned the 'promotion' of homosexuality in school teaching, this one not only survived but established itself as needing no argument: it is better to own your own home than to rent it, however secure the tenure, and even if the landlord is the community ('council housing') rather than a private individual or company. With the hindsight of that normalisation, we look back at Woolf's summer of house-love as a symptomatically early manifestation of a desire for home ownership along with the ritualised highs and lows in the process of finding, desiring and purchasing a property. It is true that not many people other than speculators would go so far, then or now, as to buy and re-sell in the space of a single month. But clearly Woolf's property-seeking heart was already beating in time to future ideological rhythms. Clearly, too, it was already normal at the time, at least for those with the means: in his history of the property market in Britain, Desmond Fitz-Gibbon singles out that same postwar year of 1919 as having been an exceptional moment of house-buying fever, seen as such at the time.[17]

It must be said, too, that the house-hunting extracts from Woolf's diaries and letters of those weeks give only a partial indication of her noted preoccupations at the time. In the fuller picture, we see constant efforts to assist Vanessa in finding servants to help her out with a new baby. For this purpose Virginia trawls the agencies that list servants (rather than houses), interviews prospects on her sister's behalf, and offers to lend her own servants as a temporary measure. These women do have some say in where they will go or not go, but mainly they need a job and put up with being moved from one place – in both senses – to another.[18] Meanwhile their employers are free to contemplate possible relocations just for the pleasure or curiosity of it (and the story, remember, is one of second not primary homes). 'Driving past, people said to each other: "I wonder if that'll ever come into the market?"'

Notes

1. Virginia Woolf, *Between the Acts* (1941), ed. by Gillian Beer (London: Penguin, 1992), 7. Further references will be included within the main text.
2. On the difference between local markets and the market economy see Fernand Braudel, *La Dynamique du capitalisme* (Paris: Arthaud, 1985).
3. On the distinctive development of the property market, see Desmond Fitz-Gibbon, *Marketable Values: Inventing the Property Market in Modern Britain* (Chicago: Chicago University Press, 2018).
4. See Rachel Bowlby, 'Motoring through History: Woolf's "Evening over Sussex"', in *Talking Walking: Essays in Cultural Criticism* (Brighton: Sussex University Press, 2018), 35.
5. See Clara Jones, 'Virginia Woolf and "The Villa Jones" (1931)', *Woolf Studies Annual*, 22 (2016), 75–89. In this connection it is notable too that it was in these terms that Woolf disparaged the large semi-detached house that she leased at the start of 1911 in the Sussex village of Firle. Writing to Violet Dickinson on New Year's Day, before she moves in, she calls it 'a very ugly villa, but under the downs, in a charming village'. A brief note at the end of the summer inviting a 'Mr Woolf' to stay is even more explicit: 'This is not a cottage, but a hideous suburban villa – I have to prepare people for the shock.' *The Flight of the Mind: The Letters of Virginia Woolf, Volume One, 1888–1912*, ed. by Nigel Nicolson and Joanne Trautmann (London: Chatto & Windus, 1983), 447, 476.
6. Woolf, *The Years* (1937) (London: Granada, 1982), 150. Further references will be included within the main text.
7. Woolf, *Mrs Dalloway* (1925), ed. by David Bradshaw (Oxford: Oxford University Press, 2000), 72–3. Further references will be included within the main text.
8. For readers today a poster in London promoting a move to Bexhill-on-Sea may look like an anticipation of DFL, short for Down From London – a twenty-first-century phrase that refers to moving out of the city and down to the coast. The concept gained traction in the period of the national Covid-19 lockdowns of 2020 and 2021. At that time working from home, and leaving London for cheaper and healthier space elsewhere, became a noted house-buying trend.
9. Bexhill was fast expanding at the time. 'COME AND SEE THE SHOW HOUSE' says a large ad on the front page of the *Bexhill-on-Sea Observer*, Saturday 18 May 1935. There is a picture of a large semi-detached house; the price is given as £625 freehold, or £1 a week rent. Elsewhere on the same page, for £1,050 – 'A bargain' – there is a 'Newly decorated house' with six bedrooms, a bathroom and 'e.l.' (electric light). It is a mere 'half minute from sea front and

new pavilion'. A prime attraction for the town, this iconic new leisure centre was the De La Warr Pavilion, designed by the modernist architects Eric Mendelsohn and Serge Chermayeff.
10. On the many scenes in this novel involving shops and shopping, see Rachel Bowlby, *Back to the Shops: The High Street in History and the Future* (Oxford: Oxford University Press, 2022).
11. *The Question of Things Happening: The Letters of Virginia Woolf, Volume Two, 1912–1922*, ed. by Nigel Nicolson and Joanne Trautmann (1976; London: Chatto & Windus, 1980), 366. Further page references will be given within the main text.
12. *The Diary of Virginia Woolf, Volume One, 1915–1919*, ed. by Anne Olivier Bell (1977; Harmondsworth: Penguin, 1981), 279. Further page references will be given within the main text.
13. The AIDA technique was standard at this time in textbooks for travelling salesmen, as well as for other modes of selling. On sales psychology in the early twentieth century see Rachel Bowlby, 'Make up your Mind', in *Shopping with Freud* (1991; London: Routledge, 2009), 94–119.
14. R. Ernest, *How to Become a Successful Estate Agent* (London: Ernest & Co., 1904), 210–11.
15. 'At the White Hart, Lewes, on Tuesday, several properties in that district [of Laughton] were offered and all found purchasers at very good prices indeed [. . .] Messrs. St. John Smith and Son then offered the following lots, which were bought as follows:- 'Monk's House,' Rodmell -street, part freehold and part copyhold, £750, Mr. Wycherley'; 'Property in the Market' weekly column, *Sussex Express*, Friday 4 July 1919, 5.
16. For more details on Woolf's many properties and forms of tenure, see Hilary Macaskill, *Virginia Woolf at Home* (n.p.: Pimpernel Press, 2019).
17. See Fitz-Gibbon, *Marketable Values*, 116. On 10 May 1919, a couple of weeks before Woolf's viewing and offer on the Lewes house, the *Times* captioned the list of its property-selling pages as 'England Changing Hands'.
18. On the lives and working conditions of the Woolfs' domestic employees see Alison Light, *Mrs Woolf and the Servants* (London: Penguin, 2007).

Works Cited

'Property in the Market'. *Sussex Express*. Friday 4 July 1919, 5.
Bexhill-on-Sea Observer. Saturday 18 May 1935.
Bowlby, Rachel. *Back to the Shops: The High Street in History and the Future*. Oxford: Oxford University Press, 2022.
——, 'Make up your Mind'. *Shopping with Freud*, 94–119. 1991; London: Routledge, 2009.

——, 'Motoring through History: Woolf's "Evening over Sussex"'. *Talking Walking: Essays in Cultural Criticism*. Brighton: Sussex University Press, 2018.

Braudel, Fernand. *La Dynamique du capitalisme*. Paris: Arthaud, 1985.

Ernest, R. *How to Become a Successful Estate Agent*. London: Ernest & Co., 1904.

Fitz-Gibbon, Desmond. *Marketable Values: Inventing the Property Market in Modern Britain*. Chicago: Chicago University Press, 2018.

Jones, Clara. 'Virginia Woolf and "The Villa Jones" (1931)'. *Woolf Studies Annual*, 22 (2016), 75–89.

Light, Alison. *Mrs Woolf and the Servants*. London: Penguin, 2007.

Macaskill, Hilary. *Virginia Woolf at Home*. n.p.: Pimpernel Press, 2019.

Woolf, Virginia. *Between the Acts* (1941), ed. by Gillian Beer. London: Penguin, 1992.

——, *The Diary of Virginia Woolf, Volume One, 1915–1919*, ed. by Anne Olivier Bell. 1977; Harmondsworth: Penguin, 1981.

——, *The Flight of the Mind: The Letters of Virginia Woolf, Volume One, 1888–1912*, ed. by Nigel Nicolson and Joanne Trautmann. London: Chatto & Windus, 1983.

——, *Mrs Dalloway* (1925), ed. by David Bradshaw. Oxford: Oxford University Press, 2000.

——, *The Question of Things Happening: The Letters of Virginia Woolf, Volume Two, 1912–1922*, ed. by Nigel Nicolson and Joanne Trautmann. 1976; London: Chatto & Windus, 1980.

——, *The Years* (1937). London: Granada, 1982.

Chapter 7

Publishing and Capitalism at the Hogarth Press

Nicola Wilson

In February 1938, Virginia Woolf sold her half-share in the Hogarth Press for £3,000 to John Lehmann. She was just over twenty years into her publishing career, and though she would continue to read manuscripts and act on the Press's advisory board, she was ready to hand over the responsibilities of day-to-day management. She was working on the notes and proofs of *Three Guineas*, up against a hard publishing deadline to make the spring lists, while recovering from influenza and Leonard's serious health scare. So the day of contract signing, like those around it, goes unrecorded. '& have said nothing here for so long', she noted in her diary on 10 March, 'nothing about the Press; how 10 days ago I signed my rights away to John'.[1] Two days later she reflects more fully on what they have achieved during two decades with the Hogarth Press:

> But this reminds me that our last Leonard & Virginia season is perhaps our most brilliant: all the weeklies I think single out Isherwood, Upward, & even Libby Benedict for the highest places. Yes: if there is success in this world, the Hogarth Press has I suppose won what success it could. And money this year will fairly snow us under. £4,000 about from The Years: then Pepita &c &c. In fact we have asked Mr Wicks to estimate a library at MH. In spite of Hitler. But its [sic] all a little – my earnings – in the air. To solidify them I bought 2 pairs of American shoes, with rubber soles, yesterday: item: a paper holder, now holding my great notebooks: item: a chair. (D5, 130)

Woolf concludes this tour-de-force on value, commodities and capital with the following quip: 'The delight of money; buying freely [. . .] The delight of spending is to say I want this & buy it outright, especially small articles of furniture & stationery.' In these playful thoughts about wealth and 'solidifying' her capital, Woolf echoes Marx and Engels' words on the triumph of modern bourgeois society. 'All that is solid melts into air', wrote the authors of *The Communist Manifesto*, 'all that is holy is profaned, and man is at last compelled to face with sober senses his real conditions of life, and his relations with his kind'.[2] This chapter follows Woolf's lead on the contradictions at play in her financially successful publishing by unpicking some of the tensions inherent in her role as capitalist cofounder and co-director of the 'radical left-wing' Hogarth Press.[3] Situating the activities of the Hogarth Press in a nuanced light, I position the Woolfs' publishing agenda and operations in the realm of ambivalence, resistance and complicity that has characterised recent scholarship on Virginia Woolf's politics and writerly engagement with capitalist culture and empire.[4] Riffing on Laura J. Miller's study, *Reluctant Capitalists: Bookselling and the Culture of Consumption*, the chapter explores Woolf's publishing at the Hogarth Press under the guise of 'reluctant capitalism'.[5]

Just as their reliance on domestic servants signalled the Woolfs' place in a distinct economic system, so co-owning a successful publishing house made them part of a capitalist class. While, as Michael Bhaskar points out,

> the printing press is not innately capitalist throughout its history [. . .] publishing has been in the vanguard of capitalism, pioneering among other things industrial process and organisation, intellectual property, trade in intangible goods [. . .] the removal of censorship and government interference in business matters, free markets, [. . .] labour organisations, sponsorship and advertising, innovations in retail experience.[6]

No matter where we date the start of modern trade publishing in Britain (the oldest firms of Longmans Green, John Murray and Thomas Nelson were set up in the eighteenth century), by the Woolfs' lifetimes, the professional associations and international standards that would lay the foundations for the global, capitalist business we know today were in place. This included the Society of Authors (established 1884) and the Publishers Association (established 1896), which the Hogarth Press had joined by at least 1935.[7] The foundations of today's dominance by European and US publishing corporations were also present in late nineteenth- and early twentieth-century British publishers' power in colonial markets. In their analysis of twentieth-century publishing, Finkelstein and McCleery argue that we might categorise British publishers' trade dominance in (former) colonies as 'an initial wave of globalisation that would give way later in the century to the rise of transnational conglomerates led by North American and European competitors'.[8] As I shall examine later in this chapter, the colonial book trade – or what was known at the time as the 'Empire market' – was by no means insignificant to the Woolfs' success and publishing profits.

And yet the place of capitalism within publishing theory as a way of thinking about the structure and practice of the industry remains complex. On the one hand, theorists like Pierre Bourdieu and John B. Thompson have drawn on Marx's theories of value and capital to show how publishers trade fundamentally in financial, symbolic and economic capital. Bourdieu uses the example of the publisher to demonstrate how the market of symbolic goods is structured by the relative positions of producers and agents within a 'field'. '[T]he most personal judgements it is possible to make of a work, even of one's own work,' Bourdieu explains, 'are always collective judgements in the sense of position-takings referring to other position-takings through the intermediary of the objective relations between the positions of their authors within the field.'[9] In *Merchants of Culture*, Thompson expands upon Bourdieu's framework to include publishers' human, social and intellectual capital. Publishing is 'both a *supply chain* and a *value chain*', Thompson argues, because the publisher adds tangible value (content development, financial investment, branding and recognition) to the author and manuscript (or commodity) they work with.[10] From its earliest instantiations, we know that the Woolfs traded on their privileged position within the literary field to create interest and boost networks. 'It is proposed to publish shortly a pamphlet containing two short stories by Leonard Woolf and Virginia Woolf, (price, including postage 1/2)' they circularised friends in an unevenly inked and erratically spaced advertisement.[11] 'I am neither an "A subscriber" nor a "B subscriber" to your Press', William Plomer wrote to them in June 1924: 'From a distance I have watched your activities with interest and sympathy, because I suspect that you are nearer the heart of things than any other publishers in London.'[12] Created in 1917, the Hogarth Press was a successful brand that – unlike many of its modernist contemporaries – continued to flourish through mid-twentieth-century consolidations and mergers. Now in the twenty-first century, it has been dusted off as a contemporary imprint by multinational conglomerate Penguin Random House.[13]

On the other hand, publishing as one of the oldest creative industries has always resisted its association with the capitalist marketplace. Publishing is 'at once an art, a craft and a business', Hogarth Press author Raymond Mortimer once said.[14] This is the nub of tension between cultural creativity and commerce, mediated in a careful balancing act of artistic values with the economic: what creative industry theorists call 'creative management'.[15] The publisher doesn't have to be a capitalist, or profit-seeker, of course; other models of radical, community-led and not-for-profit publishing remain.[16] The Woolfs did not start out to become 'a commercial publishing business' according to their own testaments, but began as an experimental, coterie start-up, seeking a satisfying manual occupation and 'to produce and publish short works which commercial publishers could not or would not publish'.[17] In *Three Guineas*, Woolf proposes radical methods of distribution. 'Find out new ways of approaching "the public"', she advises the daughters of educated men: 'Fling leaflets down basements; expose them on stalls; trundle them along streets on barrows to be sold for a penny or given away.'[18] But that is not how they operated themselves. The Woolfs wanted to produce materially attractive but affordable books – not fancy collectors' items – and the Hogarth Press business archives show that they circularised widely depending on product to broaden their reach (from the WEA, to the Amalgamated Engineering Union, to the clergy). Aside from review copies, they didn't give pamphlets or books away for free. Success meant selling books in 'a capital-intensive, risk-laden environment', as Bhasker reminds us, 'undercapitalised publishers are chronically weak and cash hungry'.[19] Like any other publisher wanting to stay afloat and shift the accent of public debate, the Woolfs' aesthetic decisions had to be tempered by good business sense. 'My wife and I both think that *O Providence* is really much the better book, though there are considerable merits in *Saturday Night*', Leonard replied to John Hampson about his submissions to the Press in July 1930:

> From the business point of view, we do not think that either is likely to sell very well, and *O Providence* has much less chance than the other. Indeed, if it were published as your first novel, it might quite easily be a complete failure. We feel therefore that it would be more sensible to publish *Saturday Night* first, which might attract some attention and so give *O Providence* a better chance.[20]

In recent years, the fact that Woolf owned the means of production and reproduction with a 'press of her own' has become a celebratory trope in Woolf studies, contributing to a wider critical re-evaluation of the Woolfs 'as not just literary figures but specifically as business people: increasingly savvy in their commercial field and constantly negotiating their own relationship with the book market'.[21] Yet shifting the mythos of the Hogarth Press from modernist little press (as it began) to acknowledging how it functioned by the late 1920s as a mid-sized publishing house 'able to manage a best seller as well as Heinemann, and with far greater distinction',[22] as Woolf boasted, has proved curiously difficult (Alice Staveley describes this as one of 'the "biomythographies" of the Hogarth Press').[23] 'The history of the Hogarth Press is exciting because it suggests the triumph of imagination over capital', Phyllis Rose argued in her introduction to John Lehmann's *Thrown to the Woolfs*, 'the creative mind over the managerial'.[24] Oddly, this characterisation of the Press as cottage industry has continued into scholarship produced in the 2000s.[25] Partly this resistance, it seems to me, is tied up in dominant critical paradigms of modernism established by scholars like Marshall Berman and Fredric Jameson who, as Mark Steven points out, see modernist artistic production as an 'aesthetic regime attempting to resist capitalism'.[26] The Hogarth Press was set up in the year that *The Communist Manifesto* made good on its revolutionary promise, and as radical creative intellectuals, the Woolfs supported Marx's 'poetry of the future'.[27] One of the first works they printed and published was Hope Mirrlees's long avant-garde poem of the alienated capitalist city, *Paris*.[28] 'Paris is a huge home-sick peasant', Mirrlees wrote, 'He carries a thousand villages in his heart.'[29] As publishers, they supported industrial writers including R. M. Fox (1891–1969) and Welsh collier poet Huw Menai (1888–1961); they published the voices of working-class women in *Life as We Have Known It* (1931); they were hugely influential in bringing Russian literature to the British public.[30] They carried a radical programme of anti-colonial titles and economic and philosophical critiques of the Great Depression, Hungry Thirties, and the rise of fascism. It doesn't sit easy that they could be anything but a small, radical press, operating somehow outside of a global capitalist marketplace.

Recent scholarship on the Hogarth Press, however, shows that this is not an accurate portrait.[31] According to the Woolfs' own accounts the success of the Press overtook them, first with Virginia's *Kew Gardens* in May 1919, and then with Gorky's *Reminiscences of Tolstoi* (1920), giving them – as Leonard recalled – a taste of 'printing and publishing [that] had given us great pleasure and whetted our appetite for more'.[32] A couple of years in they took on their first paid employee, and in 1922 they would take on a full-time manager, Marjorie Thomson (Joad), to avoid a buy-out and retain editorial and financial control.[33] They employed a book traveller from 1928, adding to their growing number of employees.[34] 'Our earnings prodigious', Virginia noted in her diary ten years later. 'Income last year about £6000. John much impressed. Press worth £10,000' (*D5* 137). As Claire Battershill argues, 'it is more accurate [. . .] to say that the Hogarth Press began with the spirit and method of a little magazine or a small press inheriting traditions from the Arts and Crafts movement [. . .] but it rapidly became a larger operation whose books found an international readership'.[35] In what follows, I draw on a few case studies to look at how what the Hogarth Press published contributed to debates about print capitalism, economic imperialism, readership and democracy; exploring to what extent they operated as publishers in an 'intimacy of complicity and critique'.[36] I begin with the Woolfs' publishing of Margaret Cole's optimistic thesis on the contemporary book world, in which Cole foresaw the overthrow of a publishing elite and the triumph of the reading masses.

The Democratisation of Books

In early 1938, while Leonard and Virginia were working out the details with John Lehmann over his potential partnership, they received a new submission from socialist and Fabian associate Margaret Cole. Cole had recently published a series of articles in the *Listener* on the 'Democratisation of Books' (these ran from 22 December 1937 to 12 January 1938) and proposed to re-use her research for a short book in Hogarth's Day to Day Pamphlet series. This would address '[t]he fact that we are only now really beginning to see the results of universal education', Cole outlined in a letter to the Press, and would look at how books and book reading were shifting 'in an ill-organized trade, existing in a capitalist world' 'from the privilege of a class into the possession of all'.[37] Cole argued that her research on the contemporary book world showed that

> what we are now witnessing is the opening stage of a real revolution, a revolution which has been economically overdue for a long time, in the world of English-language book-production, and that its effects are going to be much more far-reaching than anyone in the earlier controversies had fully realized.[38]

Books were becoming more accessible, it seemed to Cole, and catering for wider, more diverse audiences thanks to the improvements to free public libraries, 'twopenny' libraries in newsagents and tobacconists, publishers' cheap editions, and subscription book clubs like The Book Society and other reading groups offering cheap books to their members (Victor Gollancz's Left Book Club had 51,000 members in 1937 according to Cole's research; Foyles' Book Clubs had 60,000 members divided between them). Cole's thesis was that the changes in distribution and consumption shaping the 'democratisation of books' would force a change in their authorship and production. No longer would Oxbridge men dominate the world of publishing, she argued:

> He tends to publish books which will be read by persons resident, or who once resided, in Oxford, Cambridge and London; he sells them at prices acceptable to Oxford, Cambridge or London; he advertises them in newspapers and weeklies which are read in Oxford, Cambridge and London; and he gets them reviewed, if they are reviewed at any length, by ex-graduates of Oxford, Cambridge and London.[39]

'Until this present generation, reading for culture's sake, and the ownership of books, was a class privilege belonging to the well-to-do-except in so far as philanthropy or unusual enterprise provided a small cheap ration for the poor', she added.[40] The book world was witnessing an economic and social revolution, Cole argued, that might just lead to the overthrow of the book world's bourgeoise.

The Woolfs knew Cole through longstanding socialist circles, especially the Fabian Society and their joint associations with the Webbs (Cole would write one of the first biographies of Beatrice Webb, published in 1945, and edited the first two volumes of her diaries, published in 1952 and 1956). The Coles, like the Woolfs and the Webbs, were important figures in the early twentieth-century socialist and Labour movements, who combined domestic partnerships with work and a shared political life. Like Leonard, Margaret Cole served on various committees of the New Fabian Research Bureau (including its Publications Committee), which had been set up in 1931 to stimulate socialist research.[41] Leonard chaired the International Section (later the Fabian International Bureau), which published *Studies in Capital and Investment*, edited by Margaret's husband, G. D. H. Cole, in 1935. The Hogarth Press had published G. D. H. Cole's *Politics and Literature* in their first series of Lectures on Literature in 1929 and would bring out his *The Machinery of Socialist Planning* (with the New Fabian Society) in 1938. They published Margaret's brother Raymond Postgate's *What to do with the BBC* in the Day to Day Pamphlets in 1935. Neither of the Woolfs liked Margaret's proposed title for the work. 'Mrs Woolf and I both feel that the present title of your pamphlet "The Democratisation of Books" is a little unwieldy', Leonard wrote to her. 'We would like to propose to you calling it "Books and the Masses" instead.'[42] This would become *Books and the People*; the 38th title in the series.

Surviving correspondence in the Hogarth Press business archive reveals the Woolfs' questioning of Cole's claims about 'democratisation'. In the first place, Leonard's consultation with John Lehmann as incoming partner prompts the suggestion that Cole might address the formal and structural impact on books of key distributors, namely fee-paying members' libraries like the *Times* Book Club. In a report by the Society of Bookmen in 1928, 'the Big Four' circulating libraries – Boots, Mudies, W. H. Smith's and the *Times* Book Club – were found to have a significant share of the new books market and were widely seen to have contributed to a standardisation in the length, price and form of books.[43] 'For instance, a book of 40,000 words is perfectly easy to market in Paris', Lehmann wrote to Woolf, 'but here,-well you know all about it'.[44] The Woolfs offered Cole a contract on her book, encouraging her to make her argument more quantitative and less discursive, while Leonard cast significant doubt on her thesis. This editorial letter is hugely suggestive of Leonard's take on how publishing worked in a capitalist economic system:

> There is, I suggest, a pretty black side to the picture which would be worth noting. To some extent, it is true to say that in the last ten years publishing has changed into a large-scale business, and is a very good example of the effect and final stages of capitalism. It may be the democratisation of books, but, in effect, it is largely a struggle by stunts and publicity to create best-sellers of any kind or type, the best-seller being the only thing which brings in enough profits. The book-clubs, it seems to me, are mainly an attempt to snatch some of the profits from the booming and publicity method. The result is that the average life of a book becomes shorter and shorter, and, like beer and soap, people do not get the books they want, but the books that they can be induced to think they want. It is not sour grapes in my case at the present moment, because we have had two best-sellers in the last twelve months. I am sure that their being best-sellers had practically no relevance to their merits, or to any conscious idea or demand in the minds of the readers who bought them or took them out in the library.[45]

Leonard's private critique to Cole of the demands and constrictions of the marketplace chimes with some of his public rhetoric on the book world in print and broadcast media. An obvious intertext is the 1927 BBC radio debate he staged with Virginia asking, 'Are Too Many Books Written and Published'. Like many publishers of the time who subscribed to the theory of over-production (including Stanley Unwin and W. G. Taylor), Leonard answers 'yes' to this question, while Virginia debates 'no', showing rather more sympathy with Cole's sense of things. 'The making of books is now a trade, or rather an industry, and in my opinion it is in an unhealthy condition – almost as bad as the mining industry', Leonard opens his side of this scripted debate, blaming the mechanisation of production and publishers' thirst for the next bestseller on poorer outputs overall that overwhelm the reading public.[46] Leonard's critique in his letter to Cole of the publishers' 'stunts and publicity to create best-sellers of any kind or type' echoes his critique of advertising in his contribution to *Books and the Public* (published by the Hogarth Press in 1927, originally a series of essays in *The Nation*). 'This is, I think, to-day the real problem of the book-producing industry,' he adds. 'Anyone can sell a best-seller.'[47]

And yet the Hogarth Press's interactions with the kind of contemporary book clubs Cole celebrates are worth unpicking. In *Books and the People*, Cole argues that 'absolute freedom of choice, in books, as in other commodities, rests basically on the power of the purse': 'It is hopeless for anyone not constantly in touch with literary and cultured circles even to hear of many books which he would gladly read', she goes on.[48] Having your books chosen and selected for you by someone else is a sensible option, Cole argues, for the cash poor, time poor 'New Reading Public'.[49] Like other publishers in the interwar period, the Hogarth Press chased the trade of the new members' subscription book clubs which could transform a title's sales. The Book Society (established 1928), which Cole cites as one of the more prominent 'revolutions' shaking up publishing, had over 13,000 members by the early 1930s, all committing to buy one new full-price book a month. Despite what he warns Cole privately about their influence, Leonard submitted many Hogarth Press manuscripts for consideration by the Book Society selection committee (including Virginia's *The Waves*), with their first success coming in May 1930 with the Book Society Choice of Vita Sackville-West's *The Edwardians*. On receiving Vita's manuscript for *The Edwardians* in March 1930 – a historical novel, and her first fiction title for six years – Leonard immediately recognised its book club potential. 'Virginia pounced on it and I have had no chance', he explained to Vita. 'She approves so violently that I shall send it off to the printer and read it in proof to save time. Will you let me have the second MS you promised so that I may take it at once to the Book Society?'[50] The Hogarth Press achieved further Book Society success with William Plomer's boarding house murder mystery *The Case is Altered* (1932), and Virginia Woolf's own *Flush* (1933) (also selected by the American Book-of-the-Month Club). A Book Society Choice meant guaranteed minimum orders of 9,000 copies to the publisher, transforming typical print runs and sales. On the one hand, these were purchased largely by a class of well-to-do readers who could afford to buy one new full-price book a month. But as Cole pointed out, the club had a much wider impact on reading. As Freddie Richardson, head of Boots Book-Lovers Library explained, the Book Society had become 'a standard of literary advice very well respected throughout the country': 'Even people who do not belong to the Book Society are prepared to order these volumes through libraries, so that most publishers are exceedingly pleased to have one of their titles chosen.'[51]

The year after publishing *Books and the People*, the Woolfs stepped further into the new 'democratic' retail world of book clubs with their first Readers Union edition. The Readers Union, founded in 1937, was the first general book club to offer its members a range of recently published titles from a selection of publishers 'at half-a-crown irrespective of its normal publication price'.[52] Within weeks it had 17,000 members and, as Iain Stevenson points out, 'was popular with publishers since it extended print-runs and gave them the benefits of "run-on" costs to spread their initial investment'.[53] Mid-1939, Leonard agreed for the Readers Union to buy Christopher Isherwood's *Goodbye to Berlin* as a discount title. 'Have sold nearly 4000 copies of *Goodbye to Berlin*, which I think is very good', he explained to Isherwood about the Hogarth Press edition that December. 'There will also be a lot more money in March or April, when the Readers' Union edition comes out: this will be 23,000 copies at half a crown.'[54] Cole had argued that 'the new public comes from age-classes and income-classes which until now had hardly ever read a book at all except under some sort of compulsion [. . .], and from all manner of people who were afraid to be seen entering a bookshop'.[55] 'You forget that the population has increased', Virginia opened her part of the BBC radio debate with Leonard about publishing,

> Thousands of people now draw up to the table after the day's work is done and read a book or write a letter, who used, a hundred years

ago, to sit in the corner spinning or lie in the armchair snoring. For my own part, I think the increase of books is all to the good.[56]

The Hogarth Press had been making Virginia's own work more affordable at five shillings a go in their Uniform Editions since 1929.[57] Her hand is not on the editorial correspondence about the 1940 Readers Union edition of *Goodbye to Berlin*. But her public rhetoric on reading and the benefits of opening up the book world indicate she would have supported it.[58]

Pamphlet Economics

The Day to Day pamphlets in which Cole's *Books and the People* came out are the most obvious example of the centrality of politics and economics to the Hogarth Press and their commitment to exploring the contemporary crises of capitalism. Following the success of the Hogarth Essays (first series 1924–6; second series 1926–8), the Hogarth Lectures on Literature (first series 1927–31) and the annual Merttens Lectures on War and Peace (begun 1927), Leonard was keen to establish a series 'devoted entirely to politics, bound in paper, and sold at 1s or 1s 6d' for a broad public audience.[59] Other political organisations like the Fabians, Trade Unions, Trade Councils and Co-operative Society published cheap, paper-bound pamphlets for their members on topical issues. Bringing a similar series of polemical interventions to Hogarth Press readers was a significant step for the Woolfs, marking their commitment to political engagement in publishing and what Peter Morgan calls 'an intervention by high modernist circles into public political debate'.[60]

The Day to Day pamphlets were the largest in number and longest-running of the Press's various series, totalling forty produced between their optimistic beginnings with Maurice Dobb's *Russia To-Day and To-Morrow* (1930) and W. H. Auden and T. C. Worsley's *Education Today – and Tomorrow* (1939). Together, they constitute wide-ranging interventions in political economy, including work on the growth of fascism, free trade, unemployment, colonialism and international relations. As publishers, the Woolfs did not necessarily agree with the viewpoint of each contributor (their decision to make available Benito Mussolini's *The Political and Social Doctrine of Fascism* as pamphlet no. 18 being an obvious example). Rupert Trouton's 1931 pamphlet on *Unemployment: Its Causes and Their Remedies* for instance (with a foreword by J. M. Keynes who also declares that 'I must not be taken to agree with all his arguments or all these proposals') proposes 'a dole to employers' to address the 2,500,000 unemployed: 'administered in such a way that it can only be drawn by the employer who increases the number of his employees'.[61] The pamphlets came into the Press via different means. Some were speculative proposals from experts outside of the Woolfs' socialist circles. 'My qualifications for writing this study are that I have spent the greater part of my life in and around the mining towns and villages described', wrote Thomas Sharp, author of *A Derelict Area: A Study of the South-West Durham Coalfield* by way of introduction in 1934, 'By profession I am a town and country planner'.[62] Others were suggestions from external political organisations which, when taken forward (as with the Fabian Society), were sometimes published under a joint imprint. Other political Hogarth Press books were specific commissions. Sally Graves's *A History of Socialism* (1939), which grew from pamphlet to book (outgrowing the Day to Day series and eventually sold at 3d and 6d), was written to fill Leonard's sense of a gap in the market. 'I have been trying for some time to get someone to write a book which I think badly needs writing', Leonard explained to Graves (niece of Robert Graves) in November 1935, 'and it has struck me that it might appeal to you'.[63] Virginia confirmed their successful outreach in her diary. 'Sally Graves to tea: stayed till 7. A resolute cornered mind, defiant rather, balanced; pleased L.: she's to write on Socialism.'[64]

In 1932, the Hogarth Press published *From Capitalism to Socialism* by J. A. Hobson as the eighth title in the Day to Day series (this followed his essay *Notes on Law and Order* in 1926). Hobson (1858–1940) was a hugely influential economic and political theorist, author of over thirty books, whose 'constructive criticism of nineteenth-century liberalism' – as David Long explains – helped define what became known as the 'new liberalism' that 'turned away from individualism and *laissez-faire* and towards a social outlook and state intervention'.[65] The Woolfs had at least seven of Hobson's books in their library (several as review copies), and after Keynes, Hobson was the most famous, and controversial, economist they published.[66] They printed 1,500 copies of *From Capitalism to Socialism*, as was typical with the Day to Day series and not untypical numbers for serious political interventions (in a 1924 letter to Norman Leys, Leonard writes that Allen & Unwin had sold only 300 copies of his *Empire in Commerce and Africa*).[67] Hobson was in his seventies when he published with the Hogarth Press and *From Capitalism to Socialism* comprised a 53-page distillation of his influential theories on national and international poverty, 'the seeds of decay in capitalism', and the false economies of economic imperialism. '[T]his definitely economic drive was usually provided with a political covering, and needed political and sometimes military assistance for its successful execution', Hobson summarised in his pamphlet for the Woolfs.[68] As Anna Snaith observes in her chapter in this collection, Hobson's work on economic imperialism profoundly affected the Woolfs' thinking and writing.[69] In this late pamphlet for the Hogarth Press, Hobson joined Keynes in arguing for a new international bank 'vested with the power of issuing and directing the flow of money capital'.[70] But for Hobson this would be an 'internationalism in socialism': 'the opening scene of a managed world monetary policy' that might 'put economic life, in its productive aspect, on a sound basis with world socialism'.[71]

Books and the 'Empire Markets'

Hobson's influential argument that it was capitalist financiers that benefited from colonies followed Marx and Engels' warnings about global capital: 'The need of a constantly expanding market for its products chases the bourgeois over the entire surface of the globe.'[72] This was also true of British and American publishing houses, fighting in the modernist period over what was an increasingly competitive global trade. As Alison Rukavina sets out, publishers and book trade agents 'negotiated, collaborated, and competed as the international book trade developed [. . .] [and] [i]ncreasingly [. . .] thought about the world not as a vast geographical expanse but as a negotiable space in which commodities and ideas circulated'.[73] For British publishers, what were known as the 'Empire markets' (redubbed the 'traditional markets' after the Second World War) were increasingly important in the face of growing American competition. The Publishers Association fought hard to maintain British publishers' trade dominance against American 'incursions' into the huge Anglophone reading and book-buying markets of Australia and New Zealand, India, South Africa and Canada. In September 1930, for instance, Leonard explained to Vita Sackville-West that he would have to give further discounts to their Canadian agent on her bestselling *The Edwardians* because Doran were trying to sell their American edition into Canada. 'We have to give discount [. . .] already on colonial books and he presses me to give him [. . .] [more] on *The Edwardians* so that he may undersell Doran. Under the circumstances I have agreed, but it is rather a nuisance as we shall also have to give it for the big Australian orders.'[74]

In the late nineteenth century, major firms like Macmillan had launched specific series of 'Colonial Libraries' for Anglophone readers overseas, but British publishers' export of books to the colonies went well beyond house series. Leonard's publisher Stanley Unwin (who would become president of the Publishers Association in 1933) estimated that 'if the sale of rights in books as well as the actual books themselves are included, more than a third of the business done by my firm in normal times would come under the heading "Export Trade"'.[75] 'Colonial editions' were manufactured cheaper, bound in light 'colonial cloth' and printed on thinner paper; reducing production costs and making them cheaper to ship. They accounted for a substantial part of a publisher's first print run in the modernist period, making up on average between 20 and 30 per cent of a typical first edition sales. Once they were established and using commercial printers for their titles, the Woolfs were no different from the rest of the trade in this respect. Production ledgers in the Hogarth Press business archives indicate that just over 20 per cent of the Woolfs' first print runs of *To the Lighthouse* and *The Years* were sold as colonial editions (1,035 out of 4,655 copies of *To the Lighthouse* sold between 5 May 1927 and 17 March 1943; and 3,100 out of 14,482 of *The Years* between March 1937 and 1945).[76] Colonial copies of *The Years* were packaged up and dispatched for overseas customers – including Argus South African, Burma Book Club, New South Wales Bookstore, Darter Brothers (Cape Town), and the Anglo-Egyptian bookshop – two weeks before UK publication. Wholesalers and distributors who put in repeated substantial orders included Australia's Angus & Robertson and Gordon & Gotch, the Oxford Bookstore & Stationary company (an Indian book-store chain with outlets in Calcutta, Delhi, Lahore and Meerut), and Whitcombe & Tombs who worked with suppliers in New Zealand.

We know from important work by Anna Snaith and Jeanne Dubino, among others, that the Woolfs supported an anti-colonial agenda through the Hogarth Press.[77] In the Day to Day Pamphlets series especially, this aspect of their publishing programme is obvious. Number 16 is *The Case for West-Indian Self Government* (1933) by Trinidadian intellectual C. L. R. James, dedicated to the leaders of the Democratic Movement in the West Indies. Number 17 is K. M. Panikkar's *Caste and Democracy* (1933). In 1924 they published Norman Leys' *Kenya*; a trenchant critique of imperialism in Africa and 'the colonial government's harsh labour laws, disastrous land redistribution policies, forcible removal of Kenyan Africans to reservations, failure to provide education, and more'.[78] Ten years later they would publish *An African Speaks for his People* by Parmenas Githendu Mockerie, the first book in English by a Kikuyu.[79] And so it is not meant as criticism, but rather acknowledgement of the capitalist and imperialist regimes they lived within, to point out that the Woolfs benefited (like other British publishers) from a trade dominance in the dominions and colonies that the Publishers Association of Great Britain continued to fight for well into the 'postcolonial' era (the British Traditional Market Agreement lasted until 1976). It is one of industrial monopoly capitalism's fundamental contradictions that colonial intellectuals like C. L. R. James and Mulk Raj Anand would travel to London and publish with the Woolfs, and that texts like *The Case for West-Indian Self Government* would potentially reach colonial readers through an uneven publishing market that helped to suppress local and indigenous publishing and contributed to London's hold on literary and publishing 'capital'.[80]

In her influential *The World Republic of Letters*, Pascale Casanova describes 'the inequality that structures the literary world'. 'Literary resources, which are always stamped with the seal of the nation,' she argues, 'are therefore unequal as well, and unequally distributed among nations.'[81] The Woolfs' radical experiment with the Hogarth Press demonstrated their business acumen and ability to manipulate a capitalist publishing enterprise with colonial networks for their own anti-imperialist ends. But they were inevitably tied up in that system. 'Viewed from the inside', wrote W. G. Taylor in 1935 (then President of the Publishers Association and managing director of J. M. Dent), 'publishing is a highly speculative and exacting trade, calling for ample capital, considerable business ability, an appreciation of the nature of contracts, an aptitude for detail, and a capacity for almost continuous applications'.[82] The Woolfs were hard-working creatives with a flair for publishing, with the social and economic capital needed to thrive. The texts they chose to frame and amplify by writers and intellectuals including Margaret Cole, J. M. Keynes, J. A. Hobson and C. L. R. James contributed during their lifetimes to contemporary debates on capitalism, print culture and economic imperialism – '& all this sprung from that type on the drawing room table at Hogarth House 20 years ago', Woolf wrote on selling her shares (*D5* 137). It was the beginning of a valuable print capitalist brand that would live on without them.[83]

Notes

1. Virginia Woolf, *The Diary of Virginia Woolf, Volume Five*, ed. by Anne Olivier Bell (Orlando: Harcourt Brace Jovanovich, 1984), 128. Further references will be included within the main text.
2. Karl Marx and Frederick Engels, *Manifesto of the Communist Party*, trans. Samuel Moore (London: Reeves, 1888), section 1 <https://oll.libertyfund.org/page/marx-manifesto> [accessed 31 October 2023].
3. Susheila Nasta, 'The Bloomsbury Indians', quoted in Claire Battershill and Nicola Wilson, 'Introduction', in *Virginia Woolf and the World of Books*, ed. by Claire Battershill and Nicola Wilson (Clemson: Clemson University Press, 2018), vii.
4. See, for instance, Alissa G. Karl, 'Consumerism and the Imperial Nation in Virginia Woolf's *The Voyage Out* and *Mrs Dalloway*', in *Modernism and the Marketplace: Literary Culture and Consumer Capitalism in Rhys, Woolf, Stein, and Nella Larsen* (London: Routledge, 2009); Clara Jones, *Virginia Woolf: Ambivalent Activist* (Edinburgh: Edinburgh University Press, 2016).
5. Laura J. Miller, *Reluctant Capitalists: Bookselling and the Culture of Consumption* (Chicago: University of Chicago Press, 2006).
6. Michael Bhasker, *The Content Machine: Towards a Theory of Publishing from the Printing Press to the Digital Network* (London: Anthem, 2013), 141.
7. Leonard Woolf affirms in a letter to the Secretary of State for India that the Press are members of the Publishers Association of Great Britain, 6 September 1935. In Leonard Woolf, *Letters of Leonard Woolf*, ed. by Frederic Spotts (London: Weidenfeld and Nicolson, 1990), 326.
8. David Finkelstein and Alistair McCleery, 'Publishing', in *The Cambridge History of the Book in Britain*, vol. 7, ed. by Andrew Nash, Claire Squires and I. R. Willison (Cambridge: Cambridge University Press, 2019), 147.
9. Pierre Bourdieu, 'The Market of Symbolic Goods', in *Print Cultures: A Reader in Theory and Practice*, ed. by Caroline Davis (London: Red Globe, 2019), 25–6.
10. John B. Thompson, *Merchants of Culture: The Publishing Business in the Twenty-First Century* (London: Polity, 2012), 14.
11. J. H. Willis, *Leonard and Virginia Woolf as Publishers: The Hogarth Press 1917–41* (Charlottesville: University Press of Virginia, 1992), 15.
12. William Plomer to the Hogarth Press, 15 June 1924. MS 2750/351. Reading, University of Reading (UoR) Special Collections, <https://www.modernistarchives.com/correspondence/letter-from-william-plomer-to-the-hogarth-press-15061924> [accessed 31 October 2023]
13. See Alice Staveley, 'The Hogarth Press', in *The Oxford Handbook of Virginia Woolf*, ed. by Anne Fernald (Oxford: Oxford University Press, 2021); Elizabeth Willson Gordon, *Publishing, Branding, and*

Selling an Icon: The Cultural Impact of the Hogarth Press 1917–2017 (forthcoming).
14. Quoted in Bhasker, *Content Machine*, 1.
15. David Hesmondhalgh and Sarah Baker, *Creative Labour: Media Work in Three Cultural Industries* (Abingdon: Routledge, 2011), 82, quoted in Bhasker, *Content Machine*, 143.
16. Gail Chester offers a good survey of radical publishers in her contribution to *The Cambridge History of the Book in Britain*.
17. Leonard Woolf, *Downhill All The Way: An Autobiography of the Years 1919–1939* (London: Hogarth Press, 1968), 60, 66.
18. Virginia Woolf, *A Room of One's Own and Three Guineas* (London: Penguin, 1993), 223.
19. Bhasker, *Content Machine*, 97, 142.
20. Leonard Woolf to John Hampson Simpson, 30 July 1930. MS 2750/153. Reading, UoR Special Collections.
21. Claire Battershill, 'The Hogarth Press', in *Publishing Modernist Fiction and Poetry*, ed. by Lise Jaillant (Edinburgh: Edinburgh University Press, 2019), 72.
22. Virginia Woolf, *The Letters of Virginia Woolf, Volume Four*, ed. by Nigel Nicolson (London: Hogarth Press, 1978), 177. Further references will be included within the main text.
23. Staveley, 'The Hogarth Press', 249.
24. Phyllis Rose, 'Introduction', in John Lehmann, *Thrown to the Woolfs* (NY: Holt, Rinehart and Winston, 1978), x.
25. See Claire Battershill, *Modernist Lives: Biography and Autobiography at Leonard and Virginia Woolf's Hogarth Press* (London: Bloomsbury, 2018), 9–11.
26. Mark Steven, 'Introduction', in *Understanding Marx, Understanding Modernism*, ed. by Mark Steven (London: Bloomsbury, 2021), 7.
27. Alex Niven, '*The Communist Manifesto* and the Exhumation of Literature', in *Understanding Marx, Understanding Modernism*, ed. by Mark Steven (London: Bloomsbury, 2021), 41; Julian Murphet, 'Marx in the Modernist Novel', in *Understanding Marx, Understanding Modernism*, 121.
28. For the effect of this on Woolf's creative praxis see Julia Briggs, *Reading Virginia Woolf*, 80–95 (Edinburgh: Edinburgh University Press, 2006).
29. Hope Mirrlees, *Paris* (London: Hogarth Press, 1919), 6.
30. See Helen Southworth, '"Going Over": The Woolfs, the Hogarth Press and Working-Class Voices', in *Leonard & Virginia Woolf: The Hogarth Press and the Networks of Modernism*, ed. by Helen Southworth (Edinburgh: Edinburgh University Press, 2010); Battershill, *Modernist Lives*, 37–60; Claire Davison, *Translation as Collaboration: Virginia Woolf, Katherine Mansfield, and S. S. Koteliansky* (Edinburgh: Edinburgh University Press, 2014).

31. See Southworth (ed.), *Leonard & Virginia Woolf*; Staveley, 'The Hogarth Press'; Battershill, 'The Hogarth Press', 70–4.
32. Woolf, *Downhill*, 60, 67.
33. Nicola Wilson and Helen Southworth, 'Women Workers at the Hogarth Press (c. 1917–25)', in *Women in Print, vol. 2*, ed. by Christine Moog (Oxford: Peter Lang, 2022), 225, 226–30.
34. Wilson and Southworth, 'Women Workers', 233.
35. Battershill, *Modernist Lives*, 9.
36. Karl, 'Consumerism and the Imperial Nation', 43.
37. Margaret Cole to Leonard Woolf, 28 January 1938. MS 2750/59. Reading, University of Reading (UoR) Special Collections; Margaret Cole, *Books and the People* (London: Hogarth Press, 1938), 47.
38. Cole, *Books*, 6.
39. Ibid., 12–13. Recent reports indicate that social mobility in publishing is in fact declining. See Brook, O'Brien and Taylor; Shaw; and Saha and van Lente.
40. Cole, *Books*, 12–13.
41. See Betty D. Vernon, *Margaret Cole, 1893–1980* (Beckenham: Croom Helm, 1986), 83, 89.
42. Leonard Woolf to Margaret Cole, 7 July 1938. MS 2750/59. Reading, UoR Special Collections.
43. The Big Four were estimated to buy between one-quarter and two-thirds of all new work produced. Society of Bookmen, *Report of the Commercial Circulating Libraries Sub-Committee* (London: Society of Bookmen, 1928), 9–10.
44. John Lehmann to Leonard Woolf, 4 February 1938. MS 2750/59. Reading, UoR Special Collections.
45. Leonard Woolf to Margaret Cole, 9 Feb 1938. MS 2750/59. Reading, UoR Special Collections.
46. Leonard Woolf and Virginia Woolf, 'Are Too Many Books Written and Published', ed. by Melba Cuddy-Keane, *PMLA*, 121.1 (2006), 239.
47. Leonard Woolf, 'On Advertising Books', *Books and the Public*, 50–1.
48. Cole, *Books*, 45.
49. The 'New Reading Public' comes from Sidney Dark, *The New Reading Public: A Lecture under the Auspices of The Society of Bookmen* (London: Allen & Unwin, 1922). Michael Bhasker makes a similar point in the contemporary media landscape in *Curation: The Power of Selection in a World of Excess* (London: Piatkus, 2017).
50. Leonard Woolf to Vita Sackville-West, 9 March 1930. MS 2750/416. Reading, UoR Special Collections.
51. Boots Book-Lovers Library, First Literary Course, 'Ninth Paper: Publishers and Bestsellers', box 460, Alliance Boots Archive & Museum Collection, Nottingham.
52. Readers Union flyer. MS 2750/195. Reading, UoR Special Collections.
53. Iain Stevenson, *Book Makers: British Publishing in the Twentieth Century* (London: British Library, 2010), 89.

54. Leonard Woolf to Christopher Isherwood, 7 Dec 1939. MS 2750/195. Reading, UoR Special Collections.
55. Margaret Cole, 'Books for the Multitude' III, *The Listener*, 5 January 1938, 42.
56. Leonard Woolf and Virginia Woolf, 'Are Too Many Books Written and Published', 239.
57. Lise Jaillant, *Cheap Modernism: Expanding Markets, Publishers' Series and the Avant-Garde* (Edinburgh: Edinburgh University Press, 2017), 120–39.
58. See also Melba Cuddy-Keane, *Virginia Woolf, the Intellectual and the Public Sphere* (Cambridge: Cambridge University Press, 2003).
59. Leonard Woolf, *Downhill*, 161.
60. Peter Morgan, 'New Ways of Approaching the Public: Leonard Woolf and the Day to Day Pamphlets' (Masters diss., Stanford University, 2019), 7.
61. Rupert Trouton, *Unemployment: Its Causes and their Remedies* (London: Hogarth Press, 1931), 30.
62. Thomas Sharp to the Hogarth Press, 30 November 1934. MS 2750/448. Reading, UoR Special Collections.
63. Leonard Woolf to Sally Graves, 27 November 1935. MS 2750/135. Reading, UoR Special Collections.
64. Virginia Woolf, *The Diary of Virginia Woolf, Volume Four: 1931–1935*, ed. by Anne Olivier Bell (Harmondsworth: Penguin, 1983), 358.
65. David Long, 'J. A. Hobson and Economic Internationalism', in *Thinkers of the Twenty Years' Crisis: Inter-War Idealism Reassessed*, ed. by David Long and Peter Wilson (Oxford: Clarendon Press, 1995), 165.
66. See Julia King and Laila Miletic-Vejzovic, *The Library of Leonard and Virginia Woolf* (Pullman: Washington State University Press, 2003), <http://ntserver1.wsulibs.wsu.edu/masc/onlinebooks/woolflibrary/woolflibraryonline.htm> [accessed 31 October 2023].
67. Leonard Woolf to Norman Leys, 16 July 1924. Reading, UoR Special Collections, <https://www.modernistarchives.com/node/15768> [accessed 31 October 2023].
68. J. A. Hobson, *From Capitalism to Socialism* (London: Hogarth Press, 1932), 12.
69. See also Anna Snaith, 'Leonard and Virginia Woolf: Writing Against Empire'. *Journal of Commonwealth Literature*, 50.1 (2014), 19–32.
70. Hobson, *From Capitalism*, 49.
71. Ibid., 51.
72. Marx and Engels, *Manifesto*, section 1.
73. Alison Rukavina, *The Development of the International Book Trade, 1870–1895: Tangled Networks* (Houndsmills: Palgrave Macmillan, 2010), 9–10.
74. Leonard Woolf to Vita Sackville-West, 17 September 1930. Reading, UoR Special Collections, MS 2750/416.
75. Stanley Unwin, 'English Books Abroad', in *The Book World*, ed. by John Hampden (London: Nelson, 1935), 180. Unwin was one of several

publishers who offered to buy the Hogarth Press in 1922. See *Letters of Leonard Woolf*, 282.
76. See Dale Hall, 'A Woolf Abroad: The Novels of Virginia Woolf and their Sales Overseas', *Virginia Woolf Miscellany*, 87 (2015), 37–9.
77. See Snaith, 'The Hogarth Press and Networks of Anti-Colonialism', in *Leonard & Virginia Woolf: The Hogarth Press and the Networks of Modernism*, ed. by Helen Southworth (Edinburgh: Edinburgh University Press, 2010); Jeanne Dubino, 'Globalization, Inter-Connectivity, and Anti-Imperialism: Leonard Woolf, The Hogarth Press, and Kenya', in *Interdisciplinary/Multidisciplinary Woolf*, ed. by Ann Martin and Kathryn Holland (Clemson: Clemson University Press, 2013).
78. Dubino, 'Globalization, Inter-Connectivity, and Anti-Imperialism', 233.
79. Willis, *Leonard and Virginia Woolf as Publishers*, 231.
80. Snaith addresses this complexity in 'The Hogarth Press and Networks of Anti-Colonialism', 104. For the continuity of this cultural logical see Gail Low, *Publishing the Postcolonial: Anglophone West African and Caribbean Writing in the UK 1948–68* (London: Routledge, 2011).
81. Pascale Casanova, *The World Republic of Letters*, trans. by M. B. Debevoise (Cambridge, MA: Harvard University Press, 2004), 39.
82. W. G. Taylor, 'Publishing', in *The Book World*, ed. by John Hampden (London: Nelson, 1935), 50.
83. With thanks to the Society of Authors (estate of Leonard and Virginia Woolf), David Higham Associates (estate of Margaret Cole), and Penguin Random House UK as owners of the Hogarth Press archive on deposit in UoR Special Collections, for permission to share unpublished archival material in this chapter.

Works Cited

Battershill, Claire. 'The Hogarth Press'. In *Publishing Modernist Fiction and Poetry*, ed. by Lise Jaillant, 70–87. Edinburgh: Edinburgh University Press, 2019.

——, *Modernist Lives: Biography and Autobiography at Leonard and Virginia Woolf's Hogarth Press*. London: Bloomsbury, 2018.

——, and Nicola Wilson. 'Introduction'. In *Virginia Woolf and the World of Books*, ed. by Claire Battershill and Nicola Wilson, vii–ix. Clemson: Clemson University Press, 2018.

Bhasker, Michael. *The Content Machine: Towards a Theory of Publishing from the Printing Press to the Digital Network*. London: Anthem, 2013.

——, *Curation: The Power of Selection in a World of Excess*. London: Piatkus, 2017.

Bourdieu, Pierre. 'The Market of Symbolic Goods'. In *Print Cultures: A Reader in Theory and Practice*, ed. by Caroline Davis, 17–30. London: Red Globe, 2019.

Briggs, Julia. *Reading Virginia Woolf*. Edinburgh: Edinburgh University Press, 2006.
Brook, Orion, Dave O'Brien and Mark Taylor. *Culture is Bad For You*. Manchester: Manchester University Press, 2020.
Casanova, Pascale. *The World Republic of Letters*, trans. by M. B. Debevoise. Cambridge, MA: Harvard University Press, 2004.
Chester, Gail. 'Sex, Race and Class: the Radical, Alternative and Minority Book Trade in Britain'. In *The Cambridge History of the Book in Britain*, vol. 7, 616–45. Cambridge: Cambridge University Press, 2019.
Clark, Giles and Angus Phillips. *Inside Book Publishing*, 5th ed. London: Routledge, 2014.
Cole, Margaret. *Books and the People*. London: Hogarth Press, 1938.
——, 'Books for the Multitude I-IV', *The Listener*, 22 December 1937–12 January 1938.
Cuddy-Keane, Melba. *Virginia Woolf, the Intellectual and the Public Sphere*. Cambridge: Cambridge University Press, 2003.
Dark, Sidney. *The New Reading Public: A Lecture under the Auspices of The Society of Bookmen*. London: Allen & Unwin, 1922.
Davison, Claire. *Translation as Collaboration: Virginia Woolf, Katherine Mansfield, and S. S. Koteliansky*. Edinburgh: Edinburgh University Press, 2014.
Dubino, Jeanne. 'Globalization, Inter-Connectivity, and Anti-Imperialism: Leonard Woolf, The Hogarth Press, and Kenya'. In *Interdisciplinary/Multidisciplinary Woolf*, ed. by Ann Martin and Kathryn Holland, 231–6. Clemson: Clemson University Press, 2013.
Finkelstein, David and Alistair McCleery. 'Publishing'. In *The Cambridge History of the Book in Britain*, vol 7, ed. by Andrew Nash, Claire Squires and I. R. Willison, 146–90. Cambridge: Cambridge University Press, 2019.
Hall, Dale. 'A Woolf Abroad: The Novels of Virginia Woolf and their Sales Overseas', *Virginia Woolf Miscellany*, 87 (2015), 37–9.
Hobson, J. A. *From Capitalism to Socialism*. London: Hogarth Press, 1932.
Jaillant, Lise. *Cheap Modernism: Expanding Markets, Publishers' Series and the Avant-Garde*. Edinburgh: Edinburgh University Press, 2017.
Jones, Clara. *Virginia Woolf: Ambivalent Activist*. Edinburgh: Edinburgh University Press, 2016.
Karl, Alissa G. 'Consumerism and the Imperial Nation in Virginia Woolf's *The Voyage Out* and *Mrs Dalloway*'. In Alissa G. Karl, *Modernism and the Marketplace: Literary Culture and Consumer Capitalism in Rhys, Woolf, Stein, and Nella Larsen*, 43–79. London: Routledge, 2009.
Keane, Alice. '"Full of Experiments and Reforms": Virginia Woolf, John Maynard Keynes, and the Impossibility of Economic Modeling'. In *Interdisciplinary/Multidisciplinary Woolf*, ed. by Ann Martin and Kathryn Holland, 20–6. Clemson: Clemson University Press, 2013.
King, Julia and Laila Miletic-Vejzovic. *The Library of Leonard and Virginia Woolf*. Pullman: Washington State University Press, 2003.

Long, David. 'J. A. Hobson and Economic Internationalism'. In *Thinkers of the Twenty Years' Crisis: Inter-War Idealism Reassessed*, ed. by David Long and Peter Wilson, 161–88. Oxford: Clarendon Press, 1995.

Low, Gail. *Publishing the Postcolonial: Anglophone West African and Caribbean Writing in the UK 1948–68*. London: Routledge, 2011.

Marx, Karl. *Capital: An Abridged Edition*, ed. by David McLellan. Oxford: Oxford University Press, 1995.

Marx, Karl and Frederick Engels. *Manifesto of the Communist* Party, trans. Samuel Moore. London: Reeves, 1888.

Miller, Laura J. *Reluctant Capitalists: Bookselling and the Culture of Consumption*. Chicago: University of Chicago Press, 2006.

Mirrlees. Hope, *Paris*. London: Hogarth Press, 1919.

Morgan, Peter. 'New Ways of Approaching the Public: Leonard Woolf and the Day to Day Pamphlets'. Masters diss., Stanford University, 2019.

Murphet, Julian. 'Marx in the Modernist Novel'. In *Understanding Marx, Understanding Modernism*, ed. by Mark Steven, 115–23. London: Bloomsbury, 2021.

Niven, Alex. '*The Communist Manifesto* and the Exhumation of Literature'. In *Understanding Marx, Understanding Modernism*, ed. by Mark Steven, 40–9. London: Bloomsbury, 2021.

Rose, Phyllis. 'Introduction'. In John Lehmann, *Thrown to the Woolfs*, ix–xvi. New York: Holt, Rinehart and Winston, 1978.

Rukavina, Alison. *The Development of the International Book Trade, 1870–1895: Tangled Networks*. Houndsmills: Palgrave Macmillan, 2010.

Saha, Anamik and Sandra van Lente. *Rethinking 'Diversity' in Publishing*. London: Spread the Word, 2020.

Shaw, Katy. *Common People: Breaking the Class Ceiling in UK Publishing*. Newcastle: New Writing North, 2020.

Snaith, Anna. 'The Hogarth Press and Networks of Anti-Colonialism'. In *Leonard & Virginia Woolf. The Hogarth Press and the Networks of Modernism*, ed. by Helen Southworth, 103–27. Edinburgh: Edinburgh University Press, 2010.

——, 'Leonard and Virginia Woolf: Writing Against Empire'. *Journal of Commonwealth Literature*, 50.1 (2014), 19–32.

Society of Bookmen. *Report of the Commercial Circulating Libraries Sub-Committee*. London: Society of Bookmen, 1928.

Southworth, Helen (ed.). *Leonard & Virginia Woolf: The Hogarth Press and the Networks of Modernism*. Edinburgh: Edinburgh University Press, 2010.

——, '"Going Over": The Woolfs, the Hogarth Press and Working-Class Voices'. In *Leonard & Virginia Woolf: The Hogarth Press and the Networks of Modernism*, ed. by Helen Southworth, 206–33. Edinburgh: Edinburgh University Press, 2010.

Staveley, Alice. 'The Hogarth Press'. In *The Oxford Handbook of Virginia Woolf*, ed. by Anne Fernald, 246–61. Oxford: Oxford University Press, 2021.

Steven, Mark. 'Introduction'. In *Understanding Marx, Understanding Modernism*, ed. by Mark Steven, 1–12. London: Bloomsbury, 2021.
Stevenson, Iain. *Book Makers: British Publishing in the Twentieth Century*. London: British Library, 2010.
Taylor, W. G. 'Publishing'. In *The Book World*, ed. by John Hampden, 49–88. London: Nelson, 1935.
Thompson, John B. *Merchants of Culture: The Publishing Business in the Twenty-First Century*, 2nd edn. London: Polity, 2012.
Trouton, Rupert. *Unemployment: Its Causes and their Remedies*. London: Hogarth Press, 1931.
Unwin, Stanley. 'English Books Abroad'. In *The Book World*, ed. by John Hampden, 163–80. London: Nelson, 1935.
Vernon, Betty D. *Margaret Cole, 1893–1980*. Beckenham: Croom Helm, 1986.
Willis, J. H. *Leonard and Virginia Woolf as Publishers: The Hogarth Press 1917–41*. Charlottesville: University Press of Virginia, 1992.
Willson Gordon, Elizabeth. *Publishing, Branding, and Selling an Icon: The Cultural Impact of the Hogarth Press 1917–2017* (forthcoming).
Wilson, Nicola. 'British Publishers and Colonial Editions'. In *The Book World: Selling and Distributing British Literature, 1900–1940*. Leiden: Brill, 2016.
——, 'Virginia Woolf, Hugh Walpole, The Hogarth Press, and the Book Society'. *ELH*, 79.1 (2012), 237–60.
——, and Helen Southworth. 'Women Workers at the Hogarth Press (c. 1917–25)'. In *Women in Print, vol. 2*, ed. by Christine Moog. Oxford: Peter Lang.
Woolf, Leonard. *Downhill All The Way: An Autobiography of the Years 1919–1939*. London: Hogarth Press, 1968.
——, *Letters of Leonard Woolf*, ed. by Frederic Spotts. London: Weidenfeld and Nicolson, 1990.
Woolf, Leonard and Virginia Woolf. 'Are Too Many Books Written and Published', ed. by Melba Cuddy-Keane. *PMLA* 121.1 (2006), 235–44.
Woolf, Virginia. *A Room of One's Own and Three Guineas*, ed. by Michèle Barrett. London: Penguin, 1993.
——, *The Diary of Virginia Woolf, Volume Four: 1931–1935*, ed. by Anne Olivier Bell. Harmondsworth: Penguin, 1983.
——, *The Diary of Virginia Woolf, Volume Five: 1936–1941*, ed. by Anne Olivier Bell. Orlando: Harcourt Brace Jovanovich, 1984.
——, *The Letters of Virginia Woolf, Volume Four: 1929–1931*, ed. by Nigel Nicolson and Joanne Trautmann. London: Hogarth Press, 1978.
——, *The Letters of Virginia Woolf, Volume Six: 1936–1941*, ed. by Nigel Nicolson and Joanne Trautmann. New York: Harcourt Brace Jovanovich, 1980.
Woolmer, J. Howard. *A Checklist of the Hogarth Press 1917–1938*. London: Hogarth Press, 1976.

Chapter 8

'It's rather distinguished to be as ordinary as I am.' Woolf's Working Women Writers

Bryony Randall

In 1907 the Council of the Society of Authors held a lively debate about the representation (or lack thereof) of women in its governance structures. By this time a well-established organisation dedicated to promoting the recognition and rights of professional writers, the Society of Authors had decided that its governance structures were unrepresentative, and lacked robustness; so their Council proposed that a Special Committee be set up in order to review the Society's constitution. To this resolution, the highly successful novelist Mrs Humphry Ward moved an amendment: 'that the Special Committee consist of not less [sic] than twelve Members and that of these not less than three shall be women'.[1] The amendment was ultimately accepted; but not before a number of interventions on the topic of 'ladies'. Of these the most striking came from the writer and political activist George Bernard Shaw.

Shaw fully supported the amendment, opining that 'it is a disgraceful thing for us that we [on the managing committee] have never co-opted a woman'. But the language in which he then went on to defend this position betrays a striking set of assumptions about what it meant to be a working woman writer:

> I should like [. . .] to get some of the women who are not members of the Council because, believe me, we who are members of this Council really do not know what literary work is and what publishers are. We are all more or less distinguished people, and would not be on it if we were not. That means that we are all persons who are more or less at an advantage in dealing with publishers; and what is really wanted is [to] have something which corresponds to a Labour Party in our management; we want to be in contact with one or two of those men

and women who have no reputation and never will have any reputation, and who consequently understand what publishers really are when they deal with that class of worker [. . .] the more obscure they are as literary workers the better I for one shall be pleased.[2]

Although he does accept that both 'men and women' may fall into the category of those 'who have no reputation and never will have any reputation', the fact that this reflection on the need for the Society to more fully consult with 'obscure [. . .] literary workers' flows directly from the discussion about co-opting women writers is indicative of Shaw's line of thought: namely, that women writers are primary representatives of the working class in the economic structure of literary production.[3] Shaw and his like, as he admits, possess the social and cultural capital which goes with being 'distinguished people' – sufficiently well-respected in the literary world not only to be on the Council of the Society of Authors, but to exclude them from the category of 'worker' altogether – 'we [. . .] do not know what literary work is'. This phrase casts the concept of 'work' in what might seem an unusual light – particularly coming from so famed a writer as Shaw; if anyone could be said to work as a writer at the time, surely it would be him? But this expression makes more sense if we consider it in its political context. Shaw's reference to the Labour Party suggests that he is understanding the concept of work in a quite specific way, as set out by the socialist principles underpinning the trade union movements of the late nineteenth and early twentieth centuries (with which Shaw was intimately involved). In this context, we should understand the term 'work' and its cognates as referring explicitly to a member of the working class, or proletariat, rather than a member of the capitalist middle or upper class, or bourgeoisie. From this point of view, Shaw seems to be – with the best of intentions, no doubt – seeking to distinguish between his own influential position in the capitalist economy of publishing, and that of those 'workers' who have limited or no control over or access to the means of production.

This chapter examines Woolf's only extended depictions of working women writers, all of which appear in her early writing: Rosamond Merridew in her short story '[The Journal Of Mistress Joan Martyn]' (composed in 1906, unpublished in Woolf's lifetime); Miss Willatt in 'Memoirs of a Novelist' (composed and rejected for publication in 1909 and unpublished in her lifetime); and Miss Allan in her first novel *The Voyage Out* (1915). It will explore the various kinds of capital that Woolf's working women writers – who vary in terms of their distinction or obscurity, to use Shaw's terms – possess and acquire, as well as the wider structures of capitalism within which they operate. Before moving to analyse the texts, I will set out the way in which I use two key terms: 'capital' and 'work'.

I have found Pierre Bourdieu's definitions of 'capital' useful in articulating the networks and movements of capital which enmesh these working women writers. 'Capital', Bourdieu confirms, 'is accumulated labour';[4] but he expands on this key Marxist principle, lamenting the fact that analysis of capital has tended to treat it solely in its economic form, and setting out 'three fundamental guises' in which capital can present itself: economic, but also cultural, and social.[5] Cultural capital consists of those embodied characteristics, material possessions, or forms of institutional recognition (primarily through academic qualifications) which confer on their possessor a kind of capital '(or power, which amounts to the same thing)'.[6] It can, according to Bourdieu, be gradually acquired, but is also transmitted through heredity. Social capital is somewhat easier to summarise, as:

> the aggregate of the actual or potential resources which are linked to possession of a durable network of more or less institutionalized relationships of mutual acquaintance and recognition [. . .] which provides each of its members with the backing of the collectively-owned capital, a 'credential' which entitles them to credit, in the various senses of the word.[7]

Both cultural and social capital can be converted into economic capital. Indeed, Shaw's comment on the disadvantaged position of the 'obscure' writer in (financial) negotiations with publishers draws attention to precisely this process – or rather its absence – when lack of social or cultural capital results in an inability to maximise the accumulation of capital in its economic form.

The other key term which requires a little discussion before proceeding is 'work' – already identified as a slippery signifier in my discussion of Shaw's use of the term. I have identified all three figures who are the focus of my analysis here as not just women writers but specifically *working* woman writers. All three women are defined by their writing-as-work: as historian, novelist and literary critic, respectively. But it should be noted that the way in which I use this term encompasses what might in other contexts be called both amateur and professional work. The relationship between these concepts certainly interested Woolf, as a number of critics have recently demonstrated. Evelyn Tsz Yan Chan builds on (and at times takes issue with) work by critics such as Lois Cucullu and Melba Cuddy-Keane, forging a careful path through the question of Woolf's relationship with the notion of the professional (and thus, by definition, the amateur).[8] Chan produces a nuanced analysis which emphasises throughout Woolf's ambivalent and fluctuating attitude to both concepts. Although it is difficult therefore to summarise Woolf's attitude to professionalism and amateurism, Chan's provisional conclusion part-way through her chapter on 'Amateurism and the Professionalisation of Literature' is helpful in setting out key coordinates. For Woolf, Chan argues, amateurism is positively associated with writing for love not money – Woolf repeatedly articulated variations on the idea that '[t]he great desirable is not to have to earn money by writing' – but on the other hand can mean 'writing mostly for oneself; fickleness in subject and method; or even a lack of concern for form and method altogether'.[9] By contrast, while for Woolf professionalism may mean 'creating art for the sake of money', thus distorting art's purity, and thereby creating literary institutions driven by 'money, status and power', nevertheless the drive to write for an audience can achieve a desirable '"disinterestedness"', including a 'conscientious and scrupulous attention to aesthetics'.[10] More recently, Patricia May has written persuasively about what she calls Woolf's useful 'pose of amateurism', specifically in relation to her engagement with formal higher education, and the institutionalisation of English Literature in particular.[11] She argues that in adopting this position, Woolf not only offers a 'challenge to academic professionalism' but also reveals the materiality of its supposedly impersonal spaces, reminding us, in May's words, that '[s]cholars are people, not machines'.[12] A diary entry of November 1924 expresses Woolf's dynamic attitude to writing as a practice which moves between the (productive) constraint and discipline of the professional and the freedom of the amateur:

> writing must be formal. The art must be respected [. . .] if one lets the mind run loose, it becomes egotistic: personal, which I detest [. . .] At the same time the irregular fire must be there; & perhaps to loose [sic] it, one must begin by being chaotic, but not appear in public like that.[13]

The ambivalence with which Woolf approaches these concepts and their cognates forms part of my rationale for eschewing close engagement with them in my analysis. While, certainly, 'a professional identity is generally implicated in money issues'[14] and amateurism conversely associated with unpaid work, even this principle is not absolute, and when other forms of capital – social and cultural – are considered, any amateur/professional distinction is even less easy to draw. Indeed, Victoria Baena's commentary on Woolf's 'professional' status shows just how unstable these terms are in contemporary critical use: observing that '[o]nly with the 1915 publication of *The Voyage Out* would Leonard Woolf register his wife as an "author" in the London copyright office, with all the concomitant privileges and conditions the status entailed', Baena goes on to argue that 'an inheritance from Woolf's aunt [. . .] would allow her to establish herself as a professional writer, leaving behind definitively any need to work for a living'[15] – putting professionalism in precisely the opposite position in relation to economic imperatives from that set out by Chan above. The term 'work' – in its unqualified form – is however both capacious and specific enough to describe what the activity of writing constitutes for these women writers. Work can describe a myriad of activities: it can be paid, or not; it can be one's primary activity or otherwise; one can conduct many different kinds of work at the same time. But if we define work, per Baena's summary of Hannah Arendt's definition in *The Human Condition*, as 'activity that molds and transforms the world, creating human artifacts that persist beyond the span of a human life', and if we add to this that all three characters I will discuss here are remunerated for their efforts, then we can define them as, unquestionably, working women writers.[16]

From an early stage, Woolf delighted in the economic capital that her own work as a writer brought her. While more ambivalent about the social and cultural capital that her writing accrued, at least in some of its forms, she nevertheless wanted throughout her life 'to be kept up to the mark; that people should be interested, & watch one's work' (*D2* 107).[17] She was also clear-sighted in drawing attention to how much more difficult it might be to find success as a female than male writer; indeed this is implicit in the entire premise of her 'Memoirs of a Novelist', although the implication is buried fairly deep; it might be overreaching to say that this text is a forerunner of Woolf's most emphatic articulation of this position in *A Room of One's Own* (1928). It is, however, notable that Woolf never chose to present a working woman writer as a major character in any of her novels. Orlando, while a writer, is (of course) not always a woman, and his/her lifespan of at least 348 years means that his/her experience of writing changes dramatically across the course of the novel. Miss La Trobe, of *Between the Acts*, is an enthusiastic writer of plays, certainly, but the text does not give the impression that she is identified as a working playwright; and she does not appear to receive any payment for her writing. In any case, Woolf made no attempt after *The Voyage Out* to write a character whose working life closely resembled what was, by that point, her own (Lily Briscoe perhaps comes closest, as a working creative artist, but in a different medium). This chapter will argue that, in the working woman writer figures of her early fiction, we might detect Woolf testing her developing sense of what a working woman writer might be, and the ambivalence with which she regarded this identity. Miss Allan's description of herself as so 'ordinary' as to be 'distinguished' encapsulates much of the tension Woolf identifies in this figure, inserting herself into the rank of those self-proclaimed distinguished individuals such as Shaw, who would no doubt patronisingly have welcomed Miss Allan onto the Society of Author's council as one of the 'obscure [. . .] workers' he regarded as in need of greater representation. She does so by rejecting the structure which would regard the identities of 'distinguished' and 'ordinary' as mutually exclusive. Examining this nexus of characters provides a novel route into exploring Woolf's evolving feminist critique of the capitalist structures within which the work of writing is inevitably embroiled, starting with the mere fact of her paying attention to these more or less 'ordinary' women writers upon whose labour the whole economic structure of the publishing industry increasingly relied. In particular, Woolf's depiction of working woman writers reveals that this work never solely comprises the activity of writing (indeed, Woolf never actually depicts the physical activity of making words on a page), but variously generates or requires other kinds of work, including that which is measured in forms of capital other than the purely economic.

* * *

Rosamond Merridew, the first-person narrator of '[The Journal of Mistress Joan Martyn]' is perhaps the least obscure, and most distinguished (in Shaw's terms), of Woolf's three working women writers. Indeed, Merridew explains in the opening sentences of the story that 'I have won considerable fame among my profession', with her name known in Berlin, Frankfurt, Oxford and Cambridge.[18] So while her celebrity hardly reaches that of Shaw, or indeed Mrs Humphry Ward, she possesses the cultural, and social, capital that goes with the acquisition of educational qualifications and integration in well-established academic networks. And yet she immediately casts her position in terms of an (explicit) exchange – one which unquestionably would not apply were the speaker a man: 'I have exchanged a husband and a family and a house in which I may grow old for certain fragments of yellow parchment' (*CSF* 33). Merridew sees herself as having exchanged the social capital (and economic security) of marriage and motherhood for the, perhaps more precarious, but differently valued, position of working woman writer. This notion, that professional women have foregone one identity in order to assume another, is deeply familiar from the discourse around women writers at the turn of the last century. As Penny Boumelha notes in her analysis of depictions of literary geniuses in *fin-de-siècle* fiction, '[t]he incompatibility of the two roles [of writing and mothering] is poignantly imaged in the number of genius-heroines who refer to their works as their children';[19] indeed, none of Woolf's working women writers has children. In this story, the exchange evolves somewhat grotesquely: 'so a kind of maternal passion has sprung up in my breast for these shrivelled and colourless little gnomes [i.e. the text she studies]' (*CSF* 33). Merridew projects her maternal feelings onto deformed materials, presented as proxies for the human children that her professional identity has prevented her from bearing.

The text continues to be characterised by questions of the relationships between intellectual (cultural), social and economic capital. When Merridew directs her driver down an avenue of elm trees in response to 'a telegram' from her 'archaeological eye' (*CSF* 35) and finds the Hall at the end of it, the first words uttered by Mrs Martyn (the Hall's owner's wife) are '"Do you want to rent it, may I ask?"' (*CSF* 37). Although this is not the purpose of her visit, Merridew opts to keep Mrs Martyn on side by alluding to 'friends' who might be interested, and is then – as she had hoped she would be – offered a tour of the house. It becomes clear that the Martyns have a sense of the cultural capital which their property represents, in tension with the economic demands that it generates. Summarising Mrs Martyn's position, Merridew comments that

> The Hall had been in her husband's family for many a year, she remarked with some slight pride [. . .] the very chastened and clear sighted pride of one who knows by hard personal experience how little nobility of birth avails, against certain material drawbacks, the poverty of the land, for instance, the holes in the roof, and the rapacity of rats (*CSF* 37).

Merridew's implicit understanding of the Martyns' struggle to convert their cultural capital into economic capital is thus an important unspoken element of the negotiations between herself and Martyn about the house's papers. When she expresses interest in these papers – one of which, the diary of Grandmother Joan, appears as the second part of the story – she detects that Mr Martyn's 'opinion of my intelligence was lowered' (*CSF* 44). Martyn has articulated the value these papers hold for him, but the relationship is highly personal, whether practical (the papers having 'stood out for my rights in a court of law' (*CSF* 43)) or emotional (he would '"feel – well kind of lonely if you take my meaning, without my Grandfathers and Grandmothers, and Uncles and Aunts."' (*CSF* 43)). The idea that the papers could enter into a capitalist system of exchange – which was, indeed, Merridew's hope, or perhaps assumption – appears never to enter his head. His innocence on this point 'almost made [Merridew] blush when I remembered it now' (*CSF* 44) – given, presumably, the Martyns' financial precarity and thus the difficult position any offer to buy the papers might have put them in. Being permitted to borrow the papers, unfathomable though her desire so to do might be to Martyn, ultimately gives Merridew access to them without money changing hands.

Following the networks of various kinds of capital which run through this story provides a means of discerning its ambivalent attitude towards Merridew. As Clara Jones has pointed out, scholarly views differ considerably as to the extent of the sympathy the text extends to this character.[20] Jones emphasises the unreliability of Merridew as a narrator, and links this to her engagement with questions of exchange, going so far as to suggest that 'Far from characterising herself as a scholarly researcher, Merridew's use of the language of commerce, exchange and [. . .] the language of the hunt, casts her instead as a cross between a wayward cavalier and highwayman.'[21] Jones, however, reads the text's critique as directed towards 'Merridew's self-serving professional practice'[22] – in other words, towards the character rather than the system within which she operates (has, arguably, no choice but to operate). Certainly, Merridew fails to acknowledge her own position of (relative) privilege, and is largely silent on her own financial position – which is presumably not entirely precarious. Although she does count among the boons she has given up in pursuit of her vocation 'a house in which I may grow old' (*CSF* 33), suggesting that her privilege does not extend to property ownership, she can nevertheless afford (or is paid) to be driven around the Norfolk countryside in a private carriage. Similarly, the Martyns' struggles with the burden of the material form of their cultural capital is presented with a mixture of sympathy and satire, and their dismissal of the value of the papers ultimately undercut by the fact that the rest of the story consists entirely of those papers. Merridew, and thus in principle her readers – like Woolf and hers – value or are invited to value these documents in ways which are indiscernible to the Martyns. In this story, then, we are presented with a writer whose professional life is to a large extent reliant on various kinds of exchange (or possible exchange): the promise of possible economic exchange (through renting the Hall) allows her initial access; the cultural capital she embodies (assisted by the social capital she presents through offering her credentials with the local landowner) enables her to acquire, if not possession of the documents she desires, at least access to the material they contain; and her entire professional identity is presented as predicated on having exchanged the acquisition of a traditional role in the transmission of social and cultural capital, through being a wife and mother, to this more active – if ethically complex – participation in networks of capital.

Woolf composed '[The Journal of Mistress Joan Martyn]' in August 1906 while on holiday at Blo' Norton Hall in Norwich, which provided the inspiration for the story. From Blo' Norton, she wrote to her friend Violet Dickinson that she had been walking and 'making up beautiful brilliant stories every step of the way. One is actually being – as we geniuses say – transferred to paper at this moment', and later 'I have written 40 pages of manuscript since I came here' – which may well be the start of this story itself; the final manuscript was 82 pages long (*L1* 235). But her letters also demonstrate her preoccupation with writing as a means to make money. She had by this time begun writing paid reviews for newspapers and journals; on 22 July 1906 she wrote that she had received a cheque for £9.7 from the *Times*, 'the largest sum I have ever made at one blow' (*L1* 232). Interestingly, however, the same letter also indicates her awareness of the potential monetary value of (literary) manuscripts, explaining with some envy that her brother Thoby made £1,000 ('*one thousand pounds*', she repeats) from selling ten pages of a manuscript inherited from his father. 'I wish my manuscripts would sell for more than their meaning!', she concludes (*L1* 232). In these letters, then, we see Woolf playfully trying out aspects of her evolving identity as a writer: an inspired (and prolific) 'genius', but one who is nevertheless mindful of the financial rewards of her work – and indeed, albeit playfully, perhaps even of the potential economic value of the physical materials she is producing.

Clara Jones's work on the 'Morley Sketch', the then Virginia Stephen's account of her experience teaching at Morley College written in July 1905, offers another perspective on her relationship at this time with the identity of the working woman writer. Jones's careful reading of Virginia Stephen's depiction of one of her students, one Miss Williams, who worked as a newspaper reporter, shows Stephen struggling with the tension around the difference in class between herself and her student, and their similarity in what Stephen was already by this point referring to as her 'profession' (having begun publishing journalism, in very similar publications to those for which Miss Williams wrote, six months previously). Jones describes:

> the curious mixture of hostility, curiosity and fellowship that defined her relationship to her working-class student: 'So we made much of this [having] we found we had a good deal in common; & I explored some of the more rather subterranean passages of my own profession'. As well as evoking all the grime and sordid dealings of Grub Street and striking a superior tone, her reference to the 'subterranean passages of my own profession' shows how she imaginatively identified with Miss Williams.[23]

This brief sketch of another working woman writer shows that, from the very beginning of her life as a working writer, Virginia Stephen was forced to confront the way in which this identity was implicated in wider networks of class, privilege and economics.

When Woolf next depicts a working woman writer, she has emphatically become one herself, making a regular income from her journalism but also, albeit largely in secret, having begun work on her first novel. An early example of Woolf's playful sleight-of-hand around genre which would come to its fullest expression in *Orlando*, 'Memoirs of a Novelist' presents itself as a review of a biography, by Miss Linsett, of a moderately successful but now forgotten novelist, Miss Willatt, who died in 1884 at the age of 61; although Miss Willatt's first novel went into two editions, '[i]t is likely that her name is scarcely known to the present generation'.[24] Miss Willatt is the working woman writer who concerns us in this story; we get no sense of Miss Linsett having made a career of writing as her friend did. 'Memoirs of a Novelist' – intended to be the first in 'a series of lives of eccentric women' (thus partly prefiguring the 'Lives of the Obscure' of later years) – was the first piece of fiction that Woolf submitted for publication.[25] In late 1909, she sent the piece to *The Cornhill*, presumably hoping for a warm reception from its editor, Reginald Smith, who had published a number of her reviews. While the work was described by Smith as 'cleverness itself',[26] it was, however, rejected. Woolf's personal writings do not record her response to this rejection, but she presented no further short fiction for publication until the establishment of the Hogarth Press made it possible for her to publish her own work: the Press's first publication, *Two Stories* (1917), included Woolf's short fiction 'The Mark on the Wall'; and *Monday or Tuesday*, Woolf's only short fiction collection, was published by Hogarth in 1921.

Miss Willatt is presented as possessing a somewhat inconsistent mixture of extreme reticence and relative assertiveness – a combination we will also find characteristic of Miss Allan in *The Voyage Out*. We must of course remember that – as the narrator herself laments – we primarily have access to Miss Willatt through the narrator's assessment of Miss Linsett's depiction of her friend, and certainly the narrator's attitude to Miss Linsett's narrative is a critical one; see, for example, the narrator's cutting assessment of Miss Linsett's extended final chapter on Miss Willatt's death, which the narrator puts down in part to Miss Linsett's 'natural distrust of life' (*CSF* 78). The narrator's acerbity about Miss Linsett's depiction of her friend leads us to understand that Miss Willatt was less reticent and passive than Miss Linsett's version of her might suggest; indeed '[h]appily there are', the narrator opines, 'signs that Miss Willatt was not what she seemed. They creep out in the notes, in her letters, and most clearly in her portrait' (*CSF* 74). For example, by contrast with Miss Linsett's timid attitude to life, we are told that Miss Willatt rejects the life of philanthropy – 'the obvious profession for a woman in those days' (*CSF* 75) – on the basis that it 'gave one no chance of "an individual life" as she called it' (*CSF* 76). For a woman to desire an 'individual life' at this time and in this context – what is more, to articulate it – might itself be regarded as strikingly emancipated and forthright.

Miss Willatt's relationship with those female novelists who forged a path before her is also ambivalently presented in this story. Woolf's slippery narrative voice implicitly attributes to Miss Willatt the view that 'merely to sit with your eyes open fills the brain, and perhaps in emptying it, one may come across something illuminating', and then immediately continues:

> George Eliot and Charlotte Brontë between them must share the parentage of many novels at this period, for they disclosed the secret that the precious stuff of which books are made lies all about one, in drawing-rooms and kitchens where women live, and accumulates with every tick of the clock (*CSF* 75).

We might detect in this description of where material for novels can be found the seed of Woolf's substantial elaboration of her theories of gender and fiction in, most obviously, 'Modern Fiction' and *A Room of One's Own*. We are then told that Miss Willatt 'adopted the theory that no training is necessary', presumably implying that this view aligns with that just set out – simply having one's eyes open is sufficient in order to access what might become the stuff of fiction. And yet, in opting not to write non-fiction, thinking it 'indecent to describe what she had seen', she instead 'invented Arabian lovers and set them on the banks of the Orinoco' (*CSF* 75); far indeed from drawing-rooms and kitchens where women like her live. It is perhaps implied here that Miss Willatt is, nevertheless, able to convey something universal of what 'lies all about one' despite the exotic setting. Indeed, we are told that approving reviewers of her first book 'liken[ed] it to the novels of George Eliot, save that the tone was "more satisfactory"' (*CSF* 76). Yet both Miss Willatt's style and subject matter are described by the narrator – from her perspective in a more emancipated next generation, of course – with considerable satire, particularly when it comes to her attempts to convey the talk of lovers; between women in the privacy of their tents; or on such fundamental matters as birth and death. '[S]he stammered and blushed perceptibly', the narrator tells us; 'She could not say "I love you," but used "thee" and "thou," which, with their indirectness, seemed to hint that she was not committing herself' (*CSF* 76). The implication here seems to be that Miss Willatt is reticent on matters of sexual desire in particular, of intimacy and the body in general; perhaps ignorant of them, and therefore inarticulate.[27] And yet, it is also worth noting that Woolf had already by this point been working for at least two years on *The Voyage Out*, primarily set in an exotic (South American) landscape which she had never visited; a central theme in the novel is the inability of two young lovers to communicate with each other, and it features a famous passage conveying in the most elliptical (if intense) terms an erotic encounter between the young protagonist Rachel Vinrace and her aunt Helen. Ironically, then, and while Miss Willatt is placed at a considerable distance from Woolf and her readers in a number of ways (her firm location in the Victorian period; the layers of narrative through which we must reach for her), there are more resonances between the first novel by Miss Willatt and that of the young writer crafting her story than might appear on the surface.[28]

Miss Willatt's stated approach to her writing, however, casts it in rather different terms from those in which Woolf conveyed her sense of her own occupation. While, we are told, Miss Willatt 'had scruples about writing well', there was 'something shifty, she thought, in choosing one's expressions; the straightforward way to write was the best, speaking out everything in one's mind, like a child at its mother's knee' (*CSF* 75, 76). This position on writing – that it is a matter of instinct rather than craft – tends to place Miss Willatt in the position of amateur writer; indeed perhaps one for whom this was not a question of 'work' at all, if understood as an effortful expending of energy. This writing process is in stark contrast to the one Woolf went through in composing *The Voyage Out*: Julia Briggs explains that the novel was begun during the summer of 1907, and 'No one knows exactly how many times it was rewritten' before it was submitted for publication nearly six years later, reporting Leonard Woolf's recollection that his wife once found a pile of manuscripts comprising five redrafts of *The Voyage Out* (and burnt them).[29] This record of the evidently agonising process of crafting her first novel dramatically conveys how immensely hard Woolf worked at her writing.

Miss Willatt is, of the three characters under discussion, the least explicitly located in networks of production and exchange of capital – not least since, as we have seen, she does not cast her own writing as laborious. Further, while one assumes that Miss Willatt makes money from the sale of her novels, this aspect is never discussed (doubtless Miss Linsett might consider it vulgar to touch on such matters). Yet what is certainly clear is the social capital that she acquires as her identity as a 'Sibyl', as an acquaintance dubs her, develops. '[L]ike some gorged spider at the centre of her web', as the narrator unflatteringly puts it, numerous more or less distinguished people came to see Miss Willatt 'to hide themselves from the entire panorama [of the world] in the shade of Miss Willatt's skirts' (*CSF* 78).[30] The fact that this social capital acts as a substitute for the more expected form it would take for women – marriage and motherhood – is also made clear, as it is for Merridew. Having at one point fantasised about emigrating and founding a society whose disciples would call her 'Mother', her writing seems to provide a means for her to take on a comparable role: 'She knew that one must have a motive in order to work; she was strong enough to convince; and power, which should have been hers as a mother, was dear to her even when it came by illegitimate means' (*CSF* 77). This phrase also leaves us in no doubt, and despite the caveats above about the way she experiences her writing process, that 'work' is important to Miss Willatt – both her own, and that of others – but also shows that the work of a writer is more than just the process of writing. We have seen that Rosamond Merridew's work includes nuanced negotiations among networks of economic, cultural and social capital. For Miss Willatt, the identity of the working woman writer also enables, or requires, other kinds of work: interpersonal interaction which results in the acquisition of, to use Bourdieu's terms, a 'durable network of more or less institutionalized relationships of mutual acquaintance and recognition' – in other words, significant social capital.

Miss Willatt, then, acquires a certain distinction (to echo Shaw's words quoted in my introduction) through her writing. So, too, does Miss Allan, Woolf's most extended depiction of a working woman writer, although the esteem in which she is held is rather different. Miss Allan is the only woman in the novel with a career, and as such represents that part of Rachel which might aspire to find satisfaction in artistic labour – in her case, in music.[31] All those around Miss Allan recognise not only that she is a working woman, but that she relies on this work financially, as is explicitly articulated in this exchange:

> Miss Allan looked at her father's watch.
> 'Ten minutes to eleven,' she observed.
> 'Work?' asked Mrs Thornbury.
> 'Work,' replied Miss Allan.
> 'What a fine creature she is!' murmured Mrs Thornbury, as the square figure in its manly coat withdrew.
> 'And I'm sure she has had a hard life,' sighed Mrs Elliot.
> 'Oh, it *is* a hard life,' said Mrs Thornbury. 'Unmarried women – earning their livings – it's the hardest life of all.'[32]

The other hotel guests acknowledge and admire, albeit pityingly, Miss Allan's status as a woman who earns her living – by teaching, but also by writing. Elements of Miss Allan's characterisation certainly map onto the popular late nineteenth-century stereotype of the working woman, a sub-set of the New Woman characterised by eccentricity, asexuality and masculinity. Indeed, Miss Allan is cast as the inheritor of family responsibility, along with material forms of inherited cultural capital, such as her father's watch; a role (and an object) which one might have expected to pass to her brother. The most burdensome element of this responsibility is economic – she worries about the repercussions of the likely failure of the crop in her brother's fruit farm in New Zealand (*VO* 163). Her writing thus appears, at least explicitly, most important (to her and others) for its production of economic capital. Notably, Miss Allan is the only one of the writers in *The Voyage Out* who actually completes a book within the novel's timeframe, though it may not have the intellectual heft of Ridley's classical scholarship, nor the avant-garde aspirations of Hirst's poetry or Hewet's (imagined) novel: 'She was reading the "Prelude", partly because she always read the "Prelude" abroad, and partly because she was engaged in writing a short Primer of English Literature – Beowulf to Swinburne' (*VO* 93). Not only does she have a publishing contract, but the precise exchange value of the material she produces is quantified: 'They [the publishers] only allow one seventy thousand words, you see' (*VO* 299). She also understands about marketing: explaining that she has finished her book but 'omitting Swinburne' she reflects that the resulting title, 'Beowulf to Browning' is '"the kind of title which might catch one's eye on a railway bookstall"' (*VO* 299). Of the three characters discussed here, Miss Allan is the one for whom the products of her labour are most clearly set in networks of capitalist exchange.

One might assume, then, that Miss Allan would gladly have her financial burden lifted, and when she begins fantasising (towards the end of the book) about her 'imaginary uncle' the reader might initially imagine that this would be his role. But in fact this imaginary uncle – 'a most delightful old gentleman' – gives Miss Allan material objects and experiences: 'sometimes it's a gold watch; sometimes it's a carriage and pair; sometimes it's a beautiful little cottage in the New Forest; sometimes it's a ticket to the place I most want to see' (*VO* 350). Unlike the famous (imaginary) aunt of *A Room of One's Own* – or indeed Woolf's own Aunt Caroline Emelia – this relative does not provide capital in its raw economic form. One conclusion we might therefore draw is that, worrying though Miss Allan's family's economic precarity may be, her dearest fantasies do not include her being explicitly absolved of the need to resolve it.

Some further features of Miss Allan's character which undercut the other characters' and perhaps the reader's initial judgement of her are swiftly yet firmly drawn in a scene which takes place during a dance held to celebrate a young couple's engagement. Noticing how late it is getting, Miss Allan observes that 'I have to despatch Alexander Pope tomorrow' (*VO* 150), this brisk articulation indicating the somewhat instrumentalist attitude that she, by force of necessity, must at times take to her writing. Hughling Elliot, an Oxford don and thus epitome of male privilege, snorts at this suggestion, and avers that Miss Allan 'will benefit the word much more by dancing than by writing'. This demonstrates his lack of respect for her scholarship, and his crass insensitivity to her financial situation – as she immediately goes on to explain 'calmly', 'It's a question of bread and butter' (*VO* 151). It also implies that these activities are mutually exclusive: 'It was one of Mr Elliot's affectations that nothing in the world could compare with the delights of dancing – nothing in the world was so tedious as literature' (*VO* 150). And yet, as if deliberately to give the lie to this distinction, Miss Allan not only takes up her position on the dancefloor, but is the only person able to lead the other characters accurately in the next dance. Admittedly, the dance in question is the lancers, whose origins date back to the mid-nineteenth century, thus reminding us of her location in a previous generation – (possibly the same as Miss Willatt's, or a little after, coming of age with the New Women); but this knowledge nevertheless constitutes a form of cultural capital that only she of all the guests possesses. As this passage also demonstrates – and despite her explicit economic anxieties – she displays, outwardly at least, a level of equanimity and contentment with her lot not generally found in the other characters in the novel.

Miss Allan's striking capacity to be both-and (both writer and dancer, for example) is summed up in the pronouncement she makes from which I draw the title for this essay: '"It's rather distinguished to be as ordinary as I am."' (*VO* 241) This phrase irreducibly combines self-deprecation and egotism, as well as – crucially – gently implying a rejection of existing categories defining 'distinguished' and 'ordinary' as antonyms, instead projecting a world in which one achieves the one through the other. The narrative's reference to the 'reticence which had snowed her under for years' (*VO* 242) seems to refer more to her relative taciturnity, rather than a quality of passivity or timidity; indeed, the hotel guests remark upon and admire her vigour. The very structure of the sentence which first introduces Miss Allan by name models the role that she plays in the narrative:

> The thump of jugs set down on the floor above could be heard and the chink of china, for there was not as thick a partition between the rooms as one might wish, so Miss Allan, the elderly lady who had been playing bridge, determined, giving the wall a smart rap with her knuckles. (*VO* 93)

We are told that she is 'the elderly lady who had been playing bridge', as if she had been mentioned in a previous scene, but in fact she has not, suggesting a tendency to remain in the background – the narrative has not really noticed her until now. The sentence begins from what must be a particular perspective – below a floor on which jugs are being thumped down – but the source of that perspective, Miss Allan herself, only emerges belatedly, her name being embedded at the centre of a sentence; 'Miss Allan' is indeed 'snowed under' by the preceding and subsequent clauses of this introductory sentence. And yet she emerges from this sentence with perhaps surprising vigour – that 'smart rap' which indicates the assertiveness lying behind, perhaps even underpinning, her reticence.

Particularly given the text's allusions to her capacity for assertion, then, Miss Allan's relative equanimity in the face of other characters' patronising or insensitive attitudes to her may frustrate a reader wishing that she might present a more emphatically resistant, including a more feminist, model for the working woman writer. But Miss Allan's power of resistance comes from her refusal fully to align herself with the structures which would reduce her only to the economic value of her work; her implicit insistence that, while attached to her work, 'working woman writer' is not the only identity she might inhabit. She can write and dance; be reticent and rap on the wall; worry about money, but not enough to dream of giving up her means of earning it. And we are given no sense that, despite their condescension, she feels the need to compete with, or even resents, the other male writers (or aspiring writers) in the novel. Perhaps, despite the squeamishness with which the youthful eyes of both protagonist and, at times, narrator regard this representative of an earlier generation, Woolf may nevertheless have found, relatively early on in her writing career, a model of the working woman writer to admire: complex, resistant, and confident enough in her own capacities and place in the world to insist that to be ordinary – to be obscure, overlooked, everyday – might carry with it a certain kind of distinction.

Notes

1. Society of Authors, *Report of the Proceedings at the Council of the Society of Authors*, Tuesday 18 June 1907, 6. This Report is held in the archives of the Society of Authors and is quoted by their kind permission.
2. Society of Authors, *Report of the Proceedings*, 10–11.
3. Shaw's phrase 'obscure [...] literary workers' brings to mind Woolf's lifelong interest in the 'lives of the obscure', evident both in the stories under discussion here and most notably in her creative biographical essays of the mid-1920s which were gathered together under that title in *The Common Reader* in 1925. See *The Essays of Virginia Woolf, Volume Four, 1925–1928*, ed. by Andrew McNeillie (London: The Hogarth Press, 1986), 118–40.
4. Pierre Bourdieu, 'The Forms of Capital', in *Handbook of Theory and Research for the Sociology of Education*, ed. by J. Richardson (Westport: Greenwood, 1986), 241.

5. Bourdieu, 'The Forms of Capital', 243.
6. Ibid., 243.
7. Ibid., 248.
8. See Lois Cucullu, *Expert Modernists, Matricide and Modern Culture: Woolf, Forster, Joyce* (Basingstoke: Palgrave Macmillan, 2004); Melba Cuddy-Keane, *Virginia Woolf, the Intellectual, and the Public Sphere* (Cambridge: Cambridge University Press, 2003). For example, Chan's work problematises Cucullu's argument that Woolf's 'modernist aesthetics were really attempts to exploit the ideology of expert culture in professional society'; Evelyn Tsz Yan Chan, *Virginia Woolf and the Professions* (Cambridge: Cambridge University Press, 2014), 19.
9. Virginia Woolf, *The Diary of Virginia Woolf, Volume Five, 1936–1941*, ed. by Anne Olivier Bell (London: Penguin, 1985), 91. Further references will be included within the main text.
10. Chan, *Virginia Woolf and the Professions*, 82.
11. Patricia May, 'Moving Houses: Domesticity, Media and Literary Form in the Writing of Virginia Woolf' (PhD diss., University of New South Wales, 2021), 54.
12. May, 'Moving Houses', 60.
13. Virginia Woolf, *The Diary of Virginia Woolf, Volume Two, 1920–1924*, ed. by Anne Olivier Bell (New York: Harcourt Brace Jovanovich, 1980), 321. Further references will be included within the main text.
14. Chan, *Virginia Woolf and the Professions*, 73.
15. Victoria Baena, 'Labor, Thought and the Work of Authorship: Virginia Woolf and Hannah Arendt', *Diacritics*, 48.1 (2020), 90. Baena claims that this freedom from financial constraint was a result of firstly the founding of the Hogarth Press, and then an inheritance from an aunt in 1918, but the source for this latter claim is not recorded; Woolf did, however, receive a significant legacy from her aunt Caroline Emelia Stephen when she died in 1909; see Virginia Woolf, *The Flight of the Mind: The Letters of Virginia Woolf, Volume One, 1888–1912*, ed. by Nigel Nicolson and Joanne Trautmann (London: Chatto & Windus, 1983), 391. Further references will be included within the main text.
16. Baena, 'Labor, Thought and the Work of Authorship', 86.
17. For a detailed summary of Woolf's finances, and her attitude to both money and fame, see Hermione Lee, *Virginia Woolf* (London: Vintage, 1997), 556–78.
18. Virginia Woolf, '[The Journal of Mistress Joan Martyn]', in *The Complete Shorter Fiction of Virginia Woolf*, ed. by Susan Dick, 33–62, 2nd edn (Orlando: Harcourt, 1989), 33. Further references will be included within the main text.
19. Penny Boumelha, 'The Woman of Genius and the Woman of Grub Street: Figures of the Female Writer in British Fin-de-Siècle Fiction', *English Literature in Transition, 1880–1920*, 40.2 (1997), 175.

20. Clara Jones, *Virginia Woolf: Ambivalent Activist* (Edinburgh: Edinburgh University Press, 2015), 38. Of the critics Jones summarises here, it is particularly worth noting the work of Leena Kore-Schröder whose essay on this short story engages directly with questions of capital, concluding that the narrative 'refutes the Marxist historical model, by which pre-capitalist peasant, or communal society is necessarily differentiated from modern social organisation based upon capitalism and individual ownership' (para 21). This critique arises, according to Kore-Schröder, not from Woolf's direct engagement with Marxist paradigms, but through her modelling of Merridew on her friend the historian F. W. Maitland. Leena Kore-Schröder, 'Who's Afraid of Rosamond Merridew?: Reading Medieval History in "The Journal of Mistress Joan Martyn"', *Journal of the Short Story in English*, 50, Spring 2008, np. <https://journals.openedition.org/jsse/719> [accessed 1 September 2023].
21. Jones, *Ambivalent Activist*, 40.
22. Ibid., 42.
23. Jones, *Ambivalent Activist*, 45.
24. Virginia Woolf, 'Memoirs of a Novelist', in *The Complete Shorter Fiction of Virginia Woolf*, ed. by Susan Dick, 69–79, 2nd edn (Orlando: Harcourt, 1989), 70. Further references will be included within the main text. Subsequent critics have identified this work as key in the development of Woolf's experimentation with biography; see, for example, Lyndall Gordon, *Virginia Woolf: A Writer's Life* (New York: Norton, 1984), 6; Rebecca McNeer 'Pointing the Way to Orlando: Literary Signposts', *Virginia Woolf Miscellany*, 67 (2005).
25. Julia Briggs, *Virginia Woolf: An Inner Life* (London: Penguin, 2005), 113.
26. Quentin Bell, *Virginia Woolf: A Biography*, Volume 1 (1972; London: Triad/Granada, 1976), 154.
27. Woolf knew a real Miss Willett, who appears fleetingly in Woolf's memoir fragment '22 Hyde Park Gate'. This Miss Willett was moved by the vision of Woolf's half-brother George Duckworth '"throwing off his ulster" in the middle of her drawing room [...] to write an Ode Comparing George Duckworth to the Hermes of Praxiteles' (Virginia Woolf, '22 Hyde Park Gate', in *Moments of Being*, ed. by Jeanne Schulkind, 2nd edn (Orlando: Harcourt Brace & Co, 1985), 166). Woolf's dismissive attitude to her half-brother, formed not least by her experiences of sexual abuse at his hands which she would go on to recount in terms at the end of this piece, casts the Miss Willett of this vignette in a profoundly satirical light. Indeed, Woolf implies that Miss Willett's idealisation of George failed to recognise his imperfections: 'one of his ears was pointed; and the other round [...] he had unmistakably the eyes of a pig' (166). But it does link the name with an erotic charge which is in each case euphemised through its expression in a

completely different setting: classical, in Miss Willett's 'Ode'; Arabian, in Miss Willatt's unnamed first novel.
28. Clara Jones draws attention to a number of further ways in which 'the story of Miss Willatt's life echoes that of [Virginia] Stephen', including a shared interest in history – both having moved to Bloomsbury after their respective fathers' deaths – and their 'turn from philanthropy in favour of literature' – in Stephen's case, her 'departure from Morley College in 1907 to focus on the drafting of *The Voyage Out*' (Clara Jones, 'Virginia Stephen at the Dr Williams's Library', *Women: A Cultural Review*, 27.2 (2016), 125–36, 132).
29. Briggs, *An Inner Life*, 4, quoting Leonard Woolf, *An Autobiography*, Volume 2 (1964, 1967, 1969; Oxford: Oxford University Press, 1980), 55.
30. Described thus, Miss Willatt bears some resemblance to Mrs Crowe of Woolf's essay 'Portrait of a Londoner', one of a series she wrote for *Good Housekeeping* magazine in 1931 and 1932: '[i]t was in her drawing-room [in which she was apparently permanently installed] that the innumerable fragments of the vast metropolis seemed to come together into one lively, comprehensible, amusing and agreeable whole' (Virginia Woolf, 'Portrait of a Londoner', in *The London Scene* (London: Snow Books, 2004), 84). Mrs Crowe, however, has a genius for gossip, not for writing; and while people come to Miss Willatt to escape from the world, they come to Mrs Crowe to learn about it.
31. Victoria Baena sets out the various kinds of activity implicitly offered to Rachel in the novel through the other characters – all, she suggests, more or less 'unsavory' (Victoria Baena, 'Labor, Thought and the Work of Authorship', 82–105, 93).
32. *The Voyage Out* (1915) (London: Penguin, 1992), 104. Further references will be included within the main text.

Works Cited

Baena, Victoria. 'Labor, Thought and the Work of Authorship: Virginia Woolf and Hannah Arendt'. *Diacritics* 48.1 (2020), 82–105. doi:10.1353/dia.2020.0003.

Bell, Quentin. *Virginia Woolf: A Biography*, Volume 1. 1972; London: Triad/Granada, 1976.

Boumelha, Penny. 'The Woman of Genius and the Woman of Grub Street: Figures of the Female Writer in British Fin-de-Siècle Fiction'. *English Literature in Transition, 1880–1920*, 40.2 (1997), 164–80.

Bourdieu, Pierre. 'The Forms of Capital'. In *Handbook of Theory and Research for the Sociology of Education*, ed. by J. Richardson, 241–58. Westport: Greenwood, 1986.

Briggs, Julia. *Virginia Woolf: An Inner Life*. London: Penguin, 2005.

Chan, Evelyn Tsz Yan. *Virginia Woolf and the Professions*. Cambridge: Cambridge University Press, 2014.
Cucullu, Lois. *Expert Modernists, Matricide and Modern Culture: Woolf, Forster, Joyce*. Basingstoke: Palgrave Macmillan, 2004.
Cuddy-Keane, Melba. *Virginia Woolf, the Intellectual, and the Public Sphere*. Cambridge: Cambridge University Press, 2003.
Gordon, Lyndall. *Virginia Woolf: A Writer's Life*. New York: Norton, 1984.
Jones, Clara. 'Virginia Stephen at the Dr Williams's Library'. *Women: A Cultural Review*, 27.2 (2016), 125–36.
——, *Virginia Woolf: Ambivalent Activist*. Edinburgh: Edinburgh University Press, 2015.
Kore-Schröder, Leena. 'Who's Afraid of Rosamond Merridew?: Reading Medieval History in "The Journal of Mistress Joan Martyn"'. *Journal of the Short Story in English*, 50 (Spring 2008), np. <https://journals.openedition.org/jsse/719> [accessed 1 September 2023].
Lee, Hermione, *Virginia Woolf*. London: Vintage, 1997.
McNeer, Rebecca. 'Pointing the Way to Orlando: Literary Signposts'. *Virginia Woolf Miscellany*, 67 (2005), 6–8.
May, Patricia. 'Moving Houses: Domesticity, Media and Literary Form in the Writing of Virginia Woolf'. PhD diss., University of New South Wales, 2021.
Society of Authors. *Report of the Proceedings At the Council of the Society of Authors*, Tuesday 18 June 1907.
Woolf, Leonard. *An Autobiography*, Volume 2. 1964, 1967, 1969; Oxford: Oxford University Press, 1980.
Woolf, Virginia. '22 Hyde Park Gate'. In *Moments of Being*, ed. by Jeanne Schulkind, 2nd edn, 162–98. Orlando: Harcourt Brace & Co, 1985.
——, *The Diary of Virginia Woolf: Volume Two, 1920–1924*, ed. by Anne Olivier Bell. New York: Harcourt Brace Jovanovich, 1980.
——, *The Diary of Virginia Woolf: Volume Five, 1936–1941*, ed. by Anne Olivier Bell. London: Penguin, 1985.
——, *The Essays of Virginia Woolf: Volume Four, 1925–1928*, ed. by Andrew McNeillie. London: The Hogarth Press, 1986.
——, *The Flight of the Mind: The Letters of Virginia Woolf, Volume One, 1888–1912*, ed. by Nigel Nicolson and Joanne Trautmann. London: Chatto & Windus, 1983.
——, '[The Journal of Mistress Joan Martyn]'. In *The Complete Shorter Fiction of Virginia Woolf*, ed. by Susan Dick, 33–62, 2nd edn. Orlando: Harcourt, 1989.
——, 'Memoirs of a Novelist'. In *The Complete Shorter Fiction of Virginia Woolf*, ed. by Susan Dick, 69–79, 2nd edn. Orlando: Harcourt, 1989.
——, 'Portrait of a Londoner'. In *The London Scene*, 75–84. London: Snow Books, 2004.
——, *The Voyage Out* (1915). London: Penguin, 1992.

Chapter 9

The Literary Public Sphere in Virginia Woolf's *Night and Day*

Stanislava Dikova

Introduction: A Problem Novel

It is telling that just as Gerald Duckworth was considering whether to publish his stepsister's second novel, *Night and Day*, and just as 'Modern Novels' appeared in the *Times Literary Supplement*, Virginia Woolf wrote another essay for the *TLS* to mark the two-hundredth anniversary of the publication of *Robinson Crusoe*. Considering both the past and the future of the English novel at a time when the nation was reeling from the consequences of the first global violent conflict, Woolf places the genre squarely at the intersection of the cultural imaginary of the nation, its political organisation and the increased economic precarity which came to characterise the postwar period.[1] She started serious work on *Night and Day* in the summer of 1916, after visiting her sister, the painter Vanessa Bell, in Suffolk. As the novel was progressing with characteristic ebb and flow, Woolf was engaged in other modes of literary production, including reviewing mainly for the *TLS* and printing work for the Hogarth Press.[2] She had also started reading and taking notes to help with Leonard's political writing and exhibited persistent interest in questions related to wartime economy, women's education, postwar reconstruction and internationalist approaches to securing peace. During the composition period, she served on her local branch of the Women's Co-operative Guild, inviting speakers and presiding over their monthly meetings held at her home in Richmond.[3] In early 1916, she attended at least one of Bertrand Russell's lectures and reports reading his *Principles of Social Reconstruction*;[4] Leonard Woolf's own influential book, *International Government*, which played an instrumental role for the British proposals for a League of Nations, also appeared in the same year.

In 1917, she was working specifically on producing a set of notes for Leonard initially for a book on international trade, commissioned by Sidney Webb for the Fabian Society, which developed into a treatise on economic imperialism, *Empire and Commerce in Africa* (1920).[5] In 1918, she attended meetings of the 1917 Club, a gathering place of radicals and intellectuals interested in securing peace and democracy, and the League of Nations Society.[6]

These events, discussions, publications and political projects of wide public note and importance occupied a significant space in Woolf's intellectual life during the time of *Night and Day*'s composition. The novel, however, appears rather narrower in scope and more focused on the private lives of its characters. Following the romantic pursuits of five young people, members of the educated class, and set before the start of the First World War, a world many considered to be irretrievably lost in its aftermath, the novel has been subject to criticisms of nostalgic remoteness. Early reviews and more recent scholarship alike often detect a mismatch between its aesthetic commitments and the contemporary political and literary permutations of capitalist modernity that surrounded its publication. The question of why Woolf produced a novel that looked back to the changing dynamics of capitalist modernity just before the war, instead of one more firmly oriented towards the future she herself was actively engaging in constructing, is the starting point of this chapter.

Night and Day, in other words, is an incongruous novel. It presents a problem, both in political and literary terms. Early readers saw in it a shirking of social responsibility, an almost offensive aloofness, which proved controversial, while later critics have taken issue with its often unflattering commentary on processes of community building and political organising.[7] Its publication coincided with a marked decline in liberal thought, which failed to formulate progressive models of political representation in response to the emergence of mass-democratic demands and a prolific increase in internationalist and socialist thought, with which many in Woolf's circle, and Woolf herself, were directly involved. Political theorists such as L. T. Hobhouse questioned liberalism's ability to reform itself as an ideology that sought to promote communitarian ideals to rival the emerging Labour Party, against the backdrop of its inherent contradiction between the 'expansionist economic forces which drive the British economy and core liberal values' such as protecting individual liberty from the dictates of church and state.[8]

In modernist literary history, *Night and Day*, the least remarked upon of Woolf's novels, also appears out of place, with its realist form and conventional plot structure. This was an impression cemented through its reception history by Katherine Mansfield's early review, much dreaded by Woolf, where she declared it a ghost ship, a remnant of a bygone age, serene and imperturbable, 'a novel in the tradition of the English novel'.[9] Mansfield's view was that *Night and Day* shied away from the challenges and responsibilities presented by its contemporary moment and remained still in the face of early modernist demands for change and permutation in response.[10] Its genre definition has presented another challenge, with critics referring to it as a romance, *roman-à-clef*, realist, and even a social novel. The variations in classification are often based on the degree of overt social intervention different readers are prepared to identify within *Night and Day*. For Ford Madox Hueffer (later Ford) the novel as a genre has nation-building duties which extend to the fostering of moral regeneration in the aftermath of violence. In his review, he declares Woolf's text a romance, because he sees it as having failed in this regard and, in turn, as a text without consequence, in which 'it matters little of what the tale teller discourses'.[11] W. L. George's comments continue in a similar trajectory to consider modern novelists' (and Woolf's among them) refusal to 'hold up a mirror to the writer's period', thus proving themselves incapable of fulfilling

> the high function of the novel, which it took up a hundred years ago: to dispel error by exhibiting the period in which it flourishes, to use the battle-axe of understanding upon the thickets of prejudice and folly, to cut a trail through the foolish forests of the present, along which to drive the chariot of the future.[12]

The genre inconsistencies noted by the reviewers are clearly linked to the perceived political inadequacies they diagnose. In fact, the explicit connection of genre (the novel) with a specific political purpose (nation-building) betrays an order of functionality, which *Night and Day* attempts to contravene, and in this sense, following Nancy Armstrong's recent formulation, it can be termed a 'problem novel'.[13]

Problem novels, Armstrong writes, 'throw themselves out of joint with their time and the context they share with a readership' in order to break 'the contract between novel and reader that subordinates rhetoric to logic and confines literary language to the prosaic institutional framework of money and property'.[14] In doing so, problem novels locate pivotal points in the intersection between the literary and wider histories of capitalist modernity and offer opportunities for rumination over the shaping of future forms of expression and organisation, both in political and aesthetic terms. This appeared as a particularly prescient task in the interwar and postwar periods of British literary history, during which writers across the political spectrum strove to leave their mark on the reconstructive processes that were taking shape around them.[15] As Michaela Bronstein has recently argued, however, this assumed responsibility for acting on behalf of the future carried some risks, including the potential to inscribe 'our own limitations onto a world that might not resemble us at all'.[16] To be clear, Woolf herself appeared reluctant to undertake any such commitments and comes to formalise her critique of the danger of literature's ideological and institutional dependencies in articulating visions of the future in essays such as *Three Guineas* and 'The Leaning Tower' two decades later. Instead of formulating instruction for the future, in a review of Sir Walter Raleigh's book of literary criticism *Romance: Two Lectures*, she looks back to the history of English literature as an 'infinitely complex' process, made by 'a thousand influences which probably have very little to do with art' (*E2* 75).[17] The fact that she returns to Defoe and the eighteenth-century novel and its relationship to the wider histories of capitalist modernity at the same time as she is forging her aesthetic commitment as a modernist writer is not a coincidental tangent, but rather a deliberate act of genealogical reconstruction.

This is not a problem, therefore, that emerges cleanly in Woolf's mature writings, but an almost existential concern regarding the nature and purpose of literature as a way of relating to and intervening in the world that occupied her from the very beginning. As Bryony Randall's contribution to this volume shows, evidence of Woolf's engagement with these questions is preserved even in her earliest short fiction. This chapter develops the genealogical work connected to the evolution of Woolf's political thought from this early period by considering three sets of 'problems' that *Night and Day* encounters in its attempt to negotiate its position within an economy of knowledge constructed to follow capitalist norms and modes of production. The first problem is the formation of the public sphere as a method of knowledge generation and dissemination; the second is the problem of authority as pertains to the relationship between the individual and the state; and the third is the problem of political representation and the role literature plays in imagining a political future. All three posit certain obstacles that the novel tries to negotiate related to tension between a normative idea of literature as a 'common good' and the conditions of understanding that determine the knowledge economy which regulates it.[18]

The Literary Public Sphere and the Market Relations Model

Questions around the ways in which novels are conditioned by the social and moral experience of their authors and how this dependence shows through the aesthetic or stylistic features of the genre have been debated by critics for generations, as is evident in the responses elicited by *Night and Day*. The idealistic, and almost nostalgic, appeal to the higher moral purpose of the novel, exhibited by George and to a lesser extent by Hueffer in their reviews, curiously only stretches back to the early Victorian novel. It also falls in line with a tradition of Woolf scholarship that sees 'literature as that which transcends the external limits of wealth, power and privilege' and presents Woolf as a writer of impersonality and high modernist interiority.[19] However, an alternative genealogy can be formed which traces Woolf's early fiction to an eighteenth-century tradition that pays more sustained attention to concomitant processes of social transformation that accompanied the so-called 'rise of the novel'.[20] The development of the modern novel occurred simultaneously with wider levels of societal and political transformation, which altered the composition and requirements of the reading public. As Jürgen Habermas states in his study *The Structural Transformation of the Public Sphere*, the eighteenth century presented a new moment in the history of capitalist modernity, which saw the birth of a new sphere, 'a public sphere whose decisive mark was the published word'.[21] In this context, the establishment of popular reviews, literary journals, and related types of publications focusing on lifestyle and cultural topics resulted in the creation of a whole new industry around the printing and publication of books to satisfy the appetite of a growing reading public. The *Tatler*, *Gentleman's Magazine* and the *Spectator*, among others, effectively regulated the emerging market of literary commodities, dictating taste and determining their wider reception, thus constructing 'a virtual monopoly of the channels of opinion' and 'a monopoly of writers'.[22] As Ian Watt reports, some literary figures such as Defoe and Alexander Pope 'were really alarmed' about 'the subjection of literature to the economic laws of *laissez-faire*'.[23] In a comment in *Applebee's Original Weekly Journal*, apocryphally attributed to Defoe, he goes as far as to state that '[w]riting [. . .] is become a very considerable Branch of British Commerce'.[24] Nancy Ruttenburg further notes, drawing on Watts's study, that the development of the novel was linked to the construction of modern modes of government and regulation, tied to the needs of emerging markets. '[C]apitalism', she writes, 'emphasised the existential state and worldly prospects of the autonomous individual or "homo economicus", whose very individuality made him or her *representative* of a multitude of others.'[25] Woolf's early twentieth-century text was published during a similar moment of socio-political change, during which questions of democratic representation and participation of a growing reading public formed an important part of postwar political discourse around the rebuilding of the nation.[26]

In Armstrong's view, it is important for literary historians to examine this blurring of boundaries between the public and private sphere, including the ways in which 'communication technology greases the wheels for global capitalism's penetration into more areas of human life'.[27] Such questions have begun to find their way into Woolfian circles too, predominantly in relation to the later fiction and social criticism, with Marina MacKay acknowledging Woolf's pressing concern with 'the way in which literature colludes with establishment cover-ups' as well as the author's commitment to thinking about literature, and the novel form more specifically, as a participant in the formation of political and normative discourses.[28] Arguments like MacKay's further necessitate the spelling out of the commitments Woolf's fiction makes to the world-making function of the novel and its relationship to the organisation of civil society. As a literary category, the 'problem novel' probes these connections and constructions by frustrating the aesthetic and political expectations to provide a programmatic solution, choosing instead to test established boundaries. In Bronstein's formulation, instead of diagnosing injustice or seeking opportunities to offer us alternatives, though it can do that too, the problem novel stages 'pragmatic and moral debates about political action' and asks questions about the strategies and forms of motivation that may be required for 'a greater good'.[29]

This third, more discursive option is, I want to suggest, the direction Woolf chooses in *Night and Day*. The text is alive with characters seeking to ascertain a position for themselves both in their individual lives and political orientations. One such is Ralph Denham, who works as a legal clerk at Lincoln's Inn, making plans and schemes for the future with furrowed brows. 'He had always made plans since he was a small boy', the narrator tells us,

> for poverty, and the fact that he was the eldest son of a large family, had given him the habit of thinking of spring and summer, autumn and winter, as so many stages in a prolonged campaign. Although he was still under thirty, this forecasting habit had marked two semicircular lines above his eyebrows.[30]

The infiltration of market forces into the most intimate aspects of Ralph's family arrangements, his relationships with his siblings and elderly mother, and even in his individual self, embroiled in a seemingly endless battle for survival, is evident in this description. The militaristic language ('prolonged campaign') in combination with the allusion to the temperamental nature of the markets ('forecasting') express enough of the novel's sense of the association between these two forms of aggressive and merciless organisation of human potential, which sap the individual of any sense of self-determination. The seasonality of the planning process ('spring and summer, autumn and winter') described here implies an earlier, more feudal and land-based form of economic organisation, which, as the story usually goes, has been triumphantly overcome by industrialisation and capitalist modes of production, to bring the individual more freedom and more choice.

The use of free indirect discourse in the description of Ralph's economically oriented process of life construction, unclaimed directly either by narrator or by character, suggests that the very forms of thinking used to arrange the so-called private lives of citizens have been overtaken by the capital-driven dependencies, which consolidate the public sphere. Ralph's life plan at the start of the novel involves learning German at night in order to continue to make obscure contributions to Mr Hilbery's *Legal Review*, thus gaining entry into the knowledge production process legitimated by the public sphere. This higher social rank is also associated with a more privileged class position than his own, one which is characterised by Woolf as possessing 'an undefinable freedom and authority of manner' that

> seemed to indicate that whether it was a question of art, music, or government, they were well within the gates, and could smile indulgently at the vast mass of humanity which is forced to wait and struggle, and pay for entrance with common coin at the door. (ND 384).

This 'vision of his future', in association with an 'upper' class, would result in 'a seat in the House of Commons at the age of fifty, a moderate fortune, and, with luck, an unimportant office in a Liberal Government' (*ND* 128). The distance implied through this almost impersonal and indirectly presented future life between Ralph himself and the path to his social realisation further emphasises the exploratory model Woolf is following in this novel. The text locates this point of disjunction in the capitalist 'homo economicus' model through the use of free indirect discourse, which creates the conditions for another mode of thinking to be generated, and 'for the discovery of some property of universal grammar which remains hidden until the new form gives evidence of its existence'.[31] As a result, the authority of Ralph's statement seems both asserted and deficient, an ambiguity which points to the obfuscation of boundaries between the private and the public realm, between state and society, the separation on which the bourgeois public sphere is built.[32]

The public sphere, alongside the rise of the novel and other forms of modern print communication, created a space for rational discussion, largely owned by the expanding middle and commercial classes, which aimed to challenge the authority of the state with its own.[33] The foundations for this lie in the emergence of a 'market for information' in addition to the market economy.[34] In these newly emerging conditions, 'fiction [...] as opposed to economic and administrative information, becomes the medium through which the bourgeoisie articulates a distinctive sense of its own subjectivity'.[35] Habermas's argument for the original emergence of the literary public sphere is that through the cultivation of discourses of taste and the figure of the professional critic such a sphere seeks to 'maintain a position of control' by exercising 'the force of argument to legitimate and control an authority'.[36] With the advance of the historical forms capitalism takes, this initial function changes by becoming more insidious and harder to disentangle from larger, and more dynamic, processes of social regulation undertaken by the modern state and markets through their institutionalised frameworks. This sense of potential intervention was felt by Woolf directly, as the publication fate both of *The Voyage Out* and *Night and Day* lay in the hands of her stepbrother Gerald Duckworth, who, Woolf notes in a letter to Janet Case in May 1919, 'doesn't know a book from a beehive' (*L2* 354). The Woolfs' decision to establish the Hogarth Press, which was purchased and developed during this period, was directly connected to their determination to secure their own and others' freedom to write without regulation. According to Habermas, within the public sphere the published word serves to facilitate the substitution of state authority 'by the power of society', a process which mediates 'the extension of public authority over sectors of the private realm'.[37] In effect, the literary public sphere assumes 'an interventionist policy', which 'could restrict the autonomy of private people without yet affecting the private character of their commerce with each other as such'.[38] Through this interventionist power, literary production in effect takes on a regulatory function in the management of interpersonal relations, which often, as in Ralph's case, are shaped in turn by a market relations model.

Authority, Intervention and Individual Freedom

Woolf's own concern with the problem of authority in *Night and Day* at first appears as a preoccupation with generational conflict, with the influence of old Victorian morality on the lives of her own contemporaries, and with the restrictions that family duty places on following personal motivations. To this effect we often see Katharine Hilbery, grand-daughter of a great poet and an heiress of literary greatness, who disdains literary forms of expression, feeling herself trapped in a condition of 'slavery to her family traditions' (*ND* 367).[39] During the composition process, however, and throughout 1918 as Woolf was writing the final third of the novel, the deeper underlying question about the relationship between individual freedom and institutional intervention begins to make regular appearances in her private papers. On 11 March 1918, for example, she records in her diary buying a copy of John Stuart Mill's essay *On Liberty*, originally published in 1859, just outside the 1860s period that we see her researching as background for her novel three years earlier (*D1* 124). In September of the same year, the Webbs visited Asheham and left Woolf mulling over the impressions made by their discussions of political organisation, including the ideal state of the citizen, formulated as a point of balance between individuality and authority: 'My wife & I always say that a Railway Guard is the most enviable of men. He has authority, & he is responsible to a government. That should be the state of each of us' (*D1* 194).

Sidney Webb's more formal reflections on the relationship between the individual and the state, published in his essay 'Social Movements', indicate his expectation that increased forms of intervention in the private lives of citizens would become the norm and that communal types of social management, exemplified by the co-operative movement and the trade union movement, would come to dominate the organisation of civil life.[40] In Michel Foucault's analysis of the functions of state power, several decades later, he also highlights the interventionist approach as one of the connective tissues between market economy and state power. A government, in his formulation, intervenes in social organisation through the introduction of competitive regulatory mechanisms in order to facilitate 'a general regulation of society by the market'.[41] Understood in this sense, Ralph's carefully charted plan for the controlled unfolding of his life is a reflection on this system of competition at work. In contrast, imaginative work, connected with the characters' inner selves, often concealed from those around them, is protected from the principle of competition in *Night and Day* by simply remaining hidden – Katharine's mathematical proofs, Mary's political treatise, Mrs Hilbery's manuscript of her father's biography, Mr Hilbery's edition of Shelley's poetry with its meticulously observed system of punctuation. This is the process of market or state-managed intervention that the novel portrays so effectively, and the source of tension which makes it appear as a 'problem'. As Armstrong attests, instead of enabling the individual to 'ascend from one position to another within a given social classification system', the problem novel moves to 'reject' the limitations of this narrative progression and instead stages a breaking point to avoid foreclosing transformation.[42]

One such limitation recognised by *Night and Day* is the apparent imbalance of power between the citizen and the state. In Chapter 27, when Katharine visits Ralph's crowded family home, she asks: 'The question is, then, at what point is it right for the individual to assert his will against the will of the State' (*ND* 399). In Webb's formulation the state is both a side in the balance equation and a guarantor for its promulgation. The latter function can obfuscate the state's ideological work on maintaining unequal distribution of power by presenting it instead as a process of fair arbitration. The Railway Guard in effect exercises an institutional, not an individual, authority, which functions as an illusory exercise of control; as a citizen, a social position which includes both personal and professional capacities, the Railway Guard is entirely under a moral and a legal obligation to respect the authority of the state. Gender further complicates this paradigm, as women were not entitled to full citizenship rights in Britain at the time and the larger histories of citizenship in the context of the British Empire further complicate Webb's clean-cut definition.

As a way to redress the balance of power between the individual and the state, *Night and Day*, in turn, seeks a method for social organisation built on the protection of individual rights over a more collective and institutionally regulated approach. This resistance to intervention is also a resistance to control, an approach characteristic of Woolf's political vision as a whole, and encapsulated well by Katharine's provocation. The novel, however, does not reveal Ralph's response, choosing to emphasise not the arrival at a particular solution, but the discursive dialogic practice required in advancing towards one. 'For some time they continued the argument, and then the intervals between one statement and next became longer and longer, and they spoke more speculatively and less pugnaciously, and at last fell silent' (ND 399). Just as Woolf was correcting the proofs for *Night and Day*, the *New Age* serialised C. H. Douglas's book *Economic Democracy*, where he warned that the modern corporate state threatened individual autonomy, arguing that 'human autonomy in the modern world is consonant with economic autonomy'.[43] The preservation of democracy, he advocated, required the reorganisation of the modern state by using a reverse model, 'we must build up from the individual, not down from the State'.[44] This reinvestment in the individual is the broadly liberal position Woolf also seems to be espousing to counteract the insidious encroachment of state power and market forces on the most intimate aspects of self-relation.

To counter this, *Night and Day* stages an enquiry into the logic of competition, asking the reader to consider whether this principle of social organisation is not in conflict with the ideal of preserving individual liberty. To this end Woolf partitions the individual into a public and a private presence. The former is used to fulfil all professional and social functions required of the individual within the regulated representative paradigm of capitalist modernity whereas the latter is the source of meaning located in individual consciousness, which for Woolf is the true thing of value. Ralph erects solid barriers which separate his 'real' life from his professional occupation through committed acts of self-mastery in the service of his steady progression along his designated social path.

> His endeavour, for many years, had been to control the spirit, and at the age of twenty-nine he could pride himself upon a life rigidly divided into the hours of work and those of dreams; the two lived side by side without harming each other. As a matter of fact, this effort at discipline had been helped by the interest of a difficult profession, but the old conclusion to which Ralph had come when he left college still held sway in his mind, and tinged his views with the melancholy belief that life for most people compels the exercise of the lower gifts and wastes the precious ones, until it forces us to agree that there is little virtue, as well as little profit, in what once seemed to us the noblest part of our inheritance.' (ND 129–30)

Evelyn Tsz Yan Chan's chapter in this collection considers this passage as evidence of Woolf's belief that 'new ideas of work seem needed that undermine the purposeful rhetoric of capital'. The passage also speaks to a wider, more fundamental liberal critique of the principles of capitalism as a system of organising personal and institutional relations. In carving out these lacunae of individual contemplation and disinterested thought, Woolf follows the Kantian dictum for the cultivation of aesthetic judgement, refusing to allow the narrative to perform a purely representational function of the coalescence between the public and private sphere, described by Habermas. Instead, she wants to protect the 'precious gifts' from the invasive forces of capitalist modes of government and their infringement on individual freedom. This task, however, as I will discuss in the final section below, coincides with a historical moment in which liberal values' participation in the construction of the very social order Woolf was criticising undermined their representative legitimacy.[45]

Community, Representation and Democracy in the Public Sphere

Jessica Berman argues that Woolf's approach to community construction, exemplified through her writings of the 1920s and 1930s, was deeply influenced by Sidney and Beatrice Webb's belief in the city as the crucible of social reform.[46] *Night and Day*, however, appears to test this model of thought, and as a novel which explores the influence of traditional forms of organising private and public lives, considers a return to rural, pre-modern forms as an alternative. Chapter 15, which describes the main characters' Christmas escape from the busy streets of central London to the country lanes of rural Lincolnshire, starts with an unusual mediation, inspired by the village of Disham, which is located in proximity both to Mary Datchet's childhood home and that of Katharine Hilbery's extended family;

> The village of Disham lies somewhere on the rolling piece of cultivated ground in the neighbourhood of Lincoln, not so far inland but that a sound, bringing rumours of the sea, can be heard on summer nights or when the winter storms fling the waves upon the long beach. So large is the church, and in particular the church tower, in comparison with the little street of cottages which compose the village, that the traveller is apt to cast his mind back to the Middle Ages, as the only time when so much piety could have been kept alive. So great a trust in the Church can surely not belong to our day, and he goes on to conjecture that everyone of the villagers has reached the extreme limit of human life. Such are the reflections of the superficial stranger, and his sight of the population, as it is represented by two or three men hoeing in a

turnip-field, a small child carrying a jug, and a young woman shaking a piece of carpet outside her cottage door, will not lead him to see anything very much out of keeping with the Middle Ages in the village of Disham as it is today. There people, though they seem young enough, look so angular and crude that they remind him of the little pictures painted by monks in the capital letters of their manuscripts. He only half understands what they say, and speaks very loud and clearly, as though, indeed his voice had to carry through a hundred years or more before it reached them. He would have a far better chance of understanding some dweller in Paris or Rome, Berlin, or Madrid, than these countrymen of his who have lived for the last two thousand years not two hundred miles from the City of London. (*ND* 183)

This passage is significant not only through the singularity of its occurrence – nowhere else does the narrator make such an expansive intervention which strays so far away from the characters' immediate experiences – but also through its stark description of the chasm that separates communities in British civic life. It clearly offers opportunities for socialist critique. The repeated reference to the Middle Ages, the turnip fields, the simplistic characterisation of village life and labour, the grotesque descriptions of the villagers and field workers, the limitations of the religious rites and cycles which structure their lives (we must recall Ralph's planning rituals and their cyclical nature here too) all speak to an understanding of rural communities as remnants of a bygone age. The whole setting appears de-historicised, located in a pre-modern simple world, which has remained unperturbed by the forces of industrialisation and capitalist structural reforms. Poverty is not explicitly mentioned, though it can be deduced. The description of the limitation of language and communication between the modern city dweller and the villagers is patronising, perhaps even grating. Yet, the fault in failing to relate seems to lie with the cosmopolitan traveller – it is he who 'only half understands what they say' and it is he who can communicate better with the inhabitants of European capitals than with his own 'countrymen'. Furthermore, this jarring incapacity speaks to an underlying rupture in the British democratic establishment, which threatens its continued survival, a rupture that relates to the problem of the translatability of individual experience.

This moment in the novel is an early formulation of Woolf's problem with politics. More particularly, it relates to her marked refusal to inhabit the voices and bodies of those who belong to underprivileged classes, formulated in her 'Introduction' to Margaret Llewelyn Davies's 1931 collection of working-class women's writings *Life as We Have Known It*.[47] Berman reads Woolf's unwillingness to admit herself as a member of this group as a recognition of the power of capital to inscribe bodily difference and class alienation through the various modes of production it utilises in its operations. As Berman writes, there, 'she seems conscious of the ability of capitalist patriarchal society both to alter bodies in such a way as to make them appear essentially different, and then to place priority on that bodily difference within social discourse'.[48] Building a politics that can narrow the distance between these altered bodies, each class-bound in its own way, is what is at stake here, as Berman rightly states.[49] The construction of cosmopolitan communities of individual selves, which have overcome class-generated types of conflict and distinction, through radical narrative forms, also seems to be precluded by the rural passage in *Night and Day*. This is because the real problem it tries to confront here is not interpretative, neither on the level of narrativisation nor of political organisation, but epistemological. It is about the norms which govern the knowledge economy, producing and distributing forms of understanding (including self-understanding) that purposefully obscure the structural connection between the state, market interests and the public sphere. Following this train of thought, translating individual experience into communal belonging could make it more widely consumable, but would not make it more liberating.

Woolf's distrust in representative politics is also rooted in its relation with the wider sphere of public relations, dominated by a knowledge economy, which serves as a regulative instrument. Knowledge production, generation and distribution that aims to serve a purpose, bring value, have use or result in a productive outcome is vulnerable to co-option, especially within an institutional setting. Knowing without determination, she seems to be suggesting, is only possible on the level of individual, unstructured, unmediated thinking. This is most clearly expressed in the novel through the development of Mary Datchet's political commitments. The question of the representative, cumulative, common 'we' recurs in the novel, in connection with Mary's suffrage campaigning and, later on, through her involvement with the Society for Democratic Change. Sitting with Mr Basnett to discuss the work of political organising, both Mary and her interlocutor are portrayed as imposters, 'she was dressed more or less like a Russian peasant girl', and he 'had come down from one of the Universities not long ago, and was now charged with the reformation of society' (*ND* 374). Their conversation revolves around the construction of a common body and representing 'the view of someone called "we"' (*ND* 375), an inorganic, fictive construction. Mary's own identity is subsumed by this construction and she is almost persuaded that she, too, was included in the 'we,' and agreed with Mr Basnett in believing that 'our' view, 'our' society, 'our' policy, stood for something quite definitely segregated from the main body of society in a circle of superior illumination. (*ND* 375)

Establishing a new regime of legitimation is at the heart of every political project, but the methods for constructing it are always tied up with processes of de-legitimation that are incompatible with a truly democratic, in the sense of representative, vision, in Woolf's view. Mary's political evolution, the novel seems to suggest, is earned at the expense of her self-knowledge, her sense of self swallowed by an unattributable voracious 'we' that threatens to engulf the entire public sphere.

Conclusion

The tension between the aesthetic and political commitments of Woolf's intellectual vision lies in the establishment of a double standard. As shown above, through the descriptions of Mary's political work Woolf reveals a suspicion that under the conditions of capitalist modernity, political work will remain vulnerable to infiltration by the insidious models of market and power relations based on practices of domination, even within a broadly democratic structure. Yet, she also demonstrates a belief in cultural and literary education to withstand these forces despite her awareness of 'the ways in which culture has been formed in the past out of histories of exclusion, of humiliation and of resistance, and aware too of how culture can be intimate with imperial and patriarchal projects'.[50] *The Common Reader* is the critical embodiment of Woolf's belief that literature can continue to be held in common, even if politics cannot, as the novel can make legible that which (and those who) do not receive political recognition. The two collections of critical essays aimed at the lay reader Woolf published in 1925 and 1932 served both a pedagogical and commercial purpose. The texts were written accessibly and designed to provide general guidance and cultivate taste with the aims of increasing cultural awareness and education for working-class people. As Melba Cuddy-Keane notes, this was in line with efforts espoused by educational associations and organisations such as the Workers' Educational Association to provide general as opposed to technical education in order to 'prepare workers to be effective members of society in a self-governing nation'.[51] Woolf's own description of her purpose, in reference to another eighteenth-century literary predecessor, Dr Johnson, returns to the economy of knowledge generation as the problem of note by stating that one of the main differences between the critic, the scholar and the common reader is that the latter, 'reads for his own pleasure rather than to impart knowledge or correct the opinions of others'.[52] They remain 'private people'.[53] The common reader in this sense is the first member of Woolf's society of outsiders, as she seems to suggest that their liberty lies precisely in their exclusion from the knowledge generation economy.

Notes

1. Virginia Woolf, 'Defoe', in *The Common Reader, Second Edition* (London: The Hogarth Press, 1925), 124.
2. A small number of reviews appeared in other outlets such as the *Times*. J. H. Stape, 'Introduction', in Virginia Woolf, *Night and Day* (1919; Oxford and Cambridge, MA: Shakespeare Head Press by Blackwell Publishers, 1994), xii. In his Introduction to the Cambridge annotated edition of the novel, Michael H. Whitworth notes Woolf's prolific reviewing schedule in 1917 and 1918 especially, following her recovery and return to literary work – 35 reviews and essays in 1917 and 44 in 1918 (xl, xlii).
3. Woolf's own committee work and political activism has been subject to wide-ranging and persistent critical debate. See, for example, Alex Zwerdling, *Virginia Woolf and the Real World* (Berkeley: University of California Press, 1986); Naomi Black, 'Virginia Woolf and the Women's Movement', in *Virginia Woolf: A Feminist Slant*, ed. by Jane Marcus (Lincoln: University of Nebraska Press, 1985), 180–97; Laura Marcus, 'Woolf's Feminism and Feminism's Woolf', in *The Cambridge Companion to Virginia Woolf*, ed. by Sue Roe and Susan Sellers (Cambridge: Cambridge University Press, 2000), 209–44; and Clara Jones, *Virginia Woolf: Ambivalent Activist* (Edinburgh: Edinburgh University Press, 2015).
4. Virginia Woolf, *The Question of Things Happening: The Letters of Virginia Woolf, Volume Two, 1912–1922*, ed. by Nigel Nicolson and Joanne Trautmann (London: The Hogarth Press, 1976), 133. Further references will appear in the main text.
5. Michèle Barrett, 'Virginia Woolf's Research for *Empire and Commerce in Africa* (Leonard Woolf, 1920)', *Woolf Studies Annual*, 19 (2013), 83–4. As Barrett states, Woolf's research was most useful for the second part of the book, 'Economic Imperialism in Africa', which includes 'a section on Algeria, one on Tunis, another on Tunis and Tripoli, one on Abyssinia and the Nile and one on Zanzibar and East Africa' (84).

6. See, for example, Virginia Woolf, *The Diary of Virginia Woolf, Volume One, 1915–1919*, ed. by Anne Olivier Bell (1977; London: Penguin Books, 1979), 157, referring to a meeting held on 14 June 1918. Further references will appear in the main text.
7. For a reception history of *Night and Day* see Mark Hussey, *Virginia Woolf A–Z: The Essential Reference to her Life and Writings* (New York and Oxford: Oxford University Press, 1996), 189–191.
8. Rachel Potter, *Modernism and Democracy: Literary Culture, 1900–1930* (Oxford: Oxford University Press, 2006), 6.
9. Katherine Mansfield, 'Review', *Athenaeum*, 27 November 1919, 1227, repr. in *Virginia Woolf: The Critical Heritage*, ed. by Robin Majumdar and Allen McLaurin (London and Boston: Routledge and Kegan Paul, 1975), 82.
10. Mansfield, 'Review', 79.
11. Ford Madox Hueffer, 'Review', in *Piccadilly Review*, October 1919, repr. in *Virginia Woolf: The Critical Heritage*, ed. by Robin Majumdar and Allen McLaurin (London and Boston: Routledge and Kegan Paul, 1975), 73.
12. W. L. George, 'A Painter's Literature', *English Review*, March 1920, 223–34 excerpt repr. in *Virginia Woolf: The Critical Heritage*, ed. by Robin Majumdar and Allen McLaurin (London and Boston: Routledge and Kegan Paul, 1975), 84.
13. Nancy Armstrong, 'Introduction', *Novel: A Forum on Fiction*, 54.3 'The Problem Novel' (2021), 321.
14. Armstrong, 'Introduction', 334.
15. See, for example, the work of Wyndham Lewis and Ezra Pound in *Blast* and the wider Vorticist and Futurist movements, Leonard Woolf's own work for the League of Nations and involvement with Labour politics, and Sylvia Pankhurst's continued dedication to the suffrage and anti-imperial struggles.
16. Michaela Bronstein, 'Revolutionary Violence and the Rise of the Art Novel', *Novel: A Forum on Fiction*, 54.3 ('The Problem Novel', 2021), 379.
17. Virginia Woolf, 'Romance', in *The Essays of Virginia Woolf, Volume Two, 1912–1918*, ed. by Andrew McNeillie (London: The Hogarth Press, 1987), 73–6. My thanks to Clara Jones for pointing out that this is another rehearsal of a later argument developed in *A Room of One's Own* about writing's connection to 'grossly material things', see Virginia Woolf, *A Room of One's Own and Three Guineas*, ed. by Anna Snaith (Oxford: Oxford University Press, 2015), 32.
18. McManus, 'The "Offensiveness" of Virginia Woolf', 96, is particularly instructive on this.
19. Ibid., 95.
20. See Ian Watt, *The Rise of the Novel: Studies in Defoe, Richardson, and Fielding* (1957; London: Penguin Books, 1966).

21. Jürgen Habermas, *The Structural Transformation of the Public Sphere: An Inquiry into a Category of Bourgeois Society*, trans. by Thomas Burger and Frederick Lawrence (1962; Cambridge: Polity, 2021), 16.
22. Watt, *The Rise of the Novel*, 55.
23. Ibid., 56. Pope was a frequent reading companion of Woolf's during 1915, when she reports reading 'The Rape of the Lock', 'An Essay on Criticism', 'Epistle to Dr Arbuthnot' and Leslie Stephen's biography of Pope.
24. William Lee, *Life and Writings of Daniel Defoe*, vol. III (London: J. C. Hotten, 1869), 410 qtd in Ian Watt, *The Rise of the Novel: Studies in Defoe, Richardson, and Fielding* (1957; London: Penguin Books, 1966), 55.
25. Nancy Ruttenberg, 'Introduction: Is the Novel Democratic?', *Novel: A Forum on Fiction*, 47.1 (2014), 3.
26. For an insightful discussion of this context, see Natasha Periyan, '"Altering the structure of society": An Institutional Focus on Virginia Woolf and Working-Class Education in the 1930s', *Textual Practice*, 32.8, 1312 and Melba Cuddy-Keane, *Virginia Woolf, the Intellectual, and the Public Sphere* (Cambridge: Cambridge University Press, 2003), 88.
27. Nancy Armstrong, 'Introduction', *Novel: A Forum on Fiction*, 54.3 ('The Problem Novel', 2021), 321 [321–34]. This refers to Frederic Jameson's claim that 'literary space had somehow been taken over by the repetition of machinic time and instant communication at the cost of historical awareness' (321); for Jameson's full account, see Fredric Jameson, *Postmodernism or, the Cultural Logic of Late Capitalism* (Durham, NC: Duke University Press, 1991).
28. Marina MacKay, *Modernism and World War II* (Cambridge: Cambridge University Press, 2009), 27.
29. Bronstein, 'Revolutionary Violence', 393. On argument staging and the agonistic features of the political novel, see Matthew Taunton, 'Chorus and Agon in the Political Novel: Staging Left-Wing Arguments in H. G. Wells, Iris Murdoch, and Doris Lessing', *MFS Modern Fiction Studies*, 67.2 (2021), 247–71. 'Such novels', he writes, 'test political arguments against specific diegetic conditions and force us to reflect on its entanglement with rhetoric, comedy, irony, characterization, and motivation' (253–4).
30. Virginia Woolf, *Night and Day*, ed. by Suzanne Raitt (1919; Oxford: Oxford University Press, 2009), 22. Further references will appear in the main text.
31. Ann Banfield, *Unspeakable Sentences: Narration and Representation in the Language of Fiction*, quoted in *Theory of the Novel: A Historical Approach*, ed. by Michael McKeon (Baltimore and London: The Johns Hopkins University Press, 2000), 486. See also Lukács on Marx in György Lukács, *The Historical Novel*, trans. by Hannah and Stanley Mitchell (1937; Boston: Beacon Press, 1963).

32. Habermas, *The Structural Transformation*, 142.
33. Ruttenberg, 'Introduction', 3.
34. Andrew Edgar, *The Philosophy of Habermas* (Chesham: Acumen, 2005), 34.
35. Edgar, *The Philosophy of Habermas*, 34.
36. Habermas, *The Structural Transformation*, 40.
37. Ibid., 142.
38. Ibid.
39. Woolf's diaries also specifically note the period of historical research she undertook while writing the novel. See *D1* 19. On 15 January 1915, she records: 'I read about 1860—the Kembles—Tennyson & so on; to get the spirit of that time'.
40. Sidney Webb, 'Social Movements', in *Cambridge Modern History: The Latest Age*, vol. XII, ed. by A. W. Ward, G. W. Prothero and Stanley Leathes (Cambridge: Cambridge University Press, 1910), 730–65.
41. Michel Foucault, *The Birth of Biopolitics: Lectures at the Collège de France, 1978–1979*, trans. Graham Burchell, ed. by Michel Senellart (London: Palgrave Macmillan, 2010), 145.
42. Armstrong, 'Introduction', 321.
43. Potter, *Modernism and Democracy*, 74.
44. C. H. Douglas, *Economic Democracy* (London: Cecil Palmer, 1920), 7, quoted in Potter, *Modernism and Democracy*, 74.
45. See Foucault on the interconnectedness between economic freedom and liberalism, Foucault, *The Birth of Biopolitics*, 67.
46. Jessica Berman, *Modernist Fiction, Cosmopolitanism and the Politics of Community* (Cambridge: Cambridge University Press, 2001), 124–6.
47. Margaret Llewelyn Davies (ed.), *Life as We Have Known It: By Co-operative Working Women* (1931; London: Virago, 1977).
48. Berman, *Modernist Fiction*, 119.
49. Ibid., 120. Berman's discussion at this point refers primarily to women's politics. The specific question asked by Berman that I paraphrase here reads: 'How to think "women" and "women's politics" without returning to the separate bodies of "woman at washtub" or "woman in the parlor" is the problem here.'
50. McManus, 'The "Offensiveness" of Virginia Woolf', 95–6.
51. Cuddy-Keane, *Virginia Woolf*, 87.
52. Woolf, *The Common Reader*, 11.
53. Ibid.

Works Cited

Armstrong, Nancy. 'Introduction'. *Novel: A Forum on Fiction*, 54.3 ('The Problem Novel' 2021), 321–34.

Banfield, Ann. 'From *Unspeakable Sentences: Narration and Representation in the Language of Fiction*'. In *Theory of the Novel: A Historical Approach*, ed. by Michael McKeon, 515–36. Baltimore and London: The Johns Hopkins University Press, 2000.

Barrett, Michèle. 'Virginia Woolf's Research for *Empire and Commerce in Africa* (Leonard Woolf, 1920)'. *Woolf Studies Annual*, 19 (2013), 83–122.

Berman, Jessica. *Modernist Fiction, Cosmopolitanism and the Politics of Community*. Cambridge: Cambridge University Press, 2001.

Black, Naomi. 'Virginia Woolf and the Women's Movement'. In *Virginia Woolf: A Feminist Slant*, ed. by Jane Marcus, 180–97. Lincoln: University of Nebraska Press, 1985.

Bronstein, Michaela. 'Revolutionary Violence and the Rise of the Art Novel'. *Novel: A Forum on Fiction*, 54.3 ('The Problem Novel', 2021), 379–403.

Cuddy-Keane, Melba. *Virginia Woolf, the Intellectual, and the Public Sphere*. Cambridge: Cambridge University Press, 2003.

Douglas, C. H. *Economic Democracy*. London: Cecil Palmer, 1920.

Edgar, Andrew. *The Philosophy of Habermas*. Chesham: Acumen, 2005.

Foucault, Michel. *The Birth of Biopolitics: Lectures at the Collège de France, 1978–1979*. Trans. by Graham Burchell, ed. by Michel Senellart, 129–57. London: Palgrave Macmillan, 2010.

Habermas, Jürgen. *The Structural Transformation of the Public Sphere: An Inquiry into a Category of Bourgeois Society* [1962]. Trans. by Thomas Burger and Frederick Lawrence. Cambridge: Polity, 2021.

Hueffer, Ford Madox. 'Review', in Piccadilly Review, October 1919, repr. in Virginia Woolf: The Critical Heritage, ed. by Robin Majumdar and Allen McLaurin (London and Boston: Routledge and Kegan Paul, 1975), 72–5.

Hussey, Mark. *Virginia Woolf A–Z: The Essential Reference to her Life and Writings*. New York and Oxford: Oxford University Press, 1996.

Jameson, Fredric. *Postmodernism or, the Cultural Logic of Late Capitalism*. Durham, NC: Duke University Press, 1991.

Jones, Clara. *Virginia Woolf: Ambivalent Activist*. Edinburgh: Edinburgh University Press, 2015.

Lee, William. *Life and Writings of Daniel Defoe*, vol. III. London: J. C. Hotten, 1869.

Llewelyn Davies, Margaret (ed.). *Life as We Have Known It: By Co-operative Working Women* [1931]. London: Virago, 1977.

Lukács, György. *The Historical Novel* [1937]. Trans. by Hannah and Stanley Mitchell. Boston: Beacon Press, 1963.

MacKay, Marina. *Modernism and World War II*. Cambridge: Cambridge University Press, 2009.

McManus, Patricia. 'The "Offensiveness" of Virginia Woolf: From a Moral to a Political Reading'. *Woolf Studies Annual*, 14 (2008), 91–138.

Majumdar, Robin and Allen McLaurin (ed.). *Virginia Woolf: The Critical Heritage*. London and Boston: Routledge and Kegan Paul, 1975.

Marcus, Laura. 'Woolf's Feminism and Feminism's Woolf'. In *The Cambridge Companion to Virginia Woolf*, ed. by Sue Roe and Susan Sellers, 209–44. Cambridge: Cambridge University Press, 2000.

Periyan, Natasha. '"Altering the structure of society": An Institutional Focus on Virginia Woolf and Working-Class Education in the 1930s'. *Textual Practice*, 32.8 (2018), 1301–23.

Potter, Rachel. *Modernism and Democracy: Literary Culture, 1900–1930*. Oxford: Oxford University Press, 2006.

Ruttenberg, Nancy. 'Introduction: Is the Novel Democratic?' *Novel: A Forum on Fiction*, 47.1 (2014), 1–10.

Taunton, Matthew. 'Chorus and Agon in the Political Novel: Staging Left-Wing Arguments in H. G. Wells, Iris Murdoch, and Doris Lessing'. *MFS Modern Fiction Studies*, 67.2 (2021), 247–71.

Watt, Ian. *The Rise of the Novel: Studies in Defoe, Richardson, and Fielding* [1957]. London: Penguin Books, 1966.

Webb, Sidney. 'Social Movements'. In *Cambridge Modern History: The Latest Age*, vol. XII, ed. by A. W. Ward, G. W. Prothero and Stanley Leathes, 710–65. Cambridge: Cambridge University Press, 1910.

Woolf, Virginia. *The Common Reader, Second Edition*. London: The Hogarth Press, 1925.

——, *The Diary of Virginia Woolf, Volume One: 1915–1919*, ed. by Anne Olivier Bell [1977]. London: Penguin Books, 1979.

——, *Night and Day* [1919], ed. by Suzanne Raitt. Oxford: Oxford University Press, 2009.

——, *The Question of Things Happening: The Letters of Virginia Woolf, 1912–1922*, ed. by Nigel Nicolson and Joanne Trautmann. London: The Hogarth Press, 1976.

——, 'Romance'. In *The Essays of Virginia Woolf, Volume Two: 1912–1918*, ed. by Andrew McNeillie, 73–6. London: The Hogarth Press, 1987.

——, *A Room of One's Own* [1929] and *Three Guineas* [1938], ed. by Anna Snaith. Oxford: Oxford University Press, 2015.

Zwerdling, Alex. *Virginia Woolf and the Real World*. Berkeley: University of California Press, 1986.

Chapter 10

Capitalism and Woolf's Beyond-Work

Evelyn Tsz Yan Chan

At the heart of capitalism lies the idea of putting capital to work to produce more of it. This has happened historically in conjunction with waged labour, as Marx suggests when he writes of the exchange of labour for a fee as 'the hidden abode of production' in which we see 'not only how capital produces, but how capital is itself produced'.[1] Indeed, we could say that '[t]he situation whereby we cannot live except through selling our labour power characterises capitalist society'.[2] As this chapter shows, Woolf's critique of capitalism was conducted through both her representations of waged work, that linchpin of capitalism, and unwaged work, which is at times equally capitalism's hidden substructure. But these representations are not of the type that the novelists whom Woolf famously called 'materialists' in the essay 'Modern Fiction' depicted.[3] In *Night and Day*, Ralph Denham despairs about the role of work in his life: 'All this money-making and working ten hours a day in an office, what's it *for*? [. . .] Now my reasons ceased to satisfy me' (185). His existential crisis arises out of the meaninglessness of his work as a solicitor, the feeling of being trapped by waged work that he cannot escape because he lacks capital. This accounts for his need to fantasise about 'giv[ing] up his profession' (*ND* 189) and about alternatives beyond it. He is instead provided a different, much safer, socially validated outlet for his passionate nature which belies his appearance as a 'hard and self-sufficient young man' (*ND* 104) in the form of his relationship with Katharine. In this way, the narrative implies, he can marry and still continue to pursue his career.

Despite the discontent that Ralph feels, his complaints about his work as a solicitor are expressed in summative statements such as the quotation in the previous paragraph, instead of through the particulars of waged work's material detail. There is the urge here, reflected across Woolf's fiction, to escape from work instead of dwelling on its material details, even when expressing characters' dissatisfaction with the problems of its capitalist premise. This is something that Rob Breton has described as Woolf's 'near refusal to depict character in an economic and social situation in order to find the *essential thing*', and her tendency to 'downplay background' and 'material circumstances' to foreground 'the private life'.[4] Such critique is to the point: many of the descriptions of waged work in Woolf's writing have a summative, 'scaled back', partially 'cut out' aspect – terms that Mary Wilson has used to describe Woolf's descriptions of domestic work, present yet without the full presence of the middle-class characters in her fiction.[5] But as this essay shows, they are nevertheless there, serving the function of moving away, rather than towards, current modes of capitalist production.

As this chapter will discuss, Woolf's minimalisation of the materialism of waged work conveys a dissatisfaction with it that looks towards what we have come to call 'postwork', a notion distinct from 'antiwork' in the sense that it is not a radical rejection of work, but a dialogue about how to engage with the idea of work differently, how to reshape it for a better future. Why work for a wage? Ralph asks. This question, in fact, places no less significance on work – whether or not the representations include explicit descriptions of the material conditions of work. And such a form of representation, as I will explain, is important: rather than making waged labour insignificant, or incidental, the form Woolf used shows the open directions into which she tried to steer waged work.

All this necessitates a brief discussion of the term 'postwork'. Stanley Aronowitz et al. mark the twenty-first century as 'a time of postwork', of 'automation and work reorganisation replacing people at faster and faster rates',[6] and make the case for a guaranteed income so that 'we will no longer allow people to starve nor to become increasingly enslaved by and to work'.[7] Dinerstein and Pitts similarly place 'automation', which 'enabl[es] a postwork society of abundance and leisure',[8] and 'basic income' 'at the heart of the post-work imaginary'.[9] Woolf engaged with both of these themes in responding to the idea of waged work under capitalism, but perhaps the response to which Woolf's is the most similar is provided by Kathi Weeks, who discusses the notion of postwork 'as a place holder for something yet to come',[10] and in 'contrast to socialism, which is defined as a system that would redeem work through public ownership'.[11] The political project that derives from it – 'for which we would probably not expect immediate success'[12] – 'takes the form not of a narrowly pragmatic reform',[13] but 'refuses the existing world of work that is given to us' while 'also demand[ing] alternatives'.[14] The 'postwork speculative horizon'[15] would then 'includ[e] not just the more traditional [. . .] blueprints of the good society, but also [. . .] a variety of partial glimpses of and incitements toward the imagination and construction of alternatives'.[16] As we will see, Woolf engaged in a project in her time that shares some of these characteristics. The openness, the 'partial glimpses',[17] and the lack of a clear roadmap, mark her representations of work, creating what this chapter calls a beyond-work that hints at alternatives in an array of representations of work under capitalism in her writing, and that connect in surprising ways with what are considered to be essential considerations in the postwork imaginary, a basic income and automation. Woolf used these aesthetics, or what Jessica Berman has called a 'rhetoric of delay and interruption',[18] even in *Three Guineas*, her essay on work most based on facts and figures.

This essay, instead of focusing on one particular work or period in Woolf's writing, looks at various characters across Woolf's oeuvre to see how they, with different aspirations and under different economic circumstances, position themselves in relation to work. It explores what insights some of Woolf's writings can provide in light of more recent discussions about the direction of waged work under capitalism. The theoretical notion of postwork is important not just as a much-needed reconfiguration of the notion of work, but also to ask: what would we be without waged work? If we were to live not just as vehicles of labour for capitalism, if the idea of waged work shifted, then what would be our role as humans? Woolf's responses to these questions lie not only in her major essays on the topic of work, but also in snippets of beyond-work she portrays in her fiction. Instead of reproducing the tenets of socialism in her milieu, she, too, as a creative writer, eschewed only 'narrowly pragmatic reform',[19] and kept the vision open, moving away from the idea that only paid work that feeds into capitalism is valuable work towards a beyond-work imaginary, even if this could only be glimpsed behind and in between the structures of capitalism.

Waged Work, Leisure, and the Purposeful Rhetoric of Capital

One prominent ideal of work in the nineteenth century was that of the self-made man, who epitomises the material success that can be attained through diligence, determination and talent applied to work. The idea of bootstrapping oneself up from the lowest rungs of society led to such famous parodies of the self-made man as Bounderby in Charles Dickens's *Hard Times*, who lies about lifting himself up from the ditch to his present comfortable circumstances. In what we can use to start mapping the variety of Woolf's representations of waged work, Woolf's scepticism of this ideal can be observed in her parodying of it. For instance, her representations of Sir William Bradshaw's and Charles Tansley's simultaneous self-consciousness about and pride in their humble beginnings, the former with his father 'a tradesman',[20] the latter with his grandfather 'a fisherman' and 'his father a chemist', are shot through with satire.[21] The narrator in *To the Lighthouse* describes how in Tansley's assertion to Mrs Ramsay that 'he had never been sick in his life' 'lay compact, like gunpowder, that [. . .] he had worked his way up entirely himself', and 'that he was Charles Tansley – a fact that nobody there seemed to realise; but one of these days every single person would know it' (*TTL* 78). With his abilities and 'seven hours a day' (*TTL* 14) of hard work, he imagines his future success so certain that '[h]e could almost pity these mild cultivated people, who would be blown sky high [. . .] by the gunpowder that was in him' (*TTL* 78), 'gunpowder' that will explosively disrupt the existing class hierarchy.

The reason why Tansley is ridiculed is not because of his strong work ethic. Woolf's own strenuous efforts in her writing and in her work for the Hogarth Press evidence her own demanding work ethic, with Leonard Woolf writing that 'I have never known anyone work with more intense, more indefatigable concentration than Virginia'.[22] Instead, Woolf's criticism centres on the extremeness and singularity of materialist, capitalist success that the ideal of the self-made man celebrates, which becomes a prison of the self despite being lauded by society. Woolf's writing deliberately veers away from the inexorable track that Tansley imagines himself on – 'lectureships', 'fellowships', what Mrs Ramsay thinks of as 'ugly academic jargon' (*TTL* 14) – and through which he defines his work. The association in Tansley's mind between his status as self-made, and his high level of singular productivity so that 'he had never been sick in his life' (*TTL* 78), contrasts with the beauty that Woolf ascribes to illness in her essay 'On Being Ill', even as illness leads to suffering, and it is highly undesirable to require one to be ill to get a temporary break from the ruts of waged work. Once we become ill, Woolf writes,

> we cease to be soldiers in the army of the upright; we become deserters. They march to battle. We float with the sticks on the

stream; [. . .] irresponsible and disinterested and able, perhaps for the first time for years, to look round, to look up – to look, for example, at the sky.[23]

If one looks across Woolf's work, this meandering, digressive quality described in this essay, incorporating a dreaminess that Ralph embraces in *Night and Day*, is the hallmark of both the form and content of her writing, having as one of its effects the attenuation of the singular purposefulness of capitalism. Decades of Woolf criticism have revealed the many examples of this quality to be seen in her writing: to name but a few, this would include the *flânerie* in *Mrs Dalloway*, the stream-of-consciousness narrative in *To the Lighthouse*, the twisting, windy thought pathways of the narrator in *A Room of One's Own* enabled by her private income, and the criss-crossing of the various central consciousnesses in *The Waves*. Woolf's aesthetics of digression remind us of alternatives to current forms of work that are excessively narrow pursuits. For instance, Bernard in *The Waves* thinks: 'I strode into a world [. . .] braced with a thousand snares and dodges to achieve the same end – to earn our livings'.[24] Movement becomes restricted because '[s]omething always has to be done next. [. . .] So the being grows rings; identity becomes robust. What was fiery and furtive like a fling of grain cast into the air and blown hither and thither [. . .] is now methodical and orderly and flung with a purpose – so it seems' (*TW* 157). The last interjection undercuts the perspective, interrupts the conclusiveness of the seeming order that has set, and the haphazard movements of the 'fling of grain' returns us to the quotation from 'On Being Ill' earlier, with the image of 'float[ing] with the sticks on the stream' (*OBI* 12).

What makes Ralph poised for an alternative path is the need to escape these 'snares and dodges' (*TW* 157) that keep one in conformity with capitalist ideals, such as that of the self-made man that has ensnared Tansley. His starting point is not to see waged work as in itself fulfilling, in accordance with the idealistic notion of work in the nineteenth century as a 'form of self-realization',[25] but as a grave impediment to fuller being. Prior to this crisis point, he had aimed 'to control the spirit', with his current life 'rigidly divided into the hours of work and those of dreams; the two lived side by side without harming each other' (*ND* 104). But now, 'it needed all Ralph's strength of will [. . .] to keep his feet moving in the path' (*ND* 103) to a predictable, materially rewarding career. His professional trajectory is built on 'beliefs not genuinely held': 'in private, when the pressure of public opinion was removed', his mind embarks on 'strange voyages', which 'gave outlet to some spirit which found no work to do in real life' (*ND* 103). The stark segregation between his public work and future, and his private life and selves, is not useful anymore, but soul-destroying. The suggestion is that this chasm between public and private needs to be more porous, rather than reinforced even further.[26] The challenge is to traverse it, and imagine a life that does not 'compe[l] the exercise of [merely] the lower gifts' and 'wastes the precious ones' (*ND* 103–4), the best parts of him. This is to imagine a way of working so that life is not 'meaningless' (*ND* 185), as Ralph calls it.

Two historical developments of waged work are relevant to understanding the public–private split that Ralph and other characters feel so acutely due to their work: the regimentation of the working day that is a product of the nineteenth century; and the question of the boundary between work and leisure that was subsequently underscored. Morag Shiach has written on the changes to the average number of hours worked each week as it went from exceeding sixty hours to fifty-three hours from the nineteenth century to 1911, and to forty-eight hours by 1920. This 'was accompanied by the significant growth of a leisure industry', and resulted in 'tension between the persistent attempt to articulate labour as self-realization, and the very real reduction of the time spent on labour by almost all workers'.[27] Woolf's representations of work suggest that with these increasingly regimented compartments, the line between the ideas of work and leisure have become too fixed. For instance, Ralph's sense of malaise, which is mitigated by his romance with Katharine, shows that what is wrong is not the fact that one's personal passions are not segregated effectively enough from one's day job, that a solid enough wall between the public and the private spheres has not been built, but that the wall itself too tightly separates the idea of productive paid work from unproductive leisure and non-work. Rethinking the meaning of work can lead to coming closer to, although not likely fully achieving, that dreamy, elusive ideal that Woolf would advocate in *Three Guineas*, of 'do[ing] the work for the sake of doing the work', instead of doing the work only for the sake of funding the necessities of life, and a separate realm of leisure unrelated to work.[28]

The notion of postwork was conceived to address these issues, among others: to do away with work as merely something for basic necessity, and to liberate the kinds of creative impulses that Ralph is forced to segregate to the private sphere. But although this was not called 'postwork' in Woolf's time, her contemporaries were actively thinking about the future of waged work. For instance, that Ralph's work only makes use of 'the lower gifts' (*ND* 104) is a frustration that John Maynard Keynes thought would be solved in a century's time. In his essay 'Economic Possibilities for Our Grandchildren' (1930), Keynes predicts that the compound 'growth of capital' on the back of continued 'revolutionary technical advances' such as those that the past century saw – which he dizzyingly lists as 'coal, steam, electricity, petrol [. . .], automatic machinery and the methods of mass production, wireless, printing, Newton, Darwin, and Einstein, and thousands of other things and men' – will lead to 'mankind [. . .] solving its economic problem'.[29] Economic prosperity will mean that 'the standard of life in progressive countries one hundred years hence will be between four and eight times as high as it is today', and ensure that 'for the first time since his creation man will be faced with his real, his permanent problem – how to use his freedom from pressing economic cares, how to occupy the leisure [. . .] to live wisely and agreeably and well'.[30] He warns that we can hardly 'look forward to the age of leisure and of abundance without a dread', because 'we have been trained too long to strive and not to enjoy'.[31] If we do not set leisure here, with its root in the Latin word *licere* – meaning to be permitted – in opposition to work per se, and instead see it in opposition to what we currently understand as waged work that is primarily done to make a living, leisure then means the freedom to engage in activities one chooses to do for their own sake.

Keynes's argument implies that everyone can reap the benefits of such productivity, just as with a universal basic income in a postwork vision, giving 'everyone the chance to do work that is meaningful'.[32] Yet since Woolf's questioning in *Three Guineas* of the tenets of waged work, of 'leav[ing] the house at nine and com[ing] back to it at six', 'do[ing] this daily from the age of twenty-one or so to the age of about sixty-five', 'perform[ing] some duties that are very arduous, others that are very barbarous', and 'leav[ing] very little time for friendship, travel or art' (*TG* 194), society has made little progress in separating the idea of work from capitalist ideology so that it can be done more 'for the sake of doing the work' (*TG* 201). Keynes's vision has ultimately not come to pass despite the present day being only a few years away from the hundred-year timeline set by the essay. Although economic output in fact surpassed Keynes's predictions,[33] hours did not drop in the way he envisioned, and one possible reason out of many is the disconnect, as Geoff Crocker explains, 'between productivity enhanced output and falling real wages', which Crocker again argues '[o]nly a universal credit or basic income can overcome'.[34]

Ralph's revisiting of his paid work, because of his lack of fulfilment, similarly provides no practicable way out, before he problematically finds in Katharine an outlet for his dreams. This issue recurs for Woolf's characters, who very painfully separate other facets of their selves from their paid working lives and experience a similar malaise. The underlying sentiment is of there being a misfit between the work they engage in for money, and essential facets to themselves that they would like to find expression for, to be known to the outside world, to become part of their life stories. They do not wish to be only defined by their waged work identity, so that the question 'what do you do for a living?' becomes their personhoods' defining feature. For instance, in *Mrs Dalloway*, Miss Kilman's financial precarity, doing some extension lecturing and some tutoring to make ends meet, makes her of little substance to the people around her. In *The Waves*, Louis's split between his money-making self and his artistic self means he unhappily separates these parts of himself in his life, with the former becoming his public persona and the latter his private. In *The Years*, Peggy's and North's malaise – the former because she is in a rut as a doctor, the latter because he is back in London after being a farmer in Africa and is listlessly considering what to do – arises out of a dissatisfaction with the limitations of the idea of work that restrict their dreams and desires, and prevent them from viewing the future as open instead of closed, even when they do find personal satisfaction and take pride in their work. One of the main problems may be that work, in its fundamental links with capitalist structures and ideology, is defined strictly as paid work, and leisure as unpaid, as done on the side for pleasure and of much lesser importance.

Instead, new ideas of work seem needed that undermine the purposeful rhetoric of capital. In a passage in *The Years* that exemplifies the undermining of the singular ruts of capitalist labour in Woolf's writing, Rose and Martin quibble about what constitutes real work: Rose's activism and 'work in the war', or Martin's money-making:

> 'And where's your red ribbon?' he was asking. [. . .] 'Aren't we worthy to see you in your war paint?' he teased her.
> 'This fellow's jealous,' she said [. . .]. 'He's never done a stroke of work in his life.'
> 'I work—I work,' Martin insisted. 'I sit in an office all day long——'
> 'Doing what?' said Rose. (*TY* 252)

Martin, who thinks that his 'affairs were turning out well' as he 'visit[s] his stockbroker in the City' (*TY* 158), is here being challenged by Rose on his notion of work: making money, Woolf suggests, does not make work, just as not making money does not mean that what one does is not work.

One passage in *The Years* demonstrates how Woolf used narrative strategies to undermine the purposeful rhetoric of capital, in what Paul Stasi has described as the novel being 'infused with a social reality whose specific details it continually obscures'.[35] There is a telling description of a court scene, Morris's 'case at the Law Courts' (*TY* 65), described from Eleanor's perspective, which has the truncated aspect that Woolf utilises whenever she wishes to both turn towards yet at the same time turn away from the idea of waged work. Eleanor 'tried to follow what the man with a big nose was saying', and although '[s]he listened' and 'could understand parts of' it, 'how it bore on the case she did not know' (*TY* 77). Even when she describes Morris's turn to speak, she turns away from the content of the speech, despite 'tr[ying] to fix her mind upon the argument': 'He spoke with extraordinary clearness; he spaced his words beautifully. [. . .] Without hurry or flutter he opened a book; found his place; read out a passage' (*TY* 78). Eleanor describes what happens, but the frame that is described is devoid of the content: what exactly is said; what the arguments are; what the case is on at all. The details that are material to her are not those of the work of the law, but what is considered the peripheral, the irrelevant. Taking Eleanor's perspective allows Woolf to truncate aspects of paid work, to turn her gaze not inward, but already outward even as she is looking in, towards an imaginary beyond-work. So Eleanor literally turns away and towards the outside: 'She fidgeted. The air was fuggy; the light dim [. . .] And it was a sham. She wanted to laugh; she wanted to move. She rose and whispered: "I'm going"' (*TY* 79).

The contrast between the inside and the outside is like night and day, with the narrative describing Eleanor's escape from the premises of arduous legal work as akin to being liberated from prison, 'c[oming] upon her with a shock of relief' (*TY* 79). She is, 'after her concentration' inside, 'dissipated, tossed about' by '[t]he uproar, the confusion, the space of the Strand' (*TY* 79). Her random, directionless and haphazard movements give her a sense of being fully alive, and are contrasted with the purposeful waged work happening inside.

In the novel, the description of Eleanor's unpaid work *as* work, and its very different structure from Morris's job at the law courts, provides an additional perspective with which to rethink the capitalist premise of work. Although Eleanor's work – for charity, for a suffrage society,[36] and for the Pargiter household – is unpaid, she thinks of it as 'going to her work' as well: 'After the Committee,

Duffus; after Duffus, Dickson. Then lunch; and the Law Courts at two-thirty' (*TY* 67). All this makes up an endless to-do list that Eleanor finds exhausting. Since 'money dignifies what is frivolous if unpaid for', Eleanor is not accorded the recognition for her work she deserves.[37] But at the same time she is also protected from the harms of the ruts of capitalist work, from the dangers of dancing 'round and round the mulberry tree, the sacred tree, of property' (*TG* 199). The constant interruptions that Eleanor faces – with 'so many different things [. . .] going on in her head at the same time' (*TY* 22) – are both the bane of creative work that requires the sanctity of a room of one's own, and of productive work in the capitalist sense.

As we will see in the next section, in order to avoid the co-opting of work into capitalism, Woolf, ironically, endowed a significant number of her characters with a private income. This morally problematic device gave some of her characters a compromised freedom that helped the representation of beyond-work in her fiction, enabling her to get out of the constraints of existing forms of paid work. Often, the detail of such private capital is implicit in her fiction – again, ironically so, for someone who was so explicit about the quantity needed to be independent in *A Room of One's Own*.

Private Capital and the Transformation of Paid Work

In *Basic Income*, Philippe van Parijs and Yannick Vanderborght identify the five hundred pounds a year of private income paid automatically to the narrator in *A Room of One's Own* as an example of the idea of a universal basic income.[38] Such basic income, as Weeks writes, 'lessen[s] the dependence of income on work', 'not only recogniz[ing] but offer[ing] a response to the inability of both the wage system and the institution of the family to serve as reliable mechanisms of income distribution'.[39] Similar issues would find their crescendo in Woolf's writing in *Three Guineas*, where she states, for instance, with biting satire that marriage 'is an unpaid profession, and [. . .] the spiritual share of half the husband's salary is not, facts seem to show, an actual share' (*TG* 180), and advocates 'for a wage to be paid by the State legally to the mothers of educated men' (*TG* 236).[40] But we also find Woolf experimenting in various ways with the idea of a private income throughout her fiction. In *The Voyage Out*, Hewett finds it difficult to explain his identity without a paid job when pressed by Hirst for 'facts', and '[t]he fact that he had money enough to do no work', 'travell[ing] and drift[ing]', 'made his life strange at many points where his friends' lives were much of a piece', giving his autobiography an especially truncated quality:

> 'I am the son of an English gentleman. I am twenty-seven. [. . .] I was educated at Winchester and Cambridge, which I had to leave after a time. I have done a good many things since—'
> 'Profession?'
> 'None—at least—'
> 'Tastes?'
> 'Literary. I'm writing a novel.'[41]

The hesitation after Hirst asks him about his profession speaks to the ambiguous status of Hewett's writing, something he is able to do without regard for money since he has his own private income of 'between six and seven hundred a year' (*VO* 197). Hewett does not seem to fully think of himself as a writer, classifying writing immediately as his 'tast[e]', which conjures up the leisure associated with the aristocratic background he describes. This risks relegating his writing to mere leisure in the inferior, instead of the regenerative, sense referred to earlier in this essay. The trope of private means would return in *Jacob's Room*. It is as difficult to place the elusive Jacob socio-economically as it is to describe him as a flesh-and-blood human being, due in some measure to his avoidance of paid work. Such avoidance makes up part of the deliberate evasive strategies the narrative uses, omissions that it foregrounds rather than allowing them to recede into the background.

For these two male characters, the lack of paid work is used to endow them with a youthful, unfixed, meandering, carefree quality (something that Jed Esty's *Unseasonable Youth* suggests is a modernist trope), embodying future potential to be co-opted into the capitalist system, rather than necessarily as a critique of capitalism. The more direct conflicts arise for female characters with a private income who do not get paid for their work, and who suggest more strongly the idea of marginal alternatives. Mary Datchet's critique of Katharine in *Night and Day* focuses on work: Katharine 'doesn't understand about work. She's never had to. She doesn't know what work is. But it's the thing that saves one – I'm sure of that' (*ND* 332). But the implied question here is whether Mary herself knows what work is. Although Mary attempts to do meaningful, even if unpaid, work for a suffrage society, her work is represented as preoccupying her, an avoidance of her personhood rather than adequately expressing it. She says to Ralph: 'Where should I be now if I hadn't got to go to my office every day? [. . .] I tell you, work is the only thing that saved me' (*ND* 332). Work here is fixated on as a concept and fetishised, rather than adapted to her self. When Mary says that 'to have sat there all day long, in the enjoyment of leisure, would have been intolerable', the shrugging off of the generative possibilities of leisure are undercut in the same breath by the narrator's ironical tone to describe her work: 'she forgot that she was [. . .] an amateur worker, whose services were unpaid, and could hardly be said to wind the world up for its daily task' (*ND* 61–2). Nevertheless, there are other moments in the novel that, as Clara Jones has written, despite being able to 'be read as instances of Mary being distracted from her work'[42] also suggest 'something more focused and ultimately productive', when 'her ambivalence towards the cause takes hold' and leads her to rethink 'the nature and value of her activism', for instance when during a committee meeting she 'look[s] out of a window, and think[s] of the colour of the sky' (*ND* 138).[43] Mary's reconsideration of the meaning of her work might also lead to her questioning the course where, 'having renounced everything that made life happy, easy, splendid, individual, there remained a hard reality, unimpaired by one's personal adventures' (*ND* 219–20).

In subsequent novels where the narrator mostly has less of a prominent critical voice, Woolf's representations of women workers with a presumed private income, even if meagre, explore their work more fully, rather than viewing it as that of the unpaid 'amateur worker' (*ND* 62). Lily Briscoe and Miss La Trobe, who both seem to own just enough private capital to live on (with this being implied rather than specifically laid out), are able to use their time for artistic creation relatively unattached to the drive to make money, unlike the working women writers of Woolf's early fiction whom Bryony Randall discusses in her chapter in this collection. Woolf's lack of clarifying detail on the circumstances of the two women artists' presumed private income deliberately relegates this to the background. The theme that gets foregrounded instead is the strong, even relentless, work ethic the two women artists share.

However, because the two women artists do not use their art to make a living, their work at times needs justification and reiteration, even to themselves. For instance, while Mr Bankes thinks of Lily as 'alone: poor, presumably', Lily repeatedly thinks of him as 'not in the least pitiable. He has his work [. . .] She remembered, all of a sudden as if she had found a treasure, that she too had her work' (*TTL* 72–3). Here, the firm prominence of Mr Bankes's work as a botanist contrasts with Lily needing to 'remembe[r]' her work, as if this is something that can be forgotten. Nevertheless, Lily and Miss La Trobe define themselves by their work identities by choice, with Lily firmly calling this 'work' instead of classifying it as a 'tast[e]' (*VO* 131), as Hewett does his writing. The hardships both women artists endure emphasise the arduousness of their creation, of their unpaid work as work to which they devote themselves wholeheartedly. This is not represented as deadening or soul-destroying, but as self-expressive.

These depictions of creativity when liberated, even if only in part, from waged work can be understood not only as stemming from an elitist position, as feeding off Woolf's personal experience as a rentier, but also as a repositioning of meaning and creativity as crucial components of human work. A similar emphasis on the unleashing of creativity exists as the purpose of a universal basic income in the idea of postwork, especially in the face of the rise of automation and artificial intelligence. For instance, in a recent online article, Viktor Mayer-Schonberger asks:

> What's so special about us, and what's our lasting value? It can't be skills like arithmetic or typing, which machines already excel in. Nor can it be rationality [. . .] So perhaps we might want to consider qualities at a different end of the spectrum: radical creativity, irrational originality, even a dose of plain illogical craziness, instead of hard-nosed logic.[44]

Woolf's emphasis on creativity seeks similarly to emphasise the personal and the unique in work, to stop the cycle of '[w]orking, serving, pushing, striving, earning wages' (*BTA* 87) that severs us from our creative and regenerative sides, desires and instincts.

Yet the use of the trope of a private income also stipulates that dependence on capitalist proceeds would still be a prerequisite, and the fact that in Woolf's fiction this is neither earned nor universal is highly problematic. For instance, two characters who far exceed the very modest independent income that Lily and Miss La Trobe likely live on are Clarissa Dalloway and Orlando, whose representations foreground such reliance on capital to the utmost, to the point of mild satire even as the characters are simultaneously treated sympathetically and seriously. Orlando's position and money allow her the luxury of a quest for artistic fulfilment throughout the centuries. Clarissa, whose socio-economic advantages by birth and marriage to Richard enable her to enjoy her life, whose creations are not works of art but exclusive parties that provide social occasions for the upper class to 'assemble' (*MD* 158), considers that '[s]he had escaped':

'quite often if Richard had not been there reading the *Times*, so that she could crouch like a bird and gradually revive, [. . .] she must have perished' (*MD* 157). One important aspect of what she has 'escaped' is needing to earn her own living through paid work. Peter Walsh's critique of Clarissa, self-centred though this is, is of Clarissa wasting her economic idleness: although 'she enjoyed life immensely', 'she needed people, always people, to bring it out, with the inevitable result that she frittered her time away [. . .] blunting the edge of her mind, losing her discrimination' (*MD* 85–6). Clarissa also judges herself for her 'escap[e]', calling it 'schem[ing]' and 'pilfer[ing]' (157), as if it is a form of cheating, not only getting away from it, but getting away with it: 'She was never wholly admirable. She had wanted success' (*MD* 157). Miss Kilman puts it in stronger terms: 'She had always earned her living', 'whereas this woman did nothing, believed nothing' (*MD* 106). That is also why Miss Kilman's retaliatory vision is of Clarissa working. This is a punishment, a type of imprisonment: 'she should have been in a factory; behind a counter; Mrs Dalloway and all the other fine ladies!' (*MD* 105).

Adam Phillips has written that 'getting away with it is conservative of the status quo in so far as it is not an attempt to change the law but to elude it. To find where it is vulnerable, and to keep it in place'.[45] Clarissa's sense of guilt at having 'escap[ed]', and Woolf's use of characters who have private incomes, is subject to such critique: living off unearned capital allows an exclusivity within capitalist society that is not available to many. Being a rentier who makes one's capital work instead of working oneself comes with some moral culpability, some complicity in maintaining the very 'social system' that Woolf sought 'to criticise' and 'show [. . .] at work'.[46]

Thus, there is a real tug-of-war between representations of conserving the capitalist status quo, and of breaking free from it, in Woolf's writing. The dissipation of the boundaries between social classes in the wake of radical changes in waged work due to technological innovation and automation, as we have seen suggested in Keynes's essay, was something to be represented, and to be both celebrated and feared. Woolf explored such boundary-crossing in her writing, as Wilson has pointed out: for instance, the figure of the cook just outside the drawing room in 'Mr Bennett and Mrs Brown', who will not be contained easily, also becomes a representative of the transformation in human character that Woolf refers to in the essay, crossing the threshold of existing class divisions.[47] Woolf's ambivalence about the simultaneous contrast and transgression of class boundaries was expressed famously in her metaphor of the 'hot and fearless flame', 'about to break through and melt us together', in her 'Introductory Letter' for a collected volume by the Women's Co-operative Guild,[48] reminding us of Tansley's 'gunpowder' metaphor (*TTL* 78). Both automation (of which Woolf had first-hand experience: her 'new electric boiler' installed in 1926, for instance, which 'is boiling our bath water this morning',[49] would surely upend domestic work in future) and universalising basic income would free up more time for creative pursuits for everyone. This is a vision that the beyond-work imaginary in Woolf's writing, often enabled by the trope of the rentier, pushed towards, while it is at the same time also something that the conservatism of that very trope pushed back against.

Owning private capital or being a rentier in order to personalise work is, then, a far from ideal solution to the woes of waged work. It is as imperfect as requiring one to be ill to get a temporary break and freedom from the conquering industries of human activity, so vividly described in 'On Being Ill'. Woolf tried to temper the morally charged figure of the rentier in her later writing, where she depicted more financially precarious versions of personas or characters who had come before: the salaried narrator in *Three Guineas* versus the narrator with an ample private income in *A Room of One's Own*; the impecunious Miss La Trobe versus the less financially strapped Lily; even Isa versus Clarissa, in what is a much less secure, satisfactory marriage. Material concerns are more emphasised for Isa, who is married to the stockbroker Giles: she 'had only bills' which she is in charge of taking care of, and 'write[s] her poetry in a book like an account book lest Giles might suspect', the subterfuge here suggesting the stark contrast between her unpaid work as a housewife and her private self and needs.[50] But as we have seen, depicting characters and narrators with private capital or incomes in her writing also enabled Woolf, ironically, to envision beyond-work. In this vision, the rigid ideological boundaries between work and a self-generative type of leisure become blurred, and work can move away from its capitalist bounds (even while still being dependent on capitalist structures in her writing). The freed-up time a private income endows can be channelled into productive work, where 'productive' escapes the capitalist sense of generating profits.

We can therefore say that the character who owns private capital or is a rentier recurs in Woolf's writing not only because Woolf herself, 'represent[ing] *par excellence* the *rentier* class',[51] sought to depict the privileged socio-economic conditions with which she herself was most familiar, but also because she wanted to reimagine work even while trapped within the constraints of capitalism. Woolf's writing, in moving away from closely detailing the toils of waged work (although mentioning these in a truncated aspect, as we have seen), attempts new ways of conceptualising work, of thinking about how it can be possible 'to do the work for the sake of doing the work' (*TG* 201), using private capital – ironically so – to work around capitalism's tenet of waged labour. If this seems to require a redefinition of the very notions of work and leisure, that was precisely the point.

We have seen in this essay how the difficulties but at the same time hope that lies in 'contest[ing] the existing terms of the work society' and the 'struggle to build something new'[52] for the contemporary project of postwork also underpinned Woolf's engagement with work under capitalism, and influenced the way in which she expressed her concerns. Weeks argues that the 'incompleteness of the utopian demand does not necessarily diminish its force; more fragmentary forms might better preserve utopia as process and project rather than end or goal'.[53] Woolf's beyond-work, of how to 'liv[e] differently, differently' (*TY* 274), is similarly glimpsed in her various experiments, formal techniques, and a variety of characterisations, making up a necessarily open, processual vision rather than a complete, finished project.

Notes

1. Karl Marx, *Capital: A Critique of Political Economy*, Volume 1, trans. by Ben Fowkes (Harmondsworth: Penguin Books, 1982), 279–80; quoted in Kathi Weeks, *The Problem with Work: Feminism, Marxism, Antiwork Politics, and Postwork Imaginaries* (Durham, NC: Duke University Press, 2011), 6.
2. Ana Cecilia Dinerstein and Frederick Harry Pitts, *A World Beyond Work? Labour, Money, and the Capitalist State Between Crisis and Utopia* (Bingley: Emerald Publishing, 2021), 123.
3. Virginia Woolf, 'Modern Fiction', in *The Essays of Virginia Woolf, Volume Four, 1925–1928*, ed. by Andrew McNeillie (London: Hogarth Press, 1984), 158.
4. Rob Breton, *Gospels and Grit: Work and Labour in Carlyle, Conrad and Orwell* (Toronto: University of Toronto Press, 2005), 147–8.
5. Mary Wilson, 'Work', in *The Oxford Handbook of Virginia Woolf*, ed. by Anne E. Fernald (Oxford: Oxford University Press, 2021), 459–61.
6. Aronowitz, Stanley, et al., 'The Post-Work Manifesto', in *Post-Work: The Wages of Cybernation*, ed. by Stanley Aronowitz et al. (New York: Routledge, 1998), 38.

7. Aronowitz, Stanley, et al., 'The Post-Work Manifesto', 65.
8. Dinerstein and Pitts, *World Beyond Work*, 48.
9. Ibid., 2–3.
10. Weeks, *Problem with Work*, 16.
11. Ibid., 101.
12. Ibid., 176.
13. Ibid., 176.
14. Ibid., 233.
15. Ibid., 30.
16. Ibid., 176.
17. Ibid., 176.
18. Jessica Berman, '*Three Guineas* and the Politics of Interruption', in *A Companion to Virginia Woolf*, ed. by Jessica Berman (Chichester: Wiley Blackwell, 2016), 206.
19. Weeks, *Problem with Work*, 176.
20. Virginia Woolf, *Mrs Dalloway* (Oxford: Oxford University Press, 2008), 83. Further references will be included within the main text.
21. Virginia Woolf, *To the Lighthouse* (Oxford: Blackwell Publishers, 1992), 78. Further references will be included within the main text.
22. Leonard Woolf, *Beginning Again: An Autobiography of the Years 1911 to 1918* (London: Hogarth Press, 1964), 232. Quoted in Alex Zwerdling, *Virginia Woolf and the Real World*, (Berkeley: University of California Press, 1986), 108.
23. Virginia Woolf, *On Being Ill* (Ashfield: Paris Press, 2002), 12. Further references will be included within the main text.
24. Virginia Woolf, *The Waves* (Oxford: Oxford University Press, 2015), 201. Further references will be included within the main text.
25. Morag Shiach, *Modernism, Labour and Selfhood in British Literature and Culture, 1890–1930* (Cambridge: Cambridge University Press, 2004), 33.
26. For a much more extensive and thorough exploration of the public–private distinction in Woolf's writing, see Anna Snaith, *Virginia Woolf: Public and Private Negotiations* (Basingstoke: Macmillan Press, 2000).
27. Shiach, *Modernism*, 6.
28. Virginia Woolf, *A Room of One's Own and Three Guineas* (London: Penguin, 2000), 201. Further references will be included within the main text.
29. Keynes, John Maynard. 'Economic Possibilities for Our Grandchildren', in *Revisiting Keynes*, ed. by Lorenzo Pecchi and Gustavo Piga (Cambridge, MA: MIT Press, 2008), 20–1.
30. Keynes, 'Economic Possibilities', 21–2.
31. Ibid., 23.
32. Rutger Bregman, 'A Growing Number of People Think Their Job Is Useless. Time to Rethink the Meaning of Work', *World Economic*

Forum <https://www.weforum.org/agenda/2017/04/why-its-time-to-rethink-the-meaning-of-work> [accessed 1 August 2022].
33. Zilibotti, Fabrizio. 'Economic Possibilities for Our Grandchildren 75 Years After: A Global Perspective', in *Revisiting Keynes*, ed. by Lorenzo Pecchi and Gustavo Piga (Cambridge, MA: MIT Press, 2008), 28.
34. Geoff Crocker, 'Keynes, Piketty, and Basic Income', *Basic Income Studies*, 10.1 (2015), 102.
35. Paul Stasi, *The Persistence of Realism in Modernist Fiction* (Cambridge: Cambridge University Press, 2022), 119.
36. Clara Jones, *Virginia Woolf: Ambivalent Activist* (Edinburgh: Edinburgh University Press, 2016), 106; Anna Snaith (ed.), *The Years*, by Virginia Woolf (Cambridge: Cambridge University Press, 2012), 465.
37. Virginia Woolf, *A Room of One's Own and Three Guineas* (London: Penguin, 2000), 59. Further references will be included within the main text.
38. Philippe van Parijs and Yannick Vanderborght, *Basic Income: A Radical Proposal for a Free Society and a Sane Economy* (Cambridge, MA: Harvard University Press, 2017), 185.
39. Weeks, *Problem with Work*, 147.
40. Asako Nakai (who kindly recommended Weeks's book to me some years ago) has written on the influence of these requests in *Three Guineas* on the Wages for Housework Movement by Marxist feminists in the 1970s. She points out how the demand for a wage for such unpaid work threatens to make it part of 'the capitalist-patriarchal system of the state' (8), and how such contradictions derive from Woolf's 'difficult but sincere efforts to make her vision as realisable as possible in the real world' (9). I make similar points in my discussion on Woolf's use of the trope of the rentier.
41. Virginia Woolf, *The Voyage Out* (London: Penguin, 1992), 98, 131. Further references will be included within the main text.
42. Jones, *Ambivalent Activist*, 94.
43. Ibid., 94.
44. Viktor, Mayer-Schonberger, 'The Last Things That Will Make Us Uniquely Human', *BBC Future* <https://www.bbc.com/future/article/20170309-the-last-things-that-will-make-us-uniquely-human> [accessed 1 August 2022].
45. Adam Phillips, *Missing Out: In Praise of the Unlived Life* (New York: Farrar, Straus and Giroux, 2012), 106.
46. Virginia Woolf, *The Diary of Virginia Woolf: Volume Two*, ed. by Anne Olivier Bell (London: Hogarth Press, 1980), 248.
47. Wilson, 'Work', 33.
48. Virginia Woolf, 'Introductory Letter' to *Life as We Have Known It*, ed. by Margaret Llewelyn Davies, xvii–xxxxi (London: Hogarth Press, 1931), xvi.

49. Virginia Woolf, *The Diary of Virginia Woolf, Volume Four*, ed. by Anne Olivier Bell (London: Hogarth Press, 1983), 202. Pointed out in Shiach, *Modernism*, 87.
50. Virginia Woolf, *Between the Acts* (Cambridge: Cambridge University Press, 2011), 36.
51. Brenda R. Silver, *Virginia Woolf Icon* (Chicago: University of Chicago Press, 1999), 52.
52. Weeks, *Problem with Work*, 233.
53. Ibid., 224–5.

Works Cited

Aronowitz, Stanley et al. 'The Post-Work Manifesto'. In *Post-Work: The Wages of Cybernation*, ed. by Stanley Aronowitz et al., 31–80. New York: Routledge, 1998.

Berman, Jessica. '*Three Guineas* and the Politics of Interruption'. In *A Companion to Virginia Woolf*, ed. by Jessica Berman, 203–16. Chichester: Wiley Blackwell, 2016.

Bregman, Rutger. 'A Growing Number of People Think Their Job is Useless. Time to Rethink the Meaning of Work'. *World Economic Forum*, 12 April 2017. <https://www.weforum.org/agenda/2017/04/why-its-time-to-rethink-the-meaning-of-work> [accessed 1 August 2022].

Breton, Rob. *Gospels and Grit: Work and Labour in Carlyle, Conrad and Orwell*. Toronto: University of Toronto Press, 2005.

Crocker, Geoff. 'Keynes, Piketty, and Basic Income'. *Basic Income Studies*, 10.1 (2015), 91–113.

Dinerstein, Ana Cecilia and Frederick Harry Pitts. *A World Beyond Work? Labour, Money, and the Capitalist State Between Crisis and Utopia*. Bingley: Emerald Publishing, 2021.

Esty, Jed. *Unseasonable Youth: Modernism, Colonialism, and the Fiction of Development*. New York: Oxford University Press, 2012.

Jones, Clara. *Virginia Woolf: Ambivalent Activist*. Edinburgh: Edinburgh University Press, 2016.

Keynes, John Maynard. 'Economic Possibilities for Our Grandchildren'. In *Revisiting Keynes*, ed. by Lorenzo Pecchi and Gustavo Piga, 17–26. Cambridge, MA: MIT Press, 2008.

Marx, Karl. *Capital: A Critique of Political Economy*. Volume 1. Trans. by Ben Fowkes. Harmondsworth: Penguin, 1982.

Mayer-Schonberger, Viktor. 'The Last Things That Will Make Us Uniquely Human'. *BBC Future* <https://www.bbc.com/future/article/20170309-the-last-things-that-will-make-usuniquelyhuman> [accessed 1 August 2022].

Nakai, Asako. 'Materialism, Autonomy, Intersectionality: Revisiting Virginia Woolf Through the Wages for Housework Perspective'. *Feminist Theory*, 24.4 (2023), 497–511.

van Parijs, Philippe and Yannick Vanderborght. *Basic Income: A Radical Proposal for a Free Society and a Sane Economy*. Cambridge, MA: Harvard University Press, 2017.

Phillips, Adam. *Missing Out: In Praise of the Unlived Life*. New York: Farrar, Straus and Giroux, 2012.

Shiach, Morag. *Modernism, Labour and Selfhood in British Literature and Culture, 1890–1930*. Cambridge: Cambridge University Press, 2004.

Silver, Brenda R. *Virginia Woolf Icon*. Chicago: University of Chicago Press, 1999.

Snaith, Anna. *Virginia Woolf: Public and Private Negotiations*. Basingstoke: Macmillan Press, 2000.

Snaith, Anna (ed.). *The Years*, by Virginia Woolf. Cambridge: Cambridge University Press, 2012.

Stasi, Paul. *The Persistence of Realism in Modernist Fiction*. Cambridge: Cambridge University Press, 2022.

Weeks, Kathi. *The Problem with Work: Feminism, Marxism, Antiwork Politics, and Postwork Imaginaries*. Durham, NC: Duke University Press, 2011.

Wilson, Mary. 'Work'. In *The Oxford Handbook of Virginia Woolf*, ed. by Anne E. Fernald, 456–71. Oxford: Oxford University Press, 2021.

Woolf, Leonard. *Beginning Again: An Autobiography of the Years 1911 to 1918*. London: Hogarth Press, 1964.

Woolf, Virginia. *Between the Acts*, ed. by Mark Hussey. Cambridge: Cambridge University Press, 2011.

—, *The Diary of Virginia Woolf, Volume Two*, ed. by Anne Olivier Bell. London: Hogarth Press, 1980.

—, *The Diary of Virginia Woolf, Volume Four*, ed. by Anne Olivier Bell. London: Hogarth Press, 1983.

—, *The Essays of Virginia Woolf, Volume Four, 1925–1928*, ed. by Andrew McNeillie. London: Hogarth Press, 1984.

—, 'Introductory Letter to Margaret Llewelyn Davies'. In *Life as We Have Known It*, ed. by Margaret Llewelyn Davies, xvii–xxxxi. London: Hogarth Press, 1931.

—, *Jacob's Room*, ed. by Sue Roe. Penguin, 1992.

—, *Mrs Dalloway*, ed. by David Bradshaw. Oxford: Oxford University Press, 2008.

—, *Night and Day*, ed. by Julia Briggs. London: Penguin, 1992.

—, *On Being Ill*, ed. by Hermione Lee. Ashfield: Paris Press, 2002.

—, *A Room of One's Own and Three Guineas*. 1929/1938, ed. by Michèle Barrett. London: Penguin, 2000.

—, *To the Lighthouse*, ed. by Susan Dick. Oxford: Blackwell Publishers, 1993.

—, *The Voyage Out*, ed. by Jane Wheare. London: Penguin, 1992.

—, *The Waves*. 1933, ed. by David Bradshaw. Oxford: Oxford University Press, 2015.

—, *The Years*. 1937, ed. by David Bradshaw and Ian Blyth. Chichester: Wiley-Blackwell, 2012.

Zilibotti, Fabrizio. 'Economic Possibilities for Our Grandchildren 75 Years After: A Global Perspective'. In *Revisiting Keynes*, ed. by Lorenzo Pecchi and Gustavo Piga, 27–39. Cambridge, MA: MIT Press, 2008.

Zwerdling, Alex. *Virginia Woolf and the Real World*. Berkeley: University of California Press, 1986.

Chapter 11

Virginia Woolf: A Sound Investment

Brenda R. Silver

Part I. Background and Context

On 1 January 2021, Public Domain Day, Virginia Woolf's *Mrs Dalloway* was released from copyright in the US. Part of a bumper crop of works originally copyrighted in 1925, the novel appeared near the top of almost every commentator's list, preceded only by *The Great Gatsby*. Three new editions were immediately available, followed by several more. Two of the original batch, published by Penguin and Vintage, include a foreword or introduction by celebrated novelists Jenny Offill and Michael Cunningham; extracts from their essays appeared in The *New Yorker* and *The New York Times Book Review*, respectively.[1] All of this attention did not pass unnoticed on the Vwoolf listserv, where the Cunningham essay in particular elicited a discussion of why trade publishers turn to novelists rather than scholars for their introductory essays. As Mark Hussey succinctly commented:

> I think that trade publishers in general regard scholars as nit-pickers, fussing over small details that no one else cares about. What Cunningham brings to them is sales [. . .] [The] fact remains that apart from a few stars who manage to cross over, our respective silos are relatively well sealed. These gigantic publishers are not that much different from any large corporation – they answer to their shareholders, not academics![2]

Yes; and this is not new. Nor is Cunningham's appearance in these debates, having thrust himself into the centre of *Mrs Dalloway*'s relationship to capitalism with his 1998 'Pulitzer Prize winning' novel

The Hours, followed by the 'Oscar-winning' film. Hussey's evocation of stars here, or star power, is at the heart of a series of talks I gave between 2001 and 2003 about the complex intersections among Virginia Woolf's star status, Michael Cunningham's desire to become a star, the discourse of fandom, and the inter-relationship of cultural and economic capital. The essay below is based on the final version, written in November 2003 after the media frenzy that followed the opening of the film but before the Oscar nominations were announced. I have maintained the use of the present tense as it appeared in the original to reproduce the currency of the debates at that particular moment. From a cultural studies perspective, both the events surrounding *The Hours* phenomenon and my response to them cannot be read outside of the intertextual contexts that precipitated and shaped them. What brings me back to these events are the uncanny resilience and recurring provenance of Virginia Woolf as 'a sound investment' in the contemporary marketplace.

Part II. Hourly Rates: Virginia Woolf, Nicole Kidman, the Internet and *The Hours*

Setting the Stage

On 12 April 1937 Virginia Woolf became a star. The occasion: her appearance on the cover of *Time* magazine; the impetus: the publication of her new novel, *The Years*. For the anonymous writer of the *Time* article, celebrating Virginia Woolf was tantamount to putting money in the bank, as the opening of the piece makes clear:

> Last year Margaret Mitchell of Atlanta, Ga. wrote her first novel, *Gone with the Wind*. Last week Virginia Woolf of London, England published her seventh, *The Years*. Margaret Mitchell's book has sold more copies (1,300,000) than all Virginia Woolf's put together. But literary brokers who take a long view of the market are stocking up with Woolfs, unloading Mitchells [. . .] Their opinion is that Margaret Mitchell was a grand wildcat stock but Virginia Woolf a sound investment.[3]

Not surprisingly, the value bestowed upon Woolf and her novel by her celebrity appearance made the prediction self-fulfilling; by the beginning of May *The Years* had moved to the top of the *New York Herald Tribune Books*' list of 'What America is Reading'.

Sixty-five years later Virginia Woolf's star power is still at work in both our material and cultural economy, manifested not only in her well-established status as cultural icon but in the ongoing versioning of her now canonical texts. Michael Cunningham reaped the benefits when his 1998 novel *The Hours*, which owes its title and underpinnings to Woolf's *Mrs Dalloway*, first won both the PEN/Faulkner award and the Pulitzer Prize and then earned what many see as the ultimate accolade: transformation into a major motion picture. Directed by Stephen Daldry, featuring a screenplay by David Hare and an all-star cast that includes Meryl Streep, Nicole Kidman, Julianne Moore and Ed Harris, the film was touted as a sure Oscar contender before it was even completed. Virginia Woolf, it is clear, is still a sound investment, accruing for those who can claim ownership of her stock both economic and cultural capital. Given her worth, the struggle over who 'owns' Virginia Woolf and her texts becomes a more than academic argument.

Once we posit Virginia Woolf as a star we also introduce the concept of fans; we introduce, that is, the pivotal role of reception in the construction of both the 'star image' and its perceived value or worth. Here, texts dominate the discourse. For Richard Dyer, the 'star image', which is necessarily textual, is structured by 'the interplay of the various media texts that constitute the image, including the interplay of the "vehicle" developed to feature or foreground a star and the responses to it by critics and commentators'.[4] For fan theorists such as Henry Jenkins, what most defines fan culture is an interaction with texts that he describes as 'textual poaching', a term borrowed from Michel de Certeau's description of the active or interactive practice of popular reading. The analogy, Jenkins argues, 'characterizes the relationship between readers and writers as an ongoing struggle for possession of the text and for control over its meanings'. Posited as a theory of appropriation, poaching becomes an act that produces not only new texts and meanings, but new sources of cultural capital for those outside or marginal to the '"scriptural economy" dominated by textual producers and the institutionally sanctioned interpreters' of these texts.[5]

Cunningham's Pulitzer Prize winning novel, as it is now always referred to, provides an excellent case study for exploring the intersections of stardom, fandom and capital in the cultural struggles over who 'owns' Virginia Woolf and her texts. What makes this a particularly useful case is that here, the versioning of Virginia Woolf's novel *Mrs Dalloway* intersects with versions of Virginia Woolf that transform her, literally, into a star. In the film, that is, Virginia Woolf, who has a narrative presence and starring role in the novel, a novel in which stars and fame and literary prizes are woven into the very fabric of the text, is played by the star Nicole Kidman; in turn, the announcement of Kidman's role generated a conversation among Woolf's readers that sounds uncannily like the discourses associated with fans. Much of this discourse has occurred on the online Vwoolf list, where arguments about who owns Virginia Woolf intersect with stories of the star's role in enriching the participants' personal and cultural worth.

How, I found myself wondering, does hitching oneself to Virginia Woolf's star power play out in terms of fame, prestige, and both cultural and economic capital in this particular conjunction of texts? Or, to put it somewhat differently, what does this conjunction tell us about the circulation of Virginia Woolf as capital within the contemporary marketplace? My exploration of these questions takes me in two different directions: one, a reading of *The Hours* as fan fiction; the other a reading of the online discussions not only as a commentary on the versioning of Virginia Woolf and her texts but as a textual performance of its own. Ultimately the question that I keep coming back to in my exploration of Virginia Woolf's star power remains the same: who benefits, who loses, and what, both culturally and economically, is at stake?

Frameworks

Here, I want to introduce a few aspects of fan culture that come into play in my reading, starting with Jenkins's characterisation of 'the relationship between readers and writers' inscribed in 'textual poaching' 'as an ongoing struggle for possession of the text and for control over its meanings'; grounded in the unauthorised interpretation and production of texts, fan culture 'stands as an open challenge to the "naturalness" and desirability of dominant cultural hierarchies, a refusal of authorial authority and a violation of intellectual property'. The act of appropriation (and the term is not negative here) practised by these 'rogue readers' allows them to 'assert mastery over texts', making them the 'raw materials for their own cultural productions and the basis for their own social interactions'. It also provides new sources of cultural capital for those outside or marginal to the '"scriptural economy" dominated by textual producers and the institutionally sanctioned interpreters' of these texts, creating an 'alternative social community'.[6]

John Fiske, writing about 'The Cultural Economy of Fandom', shares Jenkins's emphasis on the productive nature of fan culture and goes one step further. For Fiske, fandom, which is often 'associated with the cultural tastes of subordinated formations of the people, particularly with those disempowered by any combination of gender, age, class and race', creates a 'culture with its own systems of production and distribution that form [. . .] a "shadow cultural economy" that lies outside of the cultural industries yet shares features with them'. Within this economy, fans vie to accumulate capital that is usually not monetary, though it performs the same function that money does: 'to produce social privilege and distinction'; to give the possessor power. Fan culture, in this reading, is grounded in the production and circulation of cultural capital that exists in an opposing or problematic relationship to what he calls 'official culture', culture that is 'socially and institutionally legitimated': the 'high' culture associated with not only with the educational system, including academics, but 'art galleries, concert halls, museums, and state subsidies to the arts'.[7] I would add to this list mainstream publishing, the self-declared intellectual media and the granting of literary prizes.

Appropriation, re-reading and reworking, then, define fan culture, but they would all be moot without the characteristic universally held to be its most powerful motivating impulse: talk, gossip, argument, exchange. To a great extent what gives the texts at the centre of fan culture their value/currency is the conversation and hence the community produced by them.

It is at this point that the explosive power of the internet comes into play, providing numerous forums for both the conversation and textual productions that define fan culture. In addition to the newsgroups and listservs where fans share their comments with each other, there are countless sites devoted to fan fiction, or fanfic: textual productions that use characters from existing texts and add new ones. While most fanfic arises in conjunction with popular culture, high culture proves equally generative. Go the page on books on fanfiction.net, for example, and you will find entries for *Les Misérables*, *Regeneration*, and *The English Patient*, as well as Shakespeare, the Bible and Jane Austen.[8]

The Author as Fan: Contention 1

With its intertextual relationship to *Mrs Dalloway* and its ventriloquism of Virginia Woolf's thoughts and voice, Michael Cunningham's *The Hours* can usefully be read within the framework of textual productivity ascribed to fan culture – up to a point: the point at which the cultural and financial profit reaped from his fiction and his elevation from fan to star catapulted Cunningham into an official culture only too happy to see him as cornering the market on Virginia Woolf. At this point the 'subversiveness' of Cunningham's novel, so central to fan fiction, unravels, if it was ever there. That is where I'll begin; I'll end with his elevation to star.

My starting point is the language used in the mainstream media to represent the novel's relationship to *Mrs Dalloway*. The more 'upscale' of the commentaries on the novel, the ones that appeared in the *New York Times*, for example, and praised the work, tended to talk about it as a set of extended variations on theme. Musical analogies also inform Cunningham's and others' representation of the work as a 'riff' on Woolf's novel, though here we are closer to jazz and popular music than to Bach; one reviewer, for example, describes the novel as 'an extended riff by a gifted jazz musician on the work of a genius of a classical composer [sic]'.[9] The cultural shift implicit in the jazz metaphor places the novel within the realm of textual versioning associated by Dick Hebdige with Black linguistic and musical practices that use quotation not only as an art form but as a subversive practice, privileging the 'collective voice' over the 'individual voice' and making such forms as reggae a 'rebel music'.[10]

Where does this subversiveness enter *The Hours*? Perhaps in what the *Village Voice* called Cunningham's elevation of the 'queer subcurrents' in Woolf's text to prominence in his own.[11] Not only is Clarissa Vaughan, the contemporary version of Mrs Dalloway, in a long-term relationship with her partner Sally, but Clarissa's daughter Julia is deeply involved with a teacher who is both lesbian and a queer theorist, and Richard, the award-winning poet and novelist who is dying of AIDS, was in his youth having simultaneous affairs with both Clarissa and Louis. But in 1998, the queering of *Mrs Dalloway* hardly seemed subversive. 'Few mainstream reviewers [may have] mentioned the powerful lesbian undercurrents in both works' when it was first published, as Christopher Lane notes in *The Gay and Lesbian Review*, but that changed when *The Hours* won both the PEN/Faulkner award and the Pulitzer Prize, setting off a spate of articles about the mainstreaming of gay and lesbian writing and writers.[12] Even the hostile article about what constituted the novel's cultural capital in the conservative *Wall Street Journal* treated the lesbian theme as just one part of what earned this 'exquisite and professional' novel (this is not a compliment) its prizes.[13]

What irked the writer of this last article far more than the queering of *Mrs Dalloway* is *The Hours*' discovery of the 'pretend literary density derived from retelling everything from Dickens's

Great Expectations to Nabokov's *Lolita*', suggesting that, at least within mainstream or official culture at the turn of the century, the subversiveness of the text lies less in its queering of a classic text than in its connection with that strand of postmodern fiction noted for its 'plagiarism', Kathy Acker's term. But even within this context, which easily qualifies as 'textual poaching', none of the mainstream reviewers cried foul or demanded the text be returned to its proper owner. A similar lack of controversy marked the publication of Robin Lippincott's 1999 queering of the novel, *Mr Dalloway*, where Clarissa's husband, we learn, has had a male lover for ten years; the novel ends with Richard holding hands with both Clarissa and Robbie.

To get some sense of the lack of subversiveness of Cunningham's fan fiction, we might compare it to the queering of texts in slash, the genre of fanfic that transforms characters such as Kirk and Spock or Starsky and Hutch into lovers, precipitating threats of lawsuits over copyright infringement. Or, we might compare it to the copyright infringement lawsuit brought in 2001 against *The Wind Done Gone*, Alice Randall's subversive retelling of *Gone With the Wind* from the slaves' perspective. Hinging on the question of whether the novel was a parody, in which case it was protected by law, or, as the plaintiff's argued in language that could have come right out of Jenkins, an 'appropriation of the original novel's content [. . .] so extensive that the work represents a retelling and an unauthorized sequel', the lawsuit not only highlights the act of sabotage ascribed to and claimed by fans, but illustrates the overlap between cultural and economic capital at this moment. For while economic capital would seem to be at stake here – and the Mitchell estate has long tried to maintain tight control over its property – it is no accident that the target was a book by a Black author whose intent was to foreground the racism of the original, posing a challenge to the cultural as well as economic value of the work. As one commentator on the case notes, it was the second notorious case in recent times involving a black parody of a white text, the first being the case brought against 2 Live Crew over their song 'Pretty Woman'. 'Authors who wrote parodies from an African-American perspective, and borrowed from a white book or song in order to lampoon a "white" viewpoint, did not get praised. They got sued.'[14]

The implication seems to be that at the end of the twentieth century queering is not perceived to decrease the value of a text, at least not in the 'official culture', but exploding it to expose its racial structures and the myths built on them is. The response to

The Hours bears this out; almost all of the reviews encouraged readers of Cunningham's text to go back to the original, and sales of *Mrs Dalloway* increased along with those of *The Hours*. What we have here, it would seem, is a reversal or reappropriation of versioning's resistant othering, a concept addressed during a panel discussion of *The Hours* phenomenon in June 2003. As one of the speakers, Woolf scholar Leslie Kathleen Hankins, put it, 'I think versioning looks like subversion, but if Virginia Woolf's text is the subversive text, then subverting a subversive text may be reinscribing the very things Woolf was trying to write against, which was a more heterosexual, male, ordered society.' For the scholar and writer Daniel Mendelsohn, another speaker, whose article in *The New York Review of Books* is, I still think, the best thing I have read on the topic, the reappropriation lies in the failure of the gay men who made the movie, including Hare and Cunningham, to escape the clichés about 'women on the verge which reinscribe an essentially patriarchal model'. 'It seems to me,' he added, 'and I hate to say it, but it is a guy problem really.'[15]

Cunningham himself identified the subversiveness of *The Hours* not with a queering of Woolf's text but with the appropriation of its writer, an act that fulfils one of the basic tenets of fan productions: wanting to make a beloved text part of the fan's own lived experience. He has a point: the decision to write Virginia Woolf, her thoughts and her words into the novel generated more discussion of its daringness than anything else. 'It takes courage to emulate a revered and brilliant writer, not to mention transforming her into a character', one reviewer noted.[16] Cunningham anticipated that his ventriloquism would be provocative: 'It is an act of real presumptuousness,' he commented before the book was published; 'it's a kind of violation to take a dead genius who can't defend herself and purport to imagine not just a day in her life but what was going on in her mind'. 'There's something in [the novel] to offend almost everyone,' he noted elsewhere. 'I am a man writing about a feminist icon, I am a regular guy doing the best I can writing about a genius [. . .] People have a remarkably proprietary sense of Virginia Woolf, more than just about any other figure I know.'[17]

The Author as Fan: Contention 2

For Cunningham, the appropriation of Virginia Woolf's star power brought more than elevation to official culture; it also made him a star, increasing his financial as well as cultural worth.

At this point I want to return to the language used to describe *The Hours*' relationship to *Mrs Dalloway* to illustrate yet another way in which *The Hours* can be read through the discourse of fandom, this time focusing on the metaphors grounded in adoration. 'Homage' is the term that appears most often in these representations of the text; Cunningham is repeatedly said to 'pay homage' to Virginia Woolf, described in one article as 'the high priestess of high modernism', and in this incarnation easily recognisable as a star. This homage, one commentator writes, 'brings his literary idol back to life'; another calls the work the 'emulation of [. . .] a revered writer'; still another calls it a 'reverent pastiche'.[18] In an interview after *The Hours* won the PEN/Faulkner award, Cunningham is quoted as saying that 'the word "homage" makes me slightly nervous, as if it were something gilded on a rope being draped over the head of someone elderly or august. I wanted it to be livelier'.[19] But two weeks later, after winning the Pulitzer, he described his novel as 'an act of "veneration" for the original'.[20] It is worth noting here, as Jenkins reminds us, that the term 'fan' is 'an abbreviated form of the word "fanatic", which has its roots in the Latin word "fanaticus". In its most literal sense, "fanaticus" simply meant "Of or belonging to the temple, a temple servant, a devotee"'.[21] By transforming Virginia Woolf and her novel into sacred texts, Cunningham becomes the privileged acolyte, elevated by his intertextual relationship to them, an act that can be read through the elevation in cultural status Cunningham experienced as a result of his prizes. As one commentator wrote the day after the Pulitzers were announced, 'Cunningham and seven other artists all got the news that they had become stars yesterday'. 'Don't worry,' he advises Cunningham, 'you now have the bright lights of stardom to keep you warm.'[22]

The transformation from fan to star reads just right here, especially when, in good postmodern fashion, we turn from what Cunningham says about his text to the text itself and ask where, to borrow Roland Barthes's terminology, the author appears as a guest. The answer, I would argue, is inscribed in the discourse of stars and fans and fame and literary awards that permeates the novel. The author, it would seem, wove his own desire for fame, including the desire to see his novel turned into a film, into the text itself.

To make this point one need look only at the first of the 'Mrs Dalloway' sections in *The Hours*, where the contemporary Clarissa, startled by a loud sound, looks out of the window of a downtown New York flower shop towards the 'welter of trucks and trailers' on a movie set; she is just in time to see 'a famous head emerge'. 'Meryl

Streep?' she wonders; 'Vanessa Redgrave?' Uncertain of the exact identity of the star, Clarissa is clear about one thing: she is 'an angel', whose message to those who glimpse her is one of 'watchful remonstrance'.[23] The intertext here is the scene in *Mrs Dalloway* where, startled by a loud noise, 'passers-by [. . .] had just time to see a face of the very greatest importance against the dove-grey upholstery' of a passing car. 'Was it the Prince of Wales's, the Queen's, the Prime Minister's?' Associated with authority and with religion, both presented ironically as part of Woolf's '[criticism] of the social system'[24] – her definition of what she wanted the novel to be – the 'greatness seated within' the car becomes distinctly problematic, to the reader if not to Clarissa herself.[25] Not so in *The Hours*, where Clarissa, who 'can't help being drawn to the aura of fame – and more than fame, actual immortality – implied by the presence of a movie star in a trailer on the corner on MacDougal and Spring Streets', allows herself to continue standing, 'foolish as any fan, for another few minutes, in hope of seeing the star', whether Streep, Redgrave or Susan Sarandon, emerge.[26] Clarissa, of course, is played in the film by Meryl Streep.

Others in *The Hours* are equally as desiring. Laura Brown, the forties housewife played in the film by Julianne Moore, 'revels' in the friendship of her neighbour Kitty (Toni Collette), whom she equates with a movie star; 'like a movie star she seems both common and heightened, in the way of Olivia De Havilland or Barbara Stanwyck'. Sally, Clarissa's long-term partner, a 'producer of public television' played by Allison Janney, has to struggle to keep her balance in the presence of the star with whom she lunches; 'there is no more powerful force in the world', she thinks, 'than fame'. 'There is the terrible desire to be loved by Oliver St Ives.' Clarissa, who experiences angst at not being invited to lunch with the star, argues her case for inclusion in terms of her own stardom: her recognisable appearance as 'the woman in the book' (Richard's novel), a phrase she and others use repeatedly to identify her status.[27]

The only person in the novel who does not desire to be a star or be around stars is the prize-winning writer Richard, played by Ed Harris. Cynical, or perhaps 'egotistical' (Clarissa's term), to the core, Richard both scorns and wants the recognition and fame that come with his prize; he commits suicide just before the award ceremony. In contrast, Cunningham, as he told the audience at a PEN/New Yorker tribute to Virginia Woolf after winning the Pulitzer, relished the attention, 'shamelessly' touring and touting his book. Thank you, Virginia Woolf, for making me rich and famous, is a rough translation of what he said. In this sense Cunningham, although he ends his talk by noting how thrilling it was to have the opportunity to bow down before Virginia Woolf's spirit as a devotee or a devoted fan would do, ceases to be a fan, for fans, John Fiske tells us, 'do not write or produce their texts for money [. . .] [As] Henry Jenkins has pointed out to me [. . .] there is a strong distrust of making a profit in fandom, and those who attempt to do so are typically classed as hucksters rather than fans'.[28]

I have a harder time deciding how to read the other aspect of Cunningham's stardom: his interactions with the stars in the film, in particular Nicole Kidman, whom he calls in an interview he did with her 'the essence of the term "star"'; his tone throughout shows a disconcerting combination of fanlike devotion and a sense of the status he's gained by proximity to stardom, both Kidman's and Virginia Woolf's. 'You, Nicole Kidman,' he says to her at one point, 'have agreed to wear a wig and a big prosthetic nose to play Virginia Woolf. I, of course, am not a movie star. But we do have one thing in common: We're both people who've dared to portray Woolf. The genius and feminist icon.' Later in the interview, in as self-serving a bit of preening as I've ever read, Cunningham returns to what it means for Kidman – and him – to be stars:

MC: I was wondering about that. I've found, even with a novelist's teeny-tiny recognition---
NK: Are you kidding me? You've had huge recognition.
MC: Then again, as compared to say, a movie star---
NK: Do you feel the pressure of it?[29]

Vwoolf; or, the Common Reader as Fan

Although Cunningham's capitalisation on Virginia Woolf earned him star status in both high culture and Hollywood culture, this was not the case on the Vwoolf list, where both the casting of Nicole Kidman to play the writer and what was termed the gay male appropriation of Virginia Woolf were extensively debated, illustrating a distinctly fanlike disconnect between the list and official culture.

Started in 1995, Vwoolf, composed of academics, students, common readers and people in the arts, is a lively, combative, international forum on just about everything, no matter how weighty or trivial, to do with Virginia Woolf, her writings, her friends and her representation in the texts that constitute her star image. While my initial interest in writing about the list focused on its role as media text in constructing Virginia Woolf's star image, what was designated the 'Nicole Kidman controversy' spurred me to rethink it in terms of Jenkins's characterisation of organised fandom as:

> first and foremost, an institution of theory and criticism, a semi-structured space where competing interpretations and evaluations of common texts are proposed, debated, and negotiated and where readers speculate about the nature of the mass media and their own relationship to it.[30]

Here, as in fan culture as a whole, expertise or knowledge counts. Here, what might be dismissed as trivia or gossip elsewhere becomes the coin of exchange and a source of power. And here, those who, when it comes to popular if not academic productions, have no control over what is produced, can hijack the productions for their own ends. In the case of *The Hours*, what started as a subversive intervention into a particular text – the as-yet-unmade film – became an extremely heated, deeply serious debate that ended, only temporarily, with the question 'Who "owns" Virginia Woolf'?

The particular thread I have been tracking began in September 2000 when someone posted a snippet from the *San Francisco Chronicle* that Nicole Kidman was negotiating to play Virginia Woolf in the film.[31] A subsequent article from the *Chronicle* posted to the list in December detailed the cast, director and writer, and quoted Cunningham on Kidman: 'I suspect Virginia Woolf would love to be played by a tall, beautiful woman'. The immediate response from list members to both postings was, no way. 'Thanks for the tip', one contributor wrote after the first; 'I'll try to get my family off the planet in time'. 'Nicole Kidman as Virginia Woolf is an abomination of everything I hold dear', was one of the first responses to the later news; 'Why, Michael Cunningham? Why???'

At this point in the conversation the participants switched gears, moving into a more productive mode. First, they offered a whole list of actresses they thought would be better: Meryl Streep (the most common choice), Eileen Atkins, Helen Mirren, Fiona Shaw, Janet McTeer, Tilda Swindon, Emma Thompson, Natasha Richardson, Kate Nelligan, Jolie Richardson. While one poster speculated that 'well-known actors will not satisfy us enthusiasts and will bring too much with them', another started a whole other creative thread by casting a 'just for laughs Bloomsbury movie'. 'This is much more fun than waiting for the film to come out and then criticising', one person wrote; another offered suggestions for what he'd like to see – and not see – in the film: a scene filmed in New York 'in front of or inside Three Lives Books [. . .] And please God, no shots of Kidman/Woolf going down for the third time in the river Ouse!!' All these posters, acutely aware, as Jenkins might put it, of their lack of control over official cultural productions, acted upon them in ways that not only made them their own property, but produced new texts, texts that actively subvert the industry's intentions.

Significantly, these intentions, as formulated on the list, are perceived to be explicitly and decidedly commercial. In a long post that defends the choice of Kidman, the writer posits that Kidman got the role because 'she will help "open" the film with a younger audience. Streep never opened a film wide' – never, that is, brought in the audience and hence the top dollars that come with a widely successful opening weekend. Kidman, it seems, was playing Virginia Woolf because Kidman, like Virginia Woolf, was a profit-producing star. Others defended her by arguing that she did have the range and acting abilities to carry off the role, but the economic argument would seem to be borne out by the extensive publicity given Kidman while the film was shooting. *Harper's Bazaar*, for example, sent a reporter to the set to do a story about Kidman's 'style', only to discover the actress almost unrecognisable in ugly clothes and a prosthetic nose. The accompanying photos, though, are pure Kidman elegance and glamour.[32] And it was Kidman whom Michael Cunningham interviewed for *Interview* in February 2002, where the discussion of her appearance in the film is once again juxtaposed to more star-like pictures of Kidman, this time in black leather or a man's white suit, projecting a distinctly S&M aura.

Back on Vwoolf, the discussion of the film sparked by the initial Kidman posting soon segued into a heated debate about whether Cunningham had 'gone too far' in trying to get inside of Woolf's psyche; whether the representation of Woolf as a 'tortured genius' was a cult fixation for some gay men, turning her into an icon on a par with Judy Garland and Joan Crawford; whether the novel 'appropriated Woolf's life into a gay male template'; whether gay male publishing trumped lesbian publishing in the current marketplace; whether the publishers did market research within the gay community before publishing the novel; whether the 'gay bashing' currently occurring on the list was accurate or appropriate; whether 'female appropriations' of Woolf, 'usually [involving] total identification' are any better than male ones. One male contributor wrote, 'what exactly would you like us men who love and admire Woolf's work to do? Never teach it or recommend it to friends? Never let it influence our lives and works? Die?'

About this time the conversation also became a discussion of versioning that raised the question of whether all texts are not intertextual; whether rather than being 'derivative' or 'piggy-backing', *The Hours*, like Jean Rhys's *Wide Sargasso Sea*, should be read as a 'provocative', 'challenging' – I would add postmodern – extension of a previous text. The question 'Who "owns" VW? Feminist scholars? Common Readers? Students? Men? Lesbians? Gay men?' subsequently brought the conversation squarely back into the realm of cultural and economic capital.

Where does this leave us?

Good question. Before the film opened, the hot topics in the media devoted to film and Oscar predictions were whether the prosthetic nose and Kidman's frumpiness would cost her the Oscar, and what it meant that the film was already being seen as a 'chick flick', a category, one Oscar site said, that would prevent it from winning best picture. The bottom line was, would the film make money; people thought not. How do we read the fact that at least some of these predictions were so wrong? Or the fact that the negative reviews of the film were few and far between, at least in the mainstream media; posters to online sites were a great deal harsher about the film's weaknesses, as were academics.

Or, what do we make of the fact that Miramax put an inordinate amount of effort, including a dedicated publicist, into getting Woolf scholars to hype the film; or that an article in the *New York Times* about the negative reactions to the film among these scholars led Miramax to worry whether this would ruin its Oscar chances, and the president of the Virginia Woolf Society to ask the participants on Vwoolf to write letters in support of the film. Before this, when the film was first released to a media frenzy, several participants on the list had a brief moment of transitioning from fans to mainstream commentators; during this period Woolf scholars, academics, even feminist academics, were widely quoted in a press that usually spends its time carefully disassociating itself from them. But when it came to advocating for the film at Oscar time, the list was having none of it, though many liked the film, and almost everyone agreed that anything that brought readers back to Virginia Woolf was necessarily good.

The one thing that I am clear about is that Virginia Woolf's cultural capital, her star power, remains as strong as ever, if not stronger, including her ability to make those who portray her, whether Cunningham or

Kidman, stars in their own right. On the 2003 panel about *The Hours* Mary Desjardins, a film scholar who writes about the recycling of stars, saw all the women actors as benefiting from their association with Virginia Woolf, a gain in cultural capital that compensates for the absence of good roles for women in Hollywood, especially as they get older, and the loss of economic capital that would come with those roles. This was especially the case for Kidman, she argued, who previous to the film was not a star in her own right.[33] Given all this, the battles over who gets to represent Virginia Woolf, and whose representation is a better investment, are not likely to end with *The Hours*.

Addendum

The day after I finished writing this talk I opened my email to discover a series of postings on Vwoolf headed, 'The Hours a better book than Mrs. Dalloway?' The question was a response to a recent statement by David Hare that it was.

Part III. Selling *Mrs Dalloway*

As mentioned at the start of this chapter, there have been a slew of new editions of *Mrs Dalloway* since Public Domain Day 2021. In a way the timing was propitious: in the early days of the 2020 coronavirus pandemic *Mrs Dalloway* had become the go-to book, precipitated in part by the publication of Elizabeth Outka's study, *Viral Modernism: The Influenza Pandemic and Interwar Literature*, and her chapter on *Mrs Dalloway* as a novel about the flu.[34] But readers didn't need this study to find themselves turning to the novel, as the multiple memes beginning 'Mrs. Dalloway said she would...' circulating on the web made clear. As one writer noted, there are multiple reasons 'Why Anxious Readers Under Quarantine Turn to *Mrs. Dalloway*'.[35] None of this appears in the introductory essays designed to sell the new editions, presumably commissioned long before the pandemic, although their focus raises a number of questions about the economics of book publishing and what governs the choices editors make about their target audiences. In a review of some of these editions for the *Virginia Woolf Miscellany*, Mark Hussey notes:

> The mysterious laws of copyright go on engendering new editions of classic works, and publishers often seem to worry that readers need to be eased into them by way of an introduction by a celebrity author.

The new Vintage edition has an attractive Vanessa Bell-esque cover, and an introduction by Michael Cunningham. His very successful novel *The Hours* – together with its film version – led to a spike in sales of *Mrs Dalloway*, so it might reasonably be supposed that his name on the cover will attract new readers.[36]

The question is, which readers, and why, as Vwoolf immediately saw. Who is Cunningham's essay aimed at, they asked; is there a trend these days away from the kind of information a scholar would supply to an attempt to make the novel meaningful for the contemporary moment, where biographical novels abound? Cunningham, judging by his introduction, might well say yes, including among his assertions as to why '*Mrs. Dalloway* is a revolutionary novel' a great deal of biographical information, including that she was molested by her half-brother who published her first two novels. Why, one wonders, include this. Cunningham justifies his movement into biography through the depiction of Septimus's 'insanity' and Woolf's own experiences. '[O]ut of respect for her', he notes, 'we should refrain from speculations, and to the greatest extent possible, from autobiographical anecdote. I would, frankly, refrain from it entirely if *Mrs Dalloway* were not quite so clearly a self-portrait in diptych'. And, one might add, if Cunningham himself had not contributed to the focus on her 'insanity' in his own representation of 'Virginia Woolf' in *The Hours* that this current introduction would seem to be both reinforcing and justifying.[37]

Jenny Offill's 'Foreword' to the new Penguin edition, which offers autobiography rather than biography, would seem to further support the shift towards the personal rather than the scholarly. To some extent the choice of Offill, described in the edition as 'the *New York Times* bestselling author of *Weather* and *Dept. of Speculation*', continues the history, as one person noted on Vwoolf, of having editions of Woolf's novel introduced by women novelists. Interestingly, the Penguin edition is a reissue of their 1992 one, which featured an introduction by Elaine Showalter and footnotes and commentary by Stella McNichol, both literary scholars. Here, Offill's role appears to be to make the novel more accessible to those who might be afraid of Woolf; it maps, she tells us, 'the twists and turns of my own autobiography over the years. Each time [I read it], I have found shocks of recognition on the page, but they are always new ones'.[38]

Curious to hear what an insider would say about the economic and cultural implications of the choice of the two novelists, I consulted a friend who had worked for what is now Penguin Random House. Both publishers, I learned, Penguin and Vintage, are divisions of Penguin Random House – as is the Hogarth Press; both editions are part of the publishers' 'classic' lines, which, having firm academic bases, would normally do an edition of a public domain title if they think there is a market for it, thereby putting them into competition with each other. Each one, she noted, would know who their readers were, including how many were academics, and would stick to their brand, trying to differentiate themselves not only from each other but from the plethora of new, perhaps cheaper, editions of the novel made possible by the public domain. Offill's contribution to the Penguin edition, she speculated, was to provide an appealing update to the more scholarly edition, while for Vintage Cunningham was a certain 'get'. After all, she concluded, 'Cunningham wrote a bestselling novel about *Mrs. Dalloway* that won a Pulitzer and was made into an Oscar winning movie. From a publishing point of view, I don't know how you can top it.'[39]

Where are we now?

As of March 2022 there were about seventeen editions of *Mrs Dalloway* listed on Amazon.com that were published around or after Public Domain Day 2021. Several of these have reading and study notes and are aimed at students or book groups; some are illustrated; some are combined with Woolf's earlier novels. Then, in May 2022, Michael Cunningham's own publisher, Picador Macmillan, finally cashed in on its 'star', publishing a volume where *Mrs Dalloway* is an add-on to *The Hours*. The cover of the new edition places 'Michael Cunningham' and 'The Hours' at the top; towards the bottom, under the illustration, we find, in very small print, 'Combined edition with Virginia Woolf's *Mrs. Dalloway*'. The very bottom line, in the largest print on the cover, reads, 'Introduction by Michael Cunningham'. In a way this edition is not surprising; my publisher friend pointed out that for Vintage to use a writer who is not one of theirs underlines the value accruing to his association with Woolf. No wonder his own publisher would want to capitalise on it.

Last Word

An opera based on *The Hours* commissioned by the Metropolitan Opera and the Philadelphia Orchestra premiered in New York in November 2022. The star power driving this commercial venture was not Virginia Woolf, not Cunningham, not the singer portraying Woolf, but Renée Fleming, who was making a comeback in the Clarissa role. I can (almost) live with that.

Notes

1. Jenny Offill, 'A Lifetime of Lessons in *Mrs. Dalloway*', *New Yorker*, 29 December 2020 <https://www.newyorker.com/books/page-turner/a-lifetime-of-lessons-in-mrs-dalloway> [accessed 1 November 2023]; Michael Cunningham, 'Michael Cunningham on Virginia Woolf's Literary Revolution', *New York Times Book Review*, 23 December 2020 <https://www.nytimes.com/2020/12/23/books/review/michael-cunningham-on-virginia-woolfs-literary-revolution.html> [accessed 1 November 2023].
2. Mark Hussey, 'Vwoolf Digest, Vol. 103, Issue 12', *Vwoolf Listserv*, 27 December 2020 <https://lists.osu.edu/pipermail/vwoolf/2020-December/004359.html> [accessed 1 November 2023]. Quoted with permission.
3. 'How Time Passes', *Time*, 12 April 1937, 93.
4. See Richard Dyer, *Stars* (London: BFI Publishing, 1990), 1–3; Brenda R. Silver, *Virginia Woolf Icon* (Chicago: Chicago University Press, 1999), 16–18.
5. Henry Jenkins, *Textual Poachers: Television Fans and Participatory Culture* (New York: Routledge, 1992), 23–4.
6. Jenkins, *Textual Poachers*, 24, 18.
7. John Fiske, 'The Cultural Economy of Fandom', in *The Adoring Audience: Fan Culture and Popular Media*, ed. by Lisa A. Lewis (New York: Routledge, 1992), 30–1.
8. This list was generated in 2003; today the prime site for reading fan fiction is 'An Archive of One's Own', where on 28 March 2022 there were ten stories based on *Mrs Dalloway*. The archive is a project of the Organization for Transformative Works, which promotes fan arts in multiple media and genres. It also publishes the academic journal *Transformative Works and Cultures*, see <https://www.transformativeworks.org> [accessed 1 November 2023].
9. Elizabeth Harvor, 'A Day in the Life x 3', review of *The Hours*, by Michael Cunningham, *The Globe and Mail*.
10. Dick Hebdige, *Cut 'n' Mix: Culture, Identity, and Caribbean Music* (London and New York: Routledge, 1987), xii.
11. David Kurnick, 'Virginia Territory', review of *The Hours*, by Michael Cunningham, *Village Voice*, 24 November 1998 <https://www.villagevoice.com/1998/11/24/virginia-territory> [accessed 1 November 2023].
12. Christopher Lane, 'When Plagues Don't End', *The Gay and Lesbian Review*, 8.1 (January 2001), 30.

13. J. Bottum, 'Taste: Wolfe vs. Woolf – The prizes are in', *Wall Street Journal*, 16 April 1999 <https://www.wsj.com/articles/SB924226477323159322> [accessed 1 November 2023].
14. Julie Hilden, '*Gone with the Wind* versus *The Wind Done Gone*: Parody, Copyright, African-Americans, and the First Amendment', *FindLaw*, 30 April 2002 <https://supreme.findlaw.com/legal-commentary/g-with-the-wind-versus-t-wind-done-gone.html> [accessed 1 November 2023].
15. Both quoted with permission. See Daniel Mendelsohn, 'Not Afraid of Virginia Woolf', *New York Review of Books*, 13 March 2003 <https://www.nybooks.com/articles/2003/03/13/not-afraid-of-virginia-woolf> [accessed 1 November 2023].
16. Donna Seaman, review of *The Hours*, by Michael Cunningham, *Booklist*, 18 September 1998 <https://www.booklistonline.com/The-Hours-Michael-Cunningham/pid=1038133> [accessed 1 November 2023].
17. Michael Cunningham, talk at A Different Light Bookstore, 24 November 1998 <https://archive.nytimes.com/www.nytimes.com/books/98/12/06/daily/cunningham.html#audio> [accessed 1 November 2023].
18. Troy Patterson, 'Eye on the Prizes', *Entertainment Weekly*, 30 April 1999, 88; Jameson Currier, 'Three Faces of Mrs. Dalloway', *Washington Post*, 22 November 1998 <https://www.washingtonpost.com/archive/entertainment/books/1998/11/22/three-faces-of-mrs-dalloway/6069af09-46ff-4e27-a346-bc767f0e2226> [accessed 31 October 2023].
19. David Streitfeld, 'Cunningham Wins PEN Award', *Washington Post*, 18 April 1999 <https://www.washingtonpost.com/archive/lifestyle/1999/04/08/cunningham-wins-pen-award/24e1b83a-0d9b-40f3-b04d-09a886131b50> [accessed 31 October 2023].
20. Mel Gussow, 'A Writer Haunted by Virginia Woolf', *New York Times*, 20 April 1999 <https://www.nytimes.com/1999/04/20/books/a-writer-haunted-by-virginia-woolf.html> [accessed 31 October 2023].
21. Jenkins, *Textual Poachers*, 12.
22. David Streitfeld, '*The Hours* Takes Fiction Pulitzer', *Washington Post*, 13 April 1999 <https://www.washingtonpost.com/archive/lifestyle/1999/04/13/the-hours-takes-fiction-pulitzer/b2d3f1d2-a885-432a-81ea-e4d480a2cf31> [accessed 1 November 2023].
23. Michael Cunningham, *The Hours* (New York: Picador, 1998), 26–7.
24. Virginia Woolf, *A Writer's Diary: Being Extracts from the Diary of Virginia Woolf*, ed. by Leonard Woolf (London: Hogarth, 1972), 5.
25. Virginia Woolf, *Mrs Dalloway* (New York: Harcourt Brace Jovanovich, 1990), 14.
26. Cunningham, *The Hours*, 50–1.
27. Ibid., 105, 176, 178, 93.
28. Fiske, 'The Cultural Economy of Fandom', 39–40.
29. Michael Cunningham, 'Nicole Kidman', *Interview*, February 2002, 92–101.

30. Jenkins, *Textual Poachers*, 86.
31. 'Woolf and Kidman,' 14 September 2000, *VWOOLF*. Subsequent quotations in the main text appear in this thread under different headings, ending with 'Comments on The Hours,' 02 January 2001.
32. Daisy Garnett, 'Dramatic Leanings', *Harper's Bazaar*, 1 September 2001.
33. Quoted with permission.
34. Elizabeth Outka, *Viral Modernism: The Influenza Pandemic and Interwar Literature* (New York: Columbia University Press, 2020).
35. Evan Kindley, 'Why Anxious Readers Under Quarantine Turn to *Mrs. Dalloway*', *New Yorker*, 10 April 2020 <https://www.newyorker.com/books/page-turner/why-anxious-readers-under-quarantine-turn-to-virginia-woolfs-mrs-dalloway> [accessed 1 November 2023].
36. Mark Hussey, 'Review', *Virginia Woolf Miscellany* (Fall/Winter 2001), 51–3.
37. Michael Cunningham, 'Introduction' to *Mrs Dalloway* (New York: Vintage, 2021), xii. Equally, if not more, problematic is Cunningham's assertion, scornfully noted by Vwoolf, that '*Mrs. Dalloway* is (though seldom discussed as such) one of the great novels of World War I'(xi).
38. Jenny Offill, 'Foreword' to *Mrs Dalloway* (New York: Penguin, 2021), xiii.
39. Quoted with permission.

Works Cited

'How Time Passes'. *Time*. 12 April 1937, 93.

'Nicole Kidman: She's got guts. She's been humanized. She takes risks. And she's the movie star the world has fallen in love with'. Index Articles <https://indexarticles.com/arts/interview/nicole-kidman-shes-got-guts-shes-been-humanized-she-takes-risks-and-shes-the-movie-star-the-world-has-fallen-in-love-with> [accessed 2 December 2022].

Bottum, J. 'Taste: Wolfe vs. Woolf – The prizes are in'. *Wall Street Journal*, 16 April 1999 <https://www.wsj.com/articles/SB924226477323159322> [accessed 1 November 2023].

Cunningham, Michael. *The Hours*. New York: Picador, 1998.

——, 'Introduction' to *Mrs Dalloway*. New York: Vintage, 2021.

——, 'Michael Cunningham on Virginia Woolf's Literary Revolution'. *New York Times Book Review*, 23 December 2020 <https://www.nytimes.com/2020/12/23/books/review/michael-cunningham-on-virginia-woolfs-literary-revolution.html> [accessed 1 November 2023].

——, 'Nicole Kidman', *Interview*, February 2002, 92–101.

——, Talk at Reading at A Different Light Bookstore, 24 November 1998 <https://archive.nytimes.com/www.nytimes.com/books/98/12/06/daily/cunningham.html#audio> [accessed 1 November 2023].

Currier, Jameson. 'Three Faces of Mrs. Dalloway'. *Washington Post*, 22 November 1998 <https://www.washingtonpost.com/archive/entertainment/books/1998/11/22/three-faces-of-mrs-dalloway/6069af09-46ff-4e27-a346-bc767f0e2226> [accessed 31 October 2023].

Dyer, Richard. *Stars*. London: BFI Publishing, 1990.

Fiske, John. 'The Cultural Economy of Fandom'. *The Adoring Audience: Fan Culture and Popular Media*, ed. by Lisa A. Lewis, 30–1. New York: Routledge, 1992.

Garnett, Daisy. 'Dramatic Leanings'. *Harper's Bazaar*. 1 September 2001.

Gussow, Mel. 'A Writer Haunted by Virginia Woolf'. *New York Times*, 20 April 1999 <https://www.nytimes.com/1999/04/20/books/a-writer-haunted-by-virginia-woolf.html> [accessed 31 October 2023].

Harvor, Elizabeth. 'A Day in the Life x 3'. Review of *The Hours*, by Michael Cunningham. *The Globe and Mail*.

Hebdige, Dick. *Cut 'n' Mix: Culture, Identity, and Caribbean Music*. London and New York: Routledge, 1987.

Hilden, Julie. '*Gone with the Wind* versus *The Wind Done Gone*: Parody, Copyright, African-Americans, and the First Amendment'. *FindLaw*, 30 April 2002 <https://supreme.findlaw.com/legal-commentary/g-with-the-wind-versus-t-wind-done-gone.html> [accessed 1 November 2023].

Hussey, Mark. 'Review'. *Virginia Woolf Miscellany*. Fall/Winter 2001, 51–3.

——, 'Vwoolf Digest, Vol. 103, Issue 12'. *Vwoolf Listserv*, 27 December 2020 <https://lists.osu.edu/pipermail/vwoolf/2020-December/004359.html> [accessed 1 November 2023].

Jenkins, Henry. *Textual Poachers: Television Fans and Participatory Culture*. New York: Routledge, 1992.

Kindley, Evan. 'Why Anxious Readers Under Quarantine Turn to *Mrs. Dalloway*'. *New Yorker*, 10 April 2020 <https://www.newyorker.com/books/page-turner/why-anxious-readers-under-quarantine-turn-to-virginia-woolfs-mrs-dalloway> [accessed 1 November 2023].

Kurnick, David. 'Virginia Territory'. Review of *The Hours*, by Michael Cunningham. *Village Voice*, 24 November 1998 <https://www.villagevoice.com/1998/11/24/virginia-territory> [accessed 1 November 2023].

Lane, Christopher. 'When Plagues Don't End'. *The Gay and Lesbian Review*, 8.1 (January 2001), 30.

Mendelsohn, Daniel. 'Not Afraid of Virginia Woolf'. *New York Review of Books*, 13 March 2003 <https://www.nybooks.com/articles/2003/03/13/not-afraid-of-virginia-woolf> [accessed 1 November 2023].

Offill, Jenny. 'Foreword', to *Mrs Dalloway*. New York: Penguin, 2021.

——, 'A Lifetime of Lessons in *Mrs. Dalloway*'. *New Yorker*, 29 December 2020 <https://www.newyorker.com/books/page-turner/a-lifetime-of-lessons-in-mrs-dalloway> [accessed 1 November 2023].

Outka, Elizabeth. *Viral Modernism: The Influenza Pandemic and Interwar Literature*. New York: Columbia University Press, 2020.

Patterson, Troy. 'Eye on the Prizes'. *Entertainment Weekly*, 30 April 1999, 88.

Seaman, Donna. Review of *The Hours*, by Michael Cunningham. *Booklist*, 18 September 1998 <https://www.booklistonline.com/The-Hours-Michael-Cunningham/pid=1038133> [accessed 1 November 2023].

Silver, Brenda R. *Virginia Woolf Icon*. Chicago: Chicago University Press, 1999.

Streitfeld, David. 'Cunningham Wins PEN Award'. *Washington Post*, 18 April 1999 <https://www.washingtonpost.com/archive/lifestyle/1999/04/08/cunningham-wins-pen-award/24e1b83a-0d9b-40f3-b04d-09a886131b50> [accessed 31 October 2023].

——, '*The Hours* Takes Fiction Pulitzer'. *Washington Post*, 13 April 1999 <https://www.washingtonpost.com/archive/lifestyle/1999/04/13/the-hours-takes-fiction-pulitzer/b2d3f1d2-a885-432a-81ea-e4d480a2cf31> [accessed 1 November 2023].

Woolf, Virginia. *Mrs Dalloway*. New York: Harcourt Brace Jovanovich, 1990.

——, *A Writer's Diary: Being Extracts from the Diary of Virginia Woolf*, ed. by Leonard Woolf. London: Hogarth, 1972.

Coda:

Critical/Creative Responses

Chapter 12

Scrapbooking the Present Day: The *Three Guineas* Scrapbooks

Helen Tyson

In February 1933, Virginia Woolf found herself 'quivering', 'itching' with anticipation at her next writing project, 'the sequel' to *A Room of One's Own*, for which she had 'collected enough powder to blow up St Pauls'.[1] In three large ringbound notebooks compiled between 1931 and 1937 (see Figures 1, 2 and 3), Woolf amassed newspaper clippings, letters, photographs, political pamphlets, handwritten and typewritten quotations, and other ephemera, testimonials of everyday life lived under what one newspaper clipping described (in a phrase that Woolf borrowed for her own typewritten index entry) as 'the capitalist system'.[2] Drawing on these 'scrapbooks' (as critics have come to call them)[3] in *Three Guineas* (1938), Woolf painted a portrait of women's lives in which they found themselves trapped, caught between 'the devil and the deep sea'.[4] 'Behind us', Woolf wrote, 'lies the patriarchal system':

> the private house, with its nullity, its immorality, its hypocrisy, its servility. Before us lies the public world, the professional system, with its possessiveness, its jealousy, its pugnacity, its greed. The one shuts us up like slaves in a harem; the other forces us to circle, like caterpillars head to tail, round and round the mulberry tree, the sacred tree, of property. It is a choice of two evils. Each is bad. (*TG* 155–6)

In *Three Guineas*, Woolf would draw a line from the 'tyrannies and servilities' of the English private house to the toxic growth of fascism taking hold across both Europe and Britain in the 1930s, arguing that the germ of fascism could be found in British broadsheet newspapers as much as in the speeches of Hitler and Mussolini. For Woolf, women's position as outsiders gave them a unique vantage point from which to criticise the reigning structures of capitalist, patriarchal and fascist power, and to imagine an alternative vision of society rooted in feminist solidarity, freed from servility to the 'sacred tree, of property' (*TG* 156).

The three large scrapbooks that Woolf compiled in the 1930s, now preserved in the University of Sussex Special Collections, speak eloquently to her method of critique: clippings detailing university accounts appear alongside photographs of men in ceremonial garb, quotations from 'lectures by men' on their '[h]atred of w[omen]', and newspaper cuttings recording the speeches of Hitler and Mussolini.[5] What can we learn from these scrapbooks today, and how might they speak to our own late capitalist moment? In this essay, I draw on work with undergraduate students at the University of Sussex compiling our own scrapbooks of the present day. I examine what this method of scrapbooking tells us about Woolf's research methods, as well as about the relationship between Woolf's 1930s and our own contemporary moment.

Figure 12.1   Virginia Woolf, '3 volumes of press cuttings, manuscript and typed extracts relating to *Three Guineas*', Monk's House Papers, University of Sussex Special Collections, the Keep, SxMs-18/2/B/16/F, vol. 1. With thanks to The Society of Authors as the Literary Representative of the Estate of Virginia Woolf.

Scrapbooking the Present Day 271

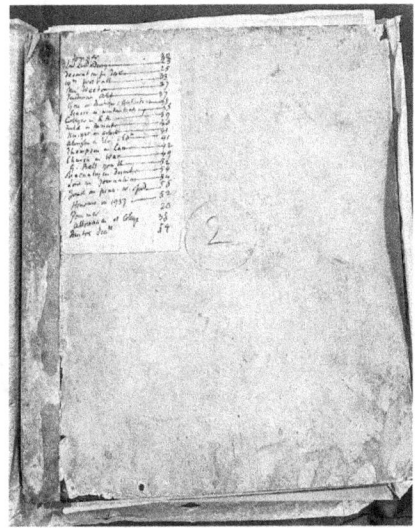

Figure 12.2   Virginia Woolf, '3 volumes of press cuttings, manuscript and typed extracts relating to *Three Guineas*', Monk's House Papers, University of Sussex Special Collections, the Keep, SxMs-18/2/B/16/F, vol. 2. With thanks to The Society of Authors as the Literary Representative of the Estate of Virginia Woolf.

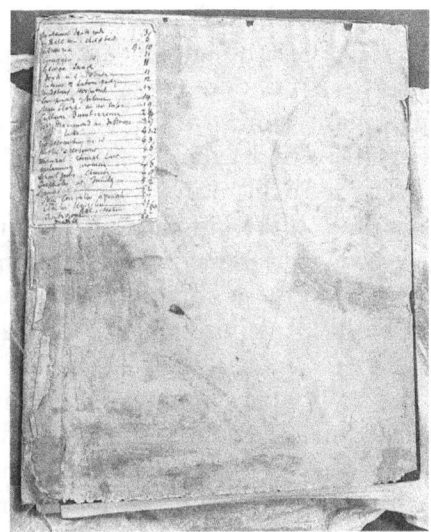

Figure 12.3   Virginia Woolf, '3 volumes of press cuttings, manuscript and typed extracts relating to *Three Guineas*', Monk's House Papers, University of Sussex Special Collections, the Keep, SxMs-18/2/B/16/F, vol. 3. With thanks to The Society of Authors as the Literary Representative of the Estate of Virginia Woolf.

The *Three Guineas* Scrapbooks and the 'Capitalist System'

In February 1935, Woolf found herself 'plagued by the sudden wish to write an Anti fascist Pamphlet' – Leonard told her she 'should have to take account of the economic question' (*D4* 282). Responding to Leonard's directive in a typically playful and yet pointed manner, *Three Guineas* both exposes the role of capitalism in shaping women's lives while also suggesting that capitalism is much more than a question of economics. Imagined variously over the years as 'a sequel to a Room of Ones [sic] Own – about the sexual life of women' (*D4* 6), as an 'Anti fascist Pamphlet' (*D4* 282) and a 'war book' (*D4* 361), and given titles including 'On being despised' (*D4* 271), 'A Knock on the door' (*D4* 28), 'Professions' and 'The Next War' (*D4* 354), *Three Guineas* was published in 1938 in the form of a series of letters. As Woolf had recognised late in December 1935, she needed a structure that would give her 'the right to wander' and 'excuse the method: while giving continuity' (*D4* 361). In order to answer the first letter, from an educated middle-class man, a barrister who has written to ask '[h]ow in your opinion are we to prevent war?' (*TG* 89), Woolf's narrator insists on the 'economic question' by arguing that it is first necessary to respond to two further letters: one from a treasurer 'asking for money with which to rebuild a women's college' (*TG* 107) and another asking for a subscription to a society to help women obtain employment in the professions. Bringing arguments about women's access to universities and the professions into her response to the 'photographs of dead bodies' (*TG* 95) arriving from the Spanish Civil War, Woolf insisted – via the interwoven letter form – on the intimate and insidious connections between capitalist greed, patriarchal power and imperialist militant masculinity, showing how these combined to sow the seeds of a latent fascism that Woolf located in the heart of the English middle-class family home. *Three Guineas*, with its emphasis on 'facts' (*TG* 127) and figures, on newspaper clippings and committee meetings, on war and militarism, may seem quite different from the book that Woolf first imagined as 'about the sexual life of women' (*D4* 6), but it is nonetheless a striking response to Leonard's injunction, revealing how the forces of capitalism, patriarchal power and imperialism penetrate, intersect and shape the most intimate realms of all of our psychic and emotional lives.

In *Three Guineas*, writing from the perspective of the 'educated man's daughter' – a self-admittedly 'clumsy term' coined by Woolf 'to describe the class whose fathers have been educated at public schools and universities', but whose historical exclusion from 'capital' and land-ownership made it 'grossly incorrect' to use the term 'bourgeois' (*TG* 218) – Woolf painted a portrait of women as trapped between patriarchal oppression and capitalist greed. For Woolf, some middle-class women may have made a daring escape from the 'tyrannies and servilities' (*TG* 215) of the Victorian household, but their entrance into the universities and the professions was fraught with the peril of submitting to the 'possessiveness', 'jealousy', 'pugnacity' and 'greed' (*TG* 156) of a capitalist higher education institution and 'professional system' that – relentlessly, unremittingly, often unconsciously – propped up war. Woolf entertains a brief fantasy of the possibilities that might open up if women were to consent to becoming 'champions of the capitalist system' – it is 'a thought not without its glamour,' comprising 'rich women', generous endowments for women's colleges, 'a woman's part in the House of Commons', a newspaper committed to free speech, 'pensions for spinsters', 'equal pay for equal work', chloroform during childbirth, and a reduction in the maternal death rate (*TG* 150). 'There seems', Woolf writes, 'at first sight nothing you could not do, if you had the same capital at your disposal that your brothers have at theirs' (*TG* 150). But Woolf checks this brief fantasy of a capitalist feminist utopia by returning to the 'photographs of dead bodies and ruined houses that the Spanish Government sends almost weekly' (*TG* 150), insisting that there is an unacknowledged link between the 'unreal loyalties' (*TG* 159) demanded of those who 'circle' round the 'mulberry tree' (*TG* 161), and the documents of war. Those 'unreal loyalties' (*TG* 159) – the conscious and unconscious ties that bind both men and women to the traditions of patriarchal masculinity ('old schools, old colleges, old churches, old ceremonies, old countries' [*TG* 159]) and the 'capitalist system' (*TG* 150) – are, Woolf argues, powerful forces in shaping the very real horror of 'dead bodies and ruined houses' (*TG* 165).

For Woolf, women's historical exclusion from sites of power allowed them to 'see the same world', but 'through different eyes' (*TG* 101), offering them a unique critical perspective on the tightly woven web of capitalism, imperialist masculinity and fascist ideology. In one of the most celebrated and oft-quoted passages of *Three Guineas*, Woolf exhorts women to respond to men's claims to 'fight on her behalf to protect "our" country' with 'indifference' (*TG* 185). Confronted with attempts to 'rouse her patriotic emotion' (*TG* 184), the outsider, Woolf insists, must be defiant:

'Our country,' she will say, 'throughout the greater part of its history has treated me as a slave; it has denied me education or any share in its possessions. 'Our' country still ceases to be mine if I marry a foreigner [. . .] [I]n fact, as a woman, I have no country. As a woman I want no country. As a woman my country is the whole world.' (*TG* 185)

And yet, as Jessica Berman has noted, Woolf's commitment to 'indifference' here is by no means reducible to inaction.[6] Throughout *Three Guineas*, Woolf searches for, and advocates, an 'active method of expressing our belief that war is barbarous, that war is inhuman, that war [. . .] is insupportable, horrible and beastly' (*TG* 96). To aid women to resist 'the seductions of the most powerful of all seducers – money', Woolf encouraged both 'active and passive measures [. . .] to break the ring, the vicious circle, the dance round and round the mulberry tree' (*TG* 177). 'The ring once broken,' Woolf wrote, 'the captives would be freed' (*TG* 177). For those who make up Woolf's 'Society of Outsiders' (*TG* 189), the task is to develop 'not merely critical but creative' 'experiments' (*TG* 190) in living life outside of the 'vicious circle' of 'intellectual harlotry' (*TG* 177).

As Melanie Micir and Aarthi Vadde have argued, the 'active' (*TG* 96) 'creative' (*TG* 190) and 'critical' (*TG* 190) 'method' (*TG* 96) of *Three Guineas* is itself rooted in the scrapbook form.[7] The 'note books' in which she kept her 'cuttings', or 'Notes & Cuttings' (as she typed onto a label glued to the front cover of the first volume, see Figure 12.1), are, as Merry M. Pawlowski has written, positioned between the overlapping traditions of the scrapbook and the commonplace book.[8] They are also examples of the intimate connections between late nineteenth-century women's scrapbooks, feminist politics and the avant-garde modernist practice of collage. Like other modernist women writers and artists, including Nancy Cunard and Hannah Höch, in her scrapbooks Woolf takes up a practice that was widespread among middle-class women in the nineteenth century, and one that was used by a number of suffragettes as a form of feminist history, but which also had strong links to the avant-garde.[9] Woolf's scrapbooks are feminist archives, documenting the material realities of women's lives in the late nineteenth and early twentieth centuries, but they also bear witness to an experimental creative and critical method of reading, responding to and intervening in her contemporary moment.[10]

The scrapbooks, Micir and Vadde argue, 'offer more than preparatory work for the thwarted "essay-novel" *The Pargiters* and the revamped project of *Three Guineas*':

They supply inspiration for the formal design and aesthetic strategy of the published work. Scrapbooking informs the work's structure of address and strategies of textual arrangement; it incorporates the democratically distributed creativity of cutting and pasting into Woolf's biting rebuke of the oligarchic hoarding of educational opportunity in a patriarchal English society.[11]

Scrapbooking, as Micir and Vadde put it, 'combats what [Woolf] calls the "hypnotic power of dominance" by restoring the connective tissue to segmented spheres of knowledge'.[12] In Woolf's scrapbooks, and in *Three Guineas*, the method of cutting and pasting, of juxtaposition and comparison, creates the effect of an avant-garde collage, a form, as Susan Stanford Friedman summarises, of 'radical juxtaposition that produces new insight'.[13] There is a kind of estrangement at work when we encounter these quotations, clippings and images ripped out of their original contexts and juxtaposed often with seemingly disparate documentary evidence of life in the 1930s – photographs of the Pope appear alongside newspaper clippings detailing men's opinions on women's nail varnishing (an 'unnatural custom'), women's football ('*too* popular') and on their ability to succeed 'in business as capitalists' (unlikely).[14] The effect of Woolf's collage is both to puncture the posture of virile masculinity and at the same time build up an argument about the very real and violent effects of a long history of bolstering the image of man as dictator. But this is also Woolf's way of tracing connections and building an argument that is itself about how women experience the intersections of capitalist, patriarchal and fascist oppression.

In the scrapbooks, Woolf gathers together a vast, often maddening, sometimes surprising, occasionally uplifting archive, bearing witness to the interwoven effects of capitalism and gendered oppression on women's lives, and tracking the links between patriarchal exclusions in Britain and sexism and misogyny in Nazi Germany and other fascist states. Woolf's typed index to the first volume (see Figures 12.1 and 12.4) reads as a list of the opinions of various men 'on' women and issues affecting women, from 'Bagehot on Girton', to 'Roberts on Abortion', 'Bowlder on propriety', 'Macready on women eating', 'Mullens on women smoking', and 'D. H. L[awrence]. on need of women'.[15] In the scrapbooks, Woolf brings together quotations and clippings from first-person biographical accounts of the various 'battles' (*TG* 146) waged by women first for the vote, and then for access to universities and the professions, and she documents the backlash against women's increased visibility in universities and the workplace in the 1930s. In the

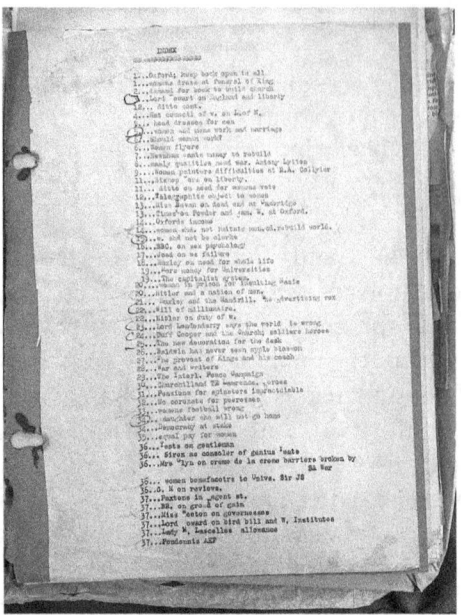

Figure 12.4 Virginia Woolf, '3 volumes of press cuttings, manuscript and typed extracts relating to *Three Guineas*', Monk's House Papers, University of Sussex Special Collections, the Keep, SxMs-18/2/B/16/F, vol. 1, index. With thanks to The Society of Authors as the Literary Representative of the Estate of Virginia Woolf.

first scrapbook, on a page that Woolf has indexed as 'Civil service on male rule' (see Figures 12.4 and 12.5), two newspaper clippings pasted alongside each other describe the backlash against women appointed to managerial positions at the Shoreditch Labour Exchange and the Wolverhampton Public Library, while another clipping pasted later in the same scrapbook describes the resistance to 'petticoat government' in the civil service.[16] On one page in the second scrapbook, Woolf juxtaposes a complaint from the Union of Post Office Workers about the 'tendency to displace men by the employment of women', with snippets from a speech by Lord Hewart celebrating England as the 'Home of Liberty'.[17] The clipping on Englishness is pasted in full on another page in the notebook, but the juxtaposition on this page suggests a wry comment on women's position within the 'Home of Liberty' and offers an ironic perspective on the line that describes 'Englishmen' as having 'proved themselves strong and even fierce when any encroachment upon [. . .] their territory is threatened'.[18] 'What has England do[d]ne for me'? Woolf asked herself in a typewritten note pasted into

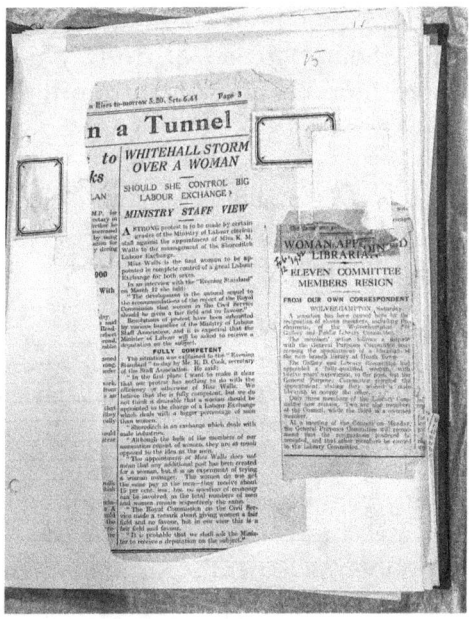

Figure 12.5 Virginia Woolf, '3 volumes of press cuttings, manuscript and typed extracts relating to *Three Guineas*', Monk's House Papers, University of Sussex Special Collections, the Keep, SxMs-18/2/B/16/F, vol. 1, 15. With thanks to The Society of Authors as the Literary Representative of the Estate of Virginia Woolf.

one of her scrapbooks.[19] 'Nothing,' was the answer – 'We are al[l] paying now £ [. . .] for the manly diversion.'[20]

The theme of men's fears about women encroaching on their 'territory' appears in a number of clippings in the scrapbooks, including the three letters to the *Daily Telegraph* that Woolf cites in the final text of *Three Guineas* lamenting that, in the wake of the war and at a time of economic crisis, women have 'too much liberty' and have effectively stolen men's jobs by 'doing work which men could do'.[21] As one of the three letter-writers puts it:

> I am certain I voice the opinion of thousands of young men when I say that if men were doing the work that thousands of young women are now doing the men would be able to keep those same women in decent homes. Homes are the real places of the women who are now compelling men to be idle. It is time the Government insisted upon employers giving work to more men, thus enabling them to marry the women they cannot now approach. (*TG* 134)[22]

In the scrapbooks, these quotations appear alongside C. E. M. Joad's misogynistic article about 'Women of To-Day and To-Morrow', beginning with three 'glorious utterances from the three leaders of the Nazi movement':

> 'The woman's task is to be beautiful and to bring children into the world.'—Herr Goebbels (Minister of National Enlightenment and Propaganda in the Third Reich).
> 'Woman—her place is in the home, her duty the recreation of the tired warrior.'—General Goering.
> 'Women's duty is to the three k's—Kinder, Küche, und Kirche (children, church and kitchen) . . . Motherhood is undeniably the aim of feminine education.'—Hitler.[23]

Placed alongside other clippings in the scrapbooks that testify further to the strict gender divisions of Nazi Germany ('Hitler and a nation of men', 'Hitler on duty of w[omen]', 'Nazi blood and race theory'), and read alongside the letters lamenting women's 'encroachment' in the male workplace, the article by Joad makes explicit the link that Woolf identifies in *Three Guineas* between misogynistic gatekeeping in postwar post-slump Britain and its role in fascist Europe.[24]

On another page in the second scrapbook (see Figure 12.6), Woolf pastes an image of Major Fey, the deposed fascist leader of the Austrian Heimwehr, in a helmet and military dress with the index title: 'head dresses for men'. This is juxtaposed with a letter to the *Daily Telegraph* that notes the 'great spectre' of unemployment in Britain and wistfully recalls a time when 'the regiment of women had not then left their natural duties to become the competitors of those who have the equally natural duty of providing for them'. A clipping from the *Times* that appears in the third scrapbook – indexed by Woolf as 'the natural and Eternal Law in Germany' – makes the same appeal for a 'return to natural and eternal law', outlining the 'Status of Women' in modern Germany and stating that 'a woman's principle work [is] family life and bringing up the children'.[25] 'There, in those quotations,' as Woolf would put it in *Three Guineas*, 'is the egg of the very same worm that we know under other names in other countries':

> There we have in embryo the creature, Dictator as we call him when he is Italian or German, who believes that he has the right whether given by God, Nature, sex or race is immaterial, to dictate to other human beings how they shall live; what they shall do [. . .] One is written in English, the other in German. But where is the difference?

Are they not both saying the same thing? Are they not both the voices of Dictators, whether they speak English or German, and are we not all agreed that the dictator when we meet him abroad is a very dangerous as well as a very ugly animal? And here he is among us, raising his ugly head, spitting his poison, small still, curled up like a caterpillar on a leaf, but in the heart of England. (*TG* 135)

For Woolf, the scrapbook method of cutting, pasting, copying and comparing helped her to reveal not just the interwoven effects of capitalism and misogyny in shaping women's lives, but also to expose the intimate and insidious links between capitalist patriarchal gatekeeping in 1930s post-slump Britain and the policing of strict gender roles in Nazi and Fascist Europe. In *Three Guineas*, Woolf compared the exclusion of women from priesthood with Hitler's statement (from a clipping in the second scrapbook) that '[t]here are two worlds in the life of the nation, the world of men and the world of women', going on to argue that '[t]he emphasis which both priests and dictators place upon the necessity for two worlds is enough to prove that it is essential to domination' (*TG* 247).[26]

Figure 12.6 Virginia Woolf, '3 volumes of press cuttings, manuscript and typed extracts relating to *Three Guineas*', Monk's House Papers, University of Sussex Special Collections, the Keep, SxMs-18/2/B/16/F, vol. 2, 5. With thanks to The Society of Authors as the Literary Representative of the Estate of Virginia Woolf.

For Woolf, in *Three Guineas*, her target is not just the way in which capitalism demands and colludes with the historical exclusion of women from the workplace, but what she reveals as the close alliance between 'the pleasures of wealth' and the 'pleasure of dominance' (*TG* 247). In a set of typewritten notes pasted into the second scrapbook under the heading 'Dictators', Woolf brings together two news items from different sections of the *Daily Herald* on 1 August 1936: first, a report that 'E. F. Fletcher urged the House of Commons to "Stand up to dictators"', followed immediately by the story of a woman whose husband 'insists' she 'call him "Sir"'.[27] The woman, applying for a maintenance order at Bristol Police Court, stated that:

> To keep the peace I have complied with his request [. . .] I also have to clean his boots, fetch his razor when he shaves, and speak up promptly when he asks [. . .] questions.[28]

Quoting these passages in the footnotes to *Three Guineas*, Woolf not only drew attention to the hypocrisy of a political culture that urged the House of Commons to '[s]tand up to dictators' while ignoring the dictator in the private home, but also offered yet another example from her scrapbooks of how women's economic dependence on men leaves them vulnerable to men's indulgence in the 'pleasure of dominance' (*TG* 247). The 'pleasure of dominance' is, Woolf argues, 'further complicated by the fact that it is still, in the educated class, closely allied with the pleasures of wealth, social and professional prestige' (*TG* 247). In *Three Guineas*, Woolf offered an acute analysis of a threatened (but therefore all the more violent) form of English masculinity, revealing the toxic combination of capitalism, imperialism and patriarchal tradition that shaped the desires underpinning both the 'conception of manliness' and 'manhood itself' (*TG* 211). By bringing together all these apparently disparate documents – from newspaper clippings demanding women's return to the home, to quotations from biographies and autobiographies about 'manly qualities' and the 'need' for war, to photographs of dictatorial and powerful men – Woolf develops a method of critique that exposes the complex entanglement and over-determination of capitalism and patriarchal power.[29] Responding to Leonard's insistence that she address the 'economic question' with a unique combination of pragmatism and creativity, Woolf goes much further than Leonard can have expected, arguing that capitalism is much more than a question of economics and insisting on an intersectional understanding of patriarchal culture, capitalist greed, imperialism and war. But she also shows how women – and other outsiders – might begin to carve a way out of this through precisely the kind of creative and critical labour that she undertakes in her scrapbooks and in *Three Guineas*. For Woolf, women's position as outsiders gave them a unique (albeit precarious) critical perspective on the stranglehold of capitalist, patriarchal and fascist power, as well as a unique opportunity to imagine an alternative society liberated from the 'tyrannies and servilities' (*TG* 215) of the old order.

Scrapbooking the Present Day

Over the past few years of teaching a final-year undergraduate module on Virginia Woolf at the University of Sussex, my students and I have compiled our own scrapbooks of the present day.[30] Inspired by the *Three Guineas* scrapbooks, and by Woolf's observation in her essay 'How Should One Read a Book?' that '[t]o read a book well, one should read it as if one were writing it', the aim of this exercise is to try to inhabit Woolf's own critical and creative methods, and to learn not just what Woolf's notebooks tell us about her historical moment, but to think about how her writing might speak to us in our own present day.[31] In 2018, and then again in 2021 (when we returned to classrooms and archives for the first time since the beginning of the Coronavirus pandemic), we visited The Keep (the home of the University of Sussex Special Collections and of the Monk's House Papers) to look at Woolf's scrapbooks and make our own virtual scrapbooks on padlet.[32] The virtual scrapbooks featured photographs of individual pages from Woolf's scrapbooks, juxtaposed with links to news items, images and social media posts from the present day. Together, these scrapbooks paint an uneasy portrait of the present day, encompassing numerous references to gender harassment, sexual violence and rape in the wake of the #MeToo movement; rampant transphobia in the British press and establishment; domestic violence; the struggle for access to abortion in Ireland and the US; the presidencies and premiership of Donald Trump, Jair Bolsonaro and Boris Johnson; the gender and BAME pay gaps; the return to power of the Taliban in Afghanistan; Instagram and the culture of perfect female domesticity; the impact of the Coronavirus pandemic in exacerbating gender inequality in the home and at work; the murder of Sarah Everard by a serving police officer during a national Covid lockdown; institutional sexism in the Metropolitan police; sexism in sport; the use of social media to propagate violence against women; sexist backlash against female politicians; the intersection of climate change and gender inequality; questions about unequal university funding and astronomical fees; a story about the proposed 'University of Austin, Texas' offering itself as an 'antidote to "cancel culture"'; and a story about a young woman opposing neo-Nazis in a small German town.[33]

Micir and Vadde write about Woolf's scrapbooking as a form of 'amateur criticism' that is 'cognizant of the changing same of structural inequality, but also responsive to the distinct conditions under which inequality endures and must be fought';[34]

> Modernist criticism as amateur blends the trivial with the serious, the disposable with the preserved. These formal choices draw from a lineage of feminist writing tactics, and show these tactics to be at the vanguard of an institutional critique that ties the professionalism of the university to larger capitalist transformations in the management of knowledge. Woolf and [Kate] Zambreno [author of the 2012 book, *Heroines*] turn to low prestige genres and use unapologetically emotional voices to reflect as well as diagnose a range of twentieth-century intensifications in the corporatization of media, the privatization of information, and the casualization of labor.[35]

Like Woolf's, the students' scrapbooks employ a method of critique that highlights the 'changing same of structural inequality' while also reminding us of the 'distinct conditions' under which different kinds of inequality endure.

In our classes at The Keep and afterwards, my students were attentive to the common themes in Woolf's notebooks and in our present day, but also wanted to highlight the differences. Reading *Three Guineas* in a period where our experiences of teaching and learning have been marked by a protracted period of industrial action related to pay, gender and racial inequality, and casualisation in UK universities, we noticed the many clippings and posts detailing the huge financial costs and unequal funding models of universities in the UK and US, and commented on the continued relevance of Woolf's analysis of universities as 'uneasy dwelling-places' ringed about with 'barriers of wealth and ceremony' (*TG* 119). There were depressing echoes between the news clipping in Woolf's scrapbook that announces 'Cleaning 5 Miles of Floor' as 'The Average Wife's Annual Work' and the BBC article shared by a student about Mrs Hinch, whose 'Instagram cleaning videos attracted more than

300,000 followers', and another article about the women forced to take on an unequal share of domestic labour during the Coronavirus pandemic.[36] More disconcerting still was the echo between Woolf's clipping describing Frau Pommer's imprisonment 'for insulting Nazis' in 1935 and the article posted by a student in 2018 about a woman protesting against neo-Nazis in the German town of Ostritz.[37] A post featuring a review of Kamila Shamsie's 2017 novel, *Home Fire* – a contemporary retelling of *Antigone* – testified to the continuing feminist resonance of *Antigone*, while Woolf's refusal to print photographs of 'dead bodies and ruined houses' (*TG* 126) in *Three Guineas* (they don't appear in her scrapbooks either, although Louis Delaprée's 1937 pamphlet *The Martyrdom of Madrid* does describe such scenes), found a new relevance in relation to a news item about the use of twitter by the Republican politician Paul Gosar to share a 'photoshopped, animated video that depicts him killing Rep. Alexandria Ocasio-Cortez [. . .] and swinging two swords at President Biden'.[38]

Despite these resonances, at least one student wanted to stress that while Woolf seemed to focus largely on questions about women's historical exclusion from universities and the professions, her own friends were (even with the huge economic costs of attending university in Britain in 2022) more concerned with their physical safety in a world where students are, as one of the scrapbook entries reported, targeted with 'spiking' and where, during the national lockdown in the spring of 2021, a young woman named Sarah Everard was raped and murdered by a serving police officer. In the student scrapbooks, references to the murders of Sarah Everard, Sabina Nessa, Nicole Smallman and Bibaa Henry, and the presence of numerous #MeToo stories, certainly mark what Jacqueline Rose has recently described as 'the crisis of the hour, the increasing visibility of gender-based violence', as well as a shift in what it is possible to say about male violence against women and transgender people in the twenty-first century.[39] And yet, the student scrapbooks – with their attention to stories about violence against women and transgender people, about rape, and about the threat to abortion rights across the globe – also helped us to see a thread in Woolf's scrapbooks on abortion, childbirth, the maternal death rate, birth control, war and male sadism that I had not quite seen before and which, writing this essay in 2022 in the wake of the overturning of Roe v. Wade, appears all the more striking.

Among the very first entries in Woolf's scrapbooks are two handwritten quotations from an article in the *New Statesman and Nation* by Dr Harry Roberts arguing for the legalisation of abortion. Woolf copied out two quotations, the first noting the widespread, even common, incidence of illegal abortion in the UK, and the second commenting on the legalisation of abortion in Russia ('the only country which officially recognises abortion as a legitimate method of terminating births'). 'From my own fairly large experience', Roberts wrote (and Woolf transcribed):

> I have come to the conclusion that not less than 25 per cent. of all women in this country, married & unmarried, have at some time in their lives, procured or attempted to procure abortion.[40]

In the article, in passages not cited by Woolf, Roberts emphasises the dangers of forcing women, especially working-class women, to resort to risky illegal abortions performed by 'unskilled and reckless' individuals who practise 'abortion for money, extorting what amounts to blackmail from poor working-girls and others already in distress'.[41] 'Surely,' he argues, 'rather than allow this state of things to continue':

> it were better to recognize the facts [. . .] and, by legalising abortion if performed by skilled surgeons in properly equipped hospitals, avoid most of the hygienic, and many of the moral, evils attendant on the present situation.[42]

In the second scrapbook, another clipping notes the high incidence of maternal deaths attributed to abortion, and describes the National Council of Women's resolution to urge the government to appoint a committee 'to inquire into the incidence of abortion and the law dealing with criminal abortion'.[43] In the third scrapbook, a newspaper clipping that Woolf has indexed as 'Maternity death rate. amenities for nurses' reports the 'urgent need for a new maternity department' at the Cardiff Royal Infirmary, and notes that the 'mortality among expectant mothers' remains 'too high'.[44] On the same page, Woolf has pasted another clipping describing the investment in 'blue uniforms' to attract more soldiers into the army, ironically juxtaposing the paucity of provision for maternal care with the lavish investment in military dress and masculine egos.[45] On the following page, Woolf similarly juxtaposes another article titled 'Postmen Want to Be Smarter' with an article that she has indexed as 'Do wo[m]en want babies to be soldiers? Birth cont.'.[46] This article, recounting the annual meeting of the National Council for Equal Citizenship, describes the '[v]igorous arguments for and against a campaign to increase the birth rate', including the resolution to undertake a campaign to 'check the declining population' through the establishment of family allowances, 'an increase in social services as would make the economic position of people with children at least as favourable as that of those without', and the 'provision of a more adequate maternity service'.[47] 'Several delegates protested against the resolution on the ground that it was advocating enormous families to provide "cannon fodder" for the next war.'[48] On page 6 of the third scrapbook, Woolf includes a letter to the *Times*, praising Lady Baldwin for promoting the availability of analgesics in childbirth. The letter includes the statistic that there are 'some 700,000 births in the United Kingdom'. Beneath this clipping, in a rare annotation, Woolf has noted in pencil: '700,000 births. 4 die in every 1000,' calculating that '2,800 die yearly'.[49] The annotation was presumably made after Woolf made the note, pasted onto a later page in the same scrapbook, from an article in the *Spectator* on 4 June 1937, that '4 mothers still die for every one thousand children'.[50] The same article (although Woolf doesn't copy this part) also, like the article by Roberts, implies that legalisation would, by reducing women's need for backstreet abortions, go some way to bringing down the maternal death rate.[51]

Looking at this collage of scrapbook entries, we can see how the method of cutting and pasting helped Woolf to reveal the close alliance between 'the capitalist system' and a gendered division of labour that turned a blind, and sometimes sadistic, eye towards women's pain and suffering. As Bertrand Russell put it in a quotation that Woolf pasted into the first scrapbook, and used in the text of *Three Guineas*, '[t]he views of medical men on pregnancy, childbirth, and lactation were until fairly recently impregnated with sadism'.[52] In *Three Guineas*, Woolf doesn't reduce misogyny, sexual or gendered oppression to a function of the capitalist system, but she does show how far that system has historically relied upon, concocted and exacerbated gendered inequality both inside and outside of the home. Although Woolf herself doesn't comment on women's access to abortion in *Three Guineas*, the clippings and quotations in her scrapbooks make it clear that she had her eye to debates taking place at the time about women's access to abortion, especially those that attended to the unequal impact of abortion law on working-class women. In fact it is quite possible that an allusion to abortion is silently at work in the title for *Three Guineas* – as Naomi Black has noted – in the drafts for *The Years*, 'Woolf has the character then called Elvira ask, "But how is that poor woman there going to Harley Street? with three guineas?"'[53] 'At issue', Black argues, 'is the financial impossibility of abortions for poor women. Then illegal, they were relatively easily and discreetly purchased by middle- and upper-class women from fashionable doctors at locations such as Harley Street.'[54] Looking at these scrapbooks, we can see just how far Woolf went in tracking the extent to which capitalism shaped the most intimate aspects of women's lives, as well as revealing the ways in which the capitalist system solicited men to capitulate to forms of violent masculinity. Woolf shows how capitalism lured men to collude with violent masculinity, revealing the over-determined nature of male violence, its complicity and intersection with various manifestations of imperialist and nationalist desires for dominance.

In the student scrapbooks, a number of posts focused on contemporary struggles for access to safe and legal abortions in the US, Ireland, and globally. Other posts included an image of Donald Trump talking to reporters on the South Lawn of the White House, the camera angled from below to capture his looming figure, hands splayed characteristically above the array of phallic microphones; an article on the election of Jair Bolsonaro and the 'return of white, male, sexist and authoritarian politics in Brazil'; and a post about Boris Johnson's refusal to 'make misogyny a hate crime'.[55] These images of men in power cry out for comparison with the final image that Woolf conjures in *Three Guineas*:

> It is the figure of a man; some say, others deny, that he is Man himself, the quintessence of virility, the perfect type of which all the others are imperfect adumbrations. He is a man certainly. His eyes are glazed; his eyes glare. His body, which is braced in an unnatural position, is tightly cased in a uniform. Upon the breast of that uniform are sewn several medals and other mystic symbols. His hand is upon a sword. He is called in German and Italian Fuhrer or Duce; in our own language Tyrant or Dictator. (*TG* 214)

But the juxtaposition of these images of masculine power with the collage of references to sexual abuse, misogyny, gendered violence and attempts to curb women's access to safe abortion also allows us, following Woolf's arguments, to see the links between what she described in *A Room of One's Own* as the 'rage for acquisition',[56] male violence against women, and a form of incipient fascism that feels almost (if not quite) as threatening today as it must have done in the 1930s.[57] Woolf herself may not have made explicit arguments about access to abortion or about sexual violence (although she alludes to both when Isa reads a newspaper report about a rape in *Between the Acts*), but her analysis of the relationship between capital, unbridled patriarchal power and fascism is as woefully significant in the present day as it was in the 1930s.[58]

The students' scrapbooks also highlighted the blind spots in *Three Guineas* in terms of Woolf's struggle to think intersectionally about the role of class and race. Although Woolf's decision to address the 'daughters of educated men' demonstrates her awareness of her own inability to speak on behalf of those whose class position and experiences she did not share, *Three Guineas* does not attend to the experiences of working-class women or women of colour.[59] In contrast to the student scrapbook posts calling for intersectional feminisms centring the experiences of Black women and women of colour, in Woolf's scrapbooks one clipping stood out as especially difficult for us to read and interpret. On a page in the third scrapbook that Woolf has indexed as 'perfumers on woms. nail varnishing', she pasted two letters to the editor of the *Times*: the first, from R. Haslam Jackson, Editor of *Perfumer and Toiletry*, disputes a previous correspondent's account of nail varnishing as having 'originated in America to cover up evidences of "black blood"'.[60] The letter claims that nail varnishing was 'a common practice of the Chinese more than 3,000 years ago', and traces it to Cleopatra and 'the Egyptian ladies', as well as pointing out that '[i]n Continental Europe and in this country women have stained or enamelled their nails for centuries' despite the 'disapproval of Queen Victoria'.[61] The second letter, from J. Wheeler Williams, accepts the account of 'the disfiguring of finger nails' as originating in America 'to conceal the traces of black blood', but asks why 'this unnatural custom [has] been adopted in this country?'[62] The letter-writer states his 'amazement that any young man can be attracted by it or by the equally unnatural painting of the lips and cheeks', and speculates that 'we are approaching the time when the customs of savage races will be copied even to painting patterns on the body'.[63] Of course, these letters fit with the many examples of misogyny in Woolf's scrapbooks, and it seems likely that Woolf was especially alert to the note here about the burgeoning 'prosperity of the ever-growing cosmetic industry', but it is hard (impossible?) to know whether Woolf also included these letters in her scrapbooks as examples of how misogyny combined in the English imagination with an exoticised racism focused on the bodies of Black women and women of colour. In both *A Room of One's Own* and *Three Guineas*, Woolf's feminism is, as Anna Snaith observes in her essay in this volume, haunted by and even predicated on the histories of colonialism and slavery. In *A Room*, Woolf famously suggested that it was 'one of the very great advantages of being a woman that one can pass even a very fine negress without wishing to make an Englishwoman of her' (*AROO* 39), simultaneously rejecting the colonising urges of imperialist masculinity while also exiling Black women from the position of the Englishwoman. It is hard to speculate about how Woolf herself – who infamously blacked up for her part in the Dreadnought Hoax, and for a party as a 'Gauguin girl'– would have read these examples of racist misogyny, although we can certainly say, as Snaith does in her essay, that Woolf's use of the 'rhetoric of enslavement' in the published text of *Three Guineas* 'both evokes but also obscures a history of racial oppression'.[64]

And yet, as I hope this pedagogical experiment also suggests, critical and creative attention to Woolf's scrapbooks can also help us to see how Woolf's idea of the 'outsider' (for all the limitations of modernist celebrations of cosmopolitanism) can still, despite Woolf's own blind spots, hold critical power for her readers. As Snaith argues in her essay, both Alice Walker and Saidiya Hartman have engaged with Woolf's writing through forms of productive resistance and the methodology of (in Hartman's words) 'speculative thought, radical narrative and critical fabulation' to offer alternative modes of resonance and influence.[65] Making a scrapbook in the 2020s allows us to engage in a form of feminism that, while inspired by Woolf's critical method and insights, is also more fully attuned to the intersection of capitalism and gendered oppression with racism, with the legacies of colonialism and slavery, and with different experiences of class. Woolf herself fails to offer a fully intersectional analysis of how, in a capitalist society, women are impacted unequally according to their different experiences of race, gender and class, but there is something in her method that opens up a space in which other 'outsiders' might do that critical and imaginative work.

Notes

1. *The Diary of Virginia Woolf, Volume Four: 1931–1935*, ed. by Anne Olivier Bell (Harmondsworth: Penguin, 1983), 77. Further page references will be given within the main text.
2. Virginia Woolf, '3 volumes of press cuttings, manuscript and typed extracts relating to *Three Guineas*', Monk's House Papers, University of Sussex Special Collections, The Keep, SxMs-18/2/B/16/F, vol. 2, 19.

Abbreviated hereafter as 'Scrapbooks'. My thanks to Karen Watson and colleagues at the University of Sussex Special Collections and The Keep for assistance in accessing the scrapbooks. I am also grateful to the Society of Authors as the Literary Representatives of the Estate of Virginia Woolf for their kind permission to reproduce images of the scrapbooks in this chapter.

3. As Merry M. Pawlowski notes, Woolf makes very few direct references other than in the notes to *Three Guineas* to the material gathered in this collection of notebooks. The current catalogue index for the University of Sussex Special Collections at the Keep describes '3 volumes of press cuttings, manuscript and typed extracts relating to *Three Guineas*'; Pawlowski uses the term *Reading Notes*, while acknowledging the common use among Woolf scholars of 'scrapbooks'. Merry M. Pawlowski, 'Virginia Woolf and Scrapbooking', *The Edinburgh Companion to Virginia Woolf and the Arts*, ed. by Maggie Humm (Edinburgh: Edinburgh University Press, 2010), 298–313 (298).

4. Virginia Woolf, *A Room of One's Own and Three Guineas*, ed. by Anna Snaith (Oxford: Oxford University Press, 2015), 155. Further page references will be given within the main text.

5. Woolf, 'Scrapbooks', vol. 3, index.

6. Jessica Berman, *Modernist Fiction, Cosmopolitanism and the Politics of Community* (Cambridge: Cambridge University Press, 2001), 115.

7. Melanie Micir and Aarthi Vadde, 'Obliterature: Towards an Amateur Criticism', *Modernism/modernity*, 25.3 (2018), 517–49 (524).

8. As Pawlowski points out, in a letter to Vera Douie, the librarian at the Women's Service Library, Woolf asked for help with a quotation, noting that '[t]he note books in which my cuttings are kept are in London, & I cannot get at them.' Pawlowski, 'Virginia Woolf and Scrapbooking', 298, 299–300; Merry M. Pawlowski, 'The Virginia Woolf and Vera Douie Letters', ed. by Merry Pawlowski, *Woolf Studies Annual*, 8.3 (2002), 3–62, 32; Woolf, 'Scrapbooks', vol. 1.

9. In her account of Nancy Cunard's 1949 scrapbook titled *Cosas de España: 1936–1946* (Things from Spain), Anne Donlon notes that its 'multivocal form [. . .] seems resonant with the forms of anthologies she created'. Anne Donlon, 'Things and Lost Things: Nancy Cunard's Spanish Civil War Scrapbook', *The Massachusetts Review*, 55.2 (2014), 192–205 (195). On Hannah Höch's scrapbooking, see Melissa A. Johnson, 'Souvenirs of Amerika: Hannah Höch's Weimar-Era Mass-Media Scrapbook', in *The Scrapbook in American Life*, ed. by Susan Tucker, Katherine Ott and Patricia P. Buckler (Philadelphia: Temple University Press, 2006), 135–52. On Woolf's scrapbooks and suffragette scrapbooks, see Barbara Green, *Spectacular Confessions: Autobiography, Performative Activism, and the Sites of Suffrage 1905–1938* (Basingstoke: Macmillan, 1997), 165–8; and Cherish Watton, 'Suffrage

Scrapbooks and Emotional Histories of Women's Activism', *Women's History Review*, (2022) <https://doi.org/10.1080/09612025.2021.2012343>

10. On modernist feminist archives, see Sara Crangle, 'Feminism's Archives: Mina Loy, Anna Mendelssohn and Taxonomy', in *The New Modernist Studies*, ed. by Douglas Mao (Cambridge: Cambridge University Press, 2021), 246–77.
11. Micir and Vadde, 'Obliterature', 522.
12. Ibid., 529.
13. Susan Stanford Friedman, *Planetary Modernisms: Provocations on Modernity Across Time* (Columbia University Press, 2015), 218.
14. 'Scrapbooks', vol. 3, 18; 'Scrapbooks', vol. 2, 33; 'Scrapbooks', vol. 1, 4.
15. Woolf, 'Scrapbooks', vol. 1, index.
16. Woolf, 'Scrapbooks', vol. 1, index, 15, 57.
17. Woolf, 'Scrapbooks', vol. 2, 12, 3.
18. Woolf, 'Scrapbooks', vol. 2, 12.
19. Woolf, 'Scrapbooks', vol. 1, 38.
20. Woolf, 'Scrapbooks', vol. 1, 38.
21. Woolf, 'Scrapbooks', vol. 2, 6; Woolf, 'Scrapbooks', vol. 2, 15.
22. This clipping from 'The "Good Old Times"', *Daily Telegraph*, 22 January 1936 also appears in part in volume 2 of the scrapbooks where it looks as though it may have been (perhaps unintentionally) ripped out or lost. Woolf, 'Scrapbooks', vol. 2, 5.
23. C. E. M. Joad, 'Women of To-Day and To-Morrow, By a Man', *Everyman*, 12 January 1934, 12, cited in Woolf, 'Scrapbooks', vol. 2, 17. On Joad as a 'lightening rod for the theme of misogyny', see Pawlowski, 'Virginia Woolf and Scrapbooking', 305–7.
24. Woolf, 'Scrapbooks', vol. 2, index, 20, 22, 47.
25. Woolf, 'Scrapbooks', vol. 3, index, 47.
26. Woolf, 'Scrapbooks', vol. 2, 22.
27. Woolf, 'Scrapbooks', vol. 2, 54.
28. Woolf, 'Scrapbooks', vol. 2, 54.
29. Woolf, 'Scrapbooks', vol. 2, index.
30. 'Special Author: Virginia Woolf' was introduced at Sussex as the first 'Special Author' module in 1989 by Rachel Bowlby, and has been taught and shaped by Elena Gualtieri, Laura Marcus, Sara Crangle, Hope Wolf and Pamela Thurschwell among others. My thanks to Rachel Bowlby for sharing this history with me.
31. 'How Should One Read a Book?', *The Essays of Virginia Woolf, Volume Four, 1925–1928*, ed. by Andrew McNeillie (London: Chatto & Windus, 1995), 390.
32. On scrapbooking and social media, see Katie Day Good, 'From Scrapbook to Facebook: A History of Personal Media Assemblage and Archives', *New Media and Society*, 15.4 (2013), 557–73.
33. Emily Tamkin, 'What is the new University of Austin for?', *New Statesman*, 9 November 2021 <https://www.newstatesman.com/the-

explainer/2021/11/what-is-the-new-university-of-austin-for> [accessed 1 November 2023].
34. Micir and Vadde, 'Obliterature', 519.
35. Ibid., 519.
36. Woolf, 'Scrapbooks', vol. 3, 21; 'Mrs Hinch: Instagram cleaner wants to make chores fun', 14 September 2018 <https://www.bbc.co.uk/news/uk-england-essex-45514306> [accessed 1 November 2023].
37. Woolf, 'Scrapbooks', vol. 2, index, 20. In *Three Guineas*, writing about *Antigone* as a potential form of 'anti-Fascist propaganda', Woolf compares Frau Pommer with Antigone, writing that: 'Antigone herself could be transformed either into Mrs Pankhurst, who broke a window and was imprisoned in Holloway; or into Frau Pommer' (*TG* 238).
38. *The Washington Post* (@washingtonpost), Twitter, 8 November 2021 <https://twitter.com/i/web/status/1457829352813498371> [accessed 1 November 2023]. Woolf, 'Scrapbooks', vol. 3, 20. On Woolf's references to the Spanish Civil War photographs, see Jessica Berman, 'Three Guineas and the Politics of Interruption', in *A Companion to Virginia Woolf*, ed. by Jessica Berman (Oxford: Wiley Blackwell, 2016), 203–16.
39. Jacqueline Rose, *On Violence and On Violence Against Women* (London: Faber and Faber, 2021), 3.
40. Harry Roberts, 'The Sanctity of Human Life', *New Statesman and Nation*, 3.51, 13 February 1932, 193–4, cited in Woolf, 'Scrapbooks', vol. 1, 4.
41. Roberts, 'The Sanctity', 193.
42. Ibid., 193, cited in Woolf, 'Scrapbooks', vol. 1, 4.
43. Woolf, 'Scrapbooks', vol. 2, index, 4.
44. Woolf, 'Scrapbooks', vol. 3, index, 3.
45. Woolf, 'Scrapbooks', vol. 3, 3.
46. Woolf, 'Scrapbooks', vol. 3, 4, index.
47. Woolf, 'Scrapbooks', vol. 3, 4.
48. Woolf, 'Scrapbooks', vol. 3, 4.
49. Woolf, 'Scrapbooks', vol. 3, 6.
50. Woolf, 'Scrapbooks', vol. 3, 11.
51. 'Maternal Mortality', *The Spectator*, 4 June 1937, 1039; Roberts, 'The Sanctity', 193.
52. Bertrand Russell, *The Scientific Outlook* (London, 1931), 17, cited in Woolf, 'Scrapbooks', vol. 1, 6 and Woolf, *Three Guineas*, 212–13.
53. Naomi Black, *Virginia Woolf as Feminist* (New York: Cornell University Press, 2004), 175; Grace Radin, *Virginia Woolf's 'The Years': The Evolution of a Novel* (Knoxville: University of Tennessee Press, 1981), 51.
54. Black, *Virginia Woolf as Feminist*, 175.
55. Mariana Prandini Assis and Ana Carolina Ogando, 'Bolsonaro, "Gender Ideology" and Hegemonic Masculinity in Brazil', *AlJazeera*, 31 October 2018 <https://www.aljazeera.com/opinions/2018/10/31/bolsonaro-gender-ideology-and-hegemonic-masculinity-in-brazil>

[accessed 1 November 2023]; 'Boris Johnson does not support making misogyny a hate crime'. BBC, 5 October 2021 <https://www.bbc.co.uk/news/uk-politics-58800328> [accessed 1 November 2023].
56. Virginia Woolf, *A Room of One's Own and Three Guineas*, ed. by Anna Snaith (Oxford: Oxford University Press, 2015), 30. Further page references will be given within the main text.
57. On why it might not be helpful to 'run the line from Trump to Hitler', see Rose, *On Violence*, 157.
58. In *Between the Acts* Isa is haunted throughout the novel by a newspaper article about a girl who was raped by soldiers on Horse Guards Parade in Whitehall. As Stuart N. Clarke has pointed out, the rape of a 14-year-old girl took place on 27 April 1938, and the trial of the soldiers was reported on in the *Times*. The girl became pregnant, and, as Clarke writes, 'Mr Aleck Bourne, a respected surgeon at one of the London hospitals, openly performed an abortion. He in turn ended up at the Old Bailey, where he was tried on 18 and 19 July 1938.' During the trial, Mr Justice Macnaghten extended the meaning of the law stating that abortion was illegal except for the purposes of 'preserving the life of the mother'. Stuart N. Clarke, 'The Horse With a Green Tail', *Virginia Woolf Miscellany*, 34 (1990), 3–4.
59. On Woolf's use of narrators to perform and probe class prejudice, see Clara Jones, *Virginia Woolf: Ambivalent Activist* (Edinburgh: Edinburgh University Press, 2016), 144. On working-class readers' responses to *Three Guineas*, see Anna Snaith, 'Wide Circles: The *Three Guineas* Letters', *Woolf Studies Annual*, 6 (2000), 1–168 (99).
60. Woolf, 'Scrapbooks', 3, index, 18.
61. Woolf, 'Scrapbooks', 3, 18.
62. Woolf, 'Scrapbooks', 3, 18.
63. Woolf, 'Scrapbooks', 3, 18.
64. See Hermione Lee, *Virginia Woolf* (London: Virago, 1997), 281–7, 291.
65. Alice Walker, 'In Search of Our Mothers' Gardens' (1983), *In Search of Our Mothers' Gardens: Womanist Prose* (The Women's Press, 2000), 231–43; Saidiya Hartman, 'Intimate History, Radical Narrative', 22 May 2020 <https://www.aaihs.org/intimate-history-radical-narrative> [accessed 1 November 2023]; Saidiya Hartman, *Wayward Lives, Beautiful Experiments* (2019) (London: Serpent's Tail, 2021).

Works Cited

'Boris Johnson does not support making misogyny a hate crime'. BBC, 5 October 2021 <https://www.bbc.co.uk/news/uk-politics-58800328> [accessed 1 November 2023].

'Maternal Mortality'. *The Spectator*, 4 June 1937. 1039.

'Mrs Hinch: Instagram cleaner wants to make chores fun'. 14 September 2018 <https://www.bbc.co.uk/news/uk-england-essex-45514306> [accessed 1 November 2023].

'Prince Starhemberg Ousts Rivals at One Stroke: Mussolini's Agent Secures Austria for Italy'. *Daily Herald*, 18 October 1935.

The Washington Post (@washingtonpost). Twitter. 8 November 2021 <https://twitter.com/i/web/status/1457829352813498371> [accessed 1 November 2023].

Assis, Mariana Prandini and Ana Carolina Ogando. 'Bolsonaro, "Gender Ideology" and Hegemonic Masculinity in Brazil'. *AlJazeera*, 31 October 2018 <https://www.aljazeera.com/opinions/2018/10/31/bolsonaro-gender-ideology-and-hegemonic-masculinity-in-brazil> [accessed 1 November 2023].

Berman, Jessica. *Modernist Fiction, Cosmopolitanism and the Politics of Community*. Cambridge: Cambridge University Press, 2001.

——, '*Three Guineas* and the Politics of Interruption'. In *A Companion to Virginia Woolf*, ed. by Jessica Berman, 203–16. Oxford: Wiley Blackwell, 2016.

Black, Naomi. *Virginia Woolf as Feminist*. New York: Cornell University Press, 2004.

Clarke, Stuart N. 'The Horse With a Green Tail'. *Virginia Woolf Miscellany*, 34 (1990), 3–4.

Crangle, Sara. 'Feminism's Archives: Mina Loy, Anna Mendelssohn and Taxonomy'. In *The New Modernist Studies*, ed. by Douglas Mao, 246–77. Cambridge: Cambridge University Press, 2021.

Donlon, Anne. 'Things and Lost Things: Nancy Cunard's Spanish Civil War Scrapbook'. *The Massachusetts Review*, 55.2 (2014), 192–205.

Friedman, Susan Stanford. *Planetary Modernisms: Provocations on Modernity Across Time*. New York: Columbia University Press, 2015.

Good, Katie Day. 'From Scrapbook to Facebook: A History of Personal Media Assemblage and Archives'. *New Media and Society*, 15.4 (2013), 557–73.

Green, Barbara. *Spectacular Confessions: Autobiography, Performative Activism, and the Sites of Suffrage 1905–1938*. Basingstoke: Macmillan, 1997.

Hartman, Saidiya. 'Intimate History, Radical Narrative'. 22 May 2020 <https://www.aaihs.org/intimate-history-radical-narrative> [accessed 1 November 2023].

——, *Wayward Lives, Beautiful Experiments*. London: Serpent's Tail, 2021.

Joad, C. E. M. 'Women of To-Day and To-Morrow, By a Man'. *Everyman*, 12 January 1934.

Johnson, Melissa A. 'Souvenirs of Amerika: Hannah Höch's Weimar-Era Mass-Media Scrapbook'. In *The Scrapbook in American Life*, ed. by Susan Tucker, Katherine Ott and Patricia P. Buckler, 135–52. Philadelphia: Temple University Press, 2006.

Jones, Clara. *Virginia Woolf: Ambivalent Activist*. Edinburgh: Edinburgh University Press, 2016.

Lee, Hermione. *Virginia Woolf*. London: Virago, 1997.
Micir, Melanie and Aarthi Vadde. 'Obliterature: Towards an Amateur Criticism'. *Modernism/modernity*, 25.3 (2018), 517–49.
Pawlowski, Merry M. 'The Virginia Woolf and Vera Douie Letters', ed. by Merry Pawlowski. *Woolf Studies Annual*, 8.3 (2002), 3–62.
——, 'Virginia Woolf and Scrapbooking'. In *The Edinburgh Companion to Virginia Woolf and the Arts*, ed. by Maggie Humm, 298–313. Edinburgh: Edinburgh University Press, 2010.
Radin, Grace. *Virginia Woolf's 'The Years': The Evolution of a Novel*. Knoxville: University of Tennessee Press, 1981.
Roberts, Harry. 'The Sanctity of Human Life'. *New Statesman and Nation*, 3.51 (13 February 1932), 193–4.
Rose, Jacqueline. *On Violence and On Violence Against Women*. London: Faber and Faber, 2021.
Russell, Bertrand. *The Scientific Outlook*. London, 1931.
Snaith, Anna. 'Wide Circles: The *Three Guineas* Letters'. *Woolf Studies Annual*, 6 (2000), 1–168.
Tamkin, Emily. 'What is the new University of Austin for?' *New Statesman*, 9 November 2021 <https://www.newstatesman.com/the-explainer/2021/11/what-is-the-new-university-of-austin-for> [accessed 1 November 2023].
Walker, Alice. 'In Search of Our Mothers' Gardens' (1983). *In Search of Our Mothers' Gardens: Womanist Prose*, 231–43. The Women's Press, 2000.
Watton, Cherish. 'Suffrage Scrapbooks and Emotional Histories of Women's Activism'. *Women's History Review* (2022) <https://doi.org/10.1080/09612025.2021.2012343> [accessed 1 November 2023].
Woolf, Virginia, '3 volumes of press cuttings, manuscript and typed extracts relating to *Three Guineas*', Monk's House Papers, University of Sussex Special Collections, The Keep, SxMs-18/2/B/16/F.
——, *The Diary of Virginia Woolf, Volume Four: 1931–1935*, ed. by Anne Olivier Bell. Harmondsworth: Penguin, 1983.
——, *The Essays of Virginia Woolf, Volume Four, 1925–1928*, ed. by Andrew McNeillie. London: Chatto & Windus, 1995.
——, *A Room of One's Own and Three Guineas*, ed. by Anna Snaith. Oxford: Oxford University Press, 2015.

Chapter 13

Mrs Dalloway said she would buy the flowers herself.
For Lucy had her **work cut out** for her.

Kabe Wilson

An attempt to create a demographic map of how British interwar capitalist society was depicted in *Mrs Dalloway*, this found poem moves through the novel, highlighting each reference to a paid occupation, named business, or personal title (whether professional or designating social rank).[1] The novel's spacing has been maintained in a condensed form, and where the editorial task required an assessment on what constitutes paid work I have endeavoured to remain faithful to both the historical attitudes of the society depicted and the novel's tone and presentation of its characters. For example, if the novel's focus, from its very opening line, is on how its titular character is specifically positioned within a social structure that allows her financial security but not commercially paid work, then 'hostess' cannot be classed as an occupation in this schema. Likewise, unlike many of those she associates with, Clarissa Dalloway does not have a title of social rank. As the novel's title famously notes, she is not 'Lady', she is 'Mrs'. The poem should therefore be read as a reflection upon the system that supports an upper-class Englishwoman – the system she is fixed in and through which she perceives the world – but her invisibility in the text should underline the fact that this is not a system within which she is necessarily identifiable. Without a job or an aristocratic title, she exists in a particular blind spot of the ruling class under British capitalism. Similar could be noted of Septimus and Rezia Smith. While originally a clerk (then a soldier) and a hat-maker respectively, when the consequences of war isolate them from their work and force them into the socially disregarded roles of patient and carer, we see that it is the medical professionals with titles of 'Dr' (Holmes) and 'Sir' (William Bradshaw) who come to dominate the textual map.

                        Rumpelmayer's men
                                            Durtnall's van

        sandwich men   Lady
          King   Queen   tapping of cricket bats
                shopkeepers
    carrying a dispatch box stamped with the Royal Arms,
           doctors.   doctors.   little job at
    Court
            barber's   Fleet
    Admiralty
      Prime Minister

         Fräulein
                                    Hatchards' shop
                    Lady
              policeman   Lady   Lady
                                                  tweed in the
    shop   fishmonger's   glove shop
              a shop where they kept flowers   her
    dismissal from school during the War
                                    Mulberry's the florists
                                              girls in
    muslin frocks came out to pick sweet peas and roses

          Mulberry's shop   Atkinson's scent shop
                    Prince of Wales's, Queen's, Prime Minister's?
              The Prime Minister's

       Mulberry's shop
                the Queen   the Queen   chauffeur,
                              butchers' boys
                          Queen, Prince,   Prime Minister
                              Queen,   Mulberry's
       the Queen.   The Queen   the Queen
                       the Queen   the Queen   Sir
           Judge   Sir   chauffeur   policeman
                    footman's   the Queen's, Prince of Wales's,
         Prime Minister's?   glove shops
    hat shops   tailors' shops   hat shops
    tailors' shops   White's
                                            with her flowers on
    the pavement   Prince of Wales   constable's
              sentries   Queen   policeman
                      the Queen   Prince   Kings
      the Queen's   Princess   Prince   Prince!
        King   Prince   housemaids,
    housemaids,   the Queen

                        dancer
                            Dr.
                nursemaid   nursemaid
        Dr.
Dr.   making hats

            clown   Dr.   Dr.
                                a post at her uncle's in Leadenhall
Street
                                            cooks
                                        missionary

                                            maid
        maid   nun   cook
    servants   cook   Lady
                    Lady   Lady
                    diver
Lady   nun
  Baron

                    old housemaid,

                    he came every summer, poor old man, for weeks
and weeks, and pretended to read German with her,

    Lady   maids
                                        Rumpelmayer's
men   baker's shop   Lady   Princess
            servants
    servants   servants   dress, one of
Sally Parker's, the last almost she ever made,   real
artist.

                        Conservative

                        Queen   guards
                    career at Oxford
                Major in the Indian Army
lawyers   Major in the Indian Army
            Major in the Indian Army,   Major
            lawyers   solicitors, Messrs. Hooper and Grateley of
Lincoln's Inn
                            Lady

   a district twice as big as Ireland;
   had invented a plough in his district, had ordered wheel-barrows from
England,   coolies

Duke
Boys in uniform, carrying guns,   boys of sixteen,
who might, to-morrow, stand behind bowls of rice, cakes of soap on
counters.   soldiers

nurse
Dent's shop

Messrs. Hooper and Grateley   butlers
            administered the affairs of a continent
    butlers;   doctors   men of business
                                                              nurse

  nurse
        nurse
                                                                            landlady
                    nurse
    housemaid   housemaid

                                            grooms   stable-boys
        coachman   old nurse,
                              botanist

    servants

                nurse's
    making hats.   nurse   nurse
nurse,   Sir
                                                Dr.
                            Prime Minister,
            shepherd boy's
    sailor

                writing quite openly in one of the respectable
weeklies about water-closets.
                                                Coal merchants.
    tradespeople.   Duke.   Princesses.
                    those poor girls in Piccadilly
        stable boys   Lady
            valet   little post at Court, looked after
the King's cellars, polished the Imperial shoe-buckles, went about in
knee-breeches and lace ruffles.   little job at Court!
                                                        secretary's
        usher's job teaching little boys Latin,   mandarin

        Duchesses,   Countesses   Lady
                                farming
    artist   writer
                                                Major
            lawyers

Work Cut Out

Sir   brewer's
     clerk,   caretaker,
   clerk,   authors
                    poet
gardener
              managing clerk   Sibleys and Arrowsmiths,
auctioneers, valuers, land and estate agents;
                cook's   officer
                                              innkeeper
  making hats,   making hats,
                 artist's   painter
    shopgirl   tea-shop
      waiters   tailor-made
                                               trimming hats.
trimmed hats   trimmed hats by the hour.
         King   hat shops, dress shops, shops with leather bags
in the window,   author?
                 cook's
                          doctor   Dr. Dr.   Dr.
          Dr.   Dr.   landlords
   Sir   Dr.
      Dr.   Dr.
   Dr.   Dr.   Dr.
   Dr.   Dr.   Dr.
                sailor
servant girl   Dr.
   Dr.   Dr.   Dr.   Dr.
             Sir   Sir
priest of science   Sir   Sir
                              sexton
took photographs, which were scarcely to be distinguished from the
work of professionals,   Sir   shopkeeper)
                                                   Dr.
  general practitioners! Sir   doctor
Sir   doctor   Sir   Sir
    Sir   Sir   doctors
Sir   nurses   Sir   Sir
   judges   sailor; poet   Lady
Sir   Sir   Sir   tradesman   Sir
         doctors   Sir
Sir   Sir   Sir   Sir
  Sir   Sir   Sir
 doctor   doctor   Sir
Sir   Lady   took photographs scarcely to be
distinguished from the work of professionals.   Sir
      Lady   Sir   Sir
                                          Sir

      Lady

doctor   Lady   Sir
              Sir   Sir   Lady
     Sir   Sir   Sir   police
                  Sir   Sir
Messrs. Rigby and Lowndes   Rigby and Lowndes
           Rigby and Lowndes   kept guard at
Buckingham Palace, dressed in silk stockings and knee-breeches, over
what nobody knew.   Prime Ministers
      held important office   servant girls
                              Lady   Lady
secretary   doing very well in South Africa,'
  Lady   Lady
   maids, handmaidens
Lady   Lady   Lady   General
    General's   Sir Sir Sir   general
                           Lady   Lady
Lady   General Sir   Lady   troops
                           Lady
        Lady   Lady
              Lady   Lady
 Lady   heads of Government offices
  Lady   Lady   Lady
 Lady   Lady
                           Lady
organise an expedition to South Africa
editors   Lady
    makers   Lady   editor of the Times, Lady
                      Lady   editor   Lady
           Prime Minister!   General's
 Lady   military men, administrators, admirals,
                 Lady   Lady   Lady
                 Lady
     nurse   commanding
battalions marching to Canada,
                                  Haymakers
                                    Lady
     editor

           championed the down-trodden and followed his
instincts in the House of Commons;
police   London police.   costermongers,
  prostitutes,

  King   Queen
                                             Lady
                 Lady
                          doctor   doctors

                    taking jobs from people like

                    the Dalloways   servants
                        a chance at Miss Dolby's school,
                               working for the Friends   teach his daughter history
                        a little Extension lecturing
            in a factory; behind a counter   Rev.
                                                            She had always earned
her living.   the Stores
                                                    Army and Navy Stores

                                                    Army and Navy Stores
                                girl serving
                                                    clergyman
                                    Duchesses   Lord
oil and colour shop
                                    waitress
                        of the Treasury,   the famous K.C.,
                                                            Rev.

Baron
                Army and Navy Stores
                                        doctor   farmer
                farmer   doctor,   farmer,   go
into Parliament,   of ships, of
business, of law, of administration,   farmer
    doctor   architects   clergymen
    Abbesses, principals, head mistresses, dignitaries,

                                                    twisting a hat in
her hands,   Dr.   Sir
                            the girl who did the room
        Dr.
    she sat sewing.   she sat sewing.
        making a hat
                        Queen   Prince
                sewing,   sewing.   sewing?
                        trimming the straw hat
organ grinder's   pinning a rose to one side of the hat.
                                            she sewed.   she
sewed,
                        Sir   girl with the evening paper

                            Sir
Prime Minister   lawgiver
                men who made ten thousand a year and talked of
proportion;   judges
Dr.
                        Dr.   Dr.   Dr.
                            Dr.

                            poor old woman who guarded

her   doctor   Dr.   Dr.
      the ambulance sped to the hospital, having picked up instantly, humanely, some poor devil;
  doctor   nurse   doctors
                                        man behind a
counter
                                   The young lady handed him
some letters
            matron   maids
         Major
                  lawyers
                                        colonels
               waiter
                     Prince
                                                  paper
boys
      young people went by with their dispatch-boxes
                              housemaid's

                              maids
                       footman
          Judge   policeman
                                        Prime Minister
                 Prime Minister   Prime
Minister
    Emperor's   (hired for
parties)
                been with the family for forty years, and came every summer to help the ladies,   Lady
  Lady   Lady   Lady
        old nurse.   Lady   Lady   (hired for
parties)   Lady   Sir   Lady
                     Lord
          Lord   Lady   Lord
                   vicar
       maids
                    politicians
                                        Colonel
Lady
        Sir   Lady   Lady
  Lady
                 Prime Minister,   Prime Minister?
                       Lady   Prime
Minister!   court footman
              coolies   Duchess
                 Prime Minister   Lady
  Lady   minor officials in Government offices

                    Prime Minister
                            Prime Minister
            Prime Minister   Sir   Sir
    Lady   Sir   Sir
Academicians   Sir   Sir
        Duke   Lady,   maid
    Professor   Professor   lectureships
                            Professor   (a very bad
poet)   Professors
    Professor   Professor   Professor   Professor
                Professor   Lord
            Lord   Lords   artists
                            Lord
Viceroys, Generals,   coolies
                        Lady   Lady
Lady   Lady   politicians   Lady
                    Cabinet   Lady   grenadier
                        Viceroys   Prime Minister
    Prime Minister   Lady   Sir
soldier's   servants   troops
                            Lady   Lady

Portuguese Ambassador   owned, it was
said, cotton mills at Manchester.
    Lady   Duchesses   Lady   Lady
    Sir   the Commons   doctor
            Sir   Lady
Sir   Sir   Sir
    Lady   Sir   army.   Prime Minister
        Lady   Prime Minister   Lady
poets   thinkers   Sir   doctor   Sir
                                        Lady
                                            Lady
            politicians   not in the Cabinet.
        merchants,   manufacturers,
            servants

        sportsman   He blacked the King's
boots or counted bottles at Windsor,

miner's   miner's   gardener
                        magician!

probably a Cabinet Minister.   Public work
                                    Sir
    engraver's   Sir
            Lady

1. The conception of this work owes a debt to Jane Goldman's 'Queer Woolf: two poems and a preamble', in *Virginia Woolf and the World of Books*, ed. by Claire Battershill and Nicola Wilson (Liverpool: Liverpool University Press, 2020), 162–88, and its completion owes the same to Merve Emre's startlingly in-depth *The Annotated Mrs Dalloway* (London: Liveright, 2021). For a comprehensive critical analysis of Woolf's use of 'work cut out' as a phrase, see Mary Wilson's 'Work' in *The Oxford Handbook of Virginia Woolf*, ed. by Anne E. Fernald (Oxford: Oxford University Press, 2021), 456–71.

Index

Books by Virginia Woolf are indicated with (VW). Page numbers followed by n are notes.

Abolition Bill, 1833, 54
abolitionists, 54–5
abortion, 283–7, 292n
Acker, Kathy, 251
Addison, Joseph, 106–7
Africa
   colonialism, 36–7
   economic imperialism, 51
   internationalism, 51
   Marx and, 49
   partition of North and East, 51
   'scramble for Africa', 40, 49, 50
aggression, 40, 50
Albania, 38
Allan, Tuzyline Jita, 60–1
Allen, Ansgar, 98
Althusserian model, 31
amateurism, 185–6
America, 49
Anand, Mulk Raj, 173
Andrews, Charles, 50
'Angel in the House', 16
Anglo-South American rubber trade, 49
anti-capitalism, 41
anti-colonialism, 49, 172
anti-imperialism, 48–52, 219n
antisemitism, 50
Applebee's Original Weekly Journal, 207

Arendt, Hannah, *The Human Condition*, 186
Armenians, 35, 37–8
Armstrong, Nancy, 205–6, 208
Aronowitz, Stanley, 225
Arts and Crafts movement, 164
authority, 211–14
'automation', 225–6, 238

Baena, Victoria, 186, 199n, 201n
Bahun, Sanja, 131n
Barrett, Michèle, 7, 18n, 51, 92, 108, 111n, 218n
Barthes, Roland, 253
Battershill, Claire, 164
Bell, Anne Olivier, 15
Bell, Quentin, 7, 11
Bentham, Jeremy, 98
Berman, Jessica, 20n, 214–16, 221n, 226, 274
Berman, Marshall, 163
Besant, Annie, 85
Between the Acts (VW)
   creativity and paid work in, 236
   domestic work in, 88n
   houses in, 137–43, 145, 150
   sexual violence in, 287, 292n
   women writers in, 187
   working-class characters in, 78, 86

Bexhill, 144–5, 156–7n
beyond-work, 224–44
Bhaskar, Michael, 160, 162
Binet-Simon, 94
biometric feminism, 92–115
Black, Naomi, 60, 285–6
Black Lives Matter protests 2020, 48
Blast, 219n
Bloomsbury group, 20n
Boer War, 50
Bolshevik Revolution 1917, 3
Bombay/Mumbai, 54
Book Society, 167–8
books
   'Colonial editions', 172
   democratisation of, 164–9
   and the 'Empire market', 171–3
   'rise of the novel', 207
Boumelha, Penny, 188
Bourdieu, Pierre, 161, 184, 195
Bowlby, Rachel, 73
Bradlaugh, Charles, 85
Bradshaw, David, 17n
Brailsford, H. N., 49
Breton, Rob, 225
Briggs, Julia, 194
British Consular Reports, 38, 51–2
British Empire, 49, 212
British Eugenics Society, 94
Bronstein, Michaela, 206, 208
Brown, Judith C., 120, 127
Budget and Economy Bills 1931, 12

Cambridge, 15
capital
   cultural, 184, 186, 188
   definition of, 184
   'emotional', 14–16
   excess, 15
   and gender, 48

Marxism, 161, 199–200n
   private, 233–9
   purposeful rhetoric of, 213–14, 226–33
   social, 184, 186, 188, 195
capitalism, 92–6
   anti-capitalism, 41
   and beyond-work, 224–44
   colonialism and violent motivations, 2
   critiques of, 3–4
   desires, 81–2
   empire, slavery and, 48–69
   'high' industrial, 3
   and imperialism, 48
   in *Jacob's Room*, 116–35
   'labour theory of value', 33
   laissez-faire social capitalism, 94, 207
   and Marxism, 32–4
   and publishing, 159–81
   as religion of modernity, 117–18
   and role of women in society, 10–11
   in *Three Guineas*, 75–6, 272–81
   ubiquity of poverty under, 2–3
   Woolf, Leonard and, 16
Casanova, Pascale, *The World Republic of Letters*, 173
Case, Janet, 71, 154, 210
Cattell, Edward, 105
Certeau, Michel de, 247
Chan, Evelyn Tsz Yan, 185, 186, 199n, 213–14
Childers, Mary, 78
Christianity, 117, 120–4, 128
citizenship, and gender, 212
Clarke, Stuart N., 118, 120–1, 292n
class
   alienation, 215–16
   in *Jacob's Room*, 29–30
   Morley College, 103–6
   in *A Room of One's Own*, 98–103, 106–8

and social differences, 138–9
and status, 35–6
stratification, 29–32
in *To the Lighthouse*, 238
in *Three Guineas*, 100, 111n, 287–8
two-class model, 33
VW's, 111n
see also middle-class; working-class
climate crisis, 40–1
clothes, 80–1
Cole, G. D. H.
   The Machinery of Socialist Planning, 165–6
   Politics and Literature, 165
   Studies in Capital and Investment, 165
Cole, Margaret, 164–5
   Books and the People, 166–7
   'The Democratisation of Books', 166–7
Coles, Romand, 118
'Colonial editions', 172
colonialism
   Africa, 36–7, 40, 49, 50
   anti-colonialism, 49, 172
   attitudes and assumptions, 36–7
   British, 36–7
   expansion, 3
   Marx and, 49, 171
   psychology of, 56
   violent capitalist motivations of, 2
   in *The Voyage Out*, 49
   in *The Waves*, 54
consular reports, 38, 51–2
consumerism
   modern, 17n
   working-class, 80–2
consumers, 83–4
consumption, 3, 13, 70–91
   under-consumption, 50
contraceptive movement, 85

co-operative economics, 73–6, 83–7
co-operative movement, 4, 7–8, 73–6
The Co-operator magazine, 74
The Cornhill, 191–2
creativity, 71, 92–3, 162, 231, 235–6, 275, 280
Crocker, Geoff, 230
Cucullu, Lois, 199n
Cuddy-Keane, Melba, 217
cultural capital, 184, 186, 188
Cunard, Nancy, 274, 289n
Cunningham, Michael, *The Hours*, 245–62

Daily Herald, 280
Daily Telegraph, 277, 278
Daldry, Stephen, 247
Darwin, Charles, *The Descent of Man*, 93
Davies, Margaret Llewelyn *see* Llewelyn Davies, Margaret
Day to Day Pamphlet series, 164, 166, 169–72
Defoe, Daniel, 207
desire
   capitalist, 81–2
   to be a star, 253–5
   to dominate and enslave, 29–47
Desjardins, Mary, 259
Dickens, Charles, *Hard Times*, 227
Dickinson, Violet, 156n, 190
A Dictionary of Marxist Thought, 32
Dinerstein, Ana Cecilia, 225
domestic work, 16, 83, 225
   in *Between the Acts*, 88n
   free, 52, 59
   'good work for nothing', 34
   'Wages for Housework Movement', 21n, 241n
Donlon, Anne, 289n
Douglas, C. H., *Economic Democracy*, 213
Douie, Vera, 289n

Dowd, Douglas, 2, 7
Down From London (DFL), 156n
Dreadnought Hoax, 288
Dubino, Jeanne, 172
Duckworth, George, 200n
Duckworth, Gerald, 72, 203, 210
Duras, Marguerite, 63
Dyer, Richard, 247
Dyhouse, Carol, 110–11n

East Africa, 51
'ecological Marxism', 40–1
economic imperialism, 49, 51
education, 94–8, 100–1
  universal, 164–5
  women's, 103–6, 110–11n, 275–6
Eliot, T. S., 16
'emotional capital', 14–16
'emotional intelligence', 21n
emotional labour in the home, 22n
empire, 48–69
'Empire market', 161, 171–3
Engels, Friedrich, 171
  The Communist Manifesto, 160
English identity, 122
Englishness, 276–7
Englishwomen, 55–7, 108, 288, 295
environment, 96–8
Esty, Jed, *Unseasonable Youth*, 234
exploitation, 36–7, 40–1
  'labour theory of value', 33
  of mass markets, 3

Fabian movement, 4, 7–8
Fabian Society, 165, 204
  Round About a Pound a Week, 74
fan culture, 247–9
fans
  author as, 249–55
  common reader as, 255–8
fascism, 41–2, 163, 286–7
  anti-fascist pamphlet, 272–81

Federici, Silvia, *Wages Against Housework*, 59
feminism, 4, 33
  biometric feminism, 92–115
  and class, 111n
  and colonialism and slavery, 287–8
  ecofeminism, 41
  and Marxism, 241n
  materialist, 48–9, 52
  in *A Room of One's Own*, 41
Finkelstein, David, 161
Fiske, John, 255
  'The Cultural Economy of Fandom', 248–9
Fitz-Gibbon, Desmond, 155
Flush: A Biography (VW), 168
food shopping, 70–3
Forum magazine, 39
Foucault, Michel, 36, 211
'Fower Marys' ballad, 64
Fox, R. M., 163
Freud, Sigmund, *Group Psychology and the Analysis of the Ego*, 38
Friedman, Susan Stanford, 275
Froula, Christine, 31
Fussell, Paul, 39
Futurism, 219n

Gagnier, Regenia, 89n
Galton, Francis, 108
  Hereditary Genius, 93
The Gay and Lesbian Review, 250
gender, 10, 12
  and capital, 48
  and capitalism, 10, 12
  and citizenship, 212
  and race, 108
  in *A Room of One's Own*, 96–8
  in *Three Guineas*, 10, 12
Geneticists' Manifesto, 95
Gentleman's Magazine, 207
George, W. L., 205, 207

Glasgow Climate Change Conference, 41
glory, 39
Goldelier, Maurice, 62–3
Goldman, Jane, 57, 120–1
Good Housekeeping magazine, 201n
Gorky, Maxim, *Reminiscences of Tolstoi*, 163
Gosar, Paul, 283
Graves, Sally, *A History of Socialism*, 170
Great Depression, 12–14, 79–80, 163
Gualtieri, Elena, 12
Guinea Coast, West Africa, 59–60
guineas, 59–60

Habermas, Jürgen, 210, 214
  The Structural Transformation of the Public Sphere, 207
Haldane, J. B. S., 95, 99
Hampson, John, 162
Hamya, Jo, *Three Rooms*, 64
Hankins, Leslie Kathleen, 252
Hare, David, 247, 252, 259
Harper's Bazaar, 8, 257
Harris, Ed, 247, 254
Hartman, Saidiya, 288
  Wayward Lives: Beautiful Experiments, 63–4
Hauerwas, Stanley, 118
Hebdige, Dick, 250
Hitler, Adolf, 269–70, 278–9
Hobhouse, L. T., 204
Hobson, J. A., 48–51, 53
  From Capitalism to Socialism, 170–1
  Imperialism: A Study, 50, 58
  Notes on Law and Order, 170
Hochschild, Arlie, 22n
Hogarth Press
  Day to Day Pamphlet series, 164, 166, 169–72
  decision to establish, 210
  owned by Penguin Random House, 261
  printing work, 203
  publishing and capitalism, 159–81
  Three Guineas, 159, 162
  Two Stories, 192
  Uniform Editions, 169
  VW as owner of, 80
  VW's freedom from financial constraint, 199n
  VW's short fiction, 192
  VW's writing for, 227
  WCG, 78
  Woolf, Leonard and, 161–72
Holtby, Winifred, 8, 108–9
home ownership, 146–55, 156n, 157n
'homo economicus', 208–10
The Hours, 246–62
house-purchase, 146–55
houses, 137–43, 145, 150; *see also* property market
How to Be a Successful Estate Agent, 149
Hueffer, Ford Madox, 205, 207
Hungry Thirties, 163
Hurston, Zora Neale, 60
Hussey, Mark, 245–6, 259–60
hyper-masculinity, 52–3
hyper-nationalism, 50

Illouz, Eva, 21n
imperialism
  anti-imperialism, 48–52, 219n
  and capitalism, 37, 48
  economic, 49, 51
  Hobson's work on, 171
  in *Jacob's Room*, 126–7
  in *Mrs Dalloway*, 56
  'new', 50
  patriarchal power and, 53
  in *The Voyage Out*, 37–8
  Woolf, Leonard and, 48–52

Index

Independent Labour Party, 50–1
India, 36–7, 49, 54, 174n
India Act 1853, 98
individual freedom, 211–14
individualism, 89n
inherited wealth, 34, 54, 93–4
intelligence, 92–6
  'emotional', 21n
  material barriers to female intellect, 96–9
  politics of, 92–115
  in *A Room of One's Own*, 96–8
  test, 94
internationalism, 51
internet, 246–62
Interview, 257
Irvine, Lyn, 98–9, 106
Isherwood, Christopher, *Goodbye to Berlin*, 168–9

Jackson, R. Haslam, 287
Jacob's Room (VW)
  capitalism and peace and war in, 116–35
  class in, 29–30
  houses in, 143
  imperialism in, 126–7
  private income in, 234
James, C. L. R., 173
  The Case for West-Indian Self Government, 172–3
Jameson, Fredric, 163, 220n
Jameson, Storm, 112n
Jenkins, Henry, 247, 248, 251, 255, 256, 257
Jews, 41–2
  antisemitism, 50
jingoism, 58
Joad, C. E. M., 'Women of To-Day and To-Morrow', 278
Jones, Clara
  on 'Cook Sketch', 82
  on houses, 141
  on inherited wealth, 93
  on '[The Journal of Mistress Joan Martyn]', 189
  on Marxism, 199–200n
  on 'Memoirs of a Novelist', 201n
  on 'Morley Sketch', 103–4, 190–1
  on *Night and Day*, 235
  on WCG, 71

Keynes, John Maynard, 11–14, 21n, 94, 169–71, 237
  'Economic Possibilities for Our Grandchildren', 230
  'The End of *Laissez-Faire*', 11–12
  'Saving and Spending' broadcast, 12–13
Kidman, Nicole, 246–62
King, William, 74
Kipling, Rudyard, 52–3
Kore-Schröder, Leena, 199–200n

labour
  'labour theory of value', 33
  Marx and, 33, 224
  see also work
Labour
  literature, 8
  movement, 3, 165
Labour Government, 12–14
Labour Party, 3, 49, 182–3, 204, 219n
  Advisory Committee on Imperial Questions, 51
  Conference 1933, 4
  Independent Labour Party, 50–1
laissez-faire social capitalism, 94, 207
Lane, Christopher, 250
Latham, Sean, 111n
Lawrence, D. H., *Women in Love*, 153
League of Nations, 203–4, 219n
League of Nations Society, 204

Lee, Hermione, 49, 89n
Lehmann, John, 159, 166
    Thrown to the Woolfs, 163
leisure, 226–33
Lenin, Vladimir, *Imperialism: The Highest Stage of Capitalism*, 50
Lewis, Wyndham, 219n
Leys, Norman, *Kenya*, 172–3
liberalism, 204
    'new', 170
Life and Letters, 95
Light, Alison, 82
Lippincott, Robin, 251
Listener, 164
literary awards, 246–51, 253, 254–5, 261
literary modernism, 7
literary public sphere, 203–23
living wage, 59
Llewelyn Davies, Margaret, 4, 13, 71, 72, 74, 76–9, 83
    Life as We Have Known It, 215–16
London County Council for Night Schools, 269–70
Long, David, 170

McAfee, Helen, 79
McCarraher, Eugene, 117–18
McCleery, Alastair, 161
MacDonald, Ramsay, 12
MacKay, Marina, 208
MacPherson, Ian, 75
Manchester Guardian, 50
Mansfield, Katherine, 205
Marcus, Jane, 7, 54, 56–7
    Hearts of Darkness: White Women Write Race, 56
market economy, 3, 4, 207–11, 49, 50
Martin, Judith, 119
Marx, Karl
    and Africa, 49
    and colonialism, 49, 171
    The Communist Manifesto, 160
    and labour, 33, 224
    'poetry of the future', 163
    as politician, 9
    and value and capital, 161
    VW and, 7–11
Marxism
    and capital, 199–200n
    and capitalism, 32–4
    'ecological', 40–1
    and feminism, 241n
    'neo-Marxism', 10
    'social reproduction', 31
    Woolf, Leonard and, 8, 10
'Mary Hamilton' ballad, 64
masculinity, 56, 280
    hyper-masculinity, 52–3
materialism, 8, 224
materialist, feminism, 48–9, 52
May, Patricia, 185
May Committee 1931, 12
Mayer-Schonberger, Viktor, 236
men
    fears of women encroaching, 277–8
    objectification of women, 56
    'pleasure of dominance', 280
Menai, Huw, 163
Mendelsohn, Daniel, 252
meritocracy, 92–6
Micir, Melanie, 274, 282
middle-class
    ignorance of poverty, 1–3
    readership, 107–8
    see also class
Mill, John Stuart
    On Liberty, 211
    The Subjection of Women, 55
Miller, Laura J., *Reluctant Capitalists: Bookselling and the Culture of Consumption*, 160
Mirrlees, Hope, *Paris*, 163
misogyny, 285–7
missionaries, 36–7, 54
Mitchison, Naomi, 95

Mockerie, Parmenas Githendu, *An African Speaks for his People*, 173
modernism, 120
modernist literature, 131n
modernity, 11, 132n
money, 49, 54, 59–61, 159–60
Moore, Dorothy, 15
Moore, G. E., 15
Moore, Julianne, 247, 254
Morel, E. D., 49
Morgan, Peter, 169
Morley College, 103–6, 190–1
Morrell, Lady Ottoline, 154
Morrison, Toni, 60
Mortimer, Raymond, 162
motherhood
  childbirth, 284–6
  in *Jacob's Room*, 87n
  maternal feelings, 188
  maternal responsibilities, 83
  'national endowment of motherhood', 59
  parenting, 15–16
  in *The Voyage Out*, 89n
  VW on, 70–91
  war-mother, 87n
Mrs Dalloway (VW)
  aesthetics of digression, 228
  The Hours, 246–62
  houses in, 143–6
  imperialism in, 56
  private income in, 236–7
  psychiatry in, 34
  Public Domain Day 2021, 245–6
  queering of, 250–2
  royalty in, 30
  and the social system, 34–8
  waged work in, 231
  working-class women in, 102
Murphet, Julian, 'Marx and the Modernist Novel', 8
Mussolini, Benito, 269–70
  The Political and Social Doctrine of Fascism, 169

Nakai, Asako, 241n
Nation and Athenaeum, 99, 106
National Council of Women, 284
National Union of Women's Suffrage Societies, 59
nationalism
  hyper-nationalism, 50
  spectacle of, 56
Nazi movement, 278–9
'neo-Marxism', 10
neo-Nazis, 283
Neverow, Vara, 132n
New Age, 213
New Fabian Research Bureau, 165
New Republic, 39
New Statesman and Nation, 283–4
New York Herald Tribune Books, 246
New York Times, 250, 258, 260
The New York Times Book Review, 245, 252
New Yorker, 245
Night and Day (VW)
  Galton, Francis, 93
  literary public sphere in, 203–23
  Llewelyn Davies, Margaret, 77
  as problem novel, 203–6
  shop window displays in, 17n
  waged work in, 224–5, 228–31, 234–5
1917 Club, 204
North Africa, 51
Norton, H. T. J., 14, 21n

'occultation', 62–3
Offill, Jenny, 245, 260–1
opera, 261–2
Orlando: A Biography (VW)
  garden imagery in, 112n
  houses in, 143
  working women writers in, 186–7
Oscars, 246–7, 258, 261
Outka, Elizabeth, 17n

Viral Modernism: The Influenza Pandemic and Interwar Literature, 259

pamphlet economics, 169–71
Panikkar, K. M., *Caste and Democracy*, 172
Pankhurst, Sylvia, 219n
Pascal, Blaise, *Pensées*, 57
paternalism, 51
patriarchalism, 41–2, 53, 56, 63
patriotism, 53
Pawlowski, Merry M., 274–5, 289n
Pearson, Karl, 108
Penguin, 245, 260
Penguin Books Great Ideas series, 40
Penguin Random House, 260–1
'pensions for spinsters', 59
Perkin, Harold, 94
Pethick-Lawrence, Frederick, 4
philanthropy, 3
Phillips, Adam, 237
photographs, 272–3, 283
Picador Macmillan, 261
Pitts, Frederick Harry, 225
'plagiarism', 251
Plomer, William, 161
   The Case is Altered, 168
plurality, 87n
Postgate, Raymond, *What to do with the BBC*, 166
'postwork', 225–6, 229–30
Pound, Ezra, 219n
poverty
   in 'Memories of a Working Women's Guild', 81–2
   middle-class ignorance of, 1–3
   ubiquity of under capitalism, 2–3
power, criticism of, 36–7
presscuttings in *Three Guineas*, 270, 271, 276, 277, 279
private capital, 233–9
private income, 233–4, 236–8
private space, 60–1

professionalism, 185–6
'Professions for Women', 16
property market, 4, 14, 140–1, 145–55
   rentiers, 4, 11, 238–9
   VW and, 4, 11, 137–58
   see also houses
psychiatry, 34, 36–8
psychology, 92–3, 98, 151
Public Domain Day 2021, 245–6, 259, 261
public sphere, literary, 203–23
Publishers Association, 171, 173, 174n
publishing, and capitalism, 159–81

Quakers, 55
queering, *Mrs Dalloway*, 250–2

race
   and class, 106–108
   and gender, 108
   in *A Room of One's Own*, 106–108
racial
   hierarchies, 50
   injustice, 59–60
   violence, 54
Raleigh, Sir Walter, *Romance: Two Lectures*, 206
Randall, Bryony, 206, 235
Rathbone, Eleanor, 59
Readers Union, 168–9
rentiers, 4, 11, 238–9
representation, 214–17
reproduction, 52, 59
Richardson, Freddie, 168
Roberts, Dr Harry, 283–4
A Room of One's Own (VW)
   aesthetics of digression, 228
   aggression in, 40
   and Black women, 59–65
   and class, 98–103, 106–8
   as 'economic biography', 49

A Room of One's Own (VW) (*cont.*)
  empire in, 48
  environment in, 96–8
  feminism in, 41
  gender in, 96–8
  intelligence in, 96–8
  materialism in, 8
  private income in, 233, 238
  race and class in, 106–8
  'rage for acquisition' in, 286
  slavery in, 48, 60–1, 287–8
  women as creators in, 83
  women writers in, 186, 193
  women's exclusion from capitalist imperialist system in, 52–7
Rose, Jacqueline, 283
Rose, Phyllis, 163
Rosenman, Ellen Bayuk, 56
Royal African Company (RAC), 59–60
Royal Opera House, Covent Garden, 29–32
royalty, 30
Rukavina, Alison, 171
Russell, Bertrand, 285
  Principles of Social Reconstruction, 203
Russian literature, 163
Ruttenburg, Nancy, 207–8

Sackville-West, Vita, 82
  The Edwardians, 167–8, 171–2
San Francisco Chronicle, 256
Sargant-Florence, Alix, 14
school prize-giving, 96, 101
Scott, David, 62–3
Scott, Gillian, 72, 84–6
'scramble for Africa', 40, 49, 50
scrapbooking, 269–94
secularity, 117–18
Sellers, Susan, 118
Seshagiri, Urmila, 56
Seton, Mary, 54
sexual violence, 285–7, 292n

Shakespeare, William, 96, 102
Shamsie, Kamile, *Home Fire*, 283
Sharp, Thomas, *A Derelict Area: A Study of the South-West Durham Coalfield*, 170
Shaw, George Bernard, 182–4, 187, 198n
Sherry, Vincent, 132n
Shiach, Morag, 229
shopping, 81, 145–6
  co-operative, 73–6
  food, 70–3
  window displays, 17n
  in *The Years*, 86
Silver, Brenda R., 31
Simon, Sheena, Lady, 39
Slave Trade Act 1807, 54
slavery, 48–69
  'rhetoric of enslavement', 288
  in *A Room of One's Own*, 60–1, 287–8
  slave trade, 54
  in *Three Guineas*, 58–60
Smith, James K. A., 117
Smith, Logan Pearsall, 96
Smith, Reginald, 191–2
Snaith, Anna
  on anti-colonialism, 172
  on feminism, colonialism and slavery, 287–8
  on feminism and class, 111n
  on gender politics, 10
  on imperialism, 37, 171
  on London capitalist economics, 2, 21n
  on plurality, 87n
  on race and gender, 108
  on women's education, 110n
Snowden, Philip, 12
social capital, 184, 186, 188, 195
social capitalism, *laissez-faire*, 94, 207
'social reproduction' thesis, 31

socialist movement, 165
Society for the Abolition of Slavery, 58–9
Society of Authors, 182–3, 187
Society of Bookment, 167
South Africa, 50
South Downs, 116–35
Soviet Union, collapse of, 7, 32
Spanish Civil War, 272–3
Spearman, Charles, 105
Spectator, 207, 285
Sri Lanka (Ceylon), 51
St Kitts, 54
stardom, 246–7, 258–9, 261–2
Stasi, Paul, 232
Staveley, Alice, 163
Stephen, Caroline Emelia, 54
Stephen, Dorothea, 54
Stephen, James, 'Mr. Mother-Country Stephen', 54
Stephen, James Fitzjames, 54
Stephen, James (Jem), 54
  England Enslaved by her Own Slave Colonies, 54
Stephen, Julia, 54
Stephen, Leslie, 31
Stephen, Virginia, 30, 103–6, 190–1
Steven, Mark, 3, 7, 163
Stevenson, Iain, 168
Streep, Meryl, 247, 253–4
suffrage, 219n
surplus value, 33, 49, 52
Sutton, Emma, 30

Tate, Trudi, 37–8
Tatler, 207
Tawney, R. H., 8
Taylor, W. G., 173
Thompson, John B., *Merchants of Culture*, 161
Thomson, Marjorie, 164
Three Guineas (VW)
  beyond-work in, 226
  capitalism in, 10, 12, 75–6, 272–81
  class in, 100, 111n, 287–8
  and economics, 49
  empire and slavery in, 48
  gender and capitalism in, 10, 12
  Hogarth Press, 159, 162
  patriarchalism in, 41–2, 63
  presscuttings, 270, 271, 276, 277, 279
  private income in, 233, 238
  problem novels, 206
  scrapbooks, 269–94
  slavery in, 58–60
  waged work in, 229–30
  'Wages for Housework' movement, 21n, 241n
  Women's exclusion from capitalist imperialist system in, 52
Thunberg, Greta, 41
Time magazine, 246
Times, 116, 190, 278, 285, 287, 292n
  Book Club, 167
Times Literary Supplement, 203
To the Lighthouse (VW)
  aesthetics of digression, 228
  class in, 238
  'Colonial editions', 172
  as 'elegy', 119
  houses in, 143
  paid work in, 227, 235–6
Tolstoyan asceticism, 15
tourism, 126–7
Tratner, Michael, 71, 75–6
Trexler, Adam, 11
Trouton, Rupert, *Unemployment: Its Causes and Their Remedies*, 169–70
Turkey, 37–8
Tyson, Helen, 58

Union of Democratic Control, 50–1
universal education, 164–5

universities, 53, 97–8, 110–11n, 272–3, 275–6
University of Cambridge, 'Legacies of Enslavement' Report, 52
University of Sussex, 270, 281–8
Unwin, Stanley, 172, 178n

Vadde, Aarthi, 274, 282
van Parijs, Philippe, *Basic Income*, 233
Vanderborght, Yannick, *Basic Income*, 233
Vintage, 245, 259–60
Virginia Woolf Miscellany, 259–60
Virginia Woolf Society, 258
Vorticism, 219n
The Voyage Out (VW)
  colonialism in, 49
  imperialism in, 37–8
  literary public sphere in, 210
  motherhood in, 89n
  paid work in, 233–4
  professionalism in, 186
  Woolf, Leonard and, 194
  working women writers in, 183, 187, 193–8
Vwoolf, 255–60

Wages for Housework Movement, 21n, 241n
Walker, Alice, 288
  'Saving the Life That is Your Own: The Importance of Models in the Artist's Life', 60
  'In Search of Our Mothers' Gardens', 60–1
Wall Street Journal, 250–1
Ward, Mrs Humphry, 182
Ware, Vron, 55
Watt, Ian, 207–8
The Waves (VW)
  aesthetics of digression, 228
  colonialism in, 54
  creativity and paid work in, 231
  school scenes, 100–1
  sensory understanding in, 82
  working-class characters in, 78
WCG *see* Women's Co-operative Guild (WCG)
wealth
  earned, 4
  inherited, 34, 54, 93–4
  private income, 234
  unearned, 4
Webb, Beatrice, 8, 165, 211, 214–15
Webb, Sidney, 8, 165, 204, 211, 214–15
  'Social Movements', 211–12
Weber, Max, 32
Weeks, Kathi, 225–6, 233, 239
Wheatley, Phillis, 60–1
Whitworth, Michael, 21n, 218n
Wilberforce, William, 54
Williams, J. Wheeler, 287
Williams, Raymond, 20n, 33
Wilson, Kabe
  The Dreadlock Hoax, 64–5
  Olivia N'Gowfri – Of One Woman or So, 64–5
Wilson, Mary, 225
Wollstonecraft, Mary, *Vindication of the Rights of Women*, 55
women
  alienation and suppression of, 52
  capitalism and role in society, 10–11
  as creators, 83
  education of, 103–6, 110–11n
  exclusion of, 52–7, 279–80, 283
  'inferiority' of, 63
  and labour, 14–16
  material barriers to female intellect, 96–9
  men's fears of women encroaching, 277–8
  men's objectification of, 56
  politics of, 221n
  'typical', 106–8

work in the home, 33
workers, 33
Women and Fiction, 40
women writers
  in *Between the Acts*, 187
  Black women, 60–1
  in *Orlando*, 186–7
  in *A Room of One's Own*, 186, 193
  in *The Voyage Out*, 183, 187, 193–8
Women's Co-operative Guild (WCG), 70–87, 203, 238
  conference, 79–82, 102
  and Hogarth Press, 78
  homemakers of the, 71–3
  Maternity: Letters from Working-Women, 72
  Woolf, Leonard and, 71
  see also 'Memories of a Working Women's Guild'
Women's Social and Political Union, 58–9
Wood, Alice, 71
Woodson, Carter G., *The Miseducation of the Negro*, 62
Wooldridge, Adrian, 95
Woolf, Leonard
  'Are Too Many Books Written and Published', 167
  and Armenians, 37
  BBC radio debate, 167–9
  and capitalism, 16
  Co-operation and the Future of Industry, 74–5, 81, 89n
  and the 'economic question', 272, 280
  Empire and Commerce in Africa, 40, 50–2, 57, 204, 218n
  and Fabian Society, 74
  and Hogarth Press, 161–72
  and imperialism, 48–52
  and inherited wealth, 34
  International Government, 203–4
  and League of Nations, 219n
  as 'Marxian Socialist', 8
  and Marxism, 10
  and Publishers Association, 174n
  and VW as author, 186, 227
  and *The Voyage Out*, 194
  and WCG, 71
Woolf, Virginia
  anti-fascist pamphlet, 272–81
  'Are Too Many Books Written and Published', 167
  BBC radio debate, 167–9
  'On Being Ill', 227–8, 238
  beyond-work and capitalism, 224–44
  The Common Reader, 217
  on consumption, 70–91
  'Cook Sketch', 11–14, 21n, 82
  on co-operation, 70–91
  on the desire to dominate, 29–47
  'The Docks of London', 17n, 21n, 49
  freedom from financial constraint, 199n
  'How Should One Read a Book?', 84, 281
  'Introductory Letter to Margaret Llewelyn Davies', 78–9, 83–4, 86–7, 102, 238
  '[The Journal of Mistress Joan Martyn]', 183, 187–90
  Kew Gardens, 163
  and Keynes, 11–14
  as 'labour woman', 4
  'The Leaning Tower', 8–10, 15, 206
  and the Left, 4
  'The Legacy', 8–11, 16, 20n
  'A Letter to a Young Poet', 21n
  Life as We Have Known It, 78, 83, 84, 86, 163
  'London Scene' essays, 17n, 49
  'The Mark on the Wall', 192
  and Marx, 7–11

Woolf, Virginia (cont.)
  'Memoirs of a Novelist', 183, 186, 191–5, 200n
  'Memories of a Working Women's Guild', 76–83, 86
  'Modern Fiction', 193, 203, 224
  Monday or Tuesday, 192
  'Morley Sketch', 103–5, 190–1
  on motherhood, 70–91
  'narrative arabesques', 118
  'The Niece of and Earl', 95, 100
  Notebook 21, 38–9
  as owner, of Hogarth Press, 80
  The Pargiters, 35, 274–5
  'Portrait of a Londoner', 201n
  and the property market, 4, 11, 137–58
  short fiction for Hogarth Press, 192
  as a sound investment, 245–67
  as star, 246–7, 258–9
  'Thoughts on Peace in an Air Raid', 38–40, 42
  Woolf, Leonard sees as author, 186, 227
  and working women writers, 182–202
  writing for Hogarth Press, 227
  see also *Between the Acts*; *Jacob's Room*; *Mrs Dalloway*; *Night and Day*; *Orlando: A Biography*; *A Room of One's Own*; *Three Guineas*; *To the Lighthouse*; *The Voyage Out*; *The Waves*; *The Years*
Woolf scholarship, 4–5
WoolfNotes.com, 38–40
work
  backlash against women in, 275–6
  domestic, 16, 33, 52, 59, 83, 88n, 225
  emotional in the home, 22n
  'equal pay for equal work', 59
  'good work for nothing', 34
  living wage, 59
  'postwork', 225–6, 229–30
  sexual division of, 38–40
  transformation of, 233–9
  unwaged, 49
  wage system, 33
  waged, 224, 226–36
  Wages for Housework Movement, 21n, 241n
  women, 14–16
  in *The Years*, 231–3
  see also labour; women writers
Workers' Educational Association, 8, 217
working-class
  characters, 78, 86
  children, 100
  men, 99
  see also class
working-class women
  intelligence of, 101–2
  in *Life as We Have Known It*, 163
  in *Mrs Dalloway*, 102
  in *Three Guineas*, 100, 111n
  WCG, 70–3, 76, 79–80, 83–5, 89n
World War I, 39, 119, 122–3
Wynter, Sylvia
  'The Ceremony Must Be Found: After Humanism', 62
  'The Re-enchantment of Humanism: An Interview with Sylvia Wynter', 62–3
  'Unsettling the Coloniality of Being/Power/Truth/Freedom: Towards the Human, After Man, Its Overrepresentation: An Argument', 61–2

Yale Review, 78, 79
The Years (VW)
  abortion in, 285–6

'Colonial editions', 172
houses in, 143–5
shopping in, 86
women's education in, 110n
VW as star, 246
work in, 231–3
working-class characters in, 78

Young, Edward, *Conjectures on Original Composition*, 106–7
Young, Robert, 49, 50

Zwerdling, Alex, 11
Virginia Woolf and the Real World, 34

EU representative:
Easy Access System Europe
Mustamäe tee 50, 10621 Tallinn, Estonia
Gpsr.requests@easproject.com

www.ingramcontent.com/pod-product-compliance
Lightning Source LLC
Chambersburg PA
CBHW050202240426
43671CB00013B/2217